Morning by Morning

Dr. Martin W. Wiles

PublishAmerica
Baltimore

First printing

All characters in this book are fictitious, and any resemblance to real persons, living or dead, is coincidental.

PublishAmerica has allowed this work to remain exactly as the author intended, verbatim, without editorial input.

Hardcover 978-1-4512-9348-7
Softcover 978-1-4512-9349-4
PAperback 978-1-4512-4640-7
PUBLISHED BY PUBLISHAMERICA, LLLP
www.publishamerica.com
Baltimore

Printed in the United States of America

This book is dedicated to the loving memory of my father, Boyce "Buddy" Wiles, Jr., who entered heaven's portals on May 14, 2009 Thanks for the example and for introducing me to Christ.

And

To my lovely wife Michelle who inspired me to pursue this work. Thank you darling for reading every word. You are the love of my life.

January

January 1
In His Image
Genesis 1

Most of us are familiar with the statement, "He is the spitting image of his mother or father." It refers to the physical characteristics found in a child that are also found in one or both of the parents. Most of the time, this is facial features and hair color. It can also refer to other idiosyncrasies-quirks if you will, that are found in the child and parent. The way they walk, talk, etc. This is only natural. Through the procreation process, the parents have "spit" that child out.

In like manner, we are made in the image of God. This doesn't mean we look like him physically. The Bible states that God is Spirit. Yet, when God chose to do something about our sin dilemma, he did take on the form of man. After the crucifixion, death and resurrection of Christ, he ascended back into heaven in bodily form-although a resurrected body. Scripture teaches that at the end of time, we too will receive new resurrected bodies that are designed to inhabit heaven.

But God's image in us means more than that. Simply defined, it means that God placed characteristics of himself in us-characteristics that were not given to the plant or animal kingdom. This makes us special and unique.

You have a special personality that enables you to interact with others, a quality that allows you to think, reflect and make decisions. You have the capacity to know and love others and to live in harmony with them. God has placed us in charge of his creation.

The image of God in us is most fully realized in a relationship with him through his Son Jesus Christ. Only when we live in harmony with Him do we realize what it means to be truly human. God's image in you allows you to fulfill the destiny God has in mind for you but only as you submit your life to Him.

God can only work through us when we are pliable-when we are soft enough for him to mold and shape. His plan is to conform us to the image of his Son (Romans 8:29). He wants us to act like Jesus for God's image was completely demonstrated in his life. As you look for satisfaction in life, remember that it comes when you let Christ shine through you.

Reflection: How is God's image changing you?

January 2

When Temptation Comes

Genesis 3

"The devil made me do it." It's a common statement we make when we want to escape responsibility for something wrong we did. In fact, it's an excuse as old as time because Eve used this same expression when God confronted her about her sin. Only she said, "The serpent made me do it." Same difference, for Satan used the serpent for his wily purposes. When this didn't work, she blamed her husband.

Move thousands of years into the future, and we often play the same game. We give in to one of the devil's tricks, consequences start to accumulate, and we want to shift the blame to someone or something else. It might be negligent parents, divorce, poverty, abuse or any number of things we might concoct, but the bottom line is that none of these things make us sin. Satan, in the form of the serpent, did not make Eve sin, and Eve did not make Adam sin. It was a free-will choice.

Satan's goal is to sow discouragement, doubt, diversion, defeat and delay in your life. Discouraged people don't have much initiative. Doubters don't have much faith. Diverted people have trouble focusing. Defeated people often lay around depressed. And procrastinators have trouble getting anything done.

Being God's child does not exempt us from temptation. In fact, Satan loves to bother us. He knows he can't steal us from God, but he can defeat our work for God through the above mentioned methods.

Though God has forgiven us in Christ, there resides in us what the Bible terms the "flesh" (Gal. 5:16ff). It's the old habits and patterns of acting that we have learned and will not forget but have to deal with so we don't fall for Satan's traps.

The good news is that we can, by God's power, overcome any temptation Satan hurls our way (I Cor. 10:13). We should never say, nor can we ever say, "The devil made me do it." The Christian armor allows us to stand firm against the assaults of our common enemy. All we have to do is put it on every day. Be prepared for battle, knowing that you have victory in Christ to defeat any temptation that comes your way.

Reflection: God has given me the power to defeat any temptation Satan throws my way.

January 3
The Power of Words
Colossians 3:17

One proverb states, "It is caged by teeth and lips but still escapes." What is the answer? The tongue. Former President Lyndon Johnson said, "You ain't learnin' nothing when you're doing all the talkin'."

Our words can be compared to toothpaste. Once squeezed from the tube, it cannot be put back in again. Once our words escape from our teeth and seethe through our lips, they are out for good. We can apologize for what was said, but we cannot literally take them back, return them to our mouth and pretend we didn't say what was said. Hence the phrase, "bite your tongue."

Even if the person you offended says they forgive you, they will never forget the words that were uttered. They may not hold them against you, but the memory of what was said is forever etched in their mind and can be retrieved if they so desire.

Perhaps this is why the Bible has so much to say about our tongues and the words that escape the cage. One good piece of advice is found in James 1:19 which tells us to be quicker to listen than we are to speak. The Bible also compares the tongue to a wild animal that cannot be tamed (James 3:7-10). It is nothing inherently wrong with the tongue-God created it. What we use it to say is where the problem arises.

It is always better to talk less and listen more. Too much talk usually leads to something being said that should have been left unsaid. Talking too much also gives the impression that our ideas are more important. We need wisdom to say the right things at the right moment.

Examples of what comes from an untamed tongue are gossip, bragging, belittling others, complaining, flattering and lying. Before speaking, ask yourself three questions: Is it true, is it necessary and is it kind? It is better to have a controlled and caring tongue than a conniving and careless tongue. Better mercy, purity, peace, consideration, sincerity and goodness than jealousy, selfishness, ungodliness and evil. Use your words to build up rather than tear down.

Reflection:Am I using my words carefully? Do I think before I speak? Do I keep my word? Do I use vulgar speech? Am I gracious with my words? Remember your words reveal what is in your heart (Luke 6:45)

January 4

Setting the Temp

Romans 12:2

In life, do you function as a thermometer or thermostat? While a thermometer only tells what the temperature is, a thermostat has the ability to control the temperature. When set at a certain temperature, it will make sure the temperature of that dwelling remains constant. One shows the effects while the other affects.

It is our challenge in life to affect. To do this, we cannot conform. We have to transform because we have been transformed by God's grace. As a modern translation of this verse reads, "Don't copy the behavior and customs of this world but let God transform you into a new person by changing the way you think."

Our minds are very important if we are to set the temperature of our families, friendships, work places, communities, civic gatherings, and world. What you think about will influence how you feel, and how you feel will lead to how you act. Since we think before we act, it is vital to monitor the thermostat of our mind if we are going to set the temperature of our world.

Decide how much worldly behavior is off limits for you. There are many moral and benevolent people who are not Christians, and most believers circulate around unbelievers every day. However, we must set the thermostat. Learn when to say, "This relationship or friendship is not good for me anymore," or "I need to speak up, let them know I am a Christian and don't appreciate their language or behavior."

Paul tells us in Philippians 4:8 what we should think about so that appropriate behavior will follow. Jesus reminds us that we are the salt and light of the world (Matthew 5:13-15). Salt is designed to give flavor and preserve, but if it doesn't do that, it is worthless. Light is designed to dispel the darkness, but a burnt out light bulb is of no value.

We must flavor our world so it will taste better. We must light our world with the love of Christ. A thermometer type person goes along with the crowd. It is always easier to sand with the grain. But a thermostat type person sets the temperature. They control their thoughts and actions and influence the same in others.

Reflection: A thermometer lets the temperature in the room change it, but a thermostat changes the temperature. Which are you?

January 5

Grace Greater Than Sin

Ephesians 2:8-10

Grace can be defined as getting what we don't deserve. Sometimes that can be very disturbing, such as when we read of the twelve-year-old girl innocently riding her bicycle through her secure subdivision and getting hit and killed by a truck whose driver accidently runs a stop sign. Or when we hear of the burglar who robs and beats an older couple yet receives a minor slap on the hand from a judge who is worried about prison overcrowding.

Thankfully, for the Christian, grace is about God giving us what we don't deserve-heaven instead of hell, forgiveness instead of punishment, mercy instead of justice. But this grace is not of merit. God doesn't look at us, see what a good person we are, and then decide to lavish his grace on us. Nor does he look at all the good things we've done, put them on a scale against the weight of our mistakes in life, and then determine whether or not we get into heaven. Sadly, many live with these misconceptions of how God operates.

God's grace leads us to salvation. We may think we're pretty good, but the Bible says all our good works are like "filthy rags" before God. If it were not for God operating in your life, you would never come to Him. God rescues us from the imminent peril we are in. We don't save ourselves. I don't deserve it and neither do you, but he saves nevertheless.

God's grace gives a proper perspective on our good works. They don't save us, nor do they put God under obligation to us. They are only outcroppings of our appreciation for what he has done in our life.

God's grace helps us with our self-esteem. It is nothing wrong with feeling good about ourselves, but that feeling must be based on truth-it must have a healthy origin. You should only feel good about yourself because you know God made you. You are his masterpiece, his work of art in process.

God's grace leads to humility. Defined, this is not thinking too much of ourselves. We are who we are because of God-nothing more, nothing less.

God's grace gives us purpose in life. A life void of purpose is a miserable life. God's children, however, have great purpose. As his masterpiece, he has work for you to do. Show him to the world.

Reflection: Do I remember that I am what I am because of God's grace? Thank you God for making me your masterpiece.

January 6
What Rocks Give
Psalm 27:5

At an elevation of over 4,400 feet above sea level, Tray Mountain, in the beautiful northern mountains of Georgia, provides a wonderful example of life on a rock. From the rocky summit, one can see in all directions for many miles. In fact, on a clear day, you can see for miles across the piedmont and catch a glimpse of Stone Mountain in Atlanta, Georgia.

The psalmist confessed that his God would place him in such a place when troubles came. In another place, he stated that God was his rock and fortress (Ps. 31:3). God was also his rock of safety (Ps. 28:1). When walking over rocks, it is easy to stumble, twist an ankle and even fall, but rocks serve an important purpose, especially when we compare them to God.

Rocks provide stability. Most mountains are made of these, but if they are blasted apart, the mountain crumbles. As long as they are intact, the mountain remains a mountain. As our rock, God can provide such stability in our life, and in an unstable world, this is a comforting thought. We can depend on Someone who is solid, unmovable, unchangeable, and able to carry us through all of life's troubles, temptations and trials. Like the wise man who built his house on rock, a life built on Christ is sure to withstand all that life may hurl at us.

Rocks give perspective. Perched on an outcropping of elevated rock with no trees to obstruct the view, one can see the miles of landscape that surrounds them. When we live on the high places with God our Rock, we are able to see life through different lenses. Our vision is clearer and not clouded by doubts, fears, worries, anxieties, and other emotions that immobilize us.

Rocks foster peace. Jesus said he left us with a gift-peace of mind and heart. The peace he gives is not like the world gives. (John 14:27) We often define peace as an absence of such things as war, pain, trials, temptations, political wrangling, strife, but this would be peace like the world gives. The peace of God is entirely different. It is a peace that surpasses our understanding-a calmness that is felt in spite of fear, anxiety, worry, war, pain and the like. It is unexplainable but experienced nonetheless. It is a peace that comes from knowing that God is in control.

Reflection: Am I resting on the Rock that will never let me down and will see me through all that life may throw my way?

January 7
A Shepherd's Lessons
Psalm 23

A shepherd's lifestyle and work is mostly unfamiliar in our post modern technological world. Even a sheep farmer's flock would radically differ from a biblical shepherd. David was a ruddy shepherd boy who played a harp, fought a giant, became a great warrior and later ruled as king over the United Kingdom of Israel. At some point in his career, he penned this all familiar psalm, taking his background as a shepherd, and comparing it to His Great Shepherd.

David reminds us that our relationship with the Great Shepherd must be personal. The Lord was his shepherd. Plainly put, we cannot get to God or heaven on the coattails of anyone or anything else. Parents, grandparents, or spouses will not do. Their relationship with God, no matter how grand and exemplary, has no merit for us. Fine material things and a padded bank account will not suffice. It is a personal matter.

Once this account has been settled, our Shepherd promises to give us everything we need. Jesus later reiterates this truth when he says not to worry about having enough food, drink or clothing. Our Heavenly Father knows about these needs. Our responsibility is simply to live for him day by day. (Matthew 6:31-33)

Sadly, we can clutter and even ruin our lives trying to get what God has already promised us. We also have that tendency to mix up our wants and needs. Never is there a promise to supply the wants-though often they are, but there are many promises to supply the needs-the things that are necessary for our existence.After all, we are his children.

Our Shepherd also promises a peaceful life. We can rest in the green meadows of knowing our eternity is secure and our needs will be met. He will guide us to the peaceful streams that will nourish us even in the most difficult and trying times of life. He promises to renew our strength. Life is tough, and it takes enormous spiritual muscles to cope with it. These muscles are developed through prayer, studying the Word, small group fellowship and involvement with a local body of believers.

Reflection: Do you have a personal relationship with the Great Shepherd? If so, take comfort in knowing he will supply your needs and guide your life.

January 8
A Shepherd's Lessons
Psalm 23

David certainly spent many nights in the open field under a star studded sky reflecting on his Great Shepherd. There was no city noise, planes flying overhead or street lights t0 dim the brightness of the stars. The fields were quiet, dark and solitary-ingredients that make for good reflection but also factors for danger. No light to see the approaching bear or lion until the baaing of the sheep let him know. Then a fight and rescue in the darkness.

Our Great Shepherd will protect us as he did David. Even when we walk through the valley of the shadow of death, we don't have to fear. As David used his rod and staff to protect and comfort his sheep, so God often uses his staff to draw us back from dangerous precipices. He brandishes his rod of discipline, though lovingly, to remind us of where bad decisions can lead us. Nothing can touch us that is not first filtered through the hands of our loving Shepherd.

And to demonstrate his great love for us, he often lavishes on us more than we need and certainly more than we deserve. God wants us to enjoy his best for us. He prepares a feast for us. Like the manna that appeared for the children of Israel in the desert, so God's goodness is all around us; we just have to take it in.

He overflows our cups with blessings like the raging stream that escapes its boundaries after a heavy storm. His goodness pursues us all the days of our lives. One has characterized our Shepherd as the "hound of heaven." It is not a pursuit of anger, hatred or revenge for our indiscretions, but one of love, grace and mercy.

Our Shepherd's unfailing love is also on our heels, pursuing us with great rapidity. His love is constant and grand. It is not conditional but keeps streaming forth in spite of our blunders. Even when rejected, his love is patient. It is agape' love at its finest.

The Shepherd's love will usher us into eternity. We will live in his house forever. Heaven is the great hope of the Christian. If this life is all we have, we are to be considered the most miserable people, but we have the assurance of a better place.

Reflection: Following our Shepherd will take us through the best of this life and the life to come.

January 9
Jesus on Crowds
Matthew 9:35-38

Crowds. In our ever expanding world, they are all around us-in the cities, on the streets, at malls, school and work, at the theater, coliseum, ball games, concerts, the beach and mountains. We make reservations for vacation; otherwise we might not get a room. As our population continues to escalate, it seems inevitable that the crowds will continue to grow.

One sociologist delineated four types of crowds: conventional, casual, expressive and acting. From just a chance occurrence of being in the same place at the same time to acting aggressively over some issue, crowds are everywhere and act in many different ways.

Jesus handled crowds in various ways-sometimes he fed them and at other times he sent them away so he could be alone, but in this instance he looked at them and characterized them as "harassed and helpless, like sheep without a shepherd."

Our challenge as Christians is to see crowds as Jesus did. He saw their true condition. Many of the people you and I meet on a daily basis can be characterized in the same terms as Jesus used for this particular crowd. They may have many other issues in their life, but their greatest need is a relationship with the Savior. The apostle Paul gave the verdict when he proclaimed the wages of sin to be death. (Romans 6:23) Jesus told Nicodemus something similar when he stated that a person had to born again. (John 3:3)

The crowds also need compassion. People often had many ulterior motives in coming to Jesus-curiosity, the need to be healed physically or emotionally, a desire for him to do something for a family member. Jesus knew they weren't all coming for the right reason, but he had pity on them nevertheless. Follow the example of Jesus-show compassion on someone who needs to feel empathy for the first time.

Jesus also said we are to pray for him to call workers to go tell the good news to the crowd. Missionaries come to mind. Take time to pray that God would send them where he has not called you specifically to go. Then again, realize you might be the one he wants to send. Maybe to a friend or work companion. It might be someone in your family.

Reflection: Take the compassion of Jesus to a hurting world.

January 10
Perspectives on Aging
Joshua 14:6-13

Getting old. Not a popular subject. In fact, most people would as soon not discuss it. When younger, we want to get older so we can leave home and venture out on our own. We want to map our day and life without having to answer to our parents. Then the years seem to accumulate quickly, and before long we wish we were back home again-enjoying the carefree life of childhood.

Yet getting older should not take away our initiative in life. Our senior adult years can be productive. We don't have to confine them to a rocking chair. Caleb is a wonderful example of having the right perspective on aging. Of the twelve spies Moses sent to scout out the Promised Land the Israelites were about to enter, only Caleb and Joshua brought back an optimistic report that they could conquer the inhabitants.

Now many years later, and at 85 years of age, Caleb approaches Joshua and asks for the land Moses promised him 45 years ago, telling Joshua that he is still strong and can fight for his "little" promised land.

Caleb shows that we don't have to fear old age. Fears that come later in life can be: physical ailments that confine, inadequate retirement money, nursing home, death of a spouse, terminal illness or debilitating falls. But Paul tells us that God is not the author of a spirit of fear. Rather he gives power, love and a sound mind. (II Timothy 1:7) God will always supply every need we have.

In our older years, we can provide models of faithfulness-most importantly loyalty to God. The younger generation always needs this example. Like wisdom, it often takes many years to learn this admirable trait. Alan Redpath, in his book, *Victorious Christian Living*, wrote, (Oh) "that the faith which was ours in youth may be undimmed in old age."

Nor do we have to grow stale in our later years. It can be a season of fruitfulness. The psalmist reminds us that we can still bear fruit even in our senior years. (Psalm 92:14) Don't go into spiritual retirement. You may have to pass some of your spiritual batons, but keep working for

God. Usefulness for God doesn't end at a certain age. Benjamin Franklin helped frame the Constitution at the age of 81.

Reflection: God can use us until our eyes close in death.

January 11
The Day of the Lord
Zephaniah 1-3

Day of the Lord. This phrase can have different meanings or even multiple meanings. It can refer to the end of time when the Lord appears, wraps up history, and ushers in eternity, or it can refer to a special visitation from the Lord, such as when he sends some form of punishment for disobedience.

This phrase can also evoke certain feelings. Some fear the Day of the Lord because they are not ready to meet him while others look forward to his appearing because they are tired of the sin and degradation of this world-they are ready for the joy and purity of heaven.

The Day of the Lord will be an event in which the wrath of God is felt by those who have rejected him. Christians have no reason to fear this aspect of the Day of the Lord, for we are no longer under condemnation. Our

sins have been nailed to the cross of Calvary. Jonathan Edwards once preached a sermon entitled "Sinners in the Hands of an Angry God." It is reported that God's wrath was made so graphic in this sermon that the congregants literally held onto the pews to keep from falling into hell.

We would rather think of God's mercy, but the Bible also speaks of his wrath. This is the anger of God against sin and those who choose to live in such a lifestyle. God would rather demonstrate love, but he will only do that to those who accept his remedy for sin-belief in the sacrifice of Jesus on the cross. We think of the verse, "If God is for us, who can be against us?" But what about the opposite? If God is not for us, how can we stand against him?

It will also be a day of repentance. Christians have had their personal Day of the Lord-when they repented and accepted him as their Savior, but when Christ comes it will be too late to repent-at least for salvation. We are told that every knee will bow and every tongue confess when

Christ returns, but this will be a forced repentance, and repentance unto salvation must be our choice.

The Day of the Lord will bring restoration. At last, sin will be destroyed, Satan cast into hell, and the earth restored to its original intent and glory. A new heaven and earth will be created, one not subject to decay and the rot of sin.

Reflection: Will the Day of the Lord catch you off guard?

January 12

The Second Coming

II Peter 3

The Second Coming of Christ, like the Day of the Lord, evokes different responses. Some try to figure out when it will happen, even though Jesus says no one can know. Books have been written announcing the date of his return. Others are enamored with prophecy, and based on occurrences they see, assume his coming is very near. Still others live with fear, believing it to be imminent, yet knowing they are not ready. And then there are those who perhaps want to get married, have children, or accomplish some goal before it happens.

While we cannot know the date, we must resist indifference to the event. It should be on our mind, and we should live everyday as if it could happen because it just might. Indifference assaulted the early church. Shortly after Jesus ascended back into heaven, word spread of his soon return. When he didn't appear, many began to abandon hope that his coming would occur. False teachings began to spread. Before long, many of the early Christians developed an apathetic attitude about his coming. Our responsibility is to watch and be witnesses.

We should also believe in the certainty of his coming. Though we don't know the time of Christ's return, his coming is as certain as the rising and setting of the sun and the changing of the seasons. It's a part of God's sovereign plan, and human actions will not prevent or delay it. Nor can liberal theology sponge it away. At God's appointed time, his Son will appear and right all that is wrong with our world.

Many things in life are uncertain, but the Second Coming does not fall into this category. Two plus two equals four is a mathematical equation that is certain. It will always be true. It has no choice but to be, and the same is true of Christ's appearing. The fact that so many years have passed has no bearing on the inevitability of it. We can attribute this to God's patience. God does not live by time nor is he bound by it.

As Christians, we should anticipate the coming of our Lord and Savior. Never has a grander event happened in history. In the meantime, God has given us work to do-take his love to all people groups. Advances in the technological field help make this a reality.

Reflection: Live each day as if Christ will come.

January 13

God's Plan for the Family

Genesis 1:26-28

The story is told of a woman getting on a bus with seven children. Her hair is a mess, and she has dark circles under her eyes. A rider asks, "Are these all yours, or is this some kind of picnic?" To which the woman replies, "Yes, they are all mine, and believe me, it's no picnic."

Families. They come in all shapes and sizes, but the majority of them are in trouble. The traditional family is almost extinct. Finances, busyness, unfaithfulness, both parents working, blended homes, and aging parents are all challenges families face. Statistics still show that almost half of all marriages end in divorce. Millions of children are in orphanages, and millions more are abused and neglected.

God intends for families to be healthy, happy and long lived. If this is to happen, there cannot be favoritism. Isaac is the second patriarch mentioned in the Bible. He and his wife, Rebekah, had two sons: Jacob and Esau. Jealousy in this family was inevitable when we read of how Isaac loved Esau because of the wild game he hunted. Rebekah, however, looked with favor on Jacob. (Genesis 25:28)

This scenario played itself out as Jacob stole his brother's birthright and his blessing, things reserved for the firstborn child. It ended with Jacob having to flee from the wrath of his brother. It was not until many years later that they reconciled.

Children perceive favoritism no matter how parents may try to hide it. This leads to sibling rivalry and the neglected child trying to gain approval from the parent that favors another sibling. Or it may lead to animosity from the child toward the parent who does not favor them. It sets the stage for disaster in a family.

Families also need faithfulness. Parents must be faithful to each other and to their children. Unfaithfulness almost always drives a death stake in the coffin for a marriage. Trust takes years to build but can be destroyed with one bad decision.

Godly teaching and example are vital in a family. Modern times have not outdated the need for a family devotion. Parents must set a godly example for their children. Children will model what they see and hear.

Reflection: What can I do to make my family stronger?

January 14

Faithfulness in Marriage

Matthew 5:27-31

The 1960's and 70's brought a sexual revolution to America that destroyed many traditional family values. The picture painted by shows like "Father Knows Best" and "Leave it to Beaver" didn't seem to fit anymore. Mom went to work, and Dad was no longer recognized as the head of the home. Unfaithfulness was also a serious side effect of this revolution.

What this revolution taught and demonstrated by example stands in stark contrast to what the Bible teaches. As we read of the first marriage in the Bible, we notice the permanence with which it was designed. The two become one. Not that one or the other lost their identity, but they were one in the purpose of taking responsibility for each other. They were also united in the sexual union-reserved for each other and only each other.

As we move to the New Testament, Jesus and the apostle Paul give two reasons for ending a marriage in addition to death-not that it is a mandate but allowances are made. One reason is for adultery, and the other is when an unbelieving spouse chooses to leave the marriage. Neither of these reasons nullifies God's original intent for the marriage-permanence.

Jesus precedes his teaching on adultery by a warning against looking with lust at the opposite sex. This can apply to a woman or man. Looks lead to feelings which in turn lead to action.

That Jesus mentions adultery as grounds for divorce shows how devastating unfaithfulness is in a marriage. Many marriages cannot survive this, not because it's impossible but because of the trust factor. Unlike forgiveness which should be instantaneous, trust takes years to build but can be destroyed with the decision to be unfaithful. To rebuild trust takes a fortitude many couples are not willing to muster. The pain is too great.

In I Corinthians 7, Paul makes allowances when an unbelieving spouse chooses to leave the marriage. At that point, the Christian is released from their vows. Again, it is not a mandate but an accommodation. This situation, while allowed for, can be avoided by following the Biblical plan for believers to marry only believers. Parents and grandparents need to teach this principle to their children and grandchildren, as well as explain to them why it is important.

Reflection: I will honor God in my marriage through faithfulness.

January 15

Honoring God

Malachi 1 and 2

Honoring God is a direct reflection of our reverence for God. God's people had just returned from a 70 year stint in the foreign land of Babylon-a land where the laws of their God were not revered. This lack of respect had infiltrated some of them, making it more difficult for them to honor God.

We too live in a society where honor of and reverence for God is often difficult to find. This lack of esteem for God's laws has a direct bearing on Christians. Yet we are instructed to honor God, for he is our Creator and Sustainer. He is the One with whom we have to do.

God wants us to honor him with our worship. In Malachi's day, a main staple of worshipping God was animal sacrifice, and while the people were bringing sacrifices, they were bringing the lame and weak. They were not giving their best to God. Therefore, their worship did not honor God.

Under the New Covenant, God no longer requires animal sacrifices, but he does expect the sacrifice of our time, gifts, abilities and money. A regular examination should be done to see if we are shortchanging God. He doesn't want leftovers in any of these areas. Are your sacrifices to your employer, family or civic organization greater than to God?

When we fail to make proper sacrifices, we in essence are saying that God is not worthy of the best of our time, talents and money. But other places and people are. As God was not impressed with the failed sacrifices of the Israelites, neither is he with our half-hearted gifts. Worship him with your best.

We need to honor God with a proper attitude about worship. Here God says he would rather shut the doors of the Temple than have this superficial worship continue. This reprehensible adoration was slandering the name of God among unbelievers who lived nearby.

Employers want employees who not only fulfill their duties but also do them to the best of their ability and who go beyond what is required to keep the job. God wants our best as well in worshipping him.

Additionally, God desires that we honor him with our actions. Israelite men were marrying heathen women. God had strictly forbidden this. Who is affecting your behavior? Christ or the world around you?

Reflection: Honor God with your worship, attitude and actions.

January 16

Living With Eternity in Mind

Matthew 25:31-46

Eternity. An infinite amount of time (well not really) that cannot be calculated. It is difficult for the human mind to comprehend this concept, yet that is where God resides-before time, outside of time and beyond time. For the Christian, we hope one day to live there also. Since we live in time, it is challenging to exist with eternity in mind. But we must.

The present verses contain teachings about the final judgment when all people will stand before God to give an account of their lives. Our final place of abode will be determined by faith first of all but by faith as it is expressed in action. In essence, we serve Christ by serving others.

We are determining our eternity now, and only what we invest in eternity is secure.

In the preceding verses, Jesus tells the parable of the talents. A man about to embark on a journey calls together his servants and gives them various amounts of money to invest while he is away. Upon his return, he finds that the first two have doubled their money, but the third hid his in a hole in the ground. The first two were rewarded with more responsibilities, but the third had his taken away.

We live with eternity in mind by investing our God-given resources. God gives us talents and abilities to use in his Kingdom work, not to squander or hide.Sharecroppers come to mind. They were given a little land for their family in return for labor. They remembered where their resources originated. Sharecroppers dare not neglect the landowner's land.

God sees a world of heartache, sin sickness and disease, and we are to use our resources to penetrate this world with his love. We serve Christ by serving the people he places in our path.

Those whom Jesus turns away from heaven must forfeit that because they did not feed him, give him drink, take him in, clothe him, tend to him while he was sick or visit him in prison. Puzzled, they ask when they had ever seen him in such dire straits and not responded. He said failing to do these things for others was tantamount to ignoring him. Those welcomed into heaven were done so because they had done these things. They did the simple things we all can do.

Reflection: Christ can return at any moment. We must allow our faith to express itself in good works. Use your God-given resources.

January 17
Considering Our Ways
Haggai 1 and 2

Times of reflection are good and necessary. We stop and think about some issue or set of circumstances. Sometimes we take vacations to do this. At times, it means looking back first before setting new goals in life. Reflection is a period of honesty with ourselves. It is a practice that believers should regularly indulge in.

Reflection also helps us evaluate our priorities. We live in busy times. Work schedules are quite different from years past. Pressures and expectations come at us from all sides. We find ourselves consumed by the urgent, and the important is often relegated to another time.

Haggai's time was similar. For seventy years, God's people had been in foreign captivity after having their temple destroyed and land plundered. A new dynasty had come on the world scene, and this new ruler allowed them to return to their homeland. They began to rebuild the temple but then stopped. Their priorities got jumbled up.

Putting God first should always be top priority. These people made a good start. The temple symbolized God's presence among them, so this was important for them, but they got busy with their own lives. Work stopped. They became enamored with things in their personal lives and put God's work aside.

"Honey, I want to watch the game tonight. Let's skip church." Or "You know I've been working all week. Sunday is the only time I have to do my yard work."

"I know I promised I'd go to the Bible study with you, but I'm just too tired. It's been a long day." The lists goes on-the list of how we tend to the necessary and often leave out the important: God. Families, jobs and hobbies are all important, but God must be first.

Not only had the people put their personal interests first, but the land was in the midst of a famine. Additionally, this temple, according to those who had seen the first one, just didn't measure up. The result-discouragement. Haggai had to encourage them. Satan loves to sow seeds of discouragement because discouraged people lose focus and energy.

Reflection: Obedience always brings blessings. God will pour out his spiritual refreshment on us when we get busy with his work, putting him first and not letting things or people discourage us as we labor for him.

January 18
Growing Spiritually
Hebrews 5:12-14

Physical growth is natural and normal. When this doesn't happen in some area, we classify that child as challenged. Babies start with milk, then baby food and finally the same thing adults eat. They start out in diapers but at some point are potty trained. Life is begun with cries of selfishness, but maturity finally wins out.

Believers are no different. When we accept the sacrifice of Christ and invite him into our lives, we become spiritual babes. There are many things we don't know yet about this new journey. We may have habits, attitudes or addictions that God will have to work on, but our route of progress should be steeply elevated. A few years down the road, and we should be farther along on the path to spiritual maturity. If this is not taking place, we are challenged, but it's not God's fault. There is something in our life that needs attention.

God equips us with divine resources that guarantee spiritual growth. Our spiritual diet should incorporate a steady infusion of his Word and prayer. These are lifelines to God. His Word is our daily food filled with nutrients needed for healthy Christian living. Good diets incorporate some foods and leave others off. There are some things from our life before Christ that we need to leave out of our diet. If we devour the Word, God will show us what these things are.

Our prayers do not change God but give us his plan for our individual lives. These two things must coalesce, for we must pray according to the teachings of his Word. One will not contradict the other.

Exercise is another part of this spiritual gain program. God says we must be "doers of the Word and not hearers only." As we exercise our beliefs, we will grow in our Christian experience. Solid food will become more inviting than milk. Lack of exercise will lead to growth in the wrong places.

Character is often formed by the environment that surrounds us in our childhood and teenage years. A Christian's character should include:

faith, virtue, self-control, patience, godliness, kindness and love. It should reflect the fruits of the Spirit delineated in Galatians 5:22-23.

Reflection: Am I growing as a Christian, or am I stuck in the baby stage? God, help me to use your resources so I can be healthy for you.

January 19

Going the Extra Mile

I Corinthians 9:24-27

Is your norm to do only what is required of you and nothing more? Or do you perform your best by putting forth extra effort in life's tasks? It is easier to do only what is mandated. Going the extra mile requires ingenuity, stamina and initiative.

For the believer, our least for God should not be the most we give. Since he has done so much for us, our best for him is the least we can do. The athletes in the ancient Greek games gave their best for the prize of only a laurel wreath. There was no money or medals, but the prize was a symbol of triumph and honor.

The Christian life is compared to a race, a race wherein we should go the extra mile. We need to strive for success. Go beyond the basics. Is your attitude, "Well, I'm just going to obey the Ten Commandments and nothing else." While the Commandments are important, obedience only to them will never result in enjoying God's best or success.

Leftovers defined are just that: leftovers. Some folks don't like them at all. Others will eat them the next day, but not after that. While some dishes are even better the next day, leftovers are not as good then as the day the food was originally prepared.

God doesn't like leftovers. Leftovers come from lukewarm believers, and in Revelation, God spits people like this out of his mouth-symbolizing his distaste for being neither hot nor cold. Success comes from giving our best.

We must train for the extra mile. Starting an exercise program without warming up is dangerous. Our muscles are cold, and this can result in injuries. Condition your muscles through Bible study, prayer, fellowship with believers, and using your gifts and talents. Take advantage of every opportunity God sends your way.

It is important to establish priorities. An absence of these leads to aimless wandering and missing assignments God puts in our path. Know the gifts God has given you, and use them faithfully. Don't try to wear hats that don't fit. Be willing to change directions as God directs.

Reflection: As you run, encourage others along the way. The race is not just about you and your rewards. It is about motivating others along the way. We want them to run the race as well and with diligence.

January 20

Who Are You?

I John 3:1-3

This may seem like a ridiculous question. If you ask who I am, I would tell you my name, and that should settle the issue. But if you say, "Well, yeah, but who are you" I might get confused, even a little irritated. Now I have to dig deeper by shoveling off the surface areas and looking at such things as my personality, character, where I work or what my position in life is.

Knowing who we are-having a sense of identity, is vitally important. It affects our attitudes, where we go, how we conduct ourselves, and what we say. Every person who has or ever will be born falls into one of two categories-saved or lost. Which division we are in is determined by what we have done with Jesus. If we believe who he is and accept what he has done on Calvary, then we fall into the saved group. Otherwise, we find ourselves in the lost class. There is no middle section.

For the believer, we are children of the King. There is no room in our life for such thoughts as, "I'm ugly, I'm a loser, I can't do it, I'm a failure, or Others are just being nice because they feel sorry for me." Nor does it matter where we are on the social totem pole.

Once our identity is settled, then we can move on to what we are becoming. As an infant becomes a child, then a teenager and finally an adult, so Christians are not static. We are in the process of becoming. John says, "We can't even imagine what we'll be like when Christ returns." God chose us and called us to himself. No longer are we under condemnation for our sins. Others may malign you, ridicule you and avoid you, but you are God's child, and you are becoming more like

28

Christ each day. God is conforming you to his image. All we have to do is submit to the process. The Bible says we can do all things because God gives us strength. (Philippians 4:13)

We also possess some things because of who we are. What are they? In a word-everything. God created all things, owns all things, and sustains all things. If you are his child, all he has belongs to you. A look at your bank account or material possessions might be disappointing, but a glance in the Bible and you can see all the riches you own. We are joint heirs with Christ.

Reflection: Can you say you are a child of the King? If so, thank God for all he has given you and for what you are becoming.

January 21

Cures for Troubled Hearts

John 14:1-3

All around are signs that troubled hearts abound. Disagreements are always part of the political scene. Crime is on the rise, and prisons are overcrowded. The family is in trouble with half of all marriages ending in divorce. Sexual immorality of all sorts is on the rampage. Children are neglected, abused and aborted. Drug use soars. Natural disasters engorge what people have worked a lifetime to accumulate.

In spite of these and other disturbing signs, Jesus tells us not to let our hearts be troubled. His disciples had reason to be concerned. One of them would soon betray him. Another would deny three times that he knew Jesus. All would desert him when the mob came to arrest him. And to top it off, Jesus was about to leave them and return to heaven.

Believing in God and trusting Christ is the ultimate cure for troubled hearts. It was for Jesus' disciples, and it's true for us as well. Their world must have seemed empty, like a haunted house. Trusting him will not alleviate all the things wrong in our world, but it will give a different perspective on life. He is in control and has our best interests at heart. Nothing happens that doesn't flow through his hands.

Believe in Christ through all your circumstances in life. Keep your focus, letting him work out all the details. Stay attentive by looking beyond the circumstances and to the great work you can do in his Kingdom. Trust him for those opportunities.

Jesus gives help for these troubling times by reminding us of our future home where all that assaults us here will be absent. There are many rooms in his Father's house-space enough for all who choose to believe in him. A "No Vacancy" sign will never appear outside the pearly gates.

Heaven is a real place, not just a soothing by-product of religious imagination. It's the place God resides and where Jesus would soon go. Robert Frost, famous poet, said of home that it "is the place that, when you arrive there, they have to take you in." Dr. James M. Conay, in a song written years ago, said; "Who could mind the journey, when the road leads home?"

Reflection: The troubles of our day seem miniscule when compared to eternity. Here is the home for all who trust Christ, a home with room for all who believe. Jesus will return to take us there.

January 22
Levels of Caring
John 10:11

Caring. Our world needs a lot of it because there is a mountain of hurt. We can do it for different reasons-recognition, a plaque in our honor, our name on a building, a guilty conscience, or because we truly want to help. Thus our motives and intentions are important.

A wonderful example of caring is Florence Nightingale. Born in 1820 in Florence, Italy, she was the daughter of well-to-do parents, but chose to devote her life to caring for the sick. When the Crimean War began, she volunteered her services and was appointed head of nurses in the military hospitals in Turkey. When Nightingale arrived, she found more men dying from fever and infection than from battle wounds. Florence established sanitary regulations, introduced special diets and reduced the death rate from 45 to 2 percent. She bought linen, shirts, food and hospital beds with her own money.

A greater example of caring is Jesus. He is the great shepherd who lay down his life for sinners so they could be forgiven. As Jesus cared for us, so we must do the same. It is a vital part of Christian living. By caring, we experience what being human is all about.

We care through inconvenience-fitting this into our busy schedules. Dual income homes, kids involved in sports, aging parents and on the list goes of why we can't fit anyone else into our day. Gone are the days when neighbors visited on front porches and helped each other. Too busy is defined as too busy to inconvenience ourselves to consider someone else.

Involvement is another method of caring. This goes one step farther than inconvenience. How well we know Jesus' story of the Good Samaritan. He took his caring to the levels of inconvenience and involvement. And Moses. Though raised in the splendor of Egypt, there came the day when "he went out to his people and looked on their burdens."Then he got involved.

The highest level of caring is identification. The plight of the person becomes our plight. We walk in their shoes and begin to feel what they are feeling. The heart of the gospel is how God identified with us in Christ.

Reflection: I can change an often uncaring world through my care. God help me to inconvenience myself and respond through identifying and involving myself in the lives of others.

January 23
Living Productively
I Peter 2:1-3

Anorexia Nervosa is a serious eating disorder affecting an impressive number of people, about 95 % of whom are women. Characterized by gross underweight, the anorexic usually perceives herselfas overweight even when they are extremely thin and emaciated. Because of this perception, they refuse food so as to maintain or further reduce their body weight. While there are psychological factors involved, the simple cure, if it could be attained, is to eat.

Most individuals desire productivity in life. Few, if any, want to be a failure. People want to make their mark on the world in some way. We want others to remember us for something special, even if it's only our family. Christians are no different, but our productivity should be in the area of spiritual concerns. We should want others to remember us because of our service to God-not for bragging purposes but because of our love for him.

Productivity requires elimination of sin-not entirely but in practice. Christians have a new nature but still contend with what the Bible calls the "flesh." The flesh is our old patterns and habits learned in the maturing process. Feeding the new nature through disciplined and methodical Christian practices helps feed the new nature and starve the flesh. We must put away malicious behavior, deceit, hypocrisy, jealousy, backstabbing, while craving those things that help us grow spiritually. These are sins of the mind, spirit, and heart.

Craving the pure milk of God's Word leads to productivity. When we yearn for godly things, we will act on our desires. Thoughts lead to behavior. Jesus says to hunger and thirst for things of righteousness. Pursue the good and hate what is evil. Spiritual growth should be foremost on our mind. As the infant craves milk so we should starve for God's Word and the guidance it gives. We cannot grow apart from drinking deeply of the Bible.

Reflection: Productivity brings the blessings of God. We should do the Lord's work without any thought of profit for ourselves. Yet God promises to reward our efforts. Receive those gifts with joy and gladness. They come in many ways: materially, physically, spiritually, emotionally and mentally. Never get so busy that you fail to recognize God's benefits. Take time to stop and count your blessings.

January 24
Five Things About Love
I Corinthians 13:13

I once knew a man who had only thirteen percent of his heart functioning. Though a fairly young man, his only hope was a heart replacement. Having his name put on the transplant list meant taking anti-rejection medicine-a cost that amounted to more than many families make in a year's time. Yet in this difficult time, cards and donations poured in from friends. It restored his faith in mankind and in God.

How unfortunate that it often takes a tragedy, illness, natural disaster or certain season of the year to bring out the "better angels" of our nature. God loves all the time. This truth is captured in the simple children's song that says, "Jesus loves me this I know, for the Bible tells me so." He loves the rich, poor, downcast, murderer, and all the people that are unlovable. His love is an example and challenge to us.

God commands us to love as he does. When asked what the greatest commandment was, Jesus said to love God with all our heart and the second to love our neighbor as ourselves. Not easy commands, but life is sweeter when love is magnified. When we love God, we will love our enemies, friends, and family. As we serve others with this love, we are serving God.

Such love cannot be mustered in our own strength but is only possible when God enables it in our life. Left to ourselves, we would love only those who are easy to love or who love us in return. Then we would forget the rest-those who are peculiar, grouchy, disagreeable and different.

Through God's strength, we can love with God's type of love-agape'. It is an unconditional love-the kind that keeps giving even when not returned. It's the kind of love that God uses to draw people to himself. God gave his all to demonstrate his love for us.

It takes faith on our part to love like this. The Christian life is lived by faith, and the believer loves others by faith. Believe that God will take your love and make a difference in someone's life. Believe that God can use you to help the ones who cannot help themselves.

Reflection: God, I thank you for showing your love to me. Enable me to love you with all my being and to love others as I do myself. Give me the strength to love the unlovable. Use me to make a difference in someone's life as you have in mine. Amen.

January 25
Living Life Abundantly
John 10:7-10

People want an abundant and fulfilling life. This conclusion is reached by appealing to any number of areas. The New Year's resolutions we make. The lucrative professions we pursue. The health habits and exercise programs we undertake. The material things we crave. We want to live long, and we want to live long with a lot. Sadly, none of these things leads to abundant life. The wealthy and toned are still unhappy, suicidal and can and do die at an early age.

Abundant life is not about whom we are or what we have but about whom we belong to and nurturing that relationship. It's about seeing life through God's spectacles. God did not design us to live life on the margin. Jesus pictures himself as the Good Shepherd as well as the door by which one enters the sheepfold. Once in, we are saved and given life, but not just life, abundant life.

While abundant living should be the norm for the Christian, we often lead defeated lives like those who don't know Christ. Abundant life may be the norm, but it takes work-it takes doing the right things. Why exist below the standard when we can live victoriously?

The abundant life is a yielded life-attracted to God and not to the practice of sin. As long as life continues, we will struggle with temptation and sin, but we do not practice sin. We cannot submit to sin and God at the same time. These are mutually exclusive situations. Christ must be our Lord, not sin. Wickedness must not reign in our bodies, for we cannot serve two masters.

Living the abundant life involves serving. Jesus' life was consumed with serving others-healing their physical, emotional and spiritual needs. He is our great example. Serving others takes our attention off our problems-the things that weigh us down and divide our minds. It puts our focus on others, and this brings happiness.

If our service to others is to mean anything, we must do it with holy attire. Service must flow out of a consistent life practice. Others who know us as Christians expect us to practice what we believe.

Reflection: Lord, help me to realize that living abundantly is not about what I have but who I am in you and allowing you to use me. Amen.

January 26
Living Life Abundantly
John 10:7-10

Harry wrote about his abundance in a book entitled, *My Wheelchair to the Stars*. At seven, he developed rheumatic fever and later severe arthritis. Wearing clothes was often torture. His father and mother worked at a textile mill and had no choice but to leave him home in the wheelchair. In time, he began to think there was no reason for him living. One day he fell from his chair and lay helplessly on the floor for several hours. His yelling finally brought the postman who picked him up and said, "With God all things are possible." Then someone suggested he paint Christmas cards. It took him six months to complete the first one. But he never forgot God's abundance the year he made one million dollars with his mail order greeting card business.

Abundant living is not only possible but natural for believers. It comes from a separated life. Christians are to be in the world but not of the world-the whole system that is opposed to God. When people look at our lifestyles, they should see something different than the norm. As different people, we impact their lives and consciences by showing them what they don't usually see from everyday interaction-acceptance, love, concern, friendship, and a helping hand.

Christians must separate themselves from the ungodliness in the world and at the same time influence it for Christ. Jesus says believers are salt and light. We are witnesses of the saving grace of Jesus but not a part of the wickedness of the world. Worldly precepts, sinful impulses and selfish motives must not control us.

Living abundantly comes from being Spirit filled. While we are given the Spirit the moment we trust Christ, we are not necessarily filled with the Spirit. To be filled means allowing God to control your life completely. We must give him power over every action, emotion and attitude. A Spirit-filled life will produce love, joy, peace, long-suffering, kindness, goodness, faithfulness, gentleness, (and) self-control.

Maturity is also a part of abundant living. As infants grow, so must the child of God. We must launch out in faith and live out God's Word in our life.

Reflection: Am I living in the fullness of my Christian life?

January 27

When the Trumpet Sounds

Matthew 24:36-44

Acts of preparation are common. Smoke alarms are placed strategically in our homes, hoping that in the event of a fire we would have time to get ourselves and some belongings out. We purchase home insurance policies hoping to replace our house and belongings if they are lost to fire, theft or natural disaster. We install burglar alarm systems to warn us or the police of intruders who would try to steal our valuables. Health insurance is acquired so we won't have to pay the full cost of medical expenses. And then there is life insurance so our spouses or children won't have undue hardships when we die. There is a certain degree of preparation undertaken at our places of employment. At school, there is preparation that must be done to pass the grade. Our lives are filled with anticipatory acts. Failing to prepare is preparing to fail.

Foresight is also needed to meet Christ, whether at death or His return. While Christians differ in their interpretations concerning events surrounding that return, most believe in the return itself. Jesus teaches that it is foolish not to prepare for such a monumental and important event.

His coming will involve surprise. It will be as it was in the days of Noah. Though Noah warned his generation of the impending flood, no one but his family believed. They probably changed their mind when the first rain drop fell and water began to burst from beneath the earth, but it was too late then. Many will be surprised when Jesus returns, but it will then be too late to prepare. Arrangements must be made in advance by trusting him as Savior now. The Bible says that today is the day of salvation.

The coming of Christ will bring separation. Jesus says people in the fields and at the mills will be separated. His point is that a division will take place-a segregation between those who have accepted and rejected him. Presently, we all live together, but a winnowing will take place as wheat is separated from the chaff.

Based on what he has taught, Jesus warns us to watch because no one knows the day of his appearing. He will come as a thief in the night, and no one knows when the robber will appear.

Reflection: Have you made preparation for the coming of Christ? Only through faith in Jesus can you be ready for this event.

January 28

Missed Opportunities

Acts 8

Opportunities. They come our way in different shapes, forms and disguises, and usually they appear on a regular basis. We must decide whether we will take advantage of them and the resulting rewards or whether we will let them pass and risk the chance that they may never present themselves again.

The Greeks had a statue named Opportunity. The head had hair on the front but was bald on the back. It signified that opportunities could be seized when coming but once past they were forever lost.

In this instance, Philip was given the chance to witness about Jesus to an Ethiopian eunuch. The eunuch, if he accepted the message-which he did, would in turn take the gospel to his country. The domino effect could be alarming. To his credit, Philip left a great mission field to take advantage of this occasion, but he could have refused.

What traits do we need to avoid so we don't miss opportunities? One is selfishness. Philip was enjoying great success in Samaria. Many were accepting the gospel. God gave him power to perform miracles. He was healing the paralyzed and the lame and casting devils from the possessed. Great joy overcame the area. Then God told him to leave and go to a desert road to talk to one man. Never let it be said that an opportunity was lost because you didn't want to be bothered.

Procrastination can lead to lost opportunities. Philip's appointment required immediate action. God had made the arrangements, but he had to act quickly. Fortunately, he obeyed promptly and instantly. Had he not done this, he could have missed the chariot. One has defined procrastination as the "art of keeping up with yesterday." We use it when faced with a matter that we really do not want to deal with.

We can miss appointments because of prejudice. Had Philip faced this with the eunuch because he was a Gentile and from another race, he could have turned away from a divine engagement. We should never miss a God-ordained opportunity because of prejudice.

Reflection: Lord, give me eyes to see each opportunity you send my way. Help me to put aside selfishness, prejudice and procrastination so I will not miss any of your important missions for me.

January 29

Remembering Our Love

Revelation 2:1-7

You can probably remember your first real love. Now surely there were those episodes of puppy love-when your heart pounded rapidly and your palms grew sweaty. But then there was the first genuine love. There was a willingness to do anything for this person. It was the first time you really cared deeply for a person of the opposite sex.

Remembering their initial love for Jesus is what John instructed the first century church at Ephesus to do. Ephesus was a city filled with immorality, idolatry and witchcraft. This church found herself in the middle of an enormously wicked environment. Their instruction was to remember how faithful they were when they first trusted Christ as their Savior. They had lost that love and once again needed to impact their society.

Christians and churches need to hear these words again. While making advances in other countries, the church in America is in some trouble. Only a small percentage of her ranks are growing. The others are either plateaued or declining. Churches were once the center of communities and societies, but not anymore. Many have lost confidence in the church.

The church at Ephesus had started well. God commended the church for working hard, persevering, resisting sin, examining false teaching, and enduring hardships. They loved God and others, but then the founders of the church died, and the second generation took over. While the church was busy, many from the next generation lost their zeal-their first love. Additionally, much of what they did came from wrong motives.

First love can be dampened by time and familiarity. Christ wants that feeling of first love for him to extend over our lifetime journey with him. It's not just something we should feel only when we first trust him as Savior. Maintaining this takes time and attention. Prolonged lapses in reading his Word, praying and worshipping can move us away from that initial love.

Take a trip back in your memory to that moment when you trusted Christ. Remember how much you loved him, and how your heart's desire was to please him in all aspects of your life. Compare that with the present.

Reflection: Does God approve of your life today? Do your actions and words match up, or are you claiming to be something you really are not? Is your life a consistent testimony for God?

January 30
Shrouding Sin
Psalm 32

This psalm was a favorite of the early church father, Augustine. Before his death, he had it along with the following motto written on his wall: "the beginning of knowledge is to know yourself to be a sinner." The psalm reveals the heavy price the believer pays when we sin and try to conceal it. It also shows the joy of confessed sin and a restored relationship with God.

The background of the psalm is the familiar story of King David's transgression with Bathsheba, the wife of one of his soldiers. Instead of out with his army fighting, David decided to stay behind. As he is walking on his roof, he sees Bathsheba bathing, sends for her, and involves himself in an adulterous affair. To conceal his evil act, David has her husband killed and he marries Bathsheba. The resulting child dies as punishment for this sin. The consequences of this bad decision were monumental.

We have heard the saying that "confession is good for the soul." When we fail to do that, it will bring inner tension that will lead to emotional, physical and spiritual turmoil. Note the imagery in the psalm, "When I kept silent, my bones grew old Through my groaning all the day long.

For day and night Your hand was heavy upon me; My vitality was turned into the drought of summer."

It was almost a year before David confessed, and all the while God's hand of discipline grew heavier. Because God loves us as a parent, he will not let us go undisciplined for our sins if we refuse to acknowledge them. How much better to confess quickly while the infraction is still fresh on our mind.

It is spiritually dangerous to refuse to own up to our sins. A failure to confess can tear our emotions asunder. Our spiritual life can dry up because God cannot use us as he wishes. Prolonged and persistent unconfessed sin can destroy our testimony.

David finally confessed his dastardly deed after God sent the prophet Nathan to confront him. God promises forgiveness when we confess our sins, and this forgiveness is unlimited. No matter how many times we fail, he is always willing to forgive.

Reflection: God, help me to remember how dangerous it is when I hold onto sin. Help me to quickly confess it so that my witness for you is not damaged.

January 31

Coming Down from the High Place

I Kings 19:1-18

Have you ever felt as if everything was going your way only to have life come crashing down on you? Elijah was a prophet during the reign of King Ahab, the most evil king of Israel. Along with his wicked wife Jezebel, they made a team to fear.

Elijah challenged 450 prophets of Baal and 400 prophets of Asherah to a contest on Mt. Carmel, a bout to see which God would answer by fire and consume the sacrifices on the altar. Elijah's God answered. He then took the wicked prophets of Baal and killed them.

When Jezebel heard of this, she put a death sentence on Elijah. This once bold prophet of God-who had everything going his way, now ran for his life into the wilderness. He found shade under a tree, and then asked God to take his life. He had had enough. Eventually, God would lift his spirits, but at this moment life had him severely depressed. How can we explain the two extremes in his life? Was he bi-polar?

Often despair can follow a mountain top experience, and we must be on guard against that. The exhilarating experiences of life can lead us to let our guard down, and Satan can slip in with a landmine. Despair can sneak into our life. We find ourselves losing hope and becoming ineffective. It is the trials and tribulations of this life that can and will bring us down off the mountain. God allows trials into our life for the purpose of teaching us some lesson or to bring a level of maturity into our walk with him. At other times, Satan will attack us. Our duty is to guard against this despair by remaining close to God while on the mountains and in the valleys.

While the threat from Jezebel was real, Elijah's fear was unfounded. So afraid was he that he ran 95 miles. His fear was groundless because God promises to protect his children.

God doesn't promise a life free from troubles, but in those times we don't have to fear. In trying times, God can grow and develop us. He can produce patience and other fruit in our lives. He showed Elijah that he wasn't the only one still serving him. There were many more who had not bowed to Baal.

Reflection: Trust God while on the mountains and in the valleys. He will protect and grow you as his child.

February

February 1
Marks of Godly Living
Matthew 26:36-56

The "Little Engine that Could" is a familiar child's story of years past. Diesel locomotives had taken over, and the small steam-engine locomotive was out of date. One day the little locomotive faced an enormous hill to climb. As he looked, he saw other locomotives sail over the hill with no problem, but he was so much smaller. The little train became intimidated and discouraged, but he finally decided he was going to climb that hill and nothing was going to stop him. As he approached the bottom of the hill, he began to say to himself, "I think I can, I think I can," and before he knew it, he had climbed the hill.

Sometimes we feel that way as we observe what God expects from us. Intimidated, discouraged, unqualified are all words that come to mind. We need the courage of the little train.

No better example exists of one who lived a godly life than Jesus. While in the Garden of Gethsemane, he struggled with what was ahead-his arrest and crucifixion. In spite of the intense battle, one so agonizing that his sweat was as drops of blood, he overcame.

We must be determined to always choose God's will over anyone or anything else. Jesus did this here and on every other occasion. As he thought of the crucifixion, he was willing to say "Not my will but Yours be done." God's plan is always best. It will never lead us down a wrong path or cause us to make a wrong turn. God desires that we offer ourselves as living sacrifices to him-ones that do not crawl off the altar when things get tough in life.

Choosing to always obey may mean we have to stand alone on occasion. It is much easier to go along with the crowd. Like sanding with the grain of the wood. Jesus found himself alone in this part of the Garden as he agonized. His three disciples chose to sleep. Later when he was arrested, they all ran.

In general, we fear being ostracized by others. It hurts when others do not accept us or treat us as outcasts because of our stand for Christ.

After a study showing how easy we compromise for acceptance, one psychologist concluded, "Some people had rather be president than right."

Reflection: God's will is always best because he has our best at heart. Choose to stand for him, even if it's alone.

February 2

Reasons to Give

II Corinthians 8:1-15

Greed. If we are not careful, it can consume our lives. Others seem to have more than we do. It may be material possessions, family life, looks, or a position, but we see things we think we deserve. Before long, an attitude of greed develops, and if not halted, jealousy and envy will follow quickly. Our thinking will lead to action. We will find ourselves doing anything to rectify what we feel is wrong in our life situation.

How much better to be give than to gather. Giving leads to true happiness, as we learn to share with others what God has blessed us with. As Paul penned this epistle to the church at Corinth, he wrote to a church characterized by wealth and influence. Sometime prior to this, they had committed themselves to contribute to an offering Paul was taking for the impoverished saints in Jerusalem. Yet for one reason or another, they had put aside this project and turned their concerns toward other things.

The example of others can encourage us in our giving. Paul appeals to the Macedonians. The church here was under great persecution which affected them economically, but still they pleaded for the chance to contribute to the offering. They realized all they had came from God. They gave beyond their means-more than they could afford to give. God loves a cheerful giver. He wants us to give freely and gladly. He can pry things from our hands, but he would rather we give voluntarily.

Jesus' example can motivate us to give. His death for our sins was the greatest gift anyone could give. Jesus said the greatest love a person could have was to lay down his life for his friends. (John 15:13) Though he possessed all the glory and majesty of heaven, he became a servant for us. He traded a heavenly home for a stable. Giving is the very nature of the gospel itself. As one so aptly stated, "It is one beggar telling another beggar where to get bread."

Human need should impel us to share. The poor will always be with us. Jesus says that as we divide with others we are serving him. This should be reason enough to give. How shameful for some Christians to live in poverty while others have the means to help.

Reflection: Remember that all you have comes from God-even the very breath in your body. Share with others as God directs.

February 3

The Race of Life

Jonah 1:1-3

It is interesting to look around and see the many ways people race or compete. Indy racing, stock car racing and horse racing are all examples. In these sports, it is fascinating to see what can happen. Often the car or horse that leads in most of the race will not win. The horse might stumble or break a leg. The person in the lead car might make a wrong move, have a tire blow or have someone run into them. Sometimes the leader fails to win through no fault of his own. Competition is all around us. Major sports such as football, baseball and basketball are built around trying to score more points than the opposing team.

Christians are in a race. God has placed a finish line before us that is encapsulated in the Great Commission. Jonah is known as the "prophet of missionary responsibilities," but in Jonah's race, he ran the wrong way. God told him to head for Nineveh, capital of Assyria. Because he didn't care for the people there, he chose to go the opposite way. It's a whale of a story (no pun intended), but God had to use such to get his attention.

We can run from what God calls us to do, but the consequences are never pleasant. They weren't for Jonah. He chose to descend in the opposite direction of where God told him to go. It cost him embarrassment on the ship he boarded to run from God as well as three days and nights in the belly of a great fish-in itself not a pleasant experience.

God wants his message of salvation taken to the world and to all types of people. Doing this requires overlooking our prejudices and seeming limitations. We should not fabricate excuses in our mind as to why we cannot do what God has instructed. Difficulties should not deter us.

How much better to run to the task God has assigned and to do so with enthusiasm. Jonah finally did this after experiencing a sour stomach, but it took God's hand of discipline to point him in the right direction. After Jonah changed his mind, God instructed the fish to spit him up on dry land. Now he would go to Nineveh, though still with reluctance.

God is with us as we run this race of gospel proclamation. He has assured us that he will never leave or forsake us.

Reflection: Are you sharing God's love with all people, no matter their race or social status. God loves all people and we must as well.

February 4

Following Christ's Example

I Peter 2:18-25

People look in many places for examples. It is characteristic of the human nature to have peers, idols or heroes that we look up to. A trait or characteristic they have is appealing. We see something in their life that is lacking in ours-something that we hope to become. It may be teachers, doctors or sports figures. We can simply admire the money they make. Christians often find their models at church. We look at the great saints, one of which may have led you to the Lord or taught you diligently through the years.

The great exemplar for all Christians should be Christ. Following his lead means suffering. Being a slave in the Roman Empire meant suffering. Employees often feel pain at the hands of uncaring employers. Christ anguished for us on the cross, and we must suffer in our Christian walk. Any distress we endure in life will not compare to the agony of Christ on the cross. Not only did he endure the torment of the crucifixion process but he also took the payment for our sin—a punishment inflicted by God and not the Roman soldiers.

We should willingly hurt for Christ in return. We are not too good to walk in the Master's footsteps. Suffering must be something God has in mind for his followers. When we live with integrity and suffer for it, it brings glory to God. It shows the lost world we are different. We live by a higher standard.

Trusting God is vital to following Christ's example. Just as he placed himself in the hands of his heavenly Father, so must we. His was a life of spotless obedience lived on a divine timetable. He patiently and courageously confided in the Father to help him carry out his will daily.

We must trust God daily, believing he has a wonderful plan for our life. The plan will probably involve suffering, and it will certainly entail sacrifice, but obedience will bring complete fulfillment to our lives.

An artist once painted a beggar. When the beggar looked at the portrait, he didn't recognize himself. The artist told him the portrait showed what he saw the man to be, to which the beggar replied, "If that's the man you see, that's the man I'll become."

Reflection: Let Christ be your example, and be the person he sees. Follow his plan for your life and know true happiness.

February 5

Successful Living

Deuteronomy 4:1-10

Walter D. Wintle wrote in a poem, "Success begins with a fellow's will: it's all in the state of mind." Most people want success in life. They want to feel they are making an impact on others. Success can come through corrupt dealing or honesty-the latter being God's method. Success is measured with different gauges. For some, it is money and material things. Others believe they have it when they are following God's will for their life, regardless of whether that meets the world's definition or not.

Moses wished success for the Israelites as they took the Promised Land after many years of wilderness wanderings. Their ancestor's disobedience almost forty years earlier had led to this. If they were to know success this time, they had to obey God. Compliance with God's ways may be costly, but it is the only way victory will happen.

Obedience to God's Word is a must. We cannot add or take away from it based on whether or not we like a certain teaching. Nor can we remove something that seems beyond our explanation or that appears politically incorrect. It will do its work of triumph in our life but not if we pick and choose which part to obey.

In John Milton's *Paradise Lost,* Adam is made to say: "Henceforth I learn that to obey is best, And love with fear the only God, to walk As in his presence, ever to observe His providence, and on him sole depend."

Successful living is also about teaching others to obey God. This was what Moses did by example and instruction. Teaching others is incorporated into the Great Commission that Jesus left for his followers.

Jesus said we were to go into the entire world and tell people about him. Then we are to baptize them in the name of the Trinity. Discipleship must follow as we teach them how to live by his commands. Christians know this as the Great Commission.

We must also teach our families to obey God, so they might know success. Our faith should be passed down to our children and grandchildren, by modeling and enlightenment.

Reflection: God, help me to know that true success comes by obeying you and by teaching others to obey you. Help me to be a shining light to my family in my example. Amen.

February 6
A Mission-Minded Church
Acts 11:19-26

The Internet. In the twenty first century, it is a way of life. Most people could not imagine living without it. With beginnings under the direction of the United States Department of Defense in the early 1960's as the Advanced Research Projects Agency Net-part of national security during the Cold War, its purpose was to withstand a nuclear war. Now people all over the world have access, as it links independent computers around the world with each other. A part of its purpose is to get more information out to others as well as have more information made available to the computer user.

The church's purpose is no different-we are charged with getting information to the world. Hundreds of ethnic groups are now represented in America alone, speaking numerous dialects and languages. The world, for the most part, has come here. A great challenge is at our doorstep for our churches to be mission minded.

Antioch was some 300 miles north of Jerusalem. Persecution of the church drove many of the early believers there, and as they arrived they found an eager audience, ready to hear the gospel.

A mission minded church is composed of people who practice lifestyle evangelism. Our actions match what we proclaim. Antioch attracted all types of people and provided the early church with an opportunity to demonstrate their faith.

Peter reminded Christians that they were a chosen group of people. He even termed them a "royal priesthood." Believers must be holy in their lifestyles so they can adequately tell others about the one who has called them out of darkness. (I Peter 2:9)

Mission minded churches are non provincial. They realize the gospel must go beyond them, their state and country to the world. Again, technology has made this much easier. The church at Antioch sent the apostle Paul on several missionary journeys-taking the gospel to many other places. John Wesley said, "The world is my parish."

Reflection: We must put our love in action. Believers must care when people hurt, are sick, hungry and in adverse circumstances. The world is our mission field. Let them see Jesus in you.

February 7
Wonderfully Made
Psalm 139

Self-esteem. Many struggle to have a healthy dose of it. Low self-esteem can result from a range of things: a threatening or neglectful home environment in childhood, unrealistic expectations from parents or employers, poor body image, an abusive marriage, or any number of other things, all of which lead us to think less of ourselves than God does.

Whether planned by parents or not, no child is an accident. God is sovereign, and nothing occurs in this world-including a birth, that is not ordered or allowed by him. Your birth did not surprise God. He knew you before you were born. At the moment of conception, we are alive.

Our parts will form in measure before our birth and continue thereafter, but at no point are we just a "fetus" that should be destroyed without thought. Fate, chance, luck or coincidence is not in God's vocabulary.

God has wonderfully made you. You are his masterpiece-a work of art that he embellishes until your death. How sad that we are often dissatisfied with our appearance. There is nothing wrong with looking our best, but remember that God made you as you are. Your features, talents, gifts and personality are uniquely created by the Master's hand.

The days of our lives have been scheduled or determined by God as well. While we can shorten our lifespan by foolish decisions and actions, it is God's intent that we enjoy all our years serving him. He gives abundant life and wants us to experience it daily.

God created you out of his love, and he has a plan for your life. He has given you talents and gifts that match your unique personality. This enables you to do things in a way that no one else can. He has a special place for you in these particular years of the world's existence.

Because God has created our bodies, we should respect them. They are temples of his Spirit. Knowing this, we should honor our bodies, not putting anything in them that would defile his dwelling. Physical exercise and eating right are important, but our thoughts and attitudes are too. Jesus says what defiles us is not what goes in the body but what's already on the inside.

Reflection: Thank you God for making me so wonderfully complex. Help me to use my gifts and talents to serve you and others.

February 8
New Life
John 3:16

The story is told of four men-two guides and two tourists all roped together, climbing the most difficult face of the Matterhorn. As they went over a particular dangerous part, the bottom man lost his footing. He in turn carried the next man with him and him the next. Three of the four were now dangling over the cliff. The lead guide, feeling the first tug of the rope, plunged his axe into the ice, braced his feet and held fast until the other three could regain their footing.

Such is the plight of mankind. When Adam and Eve chose to sin against God, they pulled all of humanity down with them. This propensity to sin is passed along like the deadly disease it is. But like the top guide, Jesus dug himself into the cross to save us from the dread consequences of sin.

Jesus shares the simple gospel with Nicodemus, a Pharisee who comes to see him at night. Why after dark? Maybe he had a busy day at work or didn't want his fellow Pharisees to know he was interested in Jesus. In his conversation with Nicodemus, Jesus makes the world's most profound statement, "You must be born again."

We must be born again because we are sinners. Many words have been contrived to tone down the seriousness of the word, but none will do. Sin is not just a mistake, failure or character flaw. It is a transgression against God-missing the mark he has established for our life. Like a drunk, humanity cannot walk the straight line of God's requirements. Beyond this, God hates sin and will not look upon it.

No matter how cultured or refined, our sinful nature cannot rise above what it is. Sin places a wall between us and God. As Shakespeare's Lady Macbeth could not wash the imaginary blood of those she had murdered from her hands, so we cannot rectify our situation.

Our only hope is to trust in what Jesus did on Calvary. As he told Nicodemus, "You must be born again" or born from above. By the power of his Spirit, God must regenerate us. We must repent-turn and go in the opposite direction. Accepting Jesus by faith is the only possible hope.

Reflection: If you have not accepted Jesus as your only hope, do so now. Pray simply: "Lord Jesus. I believe you died on Calvary for me. I ask your forgiveness for my sins, and I want to follow you in obedience."

February 9

Home Wreckers

Genesis 25:20-34

Healthy families are increasingly more difficult to find. Children with two parents in the home are shrinking. Single parent homes are skyrocketing. More and more grandparents are raising grandchildren. The wrecking ball seems poised precariously over many families.

The story of Isaac and Rebekah and their family offers wise warnings that will stave off catastrophe in our families. Partiality will destroy a home. Rebekah favored Jacob while Isaac was fond of Esau. It was a recipe for disaster. Esau was an outdoorsman-a lifestyle that apparently appealed to his father, while Jacob was a homebody. His mannerisms and personality captivated Rebekah.

Favoritism infected this family. Jacob, perhaps feeling special, stole his brother's birthright-an inheritance reserved for the oldest son. Later, he would trick his aged father and confiscate the blessing that belonged to Esau. This deception led Esau to put a death warrant on his brother, resulting in Jacob running for his life. Rebekah never saw her son again.

Partiality will foster jealousy, and this can lead to strife in a family. It can cause friction between the parents, and more often discord between the siblings. Parents must be careful to treat all their children equally. They are each a gift from God.

Having an indifferent attitude about spiritual matters will also wreck a home. Though Jacob stole his brother's birthright, it appears Esau had a very casual attitude about it. The birthright involved receiving a double portion of material goods as the oldest son but also the spiritual leadership in the family. Esau didn't seem concerned about this. In fact, the descendants of Esau became an ungodly lot.

Parents must give their children a godly foundation. They must teach them God's Word and its principles as well as live them out in their lifestyle. Our children need our diligent prayers. Parents should also submit to God's will for their children. Parenting is not about rearing a child to become what you want them to be but what God wants. Encourage them to follow his will, not yours.

Reflection: Make it your commitment to put God first in your family. Pray daily that your children will follow his will.

February 10
Wilderness Warnings
Luke 3:7-9

Following the provocative attack on Pearl Harbor in 1941 by the Japanese Empire, President Franklin Roosevelt asked Congress for a declaration of war because of the "unprovoked and dastardly attack by Japan on Sunday, December 7th." It was a warning that would take the United States into another four year war.

Warnings can come from interesting places. This one came from a locust eating, honey slurping wilderness man dressed in a camel's hair garment secured with a leather belt. Drawn no doubt by his appearance and message, people flocked to hear and see him. They confessed their sins, and he baptized them. Then came the hypocritical religious leaders, but he had a different message for them. After calling them a bunch of snakes, he gave them some warnings-proposals we need to hear even after all these years.

The first was to bear fruit. The Pharisees talked a good game, but their actions were legalistic and did not flow from sincere motives. They wanted to be seen and heard. Jesus told them they were like pretty tombs. Problem was, the grave was full of maggot infested deteriorating bones.

God brings us into his fold to bear good fruit for him. Our actions must demonstrate his love that others might want what we have. Love, joy, peace, patience, kindness, goodness, gentleness, faithfulness and self-control are supposed to be the fruit on our trees.

In Nathaniel Hawthorne's, *The House of Seven Gables*, Phoebe, the house guest, asks, "How is it possible to see people in distress, without desiring, more than anything else, to help and comfort them?"

A further warning involves depending on God for our salvation. The pious religious leaders thought having Abraham as their ancestor was sufficient. John vehemently reminded them that it required repentance, not heritage. It is the same message we must take to unbelievers today. Only in Christ is salvation and forgiveness of sins found.

We are also cautioned about God's wrath. If we do not accept the love of God, we have to face his wrath. He is angry over sin every day, and he must punish it, unless we accept Christ's sacrifice on the cross.

Reflection: Is your life bearing fruit for God. On what or whom are you depending for salvation, if not Christ?

February 11

Sightseeing

Isaiah 6:1-8

Sightseeing. It's a favorite pastime for many—mountains, beaches, birds, flowers, leaves, insects, and more. There is so much to see in this beautiful world our Creator has designed, but of all there is to observe, Isaiah captured the most important, and it transformed his life.

Isaiah's world was very wicked. Worship of Baal was prevalent. Baal worship divorced one's daily life from his religious life, emphasizing ritual over a religious lifestyle. Uzziah, their king of 52 years, had died. The throne was empty, and the people were like sheep wandering aimlessly. In the midst of this mess, God called and commissioned this prophet.

God still does the same in our twisted world. He calls us to salvation and then to a life of holiness. It is an invitation to take up our cross daily and follow him. This exciting journey that he invites us to embark on only comes after we do some sightseeing.

God wants us to behold his holiness. Isaiah, in his vision, saw God on a high and elevated throne. Angels stood above him, and one cried, "Holy, Holy, Holy, is the Lord of hosts." Unless we discern the holiness of God, we will never see the need for forgiveness. He is the Holy Other. We are not like him, and he is not like us. The writer of Proverbs reminds us that fearing God is where knowledge begins.

After a seemingly successful meeting, Billy Graham was asked if revival had taken place. He said no. According to the great evangelist, revival would involve a fresh sense of God's holiness and man's sinfulness.

Our sightseeing journey must include our sinfulness. When Isaiah saw God's holiness, he cried out in anguish over his sinfulness. The Renaissance inspired people to think they could pull themselves up by their own bootstraps with no further need for God. Intelligence will not wash away our transgressions. Only God can do that by the blood of Christ. The sight of God's holiness will magnify our sinfulness, and this is not a negative element.

The Christian must also see the world. Isaiah recognized that people around him needed the same God he saw and worshipped. When we walk in the light, our perspective changes.

Reflection: God, help me grasp your holiness, so I can visualize my sinfulness. Direct me as I take your love to the world around me.

February 12

Celebrating the Covenant
Matthew 26:20-30

Celebrating the New Covenant established by Christ through observing the Lord's Supper is a vital part of Christian worship. The church in history has struggled with different aspects of the memorialization, but not with the observance itself. One question is how often we should partake of it. Another issue is the elements themselves. Are they symbolic of the body and blood of Christ, or, as some churches have maintained, do they actually change into his body and blood?

These differences aside, all Christians agree that observing the Lord's Supper is an important rite. It is an occasion to prepare for, not a mindless habit that involves no thought at all. We need to examine ourselves for known and unconfessed sin so we don't make a mockery of the event. It is an opportunity for inspection. The apostle Paul would later caution us to examine ourselves before we take of the Supper.

The commemoration also reminds us that we are capable of disappointing Christ. Otherwise, there would be no purpose in the examination. As Jesus ate the Passover Meal with his disciples and established the Lord's Supper, he made the startling announcement that one in the group would betray him. Judas knew he was the culprit, but no one else did. The disciples entered a state of shock over this declaration.

Betrayal comes in other forms than in outright denial, as was the case with Judas. When our actions, words and attitudes are not in keeping with the ideals of God's Word, we betray our Savior by emitting mixed signals. It confuses other Christians and fosters doubt from unbelievers.

Communion symbolizes the death of Christ. The elements are vivid reminders of what happened on the cross. The bread is broken as was his body prior to and on the cross. Merciless beating preceded the actual crucifixion, but the spear in the side and the spikes added to the agony. Blood flowed from the crown of thorns, the spear entrance, and the nails.

Eating the bread and drinking the juice reminds us of the pain Christ endured as he died for our sins. Our behavior after the celebration testifies of our love and loyalty to the Savior. We leave the Supper to face times of testing and trials but with renewed vigor to endure.

Reflection: Let the Supper remind you of God's amazing love.

February 13

The Christian's Liberty

I Corinthians 8:1-13

Believers are free in Christ, but what exactly does that mean? Now that Christ has forgiven my sins, can I do anything I choose? Exactly how far can I go before it damages my testimony?

A student once asked his Bible teacher if it was wrong to drink. The teacher cautiously answered that it was unwise to drink. The teacher explained that while no biblical mandate prohibits drinking completely, there are numerous places where the Bible speaks against drunkenness, drinking to excess, and about the foolishness of drinking.

Other examples could be given of things the Bible doesn't strictly address but that could be damaging to us physically or to our witness. Over time, Christians have debated such matters as smoking, drinking, dancing, playing cards, going to the movies, wearing makeup and listening to certain styles of music. Disagreements over these issues abound.

The apostle Paul dealt with such a matter in the first century. It involved Christians eating food that had been sacrificed to idols. This food was encountered at the marketplace where it was sold after being offered to an idol. Or they may be asked to eat it as a guest in someone's home unaware that it had been used in an idolatrous setting. Was it right or wrong?

While we have liberty in Christ, it is not license. We do not have the freedom to sin or to lead others into sin by our example. Christians have gravitated toward one of two extremes: legalism or license. Legalists live by rules not liberty. Everything is black or white whether the Bible specifically deals with it or not. For them, spirituality is living by a list of rules. Living by license is the opposite. If the Bible doesn't specifically forbid it, or if it doesn't bother my conscience, I can do it.

Paul's advice is somewhere in the middle of these two extremes. He offers a third option: not offending the conscience of another believer-one probably not yet mature in their faith. If eating meat offered to an idol offended them, the mature believer should not eat it.

Reflection: While we are free in Christ, we are not free to disobey biblical commands and thereby ruin our witness. Nor are we free to violate our own conscience with a questionable matter. Furthermore, we certainly should not offend a fellow Christian by our actions.

February 14

A Samaritan's Love

Luke 10:30-37

Valentine's Day celebrates love. Cards and flowers are sent to loved ones, often in the shape of a heart. Love is most assuredly an important characteristic. Some feel it makes the world go around. According to the apostle Paul, it is the greatest gift.

S. E. Hinton's book, *The Outsiders*, tells of two rival gangs: the Greasers and So-shes. In one scene, Johnny and Ponyboy, both Greasers, instinctively rescue children from a burning church. It was not normal behavior for a gang living on the wrong side of the tracks. Johnny was seriously injured. Just prior to his death, he admitted to Ponyboy that it was worth it to save those kids. It was an act of love.

While love was most vividly demonstrated on the cross, Jesus tells the story of the Good Samaritan to illustrate how love should be acted out. A man was making his way from Jerusalem to Jericho when he fell into the hands of robbers who beat him and left him for dead. A priest and Levite pass by. Neither offer any help. Finally a Samaritan stops, a man from the wrong side of the tracks. He bandages his wounds, takes him to an inn, and pays for his stay until he recuperates.

Love should tear down barriers. The Samaritan came from a mixed race of people and was despised by the devout Jew. In fact, most Jews, if traveling to the northern part of their country, would avoid the area of Samaria completely. The only way to truly love others is to destroy the man-made barriers separating us.

Love is also familiar with sacrifice. The Samaritan willingly gave of his supplies and time to help the wounded man, who was most likely a Jew and his sworn enemy. Love is most eloquently manifested by actions that inconvenience us in some way. It is the true test of the sincerity of our love. In all love relationships, there must be that willingness to give up for someone else.

Reflection: We love when we risk being misunderstood. The Samaritan's peers would not have understood his actions. Seemingly, this was of no concern to him. His love motivated him to help and risk misunderstanding. Make up your mind to love, regardless of what others think, because it is the right thing to do.

February 15
Soul Harvesters
Matthew 28:16-20

Harvest. It's what all gardeners and farmers hope for as they plant seeds. They envision fields bulging with corn, wheat, soybeans, cotton-all spouting from the seeds they have scattered. The hope is to reap more than was sown.

S. D. Gordon, in his book *Quiet Talks With World Winners*, tells of a group of climbers about to ascend Mont Blanc in the French Alps. On the evening prior to the climb, the guide shared the one basic requirement for success-take only the necessary equipment.

Christians are soul harvesters. Programs, activities and fellowship are good, but our main business is to sow seeds of godliness across our world so we can reap a harvest of unbelievers. While sometimes demanding and often difficult, it is our mission. To adequately accomplish this, we must take only the basic tools.

Be available. When someone is dying, their last words are vitally important. Jesus had already died, then was resurrected, and was now about to ascend into heaven, so these words swelter with significance. Jesus had instructed his disciples to meet him on a mountain in Galilee. They went, and Jesus met them. They were accessible.

Our greatest ability is availability. God grants gifts and talents to his people, but if we don't make ourselves available, they are of little value. God desires to work through us so a great harvest of souls might be reaped.

Be a genuine worshipper. When the disciples saw Jesus, this is what they did-though some doubted. These were the ones still confused about who Jesus was and why he had not set up his kingdom on earth. Apart from truly worshipping Christ for what he has done, we will not sow the seeds or reap a harvest. Worship inclines us to serve.

Submission is necessary for the harvest. All authority on heaven and earth is given to Jesus. Unless we submit to this authority, we will miss the harvest. We need his direction on the planting. He knows what nutrients the soil needs. He knows where we need to plow. Jesus' authority makes success possible.

Reflection: Are you committed to the harvest? Depend on God to guide you as you share his love with others.

February 16

Defining Revival

II Chronicles 7:14

Recent studies show Americans of all ages don't get enough sleep. I once required my high school Psychology class to keep a record of their sleep habits for a week. Results were astounding. Some were staying up until two a.m. Others were working until midnight. No wonder many of them came to class tired. We can grow spiritually tired as well. Just as sleep will regenerate our bodies, so spiritual nourishment will refresh the soul.

Spiritual restoration takes place during revival. God desires those times of renewing, but they depend in large part on us. Are we willing to do what is necessary? What does spiritual restoration entail? Humility, prayer, an earnest seeking for God, and a willingness to turn away from what we know to be wrong. These are our responsibilities. God will enable us, but the effort must be ours.

Revival is for the Christian. It has nothing to do with individuals trusting Christ-though that might happen during a revival. Evangelistic meetings and revivals are not the same, though evangelism is what the Christian does. For something to be rejuvenated, it has to be alive, and only believers are living spiritually. Unbelievers are diagnosed by God as spiritually dead.

Times of renewal are for believers who have grown cold in their faith. The fire of excitement has diminished. It may be from unconfessed sin, or from living with sinful habits that don't fit who we are.

Revival should be a continuing experience throughout our life span. Jewelry will dull over time if not polished. When polished, the luster is as if it was just purchased. The same is true for the Christian. Revival shines us up spiritually, and we need this periodically. It can be painful, as God confronts us with changes we need to make. He chisels away at things in our actions, attitudes, and relationships. It may take him a short time or long period to conform us.

Such times of renewing involve repentance. We recognize we are going in a wrong direction spiritually, and we ask God to help us make that U-turn.

Reflection: God, chisel away at those things in my life that hinder me from being spiritually zealous. Revive me today.

February 17

Defining the Church

Ephesians 4:1-16

The Church is alive and well. Attendance charts and giving records may seem to shout otherwise, but God's church is marching forward triumphantly. In fact, Jesus says the gates of hell shall not prevail against her. We are not fending off the onslaught of evil but rather are pressing against the doors of hell and all it represents.

As the body of Christ on earth, the church is a chosen community. We are his hands, feet, arms, ears and eyes. In the Old Testament, Israel was God's selected people with certain responsibilities. One was to be a light to the pagan people around them.

Applying what was once said of Israel, Peter said of the church that they are chosen by God with a purpose. As royal priests, they must proclaim what God has done for them to others. God has delivered them from a sinful lifestyle.

The church was birthed by God. So great was his love for her that he sent Christ to the cross. Individual churches may be organized and built by human hands, but God conceived the idea. God's church is a community. Christians do not live in isolation but are connected to each other by the common bond of Christ. As a group, we should manifest God's glory to the world with a unified stance on the core of the gospel. While varied in our parts, we are unified in our commission.

Since Christ gave his life for the church, he is the head. No individual, group or board controls the church. Decisions should be made under the guidance of the Holy Spirit, not by tradition or out of fear from a power structure. We acknowledge his headship by living lives that honor him.

As our head, Paul compares the relationship to a marriage-Christ is the groom and we are his bride. He is the cornerstone that holds the building together. Christ is the vine and we are branches. We draw our sustenance from him and would wither and die if cut off.

Reflection: God's church is a fellowship of redemptive love. While composed of different denominations, races and cultures, our goal remains the same. We must take the love of Christ to our world by a holy lifestyle and practical ministry methods.

February 18

True Freedom

Galatians 5:13-15

Freedom movements are prevalent in history. In America, our great trek for freedom came when we shook off the chains of Great Britain. No longer would a far-away nation control us with their injustices. Yet many years into the future, groups in our country continue to cry for freedom from some type of oppression or injustice. Ours is a day of individual rights where authority is dismissed or at best flouted in the name of "me."

Jesus taught that only he could give a person true liberty. He said those made free by the Son were the only ones who were truly liberated. Paul taught this same freedom-one found in knowing Christ as Savior but also in understanding the nature of this freedom and the provision God has made for us to live in it.

As emancipated people, we must oppose our flesh. The flesh is not identical to the sinful nature we are born with. God removes that at salvation and replaces it with a new nature. However, we still contend with the flesh. It is the old habits and patterns of behavior that we learned in the maturing process. Satan works through this aspect of the Christian's life, and we must do battle with it. The difference is that we now have new power from Christ to be victorious over the flesh. He will not allow us to be tempted to the degree that we cannot resist.

In John Bunyan's classic, *Pilgrim's Progress*, Christian is on his way to the City of Zion. Passing through the Valley of Humiliation, he comes upon Apollyon, his enemy, who entices him to return to his service. Christian's response should be ours when we are tempted, "But I have let myself to another, even to the King of princes, and how can I with fairness go back with thee?"

Freedom is not about doing anything we want without restriction. It is not about indulging in those things Christ has delivered us from. Liberty is about possessing the power, for the first time, to live according to God's requirements. It is loving what is right and hating what is wrong, for we cannot love the wrong and live for Christ. Some things are mutually exclusive.

Reflection: God has given us the necessary equipment to oppose the flesh and live victoriously.

February 19

Continuing in Freedom

Galatians 5:13-15

The Civil Rights era in America was one with marches for freedom in various areas: women's rights, African American rights, gay rights, and privileges for other fringe groups-even right-wing militant ones. An accurate understanding of freedom, however, requires looking at its spiritual dimensions.

True freedom expresses itself in serving others. Paul says we are to have the same mindset as Christ, who, although he was God himself, did not let that deter him from emptying himself to serve us on the cross. We often think of serving as a painful sacrifice that is unpleasant. Yet giving of ourselves in some way brings a form of happiness not found in any other place. Because Christ has made a deposit of love in our hearts, serving should come natural to us.

Jesus demonstrated the concept of serving by washing his disciples' feet. Such was the duty of the lowest servant, but it was not beneath Jesus as he taught his followers what life is all about-not taking but giving.

In Hannah Hurnard's allegory, *Hind's Feet on High Places*, Shepherd says, "The High Places are the starting places for the journey down to the lowest place in the world. For it is only up on the High Places of Love that anyone can receive the power to pour themselves down in an utter abandonment of self-giving."

Liberty is fulfilling God's moral law. This is done by loving our neighbor. God's standards have never changed, and a part of his plan is loving our neighbor as ourselves. Normally, it is easy to look out for myself. We're taught the "number one" principle early in life, but it is one the believer must forget. Jesus frees us to love those we could not or did not want to love before we trusted him. He even empowers us to love our enemies.

Living in freedom avoids harming others. If we bite and devour one another, we will consume each other. Like wild animals in the fury of a deadly struggle for existence. True freedom is always limited because it takes other rights into consideration. We must serve wrapped in the cords of unity.

Reflection: Be a freedom fighter. Take your eyes off self and love your neighbor. According to Jesus, the two greatest commands are to love God first and then others.

February 20
Words for the Home
I Peter 3:1-6

While serving as Secretary of State, John Dulles once phoned Douglas MacArthur II's home. Mistaking him for an aide, MacArthur's wife snapped at him, telling him MacArthur was where he always was-at the office. Indeed, he was a hard worker. Moments later, Dulles phoned MacArthur's office and told him, "Go home at once, boy. Your home front is crumbling."

God has directions for the home. In addition to the instructions here, the New Testament contains two other passages pertaining to the home, the others being found in Ephesians and Colossians. None of these are favorites of women's rights groups or of those who think children should be allowed to express themselves and their emotions without consequence. Yet, they give injunctions, which if adhered to, would heal the hurts in many families.

Wives are to show redemptive behavior in the home by being submissive to their husbands. While such mandates seem oppressive from a twenty-first century viewpoint, they were actually very revolutionary for the time. In the first century, women had little if any rights. The Jewish wife was considered the property of her husband. The Greek wife was to remain indoors and be obedient to her husband. Under Roman law, the woman had no rights at all.

Peter and the apostle Paul recognized mutual responsibilities between husband and wife. This was progressive thinking for the period. The submission was voluntary, even as the believer voluntarily submits to Christ. It is not a command to submit to men in general, but only to her husband. If a woman is married to an unbelieving husband, it might be this very act that leads him to Christ. The wife should be clean, pure and above reproach.

The wife should also show her inner person. The warning is against becoming obsessed with what she wears or how she looks, and using that as a measurement of her self-worth. A godly woman's adornment is not outwardly but inwardly. The Christian wife is to be modest, discreet and

66

is to put away all appearances of worldliness. She is attractive because of Christ.

Reflection: God, as your follower, help me to remember that I am beautiful because you live in me.

February 21

Home Recipes

I Peter 3:1-9

While some dishes are thrown together without a recipe, most of what we eat-especially our desserts, meats and casseroles, results from a recipe. It is possible to leave some ingredients out of most recipes without affecting the outcome, but other components are vital to the end result. For example, baking a cake without flour would be disastrous.

Likewise, there are vital ingredients for a successful family. Just as the wife has the responsibility to submit to her husband and let her inner character show outwardly, so the husband and children have duties as well.

Husbands are to be considerate and respectful of their wives. If they are not, their prayers will be hindered. Just as unconfessed sins affects our relationship with God and keeps him from working in our life as he wishes, so the same will happen in the marriage. There is a spiritual connection between how the husband treats his wife and his relationship with God.

Paul says the husband should love his wife as Christ did the church. He loved the church so much that he died for it. The husband is to love his wife as he does his body. Our bodies are temples of God's Spirit and should be held in high regard by caring for them physically. When a husband chooses to mistreat his wife, his relationship with God will suffer.

Children are also involved in the recipe. They are to obey and honor their parents. This doesn't mean they must always agree with them, but they should always honor them. While obedience in some matters may end when children leave home, honor should be shown for a lifetime. Honor involves respect and love, and children owe this much to the parents for all they have done for them. This command reflects one of the Ten Commandments and establishes a foundation for healthy societies.

Authentic Christian families should have unity. This does not mean husbands, wives and children will always agree. God has given us different personalities, but overall harmony should exist. Sympathy will be present as all parties care for one another. Love will be the yeast that causes tenderness to grow. Humility will help each member look out for the other's interests.

Reflection: Father, help me be faithful to my position in my family. Help me understand that my family is a reflection of the church and the harmony, respect and love that should be found there.

February 22
Handling Stress
John 16:33

Jesus said he came to bring peace yet stress seems to be the dominant theme in our world. Couples living from paycheck to paycheck. Single parents caring for children.Soccer moms worn out from travel. Retirees living on fixed incomes. Rapid growth in technology leaving many behind and frustrated. On and on the list goes.

We often focus on the negative aspects of stress, but there are some positive qualities. Children with negligible stress develop better than those with none, and stress does challenge us. When negative, stress can destroy us, but positive stress will move us farther up the mountain. Adapting positively to stress is important. Otherwise it will affect us emotionally, physically and spiritually.

Avoiding fleshly patterns in dealing with stress is essential. Christians should know better, but often, in a lapse of judgment, we damage ourselves by such patterns. We turn to drugs-prescription or not, alcohol, or tobacco. Church attendance weakens. Un-Christlike attitudes creep in. Materialistic thinking takes over. We work more. A drive for power infiltrates. I must control situations to avoid stress.

Such things only increase the damage of stress and do not fit the Christian's life. Letting God have control helps us deal with negative stress. After all, he is in control anyway. We just need to acknowledge it. Ironically, the stress comes when trying to govern our lives. Since he is all knowing and all powerful, why not let him take charge?

Stress can result from making decisions without consulting God first. This leads to bad decisions and often financial duress. Human nature causes us to want control and to tackle life alone. Christ wants to be involved in every detail of your life.

Along with stress comes fear, and we need to leave this behind. God has not given us a spirit of fear, but of power, love and a sound mind. Fear will enslave. Many situations lead to caution, but fear for the believer is unfounded.

Reflection: Often things we do that lead to stress are an attempt to boost our self-esteem. Ask God to enable you to remember that you are important because you are His. He controls every situation.

February 23
Kingdom People
Matthew 5-7

The Kingdom of God is often misunderstood. It can refer to heaven. Some define it as a literal thousand year rule of Christ prior to the end of time. Still others see it as the period between Jesus' first coming and when God ends it all. Ironically, all three definitions fit. When we trust Christ as our Savior, we enter the kingdom of God. From that moment on, life isdifferent because we are changed people.

As kingdom inhabitants, our internal motivations are more important than the external. Jesus says our righteousness must exceed that of the religious leaders of his day. They were very meticulous in observing God's laws. However, most of them did it for the wrong reasons. A pat on the back, to be seen by others, and thinking it would gain them entrance into heaven were all reasons for their good works. Our good deeds should emanate from a heartfelt appreciation for what God has done for us-nothing more. We can keep the letter of the law and miss the heart of it.

Our responsibility to God is more important than the behavior of others. People will disappoint us, but God never will. The religious leaders taught the people to love their neighbors and hate their enemies. God's law did not teach this. The law taught people to love their enemies and pray for those who persecuted them. Others will often malign and ridicule us because of our stand for Christ, but keep your behavior clean and pure.

For kingdom people, the eternal is more important than the earthly. We store our treasures in heaven, and this is done by clean actions, words and attitudes. Here, they will not corrode nor can thieves steal them. Some things in life are more important than others. Our eyes and efforts should be on the eternal not the temporal.

Additionally, our character is more important than our behavior. What is on the inside is reigns supreme. While others may look at our outward behavior, God looks on the heart. The heart-who we really are, controls our character. What we think leads to what we feel, and this leads to actions.

Reflection: Kingdom people look at their actions before that of others. We cannot help others until we deal with those things in our life that shouldn't be there. Treat others as you want to be treated.

February 24
Healthy Churches
John 5:1-15

A trip the family doctor for a physical is often where we begin to determine the status of our health. The doctor will check such things as blood pressure, pulse, and weight. Blood work is normal. Then comes the prodding and poking in different places. After all results are in, the doctor will tell us what health issues we may or may not have.

God wants his churches to be healthy. Our period in time finds Christians pulled in many directions by busyness. As Jesus went to Jerusalem, he came upon a collection of people with all types of infirmities: blind, lame, and paralyzed. He approached one man who had been an invalid for 38 years. His question seemed senseless, but it made perfect sense. Jesus asked him if he wanted to get well. Churches must want to get well.

A healthy church will takes steps of faith. After asking the question, Jesus told the man to get up, take his mat and walk. The command must have seemed absurd. He had been lame for such a long time, but he obeyed and took that step of faith which led to many other steps.

As head of the church, Jesus will not permit its death. Therefore, we can faith walk with confidence. We must renew our commitment to spread the gospel, teach the Bible, help the needy, and give hope to a hurting world, all the while letting God's Spirit guide us in our endeavors.

Healthy churches will put away some things. Jesus told the man to pick up his mat, but in reality he was telling him to put it away. He would not need to lie on it anymore as he had been doing.

While some traditions are healthy, others can keep us from moving ahead in God's work. Tradition for tradition sake is devastating. We have to change our methods while clinging to the core of what we believe. Methods are not sacred. Only the message is. Positive attitudes are just as contagious as the negative ones. Some toys are age appropriate, and so are some programs.

Jesus told the man to do something-walk. His problem had become a way of life, so no doubt he lay there without hope. Healthy churches want to do something for God. Good intentions without actions are only that-good.

Reflection: What am I doing to help my church have a clean bill of health?

February 25

Life's Most Important Question
Matthew 19:16-22

Many things in life can be summed up by Sir Winston Churchill's statement concerning Russia's actions: "It's a riddle, wrapped up in a mystery, inside an enigma." Life can hold questions that are unanswerable. They may disturb us and baffle our minds, but there is no answer.

The question of how to have eternal life is life's most important matter. Obviously, this was recognized by a rich young man who came to Jesus with this very question. Rather than immediately answering his inquiry, Jesus gives him a test of sincerity that would examine his motives. In the question posed and the answer given, we find the way of salvation as well as the answer to this most important query.

Recognizing our need is a part of the solution. The rich young man needed to realize that eternal life was not gained simply by obeying the commands. There were internal issues at hand. Jesus told him to sell all he had and give the proceeds to the poor. The young man left grieving, for he had much wealth. His treasure was in the wrong place, and his priorities were out of sequence.

Our need is forgiveness, plain and simple. Sin separates us from God, and until this is recognized, we will never have eternal life. The forgiveness has been made possible through Jesus' work on the cross, but we must accept it. Religion and good works will not suffice. While we have many real needs in life, forgiveness is the greatest.

God does expect adherence to his commands. While obedience doesn't bring eternal life, appreciation for our forgiveness will motivate us to conform. The rich young man Jesus spoke to was obeying for the wrong reason. God's commands are for our good, not to make life miserable. Compliance with God's demands leads to hating sin-what each Christian should do.

Paying a cost is a part of attaining eternal life. The young man was instructed to sell his possessions. We are to put away whatever comes between us and God. There is a price to pay in following Christ.

Reflection: Are you sure of your eternal life? Have you recognized your sinfulness and asked Christ for forgiveness? If so, are you putting away those things that hinder you from following him in obedience?

February 26

Portrait of a Christian

I Peter 1 and 2

Are you happy as a Christian? Do you feel as if something is missing? Is there something you wish you would have done today? Comfort comes in knowing that God is not through with you yet. But we must respond in the correct manner for his portrait to turn out as he desires.

Definitions of a Christian vary. Is it a person who attends church every time the doors are open? Some insist it means avoiding the known vices: drinking, smoking, gambling and cussing. Others suggest that a person can be born or raised a Christian. These definitions are only important if they match God's Word.

Peter states that Christians are obedient children. Parents are proud when their children are obedient to them and other authority figures. It demonstrates a sense of respect instilled in them. God is no less proud when his children obey him. In fact, he demands it. Peter says we are not to be conformed to those things that characterized our life before Christ.

Our obedience to Christ should result from love, not fear of reprisal or punishment. While God does discipline us because of disobedience, this comes out of concern for our well being. Parents do the same if love is the source of the punishment. We obey because we love. God can force his children to submit if they act stubbornly, but voluntary compliance out of love is what he desires.

In our submission to God, we are to act as newborn babies. Newborns have a craving for milk. It's the first thing they want after entering the world, and the desire continues until they are weaned. We should long, yes crave, God's Word. It is our source of nourishment wherein we discover God's will and plan for our life. The principles therein will satisfy our God-given thirst.

Christians should display unity. This is the only way we can erect God's spiritual house. Jesus is the cornerstone, but we are living stones joined together. We are also aliens and exiles in this world. It's not our eternal home. As such, we should not be excessively concerned with what happens here.

Reflection: When others look at you, who do they see? A phony, a hypocrite or one truly following Christ. Be genuine in your faith walk.

February 27
The Spirit Filled Life
Galatians 5:22-23

Suppose you purchase a small seedling with no leaves or fruit. There is no tag, so the identity of the tree is uncertain. But you want a tree in your yard, so you buy it anyway. In time, leaves begin to appear. You are not an arborist, so the name of the tree remains a mystery. The second year after planting, suddenly fruit appears. Since you know what an apple is, you now know what type of tree it is.

Like trees, believers are planted and rooted in God's love. We have his Spirit indwelling us. Because of nutrients associated with that connection, certain fruit should appear in time. The apostle Paul lists the type of fruit that others should see in our life and thus be able to identify us by.

Love is the foremost fruit. It is the greatest virtue that can grow. God's entire law is summed up in the command to love our neighbor as we do ourselves. This love will motivate us to give unselfishly and unconditionally as God did to us. He showed his love while we were still sinners by allowing Christ to die for us. Our love should extend to all people.

At Christmas, a young wife sent a note to the woman her husband had been unfaithful with stating, "Because of Christ's love for me and through me, I can love you!" How deep is your love?

Joy is a fruit that should dangle on our tree. Sadness abounds in our world, and there are many reasons for it. The Christian, however, has great cause to have a smile on their face. Christ has forgiven our sins and assured us of a home in heaven. Our happiness is based on spiritual realities. It is a sense of contentment that comes from knowing that all is well between us and God. Circumstances do not affect it and people can't steal it.

When love and joy hang heavily in our life, peace will result. Like joy, peace has nothing to do with circumstances. The Bible terms it a peace beyond our understanding. Like a soothing balm, it coats troubles and trials with a sense of well being.

We have the promise that God will work all things together for our good and his glory. Peace comes when we know God is in control. Jesus says he is the giver of peace, and it is a peace unlike the world tries to give us.

Reflection: God, help me remember that my fruit shows others what I am. Help me to know your love, joy and peace.

February 28
The Spirit Filled Life
Galatians 5:22-23

Fruit is a healthy part of good diets. It contains vitamins, minerals and acids that aid the digestive process. Fruit can be eaten fresh, canned, frozen, and dried. Bottom line, fruit is beneficial for our body. Fruit is also good for the Christian's body. It is proof positive that we belong to God.

Patience is an important fruit. It is a virtue and often takes a long time to develop. Situations arise regularly that test our endurance. When injured or wronged, patient people are tolerant and longsuffering. It is a calm willingness to accept situations that are irritating and painful. This is done without a desire to retaliate or get revenge. Instead, we are kind and compassionate. We interact with others on the basis of understanding not criticism.

We must exercise patience in doing God's work. Others will oppose us. The work can be tiring. If not careful, we can get discouraged. Even in the church, we find some who are not excited and even seem lazy. Yet, we calmly move forward in the most exciting work to be found.

This virtue is seen in Jesus' life. Many doubted his authenticity. He was maligned, tested, and falsely accused, yet he diligently moved ahead with his Father's work. He was finally crucified, but patience was a fruit dangling from his life tree. Joseph demonstrated this virtue even after cruel treatment from his brothers. God is patient with us, and we must emulate that example.

Our lives should also exude with kindness. Kindness involves tender compassion and concern. It is a genuine desire to treat others as God treats us and should permeate every fiber of our being. We will weep over sin and sinners as we see their condition apart from God. Jesus brought kindness to his world by healing the sick, lame, blind, and deaf. He showed compassion to those ostracized by the society of his day.

Goodness is another fruit of the Spirit. This is active goodness. It is possible to be morally upright, yet not show goodness to others. We must sacrifice self. Goodness is not shown because we expect a medal or reward but because God has been inclined favorably toward us.

Reflection: Lord Jesus, help me show patience with others as you do with me. Help me to see people as you see them, and give me opportunities to show kindness and goodness to others.

March

March 1
The Spirit Filled Life
Galatians 5:22-23

By now, we know the importance of fruit in our diet. Doctors and health experts continually remind us of this. According to the Food Guide Pyramid, a daily portion of two to four servings should be in our daily diet. Grocery stores usually put fruit on the first aisle.

All of the fruits of the Spirit should be evident in our life. Because of our relationship with God, we have the power to produce them all and thereby honor him. Manifesting these fruits gives witness before others of what he has done for us.

Faithfulness is a must in the believer's life. This is not the faith we exercise when we first accept Christ as our Savior. It is the loyalty and trustworthiness that follow thereafter. This is one of the surest tests of our character. Jesus says if we love him we will obey his commands. Obedience demonstrates our faithfulness. Jesus exemplified loyalty by his obedience to the Father, even when it meant his death.

Being faithful means adhering to the right and opposing the wrong. To do this, we must continually discover the right in God's Word. There is a difference between right and wrong, and the Christian must show faithfulness to what is right. We should be devoted to God's plan for our life. He has an individual plan for us, and it is up to us to let him reveal what it is. Our steadfastness will help us grow spiritually.

Gentleness should adorn our life. The word is sometimes translated meekness. It is power under control, like the horse that has enormous strength but is controlled with a bit and bridles. We remain humble and gentle, even when mistreated by others. It is submission to the will of God, a willingness to be taught, and consideration for other people. When hurt, we do not rise up defensively, and God receives all the glory from our lives.

Self-control is a difficult but necessary fruit to grow. This involves learning to restrain our passions and appetites. It also entails controlling our thoughts and actions. Unkindness, pride, jealousy, gossip, tempers and immorality are all areas where we often need restraint.

Reflection: Lord, thank you for producing spiritual fruit in my life. Help me to show faithfulness and gentleness to others and self-control in my life.

March 2

Sufficient Faith

Genesis 4:2-4

The story is told of a man driving his truck along a narrow mountain road. As he rounded a curve, he suddenly lost control, and the truck plummeted over the side. He managed to grab a bush as the truck fell to the rocks below and burst into flames. As he dangled over the edge, he cried out in desperation.Suddenly the Lord answered and asked what he wanted. Help of course was his answer. The Lord told him to let go of the bush and he would catch him. Looking at the valley below and the burning truck, he asked, "Is anyone else there?" Insufficient faith.

While we exercise faith in people and things every day, the acid question is whether our faith in God is sufficient. Do you worry that a tragedy or life changing event would destroy your faith in God? Has it already?

The story of Cain and Abel is familiar to most Bible students. So is the story of their sacrifices. Abel's was accepted by God but not because it was a blood sacrifice. Cain's was rejected but not because it was not an animal. Attitude determined acceptance. Abel approached God with a proper one but Cain did not.

Sufficient faith will bring the right sacrifice. Abel brought the best of what he had. Cain just brought something. The contrast was between a careless thoughtless offering and a generous one. Cain thought he could approach God with any attitude he chose. He tried to worship God the way he wanted and not how God required.

After recognizing our sinfulness and accepting Christ, we must live by faith. It must embellish every decision we make. Such faith recognizes that God is active in every detail of life. We are not accepted because of good works but because we are loved by God and we bring the faith sacrifice.

Sufficient faith leads to righteousness. Cain and Abel were both sinful. One just had the right kind of faith, and that led to God's acceptance.

God wipes the slate clean when we ask for forgiveness. He declares us righteous. We are justified-just as if we never sinned. Our sins are cast into the depths of the ocean.

Reflection: When our faith is sufficient, it will speak to others as Abel's has for centuries. Give your best to God, not just the leftovers. Thank God for his forgiveness of all your sins.

March 3

The Final Evaluation

Romans 14:10-12

Evaluations are common in the work world. On a time frame determined by the company or proprietor, employees are evaluated on their performance, attendance and attitudes. Based on the results, an employee may secure a raise, be reprimanded or even terminated.

God's Word speaks of a final evaluation, a time when we will stand before God and give an account. The Bible says it is appointed that man die and after that be judged. We will stand before the judgment seat of Christ. While we may differ in many respects, death is the great leveler of humanity.

Since we are assured of a final evaluation, it is important to know on what God will judge us. He will judge us on the matter of salvation. What have we done with his Son? This is the ultimate evaluation for it determines one's destiny. The answer to this question is of vital importance. Heaven or hell results from the decision.

In the evaluation process, baptism is essential. Nowhere does the Bible teach that baptism is required for salvation, but it does instruct us to be baptized after trusting Christ. What is its importance? It is symbolic. It shows others that we have died to the old way of living and have been raised to new life in Christ.

Many methods of baptism have been used throughout Christian history: immersion, pouring, and sprinkling. The correct method is not the issue. That one has done it is the important fact. By doing so, we proclaim to others that we are not ashamed of our Savior.

Our work for Christ will enter into the final evaluation. Salvation and baptism are only the beginning of the Christian walk. Using our gifts and talents to work for God is the other part of the lifelong journey. It is a pleasure to serve him not a burden. While our talents and gifts differ, we all have them, and God expects us to use them. The greatest ability he gives is to love others.

We are also instructed to tell others about Christ. Jesus tells us we are his witnesses. Don't keep the good news to yourself.

Reflection: Are you ready to stand before God for the final evaluation? If not, accept his Son today, be baptized and follow him in obedience.

March 4

What's In a Voice?

I Kings 19:11-12

The voice is one of the most widely used methods of communication for humans and animals. While many higher vertebrates can make some vocal sounds, only humans have the capacity to laugh, cry, sing and speak. Different parts of our body must work together for the voice to function. We might think how different our world would be if our voices failed.

Elijah, a great prophet of God, had encountered some voices. He had heard the voices of the prophets of Baal as they cried out to their god to send fire, consume their sacrifice and prove he was god. He had heard the voice of wicked Queen Jezebel, threatening to put him to death. After fleeing far into the wilderness, and now entering a cave, he hears another voice.

The voice Elijah senses this time is God's, but it came in an unexpected way. Elijah was accustomed to God speaking in miraculous and magnificent ways, so when he felt the wind, saw the fire and felt the earthquake, he was quite sure God was communicating in at least one of them. He was wrong. Yahweh spoke only in a still small voice.

God still speaks in the same manner. On the Day of Pentecost, God sent his Spirit upon believers. Now all who believe have God's Spirit residing in them. God talks to us by his Spirit in a quiet voice. It comes when we read his Word, pray, and interact with other believers. We hear it in our consciences as God pricks them when we stray from the narrow path. It is God's Spirit that initially draws a person to Christ, helping them realize they are sinners. This still small voice leads us to abundant living.

How many times have you been so engrossed in a television show, movie or book and have missed someone walk through the room or fail to hear what someone says to you? Have you missed God's voice?

God's still small voice gives instructions. God gave Elijah several tasks to complete after he left the cave. God's Spirit gives us directions, which will lead to success in our ministries. He tells us to care for the physical, mental, emotional and spiritual needs of others. Have you heard, and have you obeyed? He tells us to love him above all else. Are you?

Reflection: How wonderful to establish communication with the God of the universe. Even more wonderful is that he chooses to speak to us. Learn to identify God's voice in your life.

March 5

Getting Out of the Rut

Acts 9

The Appalachian Trail is a footpath extending more than two thousand miles from Georgia to Maine. Each year, thousands of people begin thru-hiking the trail. Very few actually finish. Many more day hike. Some of the more popular spots have been trekked on so heavily that ruts have developed-ruts that are very difficult to walk in.

Ruts are akin to a daily routine. Most of us have morning habits. Up at a certain time, get the kids ready for school, leave for work, come home and eat, shower and off to bed. Ruts are formed when we do the same thing over and over again. While some routines have merit, there are times when we need to get out of life's grooves.

Saul was on a religious treadmill. He arrested Christians and dragged them off to prison. They threatened his religion of Judaism. As he was on his way to Damascus to do this very thing, a bright light appeared. God met him face to face and interrupted his religious rut.

Traditions can be important, but they cannot replace timeless truths. Saul's religious customs were only that. They had little meaning and were making no difference in his life. Ruts can grow out of personal or cultural convictions. They may or may not be biblical. We get into trouble when we judge others by our traditional mores and not by what God says. Our sacred customs must align themselves with God's Word. It is the same problem Jesus had with the religious leaders.

Ruts keep our eyes focused on "me" instead of others. Being a Pharisee, Saul no doubt had this problem. Life was all about him. Jesus constantly confronted the Pharisees with their selfishness and self centeredness. We must put our eyes on others.

Ruts also cloud our vision. We can only detect the same old thing. Churches and believers need dreams. What do you envision God doing in your life and in your church?

Reversing mindsets leads us out of the rut. Believers are no longer sinners. We are saints, and as such we can rejoice in who we are and what God can do through us. His power is unlimited.

Reflection: Are you in a religious rut? Ask God to grant you a vision of what he can do in and through your life.

March 6

Surviving the Integrity Crisis

Genesis 39:11-13

Integrity is doing the right thing when no one is looking or when everyone is looking. It is a determination to make the right decision in all situations. Webster defines it as "an unimpaired condition: soundness." True integrity goes beyond actions to motives. Yet our world finds itself in an integrity crisis. All types of actions are taken to protect ourselves against those who would cheat us because they lack integrity.

Joseph was a man of integrity. Sold by his brothers because of their hatred, he finds himself in an Egyptian prison. After finding favor with the captain of Pharaoh's bodyguard, he was elevated to overseer of Potiphar's house. But Joseph was a handsome young man, and Potiphar's wife wanted him to sleep with her. Being a man of integrity, Joseph ran instead of succumbing to the temptation. He paid for his integrity with another trip to prison, but he did the right thing. Believers should lead the way in being people of integrity.

We need to do the right thing even if it seems everyone else is compromising. Daniel was such a man. Taken captive to Babylon, he in time finds himself promoted to a leadership position. Some of his work cohorts became jealous and tried to find some fault in him. They persuaded the king to issue an order prohibiting worship of any other god. This presented an integrity crisis for Daniel. He chose to do as he had always done-pray three times a day to his God. It cost him a trip to the lion's den, but God rewarded his decision.

Doing the right thing when many around you choose to compromise will not always win you friends, but you will stand out as a shining example of righteousness. God will bless you. Make it a point to reflect this characteristic of God in your life.

Choose to show integrity even when life seems to throw you a curve ball. Life is full of the unexpected. When times get tough, we are tempted to take short cuts or do things we would not normally do to get ahead. Integrity maintains itself even in difficult circumstances.

Reflection: Anytime we compromise our integrity, consequences follow. They did with David and Bathsheba and when Peter denied Christ. Make a daily commitment to God that you will be a person of integrity.

March 7

How to Have Healthy Families

Genesis 27:31-34

Brian had flown halfway across the country to reconcile years of resentment and misunderstanding between him and his father. As he leaned over his father's hospital bed, listening to the heart monitor, he cried, "Please, say that you love me. Please." He had searched for years to gain his father's approval, but it was always just out of reach. He had grown up as a Marine's son where words of love and tenderness were forbidden. After a dishonorable discharge from the Marine's, Brian was no longer welcome in his father's home. His father died with the wall erected. Brian never received his father's blessing.

Jacob and Esau are only two examples of the biblical blessing being administered. Parents would give words of encouragement, love, and acceptance, usually just prior to death. Parents today have daily opportunities to give the blessing so their children can grow up emotionally stable.

Wholesome families touch. Biblical blessings involved touching-a hand on the head, kiss on the cheek or hug, but touch preceded the blessing.

Touching between spouses and parents and children is essential. It communicates warmth, acceptance and affirmation.

Speaking the right kind of words promotes healthiness. Normally, the biblical blessing contained encouraging words about the child's future. Touching without words of love and acceptance does not glean the same effect. Nor does presence with silence. Hearing is important.

We need to place a high value on our families. Next to God, they should be the most important commodity in our life. When we treasure something, we will honor it. Families are high on God's priority list. In fact, he created the family before the church.

Picturing a special future for your family is also beneficial. Usually the biblical blessing addressed this. As parents, we need to detect special gifts and talents God has placed in our children and then encourage them to use them. Spouses can do the same for each other.

Reflection: As a flower cannot grow without the proper nutrients, neither can a family. Make sure meaningful touch, encouraging words and value are instilled in your children and spouse.

March 8

Heroes for God

Joshua 1:1-9

It is quite typical to have heroes as we are growing up. They can be found in families, actors and sports figures. Having heroes leads us to raise our sights above the horizon of the mundane. We look at them and suddenly think we can attempt what seems impossible or improbable.

Joshua was a hero for God. He was chosen as Moses' successor to lead the children of Israel into the Promised Land. Moses had disqualified himself from this task because of disobedience. Many conquests and foreboding people groups stood in Joshua's way, but his dependence on God carried him through and gave the people a great model. Being a hero for God is simply living in such a way that we are an example to others.

Heroes for God have courage and strength. Joshua's first great task after actually leading the people into the land was to conquer the mighty city of Jericho. This was done through psychological warfare and obedience to God.

God never promised our work for him would be easy, but he always equips us for it. There is no room in God's army for quitters or cowards. It takes great courage to stand for right. Strength is needed to trust God through life's difficulties. Composure must be maintained in spite of adversity.

Honesty is a hero trait. Dishonesty should never be found among God's people. His work must be carried out with high esteem. We all fail at some point, and it is not that God will not forgive dishonesty; it is simply that it scars the impact of our work.

Some of our most cherished historical figures are known for their honesty. Abraham Lincoln was known as "honest Abe." It is purported that George Washington could not tell a lie.

We also need to be kind, generous and loving. While heroes courageously stand up for what they believe in, they do so with compassion. Joshua did this with Rahab the prostitute after she safely hid the spies he had sent into the land.

Reflection: God, help me to leave an admirable example for those who follow me. Give me strength to march forward daily knowing you will guide me through all of life's challenges.

March 9

Hanging on in Difficult Times

Jonah 2:1-7

Life is difficult. Having a large bank account or an abundance of material possessions doesn't prevent adversities. Nor does having the right social contacts. A good family is not preventive medicine. Hardships come with being human and living in this world. How we deal with them determines whether we grow closer to God or drift farther away.

Jonah was in a troublesome situation. Running from what God tells us to do always puts us in a precarious position. Jonah's bad decision put him in the belly of a great fish. He could have avoided the pain by obedience, but to his credit he came to his senses. And since he was in the fish three days and nights, he had sufficient time for meditation.

While in the fish's belly, Jonah remembered the Lord. This is a good thing to do in challenging times. After all, God is in control of the situation, so it makes good sense to turn to him. Imagine Jonah's scenario: in darkness, the contents of the fish's belly swirling around him, the stench. It was probably a no brainer for him to remember God.

We have a tendency to almost dismiss God in the good times and rely on ourselves. Then when misfortunes arise, we immediately turn to him. Now that's a good move, but we need to remember the Lord in pleasant and difficult situations. God wants to be included in each day and the activities thereof. Why force God to bring adversity to get your attention?

As Jonah's life was ebbing away, he prayed. He knew his mistake and realized that only God could get him out of this mess, literally. Prayer is our communication line to God. It should be a daily practice, and it is certainly comforting in difficult times. Be in an attitude of prayer every waking moment. Draw on God's strength when life goes sour.

A church family can encourage us in hard times. Jonah had no church to attend, but he maintained that his prayer went into the temple of the Lord. Nothing can compare to a loving church family when we need help. We can share experiences and learn from each other. Being there for one another is important.

Reflection: Don't let the difficulties of life get you down. Search to see if bad decisions or wrong actions have led to your circumstances. If not, ask God for strength to see you through. He won't let you down.

March 10

Patterns for Church Growth

Ephesians 4:12-16

People who enjoy crocheting, sewing or cross stitching normally have patterns to follow. Without a pattern, whether memorized or on paper, the result will be disappointing and probably unusable.

Patterns are also important for church growth. Otherwise, growth may not happen, stagnation will set in and God's work will suffer. It is easy enough to find articles, programs, seminars and books on church growth, but unless God's Spirit guides a church to these things, what the church does may not be in God's plan for that particular church. Yet, there are some patterns that are universal for all churches.

God's pattern involves equipping, service, and building up. While entertainment is not in the mix, sadly many churches have resorted to this for increased attendance. Methods vary, but they must include the core ingredients. Equipping is an individual and corporate process. The church must equip or fit the individual to serve God properly. Then the entire body must be equipped to look more like Christ. God's Word, prayer, times of testing and suffering are the tools that equip us.

Service is the duty of all church members. No one person can do it all, including the pastor. When the church equips and serves, the body will be built up. Spiritual edification will take place.

God's pattern for church growth is not without purpose. The ultimate target is unity of faith. There will be an oneness where the core Christian doctrines are concerned. Sound doctrine is necessary for God's church. Studying the great teachings of our faith leads to deeper knowledge of spiritual truths. Shallowness is the bane of the twenty first century church. Growth in knowledge leads to spiritual maturity. When this happens, the church will emit a sweet testimony to the world.

Water stagnates for lack of movement. The same can happen to the church. Heinrich Heine, German skeptic, said to Christians, "You show me your redeemed life and I might be inclined to believe in your Redeemer."

Great leaders, structures, entertainment and activities do not lead to authentic church growth. This comes from the authority, direction and power of Christ for churches who follow the correct strategy.

Reflection: Is your church following God's pattern for growth?

March 11

A Saved Church Member

Amos 5:18-24

The title seems almost ironic. "Aren't all church members saved," you might ask. Truthfully, the answer is no. We would like to answer in the affirmative, but we cannot. Talk to any pastor, church leader or read survey results, and the truth becomes alarmingly clear.

While the church had not yet been born in Amos' time, he faced a similar situation. His audience was guilty of playing church. Because of this, his assignment from God was to preach against their wickedness-to his own people and the nations who surrounded them.

Being a lost church member is of no worth. Church membership has no saving value. The Bible does not teach salvation through the church, though the church does play a meaningful part in the believer's life. What are the requirements to be a saved church member?

A personal relationship is necessary to be a saved church member. Amos faced listeners with misconceptions. Many thought being born an Israelite automatically made God receive them. This can be compared to people who think God accepts them just because their parents were Christians or because they live in a godly nation. Nor is universalism the answer. God will not eventually save everyone as wonderful as that sounds. He accepts only those who have a personal relationship with his Son.

Saved church members pursue righteousness. Though Amos' audience was going through the right motions, their works were unacceptable to God because they left out the personal relationship. Apart from that, the Bible says our offerings are filthy rags in God's sight. Jesus says the person who pursues righteousness will be happy.

Houses quite commonly have junk rooms or a junk drawer. It's the place that accumulates stuff-items we plan to put away later or things we just don't know what to do with. Left unattended, the accumulation can become overwhelming. Periodically, we need to clean out. Our lives are the same. We hunger after righteousness by regularly tossing junk from our life that doesn't fit who we are.

Reflection: A saved church member will touch the lives of others with their Christianity. Are you moved to love others? Are you serving them in practical ways? What are you depending on for your salvation?

March 12
Neighborly Advice
Luke 10:25-37

Can you remember the time when neighbors were actually neighborly? They were not only the people who lived next door. They were the people who lived in your community. Their children played together. If they had a problem or need, you helped them. You probably ate meals at their house. Now we may not even know their names.

Though this parable does not use symbols as many of Jesus' stories do, it leaves an impact on our conscience. We read it and feel as if there is something we must do; something we must change about our life. It is simple enough for a child to understand yet so profound that it takes a lifetime to learn to practice all it teaches. It reminds us that our Christianity is a lifestyle.

The parable challenges us to demonstrate compassion. A certain man was traveling from Jerusalem to Jericho when he fell into the hands of thieves and robbers. They did to him what their names imply. A priest and Levite happen by, but neither stops. It was a Samaritan who showed compassion. Since the injured man was probably a Jew, this makes the story interesting and conscience pricking to Jesus' listeners.

Technology has hurt individual contact. When calling places of business, it is common to get an automated service that will answer our question. No human voice. We text, email or live chat instead of calling. Technology has led to a very impersonal world making it more difficult to exercise compassion. Yet this is exactly what Jesus teaches. Think of ways you can be compassionate to someone.

We need to monitor our conduct. The Samaritan did this. He tended to the man's wounds, took him to an inn, and paid for his stay. Compassion can only be that if it moves beyond kind thoughts for someone to action on their behalf. Life is to be lived by the golden rule. John Wesley said, "Do all the good you can by all the means you can."

The Samaritan also encourages us to enlarge the circle of our friends. Make friends with someone unlike you-with different interests or who has a different personality.

Reflection: God, help me to be neighborly to all people no matter what their race, culture or creed. Help me to see people through your eyes.

March 13

Results of Curiosity

Luke 19:1-10

Between the 1400 and 1800's, Europeans set out to explore, trade and settle in distant countries. There were many reasons for doing so, but curiosity was one. One of the more famous explorers was Christopher Columbus, an Italian navigator. He thought the world was much smaller than it was, so his inquisitiveness led him far away to find out. Sometimes curiosity leads to new inventions and at others it kills the cat.

Zacchaeus is a familiar biblical character, even to small children who often sing a song about him. Since his occupation was tax collector, he was not well liked in his time. The title usually equaled thief. Additionally, he was short. This led him to shinny up a tree when he heard Jesus was coming. He wanted a peak at the master teacher. The story illustrates the merits of curiosity.

Zacchaeus was a man of action. He had heard of Jesus and wanted to see him. Perhaps he was also aware that Jesus was a man of compassion. He may have even overheard that Jesus associated with tax collectors. Then the day came when Jesus came to Jericho, Zacchaeus' hometown. Being a short man and a tax collector, he may have been accustomed to being jostled and insulted, but today he would show the crowd. He ran ahead of Jesus and found a box seat in a sycamore tree. His efforts were rewarded. Jesus invited himself to Zacchaeus' home.

What action has your curiosity led you to take? Is Jesus merely a great historical figure to you, or have you recognized and accepted him as your Savior? Knowledge must lead to action to be of benefit.

Zacchaeus teaches us about adjustments. Before meeting Jesus, he was out to steal all Roman law would allow. Now he wanted to rectify his wrongs and give back more than he had taken. He also wanted to help the poor. His adaptations were financially liberal, and Jesus pronounced that salvation had come to his house. Following Christ requires changes and adjustments that move us from selfishness to selflessness.

This tax collector now wanted to serve those he had cheated. We can only imagine how much he did for the biblical record is silent. Because Jesus served his spiritual need, he wanted to serve physical needs.

Reflection: Is curiosity leading you out of your comfort zone?

March 14

Assuring God's Blessings
Nehemiah 13

All of us want to be blessed by God. Many of God's blessings descend on the righteous and unrighteous simply because of God's goodness. Rain and sun are examples. The wicked experience them just like the Christian. Other blessings are reserved only for believers.

Nehemiah led the third group of returning exiles from Babylon after Cyrus, the new Persian ruler, gave them permission to go home. His heart was broken by the collapsed walls that once protected the city of Jerusalem. While Nehemiah was on a return trip to Persia, the people reverted to their old sins. When he returned for his second term as governor of Judah, he confronted the people with their sins-transgressions that were hindering God's blessings.

The people were not obeying God's Word. He had told them not to associate with or marry the pagan people that lived among them. God knew this would turn their hearts from him, and they would begin worshipping foreign gods. Jesus says our obedience to him is proof of our love for him. Anytime we willfully disobey God's teachings, we forfeit his blessings.

We must respect God's house. During Nehemiah's absence, the high priest had cleaned out a storage room in the temple and was allowing a pagan neighbor to use it. This infuriated Nehemiah. God's temple was being desecrated. God's house is a testimony of his holiness, justice and righteousness. Anytime we desecrate it in any form, we negate his blessings.

God wants us to give cheerfully to his work. The people were to bring their tithes to the priests and Levites who worked at God's Temple. They had neglected their duty, and the leaders now had to labor in the fields.

God has given us so much. When we give back a portion to him, he will bless and multiply it.

Respecting God's Day is fundamental for his blessings. The people were commercializing the Sabbath, making it just an ordinary day. As the early Christians met on the first day of the week to worship, so should we. As we do, we commemorate our risen Savior.

We should also separate ourselves from the world. One has said, "A single generation's compromise could undo the work of centuries."

Reflection: What is hindering God's blessings in your life?

March 15

Rethinking Our Roots

I Peter 3:15

Roots are important. Perhaps the book and saga that portrayed this so vividly was Alex Haley's *Roots*. In the novel, the author traces his ancestors back to their African origins. Many people today do this same thing with their family genealogies-some for just a few generations and others for many generations. Genealogical histories give connection with the past.

Christian roots are also important. While saving faith is not passed down from generation to generation, the great doctrines of God's Word should be. Peter tells us to ready ourselves to give an answer to those who question the hope we have. Only as we are familiar with our spiritual roots can we do that.

One vitally important root is the sovereignty of God. Sovereign means superior and above all others. God is the creator and sustainer of all things, good and evil. He does not author evil, but it exists by his permission. God is perfect and good and can do anything he desires so long as it does not violate his nature. He answers to no one and is not under obligation to anyone. Such a picture should not frighten us, for he is benevolent ruler.

God is also love. In John 3:16, we are reminded of how great that love was. There are many facets of God's character, but they all flow from this one. The basic dimensions of his love are benevolence, grace, mercy and persistence. God looks on humanity with pity. He sees the predicament we are in, knowing that only he has the solution to our problem. Mercy is what he gives that we do not deserve. Fortunately, God tolerantly pursues us even when we want nothing to do with him. The Bible says he is patient, not wanting any to perish.

Freidrich Nietzsche, a German philosopher who declared God dead, rejected Christianity, saying it involved a "slave morality." He was wrong in that sense, but the Bible does teach that we are slaves to sin. We can invent friendlier terms for sin, but they do not change the fact that we are sinners. And the wages of sin is death. It is a universal malady.

Reflection: Our only hope is found in Jesus. The gift of God is forgiveness and eternal life. There are not many ways to spiritual healing. Jesus will come again, and all humanity will stand before him. Trusting him as your Savior is the only hope of enjoying heaven.

March 16

Why Be Thankful?

Psalm 100

In 1620, about one hundred people set out from Plymouth, England on a ship named Mayflower. The winter that followed their landing in America was severe with many of them dying. Fortunately, there was an English speaking Indian in the area named Squanto who showed them how to plant, cultivate and fish. After the first harvest, they invited the Indians to a feast as an expression of their thankfulness.

Believers have many reasons to be thankful. We thank God for the offer of salvation, realizing he could have let us perish in our sins. He was under no obligation to save us. The psalmist thanked God because he made him and because he belonged to him. Paul thanked God for this indescribable gift (II Corinthians 9:15). Thinking of who we were before God did his work of grace in us, and then reflecting on who we are now that the work is complete, should lead to daily gratitude.

Around 425 B. C., Protagoras wrote, "Man is the measure of all things." But man did not concoct the plumb line. God did. Though we did not measure up, he made a way that we could be accepted by him.

We should thank God for his goodness and mercy. He is a faithful God whose love endures forever. God is good all the time, and he works all things together for the good of his people (Romans 8:28). Mercy is getting what we do not deserve. In salvation, God gives us what we do not merit. He has a tender hearted concern for the needy. God will sustain you every day, no matter what your burdens and trials are. He promises us food, shelter and clothing, and lovingly gives much more than that (Matthew 6). God's mercy releases us from worry and anxiety over life's necessities.

God should be praised for his abiding truth. His truth is absolute and never changes. People have always searched for truth that is reliable and trustworthy. Such certainty is found in God's Word. Jesus said he was the way, the truth and the life (John 14:6). Two basic truths are that we need a Savior and that we will exist beyond death. The first has a direct bearing on where we spend the second. God's truth will endure forever.

Reflection: Focus on the good things in life instead of those things that speak of misery and pain. Thank God for all that is pleasant, wholesome and good in your life. Most of all, thank him for saving you.

March 17

Characteristics of Good Fishermen

Matthew 4:18-22

My grandmother was a fisherman. She fished in an old boat-barely seaworthy. Rods and reels were absent from her gear. She preferred cane poles. A small motor adorned her wooden boat. She avoided the open water, choosing to fish in coves. But if one were to measure her success over a lifetime, she would be classified a good fisherman.

Churches, and by extension believers, are fishermen as well. Jesus told his first disciples he would make them fishers of men. The church has many responsibilities, but leading others to Christ is of top priority.

Sadly, many churches have become social clubs instead of life giving stations. We gather to visit and only talk about the work that needs doing-work many churches never get around to. Statistics on church growth bear this out. The Bible tells us we are people on a mission. People on mission are going somewhere, and we have been commissioned to tread on the entire world (Matthew 28:19, 20).

Good fishermen are patient. In a vast expanse of water, how is a person to know where fish are? Apart from a fish finder, one must look for signs: a rolling of the waters, piled up brush, or shade. This is called good instinct. Sometimes the fish are there and just do not bite.

Believers must exercise patience in our fishing. The lost are around us every day. We must await the right opportunity to share our faith. It may mean building a relationship with them first. Let God bring about the circumstances in which you share his love with others.

Fishermen persevere. If the fish do not bite in one place, they move to another. They may relocate many times on one trip or simply trolley along while casting at the same time. We cannot give up if everyone we tell does not respond positively to the gospel. They didn't with Jesus. In spite of this, we must continue to tell the story and let God deal with the person's heart.

Courage characterizes a good fisherman. Fishermen have to contend with the threat of bad weather. In our mission for Christ, we will face trials and even dangers as we fish. Many have even lost their lives throughout Christian history.

Reflection: God, help me to realize that others need what I have. Give me opportunities to share your love and the courage to do so.

March 18
Steps to Christian Victory
II Corinthians 1:1-11

Discouragement is no respecter of persons. It runs the gamut of life. Charles Spurgeon, the greatest preacher England ever produced, said, "I am the subject of depressions of spirit so fearful that I hope none of you ever get to such extremes of wretchedness as I go to." Even the apostle Paul spoke of being so burdened that he despaired of life.

God does not expect his people to live in a state of discouragement or defeat. The key is how we respond. Though we may experience periods of each, victory should be the pattern of our life. Paul faced many difficulties, but one of his crucial words was comfort or encouragement.

Victory comes in remembering what God is to us. We worship a God who is control of all circumstances, no matter how daunting they appear. Nothing happens apart from his directive or permission. If it did, he would not be sovereign. He is God, and there is no other. God has done wonderful things in your life in the past. Remember those times when despair lurks near you. He will do great things in the future as well.

God is the Father of our Lord Jesus Christ. We have victory because of our relationship with the Son. He is the father of all mercies who allows his undeserved favor to rain down in abundant showers.

God comforts us in all of life's tribulations. Who controls life for you? Fate, you, or God. Your answer determines your perspective in hard times. If it is fate, you have no control. Hardships quickly let us know we are not in control. It is much more comforting to believe God is in control- and it's biblical. No human can comfort you as God can when life gets tough. He gives a peace beyond our understanding.

God gives us strength to bear our trials. Though it is in our nature to try and handle them, the hurdle quickly shows us we need someone far more powerful. Trials drive us to God in prayer. We are pulled to his Word for comfort and instruction. Here we discover that God promises to bring us through these times and increase our faith along the way. God is also glorified through our trials. As people see how we respond, we give testimony of God's delivering power.

Reflection: As God comforts you in the trials of life, learn to be an encourager to others. Reassure someone today.

March 19
How to Be a Healthy You
Luke 14:7-11

Love of self is easy for some and difficult for others. Growing up in a healthy home environment makes it easy for a child to love and believe in themselves. But for those reared in unhealthy circumstances, life is different. An absence of praise and encouragement can lead to low self-esteem, negativity, poor body image and a general state of insecurity.

Through the story of the wedding feast, Jesus teaches how we can have a wholesome appraisal of ourselves. Selfishness must be crucified. Jesus imagined a person invited to a wedding feast. He chose the seat up front-a foolish decision. Someone more distinguished might have been invited. Then the egotistical fellow would be asked to take a seat in the rear.

Seeking the best in life for selfish reasons is thoughtless. When egotism and disregard for others is your life pattern, you will never hold a position of honor in God's sight. Not only will such a person know shame in this life, but he will also experience it as he stands before the judgment seat of Christ. God will ask why he did not concern himself with the needs of others. Crucifying self is a daily exercise.

Sincerity and humility are the better choices. Jesus says to take the lowest seat. Then the host will lead us to a seat of honor. Humility is praised by God, and the rewards are enormous. Sincerity is a mark of greatness. God will honor us when we do not try to honor ourselves. Being sincere does not mean we are weak or self-deprecating. We simply realize that worth is found in Christ, not ourselves. You are what you are because of God's grace and mercy. When that relationship is secure, you will not have to fight for the world's badges of recognition.

Our spiritual honor is given by God. He is the one who exalts and abases. An exalted view of oneself leads to God bringing us down to size. He does this in various ways, but the result he intends is recognition that he elevates, not us. A spirit of humility is his desire for us.

Andrew Murray once said, "Humility is perfect quietness of heart. It is to expect nothing, to wonder at nothing that is done to me, to feel nothing done against me."

Reflection: God, help me realize that genuine humility is honored in your sight. Help me to remember who I am and who you are.

March 20

Guaranteeing Failure

Genesis 11:1-9

History is full of examples of failure. Adolph Hitler led Germany to great heights during the Second World War, but in the end would not admit failure and defeat. He stated, "I will not fall into the hands of the enemy dead or alive!" He chose suicide. His mistress took the same route by another method.

Success is a more popular subject. For example, if we set ambitious goals, plan and work hard, we are guaranteed success. The formula, however, does not assure achievement. The building of the Tower of

Babel was one of the most signal failures in history. It was an ambitious goal, but a fiasco.

When we leave God out of our plans, we guarantee failure. Never in the story is God mentioned. The builders went about their endeavor with never a thought of him. The Tower was designed to promote unity of the human race but in a society devoid of God. It was an act of insensitivity and pride.

Plans are essential. An old saying states, "To fail to plan is to plan to fail." The statement is pregnant with truth. Building a house, making a budget, going on vacation, searching for a job are all examples of times when we plan. A better form of the statement would say, "Failure to include God in our plans is a plan to fail."

We should include God in all our endeavors. Leaving him out is the utmost of foolishness. He is concerned about our big and small plans in life. Many failures could be avoided by including God in the preparation process. Churches often make the same mistake by developing strategies without consulting God. How often do we ask him to bless what we've already decided on?

Failure is guaranteed when we have selfish motives. The builders did. They wanted fame and recognition for themselves. Life is about glorifying God, not us.

We guarantee failure when we adamantly deny the express will of God. God's instructions for the human race were to be fruitful and populate the earth. The Tower would keep them from being scattered over the earth. God intervened and halted the project.

Reflection: Include God in all your plans so you can succeed.

March 21

Making Peace with the Past

John 8:1-11

In one verse of Robert Frost's poem, *The Road Not Taken*, he says, "I shall be telling this with a sigh/ Somewhere ages and ages hence:/ Two roads diverged in a wood, and I-/I took the one less traveled by,/ And that has made all the difference."

Frost speaks for all people, for life is full of choices. We make decisions but often look back with regret. If not remorse, we wonder what would have happened had I made another choice-a different job, spouse, home, vehicle. The "what if" game can cause deep disappointment. Some bad decisions can be undone, but most require living with the consequences and learning.

If we are not careful, we can imprison ourselves in self-pity, regret, guilt, depression and indecision. This in turn holds us back and keeps God from using us. We have to make peace with our past. Remember, it is that-the past. All people have one, and sometimes we are not proud of it, but we cannot move forward while looking backwards.

Jesus encounters a woman who needed to make peace with her past. The religious hypocrites brought her to see if he would uphold the law. According to the law, stoning was the penalty for adultery. But Jesus did not condemn her. He forgave her, told her to leave that lifestyle and sin no more.

Regret can poison life. It could have for the adulterous woman. She was running around with a married man. Though Jesus forgave her, she could have failed to forgive herself. The woman needed to grasp what Jesus did for her. He does the same for us. Upon request, he forgives our sin. No longer are we "sinners." The Bible refers to believers as "saints." The slate is wiped clean. Live in the joy of that reality.

We should not dwell on the past. It is that, and for the believer it is forgiven. Jesus did that for the woman. She needed to put that lifestyle behind her. We should do the same. Instead of asking ourselves "Why," we need to ask, "What next?" One has said, "Learn from the past, live in the present, and plan for the future."

Reflection: Lord God, free me from my prison of regrets and failures. Help me to know that in Christ I have been forgiven—my past is clean. Help me to move forward with renewed zeal to serve you.

March 22
Shape Up!
Matthew 26:36-46

The prevailing message in America is "Shape Up!" From diet programs to television shows, we are told to exercise and eat right. No doubt, our technological advances have birthed a generation of couch potatoes. And while physical health is important, spiritual health is even more vital.

Believers and churches are both in need of spiritual exercise that will tone our muscles and make us more effective in God's work. The fat of complacency and indifference often holds us back.

The Garden of Gethsemane experience was a shaping up occasion for Jesus. He was, in essence, asking the Father to tone him up. The cross was just ahead, and he requested renewed strength to forge ahead to the Father's ultimate will.

Shaping up requires a life of holiness. God's Word refers to believers as a "holy nation." Our purpose is to declare the work of God to unbelievers and to glorify the One who has called us out of darkness into light. Our body is a temple of God's Spirit. When we speak, walk and think, God is present. Christians live in the world but are not to reflect the world.

Serving our generation is an important part of good spiritual health. Jesus did this. His entire ministry was filled with serving the needs of others-physical, emotional and spiritual. Even when it led to the cross, he was willing to go.

Are you investing yourself in something that will serve your generation spiritually? What will you leave behind when your life is over? Prayer is important, but we need to leave the closet after we are through and move into the streets of neediness.

Evangelism keeps us in shape spiritually. Testifying to the character and redemptive work of Christ is a must. This is carried out in our lifestyle-words and actions. It is not an option for the believer, nor is it reserved for the "professional clergy."

Reflection: Devote yourself to being in good shape for God. His work is exciting and carries long range effects. Kingman Brewster, past president of Yale University, said, "There's a tremendous satisfaction in losing your own identity in something that is much more important than you are."

March 23

Having Beautiful Souls

Romans 5:3-4

"Beauty is only skin deep." Perhaps you have told yourself that because you were not satisfied with your outward appearance. In spite of your poor self image, it helped you feel better. Or perhaps there are some prejudices that haunt you, so you repeat the phrase in your head to help you treat others as they deserve.

But the saying is true. What's on the inside is who we are. The heart is where our character flows from. As a forgiven child of God, our heavenly Father sees this beauty regardless of whether others label us as "beautiful." Soul work must be done relentlessly and endlessly. We are works in progress.

Beautiful souls please God above everything and everyone else. Jesus reminds us to love God with all our being. He deserves it and will not settle for less. Typical behavior pleases the one who is most important to us. When we worship and serve God with all we are, it brings pleasure to him.An entertainer thrives on pleasing the audience, for this is where his livelihood derives. Our very essence stems from God.

A soul that is beautiful will take responsibility. Here is a message that needs a megaphone, for we see it silenced on every corner. We are responsible for our actions and words. Therapists get wealthy helping people find someone to blame for bad or abnormal behavior. Everyone is a victim: bad family situation, poor teachers, school that didn't care, or a government who let me slip through the cracks.

While people and situations do affect us, we are responsible for our actions and words. The Bible teaches individual accountability for sin. We can't blame anyone. At the final judgment, God will confront us about our sins, not someone else's.

We need to accept ourselves for who we are. Comparison is a way of life for many people. We want something someone else has or to look like someone else does. Our souls cannot be healthy when they are constantly in a competitive mode. God uniquely created us and, we must accept his plans and live accordingly. You are beautiful to him.

Reflection: God, help me to see myself as you do-a beautiful soul that needs to love you above everything else. Help me make wise decisions, knowing that I am responsible for my actions.

March 24

Living Successfully
Daniel 1:1-8

Larry was preparing for his first 10K run. While in shape physically, he needed mental preparation. A veteran runner, familiar with the course, gave him some needed advice. The first portion of the course was flat. She advised him to pace himself because the last two miles were hilly, and he would need his energy. Sure enough, the hills made his body ache, but because he prepared he finished the course.

Hills are part of life. They come in disappointments, defeats and sorrows. It is essential to prepare for them. Daniel faced the hill of Babylon. He was one of the Israelite captives who now finds himself in a foreign land with pagan gods. How could he live successfully for his God here? How can we live in a world that is often not friendly to Christianity?

Success comes from pure living. Daniel was one of the captives chosen to serve in the king's palace. This involved eating and drinking what God had forbidden. Daniel resolved that he would not defile himself. Even when impurity seems to surround you, determine to keep your thoughts, actions and words pure. Make up your mind to keep your body undefiled.

We must prepare for success. Daniel successfully lived for God in a pagan culture, but it didn't happen by accident. It took forethought. He became familiar with Babylonian literature, thereby becoming smarter than his captors. This gave him the opportunity to influence them.

Our responsibility is to accurately handle God's Word. Doing that enables us to give a reason to those who ask about the hope we have. This takes preparation. It takes time in God's Word. Only as God's Word flows continuously through your mind can you thwart the attacks of evil.

Success involves productivity. After a period of time, the king examined Daniel and his friends and found them smarter than any others. Because of their productivity, he placed them in charge of entire provinces. They did what the prophet Jeremiah told the people to do: be productive because they would be in captivity seventy years. In spite of living in a culture gone sour, it is still our responsibility to be industrious in God's work.

Reflection: One has said, "When the country temporarily goes to the dogs, cats must learn to be circumspect, walk on fences, sleep in trees, and have faith that all this woofing is not the last word."

March 25

Living Successfully

Daniel 1:1-8

Delos Miles found himself in a bunker in North Korea. As he lay on the ground, a Chinese soldier put a gun to his head. Miles prayed a fox hole prayer, telling God he would do whatever he wanted if he would bring him out alive. The soldier fired, but instead of going through his head, the bullet grazed the side of his head. After eighteen hours pretending to be dead and three days of searching, he finally made it to the First Marine Division. He would later serve as a Professor of Evangelism at a Baptist Seminary.

Sometimes the mountains of life appear insurmountable. Daniel gives a wonderful example of how to scale them successfully. A vibrant prayer life is necessary for success. Many see no need of prayer, and others feel it has little if any affect on anything. Daniel disagreed.

The King of Babylon had a dream that none of the wise men could interpret. He ordered them all killed. This included Daniel and his friends. Daniel pleaded for time, and asked his friends to pray. God gave him the interpretation. On another occasion Daniel was the victim of jealousy. Even though an order was given not to pray to any other god, Daniel continued his practice of petitioning his God three times daily.

Our culture desperately needs the prayers of God's people. Wickedness in many forms clings to our society. We need to petition God in its behalf. We must also ask for guidance on how to influence our civilization for Him as Daniel did his. Presidents, politicians and doctors cannot cure our ills. Only the Word of God applied to the wound will bring healing. It is up to believers to apply the salve.

Success involves proclaiming the love of God. Though there were no wise men who could interpret the king's dream, Daniel told the king that there was a God in heaven who could. And he did. God gave Daniel the meaning of the dream. Daniel was not afraid to proclaim the superiority of his God before a pagan ruler. His three friends shared how their God could deliver them from the fiery furnace, and Daniel would later tell the king that his God could liberate him from the lion's den.

Reflection: Hurting people need a healing message. We do not share out of arrogance but in love. Have you prayed for those you are around daily? Ask God for courage to proclaim your God to others.

March 26

Staying Clean

I John 2:15-17

Gravity is the attraction that masses of matter have for each other. It also keeps your feet on the ground. Otherwise you and other small objects would fly off the earth. Gravity keeps the planets in their heavenly paths and the stars on their courses. Its pull on our moon causes the tide to rise and fall.

There is another force that pulls, and the Bible calls it sin. It is that force that pulls us in directions that are opposite of where God wants us to go. It's the force that draws the teenager to smoking, drinking, cursing, drugs, and premarital sex. It bothers adults too. Stopping by the bar after work for a drink with the guys, extramarital affairs, and gambling are all results of the force.

How can we stay clean with such a powerful force? Fortunately, believers have an even more powerful force. God has given you a new nature, and he will enable you to stay clean. He has also sent his indwelling Spirit.

It is important that we are selective in what we look at. We are warned against the lust of the eyes. We usually associate this with sexual things, and it can be that, but it is certainly not limited to that area. It is impossible to remove any and everything from our sight that might tempt us. Rising above this is the key. Isolation is not the answer. Monks and nuns tried that. It didn't work.

Through our eyes, we bring visual images and information into the processing station of our mind. What we see feeds our imaginations. We are tempted to look at alluring and attractive things. Since Christians are not to love the things of this world, there are many things we do not need to stare at or look at for very long.

John reminds us that the lust of the flesh and the eyes as well as the pride of life is not from God but is of the world. We are assaulted by a thousand protruding arms that entice with fame, power, fortune and pleasure. Most of this, however, will come only by disobedience to God. Focusing on things that are good often puts us at odds with friends, family, work associates and often society's traditions.

Reflection: God, help me stay clean. Guide me to only look at those things that are pure in your sight.

March 27

Remaining Clean

I John 2:15-17

In the movie, *Star Wars*, "May the force be with you" was a phrase used to wish good luck to someone. Christians do not need good fortune to stay clean. We have the power of God's indwelling Spirit to facilitate us.

Thinking more about the consequences of sin than its pleasures will aid in keeping clean. It has been said, "Sin will take you farther than you want to go, keep you longer than you want to stay, and cost you more that you want to pay." One of Satan's chief ploys in temptation is to leave out the consequences of sin. Watch a few commercials or e-ads. The pleasure is highlighted but never the consequences.

When Satan tempts you in some area, run through the possible results of that sin in your mind. Think before acting. Our actions are a reflection of the one we serve. The Bible says believers are to be holy even as the one who calls us is holy. (I Peter 1:15)

Being different is a daily challenge faced by the Christian. We cannot adopt a passive attitude about sin, thinking we do not have to worry about that anymore since we are born again. Satan wants to change our focus and distract us. He cannot steal what God has given in salvation, but he can destroy our effectiveness by leading us into sin.

In the 1988 Summer Olympics in Seoul, Ben Johnson of Canada won the one hundred meter dash. Carl Lewis, the American contender, came in second. After the race, the judges learned that Johnson had an illegal substance in his body. It must have been pleasurable for the moment to use this to aid in victory, but the consequences were not worth it.

We need to begin each day with a renewed reverence for God. Jesus' precious blood was shed for our redemption. Remembering the cost of our salvation enables us to stay focused. His grace and love both need to constantly assault our mind. When they do, we will look at things that are pure, holy, clean, that have virtue and are pleasing in God's sight. The consequences of sin will frighten us, and our aim will be avoiding anything that displeases our heavenly Father.

Reflection: Lord, I set apart my mind for you today. I set apart my passions, my eyes and my ears. Today, I set apart every limb of my body to you as Lord of my life.

March 28

Magnetic Personalities

Matthew 5:14-16

Light attracts bugs. Leave one on outside your door, and, if it's not a bug repelling light, in a short time the little creatures will surround it. Hang a bug light and listen to the constant zapping. Like magnets that draw items with a certain makeup, so the light lures the bug.

Jesus had a magnetic personality. How else do we explain the people that constantly surrounded him? They came for healing and teaching. Some came in an effort to trap him and assure his demise. One came at night. But they came and they came. They were drawn to him.

Believers are salt and light. As light, we want to draw others to the One we serve. When they see him, we then have opportunity to share the good news. Believers are like a city on a hill. The light of such a city can be seen from a great distance. And our light should shine brightly. Others should readily know by our actions and words that we are Christians.

Gratitude attracts. Our world is a "give me" society because I deserve. Since I deserve, there is no reason to show appreciation. Jesus once met ten lepers. He healed them and sent them to the priest, who was required by the law to assure cleansing had occurred. Of the ten, only one returned to thank Jesus. Learn to say "thank you."

Honesty is important. Zacchaeus comes to mind. Jesus met him in Jericho, in a tree. He was a tax collector and hated by most because of his dishonesty. Jesus went to his house, but he also entered his life. Zacchaeus became a changed man-he became a honest man, vowing to return fourfold to any he had taken from and to give half his goods to the poor.

The old saying is true: "Honesty is the best policy," and it attracts people. It should be seen in our eyes and actions. Honest people smile with their eyes and mouths. Let honesty be your guide.

People are also attracted when we forgive. Peter once asked Jesus how many times he should forgive someone who sinned against him. Jesus' answer was, "No limit." It takes time to restore trust, but forgiveness must be instantaneous. God keeps no record and constantly forgives. We can do no less.

Reflection: Form a magnetic personality so you can attract others to the God you serve.

March 29

Somebody for God

Judges 6

Have you ever felt like nobody in a world of some bodies? Do you suffer from low esteem, thinking there is little contribution you can make to this world? Do you lack confidence in yourself? If so, you are in good company. The Bible is full of nobodies that God used.

Gideon was one. He belongs in the period of the judges and to the tribe of Manasseh. God's people had no king, and everyone was doing what seemed right in their own eyes. Their pattern was disobedience, punishment, return to God, deliverance, and disobedience again.

Because of their waywardness, God used the Midianites in a seven year stint to harass the Israelites. They were forced to live in caves and shelters. Their crops and livestock were being destroyed. The Midianites had swift camels and showed great effectiveness in battle. It was a self inflicted time of misery.

In such a time, God called Gideon. We find him threshing wheat in a winepress, not the normal place to process grain. This was usually done on a high place where the wind could blow away the chaff. Fear had driven Gideon here. In the dungeon of despair, God appears to him, calls him a mighty warrior, and tells him he was going to deliver his people from those who were chafing them.

Gideon was not impressed with the assignment, reminding God he was not from a noteworthy tribe. In fact, God had to fleece him (pun intended) to get him going. Out of 32,000 original soldiers, Gideon's army was reduced, by God, to 300. With them, he soundly defeated the Midianites.

God uses ordinary people. Gideon fit the bill. God is not looking for wealth, influence, prestige or the right last name. Obedience and willingness are the only requirements. In our world, "it's not what you know but who you know." God's arena is different. He uses the ordinary to do the extraordinary, so he can receive the glory and not us.

When doing God's will, we are always doing more than we can imagine. What seems small can be used of God to infect a great number of people. God only wants us to depend on him and realize he is all we need to be somebody for him.

Reflection: When God calls you to a task, go willingly.

March 30

Successful Money Management

Proverbs 3:9-10

Seminars and books abound to help us manage our money more effectively. And money is of the utmost concern, especially as America suffers through the current recession. Debt levels are rising. Saving rates are declining. Our country's national debt will haunt our children and grandchildren for years. While seminars and books can be beneficial, God's Word is the best place for advice on successful money management.

Managing our money effectively starts by honoring God with our possessions. The Israelites were to give God the first fruits of their crops.

The firstborn son and animal were also to be dedicated to God. Giving this first portion to God symbolized dependence on and dedication to him.

All we have has been given to us by God. We own nothing. He owns it all. He gives us the ability and ingenuity to work and then buy with our pay. Only as we recognize this will we honor God with all we have. He wants our best. Giving back to God should be a priority. If God is not first, successful money management will always be elusive.

We need to work diligently, not be lazy. God praises the resourceful person and rebukes the lazy person. The have and have nots can usually be traced to the did and did nots. Work honors God, and work is good for us physically. Work teaches us how difficult it is to earn money but how quickly it can be spent on our monthly responsibilities. Whatever profession God places you in, work vigorously at it.

Be honest with your money. The Bible reminds us that it is better to be godly and poor. (Proverbs 16:8) The root cause of dishonesty is greed. When this runs unchecked, we can fall victim to get rich schemes or other unscrupulous activities. The oft quoted advice is still true: "If it sounds too good to be true, it usually is." You cannot live right and get things the wrong way.

It is important that we live within our income. Most Americans and Christians do not do this. We want now what it took our parents years of hard work and saving to get. The result: huge amounts of credit card debt.

Reflection: Remember; "If your outgo is greater than your income, your upkeep will be your downfall." Honor God with your money and possessions.

March 31

Money Management 101

Proverbs 3:9-10

Jesse Jackson once said, "Both tears and sweat are wet and salty, but they render a different result. The tears will get you sympathy, but sweat will get you progress." Progress will also come from successfully managing our money. Another has said, "The most nerve racking place on earth to live is just beyond your means."

Saving is a word we are familiar with but something few of us do. The popular phrase tells us to "save something for a rainy day." By the way, the rainy days do come, sometimes in downpours. The Bible says the wise person will save for the future while the fool will spend and spend. (Proverbs 21:20) George Burns used to remark, "People tell me I should save for a rainy day. But with my luck it will never rain and I'll be stuck with all that money." It usually rains.

Unexpected occurrences are a part of life. When we do not save for such times, we are often forced into debt or dishonest dealings. A vital part of good money management is planning ahead. A good rule of thumb is to save ten percent, give ten percent and enjoy the rest.

We need to use our resources to help the needy. The Bible purports that the person who is kind really lends to the Lord, and he will be rewarded. (Proverbs 19:17) Jesus reminds us that the poor will always be with us. Our world is filled with people who go to bed and wake up hungry. Even in America, the land of plenty. While some are in this position because of laziness, many are here simply because of poverty. God has a special concern for the poor, and we must also.

Have a proper perspective about your possessions. Realize they are temporary. Wealth has wings and can fly away in a moment. Possessions can be stolen or destroyed by disasters. If not cared for, they can rust and wither away. God gives them to us to enjoy, but our true treasures are in heaven, not here. One said, "It's almost impossible to overestimate the unimportance of most things."

Reflection: Money and possessions are sensitive subjects. Money is necessary for almost anything we do. We do not live in a bartering society. Our economy is based on the dollar. Remember where your money comes from. Keep it and your possessions in the right perspective.

April

April 1
A Wise Person's Secret
Matthew 2:1-12

On a night prior to the Battle of Bull Run, Abraham Lincoln kneeled before an open Bible and prayed, "O Thou great God who heard Solomon in the night when he prayed and cried for wisdom, hear me. I cannot lead these people. I cannot guide the affairs of this country without Thy help. O Lord, hear me and save this nation." A wise man.

Nestled in Matthew's gospel, is the favorite story of the wise men and their visit to Jesus. No doubt, tradition has distorted some of the details of when they came and how many there were, but the warmness of the story lives on. They came because they saw a star-a star that led them to the baby King of Kings.

Wise people make seeking God a priority. It was for the wise men. No one forced them to make the journey. They were probably busy, but a star appeared, and somehow they knew what it meant. They traveled to recognize a king in whose coronation they had no part.

The magi teach us how important it is to make spiritual things our main concern. Busyness consumes our life, and if we are not careful, spiritual things take a backseat. The urgent outpaces the important. We find ourselves giving time and attention to things that in the long run are not that significant. A periodic check list is a good idea. Our jobs, families, church activities, and recreational pursuits can all steal God's time.

Wisdom involves acknowledging our limitations. Though the wise men were trained in studying the stars, they still required help finding the Christ child. As they began to ask where he had been born, no one seemed to know what they were talking about.

Though we must admit our limitations and weaknesses, they should not prevent us from giving our best to God. Limitations are not excuses. God grants each of his children gifts and talents for use in his service. We have different personalities and opportunities, but we can use our gifts for God's glory.

Wise people give to God. They recognize all they have belongs to him and has proceeded from him. Tight fists are not their pattern.

Reflection: God, help me to worship and serve you above all else.Help me live with wisdom as I do your work.

April 2

Gaining Control of Your Life

Romans 6:1-13

Slavery was a dark period in American history. It took a war, Voting Acts and Amendments, and bloodshed to finally settle the issue. Slaves had very little if any control over their lives. The master mapped out their day and duties. Though some slaves had benevolent masters, many of them were treated with wretched cruelty.

Many live today with no authority over their lives. In fact, the person apart from Christ is out of control. They may think they manage their decisions and actions, but the Bible says they are slaves to sin. A slave does the bidding of his master. Long work hours, hectic family lives, and binding habits are all evidences of out of control pursuits.Sadly, many believers' fall into the same trap.

Control comes from knowing our position. Believers are not mastered by sin any longer. Sin is not our slave driver. We have been cleansed from that old nature and set free. Sometimes we do not realize it. Like a dog accustomed to the chain does not realize his freedom when the owner secretly unleashes him, so some believers still live as if controlled by evil impulses. God gives us power each day to live as he requires. He wants us to enjoy the abundant life that is ours for the taking.

The key to such a lifestyle is to consider ourselves dead to sin and alive to Christ. Instead of a habit we cannot help, acts of sin can be seldom occurrences. When the Bible says the believer does not sin, it is referring to a pattern of sin, not individual acts. (I John 1) Perfection is not reached until heaven when we receive new bodies. Major on the control Jesus now has over your life.

No longer are we to present our bodies to sin but to God as instruments of righteousness. Our society desperately needs to have godliness woven into every fabric. Christ gives every believer the power to do this. Every place you are each day, shine the light of Christ into it. Be the salt and light that will suffocate evil. Rather than your body controlling you, control your body. No longer are we victims but victors.

Reflection: If you know Christ as your Savior, sin is no longer your master. You do not have to practice sin. It is a choice. God's forgiveness is complete. Live in the victory that is yours.

April 3

Three A's of Success

I Peter 5:5-7

Driven seems to be a proper word for the average twenty first century person. Our self esteem is often measured by how much we accomplish in a twenty four hour period. The more I can do, the more important I am. One Andy Griffith episode casts a visiting preacher who warns his constituents against hurrying. An almost hilarious admonition as we compare the 1960's with the present. We hurry for success.

God's definition of success if often radically different from ours. One has remarked that "there is never enough success in anybody's life to make one feel completely satisfied." Another stated, "The trouble with success is that the formula is the same as the one for a nervous breakdown." Not so with God's formula. The vertical dimension of success is often missing from the world's recipe.

Recognizing and respecting authority brings victory. Peter tells the younger men to respect the elders. All of us are then to clothe ourselves with humility for one another. Why? God gives grace to the humble.

Our practice and habit should be to respect those in authority over us. Respecting them involves praying for them that they would look to God for wisdom in their decisions. It involves supporting and obeying them as long as it does not entail disobedience to God.

Christians should respect their elders in the faith. They have been believers for a long period of time and have much to teach. We should watch their lifestyle and follow their example. Their warnings and wisdom are of inestimable value.

Success involves an attitude of humility. We are to humble ourselves under the mighty hand of God. God's hand symbolized discipline and deliverance. We must accept both when they come. Humility keeps us from manipulating others to get ahead. It teaches us to wait on God's timing, not create our own. It encourages us to follow God's pace. God should be in control of our life time table.

Believers must let God handle their anxieties. Peter says cast them on the Lord. We can trust the mercy of God to care for us. Only God can give us a sense of peace regardless of our circumstances.

Reflection: Determine to follow God's definition of success.

April 4

Marching Orders
Luke 9:23

The story is told of the little boy whose hand got stuck in his mom's antique flower vase. Nearly in tears, he cried out to his mother that he could not get his hand out. She tried soaking his hand in warm water and then swabbing it with jelly, all to no avail. Then she scolded him for putting it in there in the first place. She finally realized breaking the valuable vase was the only solution. Just before she did, the little boy said, "Mom, would it help if I let go of the penny."

Life is full of marching orders from various people, but our most important orders come from Christ. Obeying them always requires letting go of some things. As we attempt to carry out God's work, we face as many as three temptations-the same three Jesus faced. There is the temptation of materialism, sensationalism and compromise.

The first command is to deny self. This in itself makes the gospel unpopular to many, for our society feeds the notion that self should be preeminent. Such a mandate goes against human nature. The message we normally hear is to analyze, improve, love and protect ourselves.

Denying self is out of step with modern psychology. Putting self aside is not equal to degrading ourselves. It is simply recognizing that God's business is more important than my business. Joy is not found in a hedonistic lifestyle but in serving others. The cause of Christ is a higher mission.

Denying self allows us to serve others. Slain civil rights activist Martin Luther King, Jr., said, "Everybody can be great because everybody can serve."

We must also take up our cross daily. The cross is not some burden in life-like allergy season or a grumpy spouse, but it is the sacrifice involved in following Christ. The cross is the ultimate picture of self giving. We make a daily decision to choose the cross over self-contentment.

Once we deny self and take up the cross, we then follow Christ. It is a call for a definite direction. This is the same call Jesus issued to his disciples. He is going somewhere, and he invites us to follow.

Reflection: Lord Jesus, I realize you have given your all for me. Help me give my all for you. I take up the cross and willingly follow you.

April 5

Overcoming Temptation
Matthew 4:1-11

The story is told of a Christian man who began stopping by a local bar after work to spend time with his work buddies. He figured one beer would not hurt him, and it would give him the opportunity to witness. But one beer became two and then more. Before long, he was going home drunk. Soon after, he had lost his wife and kids.

Jesus' temptations in the wilderness demonstrate that no one is exempt from Satan's tactics. The temptation itself is not a sin. If this was the case, Jesus would have sinned. None of us are immune.

Our temptations are the same as Jesus'. The specifics may vary, but the broad areas are the same. Our focus should be on overcoming. The Bible reassures us that God will not allow temptation beyond our ability to bear it. We can always be victorious, and Jesus gives an example of how to succeed.

Satan will tempt us to meet our needs by our own power and in ways that are unpleasing to God, even wrong. Jesus had fasted forty days and nights and was hungry. The tempter comes and encourages Jesus to turn stones into bread to satisfy his hunger. The act itself would not be inherently wrong, but Jesus would have demonstrated reliance on himself for his needs instead of the Father. Satan's ploy was to get Jesus to doubt the Father's care, as he did with Eve in the Garden of Eden.

God promises to meet all our needs. Food, shelter and clothing are things we never have to worry about. We often get into trouble when we take matters into our own hands instead of trusting God. We do our part by working, and God does his by supplying.

Satan also wants us to presume on God. He told Jesus to jump from the Temple and prove that angels would keep him from injury. He could have, and they would have, but there was no point. Nor should we live recklessly and carelessly and then expect God to get us out of our dilemmas.

Satan's final ploy was asking Jesus to worship him and he would give him all the kingdoms of the world. The temptation was to rule without the cross. Some temptations are simply to cut corners, but the corners often have dangerous edges.

Reflection: Remember God will not allow you to be tempted beyond your ability to overcome. Trust God when Satan attacks.

April 6
Find Your Place
John 12:1-11

Imagine the high school band. It does not consist solely of trumpets, drums, clarinets, tubas or any other one instrument. A band that lives up to the name has variety and people who know how to play the right notes.Just a collection of people blowing into instruments and beating on drums does not make a band. Each one must know their place.

Paul uses this same illustration when speaking of the church. He says it is comprised of many members yet is one body. This organism only lives up to its name as each member recognizes their gifts of the Spirit and uses them accordingly.

Jesus had a special friendship with Mary, Martha and Lazarus-siblings from Bethany. Prior to this occasion, Jesus had raised Lazarus from the dead. To celebrate the occasion, they hosted a party in Jesus' honor. At this party, they each filled their own position.

Martha's gift was serving. She was a busybody who was in her prime when serving others. Picture her. Running here and there. Hair pulled back. A little sweat on her brow. Sleeves rolled up. But she knew what her gift was.

Every church needs some Martha's. They keep the church focused on its mission. The budget gets passed because of them. Activities that promote involvement are a part of their assignment. They make sure offices are filled and the babies are taken care of. Hats off to the Martha's. If you are one, just make sure your religious activity does not outpace your time with the Master.

Mary sits at Jesus' feet and worships. Martha gets steamed and asked Jesus if he cares that she is doing all the work. Jesus reminds Martha that Mary has chosen the most important thing. Busyness in God's work is good, but it cannot take the place of time with our Father. Stop and know he is God.

Lazarus had a story to tell. Fresh back from death, he was a walking testimony to the power of Jesus and who he was. Because of him, many believed in Jesus, and this infuriated the religious leaders. If you are a believer, you have a story to tell.

Reflection: Lord, help me to know my place and serve you faithfully where you put me.

April 7

The God of Perfect Timing

John 6:15-21

"I don't have enough time." Ever uttered those words? Interestingly, we all have the same amount of it. Each day contains twenty four hours. While some may use theirs more wisely, we all have the same amount.

Then there is timing. This is the when or how of circumstances—what order they come in or their convenience. The timing of something is just as important as the time that that particular thing takes.

While our timing is seldom perfect, God's always is. Jesus had previously fed the thousands with five loaves of bread and two fish. He now retreats to the hills for some down time. His disciples wait on the shore until dark. Jesus never shows up. They decide to do what he told them—ford the Sea of Galilee to Capernaum. While on this unpredictable lake, they encounter a significant storm, but also the God of perfect timing.

Following Christ does not eliminate suffering. It didn't for the disciples. They still encountered a storm that threatened their very existence. Had

Jesus knowingly sent them into a death trap? Mark's account says Jesus was watching them as they fought against the wind and waves.

The storms of life will come even for believers. Ask the woman who cannot have children or the husband whose wife was unfaithful. Question the businessman who lost all in a recession or the parents who lost a child in a tragic accident. Storms are not necessarily a sign of disobedience. If we know of no infraction in our life, then we have to view the storm as sent or allowed by God for a reason. Trust him in the storm.

Jesus prays for us in our squalls. While the disciples were fighting the tempest, not knowing whether they would live or die, Jesus was on the mountain praying. No doubt, a part of his prayer was for their safety. Though they could not see him, he could see them. He does no less for us. He is our great High Priest who intercedes for us.(Hebrews 7:25)

We must also keep going in the storm as the disciples did. When Jesus did not come, they kept rowing. Much of our life is spent rowing against the waves, but we cannot bail out. Jesus is there, and in his perfect time, will calm the storm.

Reflection: God, help me to trust you in the storms, knowing that your timing is perfect.

April 8
The Cure for Calamity
John 2:1-12

You just had your car serviced. The oil was changed, pressure checked in the tires, fluids confirmed, and to top it off, they vacuumed the inside. Now you are off to a friend's house.After the visit, you walk outside only to discover that you have a flat tire. Your friend remarks, "Oh, I forgot to tell you not to park in the driveway. They are reroofing the house." Calamities. Life's regular occurrences.

Jesus' mother Mary faced one. While attending a wedding feast in Cana of Galilee, the wine ran out. This was a bad reflection on the groom. While this calamity might seem insignificant from a modern perspective, in Jesus' time it was equivalent to forgetting the wedding cake. Perhaps Mary was involved in preparing for the wedding. What would she do?

Dealing with calamities involves indentifying the problem. The wine had run out. The groom, no doubt, was embarrassed. Mary had some responsibility. She could have lost her cool or started blaming someone or even herself. Mary took the right approach. She approached Jesus. John Dewey once said, "A problem well stated is a problem half solved."

Many waves in life are relatively small-losing something important, being late to work, or having a friend betray us. Small waves, if left unattended, can become crashing curls.

We need to take our calamities, large or small, to Jesus. Mary did. She could have gone to any number of people, but this was a major problem, so she went to the problem solver. Jesus took some water and made wine.

Prayer is the way we take our calamities to Jesus. Sadly, we often wait until we have exhausted all other means and failed in our attempted solutions. Then, in a last ditch effort, we try what we should have tried first. Jesus is concerned with every detail of your life.

After taking our calamity to Jesus in prayer, we need to obey what he says. Jesus told the servants to fill the water pots. When the master of the feast tasted it, it was wine, and a fine quality at that. The Father gives guidance during our times of calamity. We do not need to analyze or question the instructions. We just need to obey.

Reflection: Trust God in times of calamity. His answer is always best.

April 9

Living with Expectation

Matthew 24:42

Imagine the young child playing on the beach. He fills his bucket with the right mixture of sand and water, packs it down, and then gently turns it over. He molds and shapes, even as the water laps at his feet. Finally the masterpiece is finished, and he stands back to admire it. A beautiful sandcastle. But soon the tide creeps in, and his work of art is destroyed. He is not disillusioned, however, because he knew it was going to happen.

Such is a picture of the one who expects Christ's return. She will not be caught unaware nor will she be disillusioned because he appears. God's Word, in many places, instructs us to prepare for his coming.

The coming of Christ is a certainty. Early Christians expected it, and Christians throughout church history have savored the hope. Still he has not returned. The apparent delay gives no reason for discouragement nor is it justification for abdicating the doctrine. Though Jesus comes to us in other ways, his final return will be a literal appearing.

Time is of no concern to God, for he lives outside of it. One reason he delays his Son's return is so the elect can be gathered in. He is patient, not wanting any to perish. While life is filled with uncertainties, this is not one of them.

His coming will bring a conclusion. The world will end and eternity will begin. A new heaven and earth will be formed. The end of things often upsets us, such as when a loved one dies. We see the breathing stop. We place the body in a casket, close the lid, and then bury them. It's over. They won't come back. Jesus' coming brings finality.

Jesus' return also involves a time of separation, a partition that will be eternal. What we do with Jesus during our time on earth determines what he will do with us in eternity. Jesus speaks in many of his parables of a separation that will occur at the end. The righteous will be separated from the wicked. One group will enter heaven and the other hell. Hell is the place prepared for the devil and his angels, not humans, but those who reject Christ must face this punishment to satisfy God's wrath against sin.

Reflection: Have you prepared for the return of Christ? If not, accept him as you Savior now. Ask him to forgive your sins and commit yourself to follow him in obedience.

April 10
Success in God's Church
John 13:13-15

April Thomas' love for gymnastics started early. She practiced hard. During high school, she ran a paper route to pay for the cost. Her mom was a single mom and could not afford the monthly tuition. Though April excelled and won many trophies, she had to quit after injuring her back. Still her love persisted. From participating, she moved to coaching. She now teaches other boys and girls to love and excel in the sport.

Success seems to be ingrained in human nature. We yearn to excel. We crave recognition. We want to leave some legacy when our days on earth are over, something that will benefit mankind. God's church should desire success as well.

Triumph in God's church will only come as we learn to serve. Jesus performed a menial servant role for his disciples by washing their feet. Then he told them to do the same. Not literally. It was an example of servanthood. Only those churches that are willing to serve will accomplish much for God.

A church must have unity. Lack of this in God's churches gives a black eye and is very damaging to our witness. Unbelievers expect Christians to get along. Jesus told his disciples to wash each other's feet. Only as they had unity would they be willing to do that.

Unity is not always easy, but accord is one of our greatest witnessing tools. Where there is harmony, there will be love. Later in John's gospel, Jesus would pray that his followers be "perfected in unity." The literal translation is "perfected into a unit." A unit is a team. Teams must function as such to know success. They support, encourage and forgive.

Successful churches love. Jesus' disciples did not always show that. Washing their feet would show them the necessity. Much of what we call love is selfishness. We tell our children we love them if they act a certain way. We show love to our employers hoping for a raise. A young man tells a young girl this only because he desires sex. The church must love unconditionally.

Believers need to support each other. A servant attitude helps this happen. We need to put our arms around each other's shoulders and carry burdens. Concern is needed, not judgmental spirits.

Reflection: As you serve in your local church, ask God to help you promote a spirit of unity and love. Encourage someone today.

April 11
Obstacles to Spiritual Health
Romans 12:1

Good health is a concern of our century. Exercise is constantly emphasized. Vitamins and natural herbs are popular. At the same time, advanced technology continues to create an atmosphere where we get less exercise at our jobs.

Spiritual health is more important, but it cannot be in just any form. Spiritual health is only advantageous when it is tied to Christianity. When it involves mediums, yoga, eastern mysticism or other forms of spirituality, it falls short.

Accurate vision of who we are is foremost. The picture is not pretty, and many have tried to dampen the seriousness of it. Biblical teaching is clear. We are sinners. Whether we sin because we are sinners or are sinners because we sin is immaterial. We are entangled in the web. The price we pay for this situation is death-spiritual and physical. Spiritual health comes when we acknowledge our condition and run to Christ for forgiveness. We must recognize the plague of our heart. Otherwise we will see no need for a Savior. Actions manifest who we are, and the pattern for humanity is evil.

Spiritual healthiness recognizes our behavior matters. While actions have nothing to do with salvation, they are important thereafter. They demonstrate our faith. Our actions show others who we are.

In Greek thought, spirit was good and matter was evil. This led to believing that one could act any way he desired in the body without affecting his spiritual state. We cannot separate our flesh from our spirit. What we do matters. We are a whole entity, not compartmentalized. Jesus said others would know us by our actions.

Believers must also be careful of the grandstand. At the old county fairs, the grandstand was where special events took place. Bleachers were about so people could sit and watch. The grandstand is those who watch us.

We must be careful lest we become people pleasers instead of God pleasers. Our actions should please God, but our motivation must be the same. God is the most important person in our grandstand. God's expectations are primary.

Reflection: Heavenly Father, show me those things in my life that are hindering my spiritual health.

April 12

Words from the Widow

Mark 12:41-44

Osceola McCarty spent most of her life making others look good by washing their clothes. She had to quit school in the sixth grade, never married, and never had children. Yet she considered herself fortunate because she had more than most other black people in rural Mississippi. Over the years, the dollar bills and change for her work grew to $150,000 in savings. McCarty decided to give it to the University of Mississippi to finance scholarships for students living in her hometown. The Executive Director of the school's foundation said, "She gave almost everything she had."

Jesus was sitting at the Temple observing people put money in the treasury. Various amounts were tossed in. Then comes a widow who puts in a fraction of a penny. It was the smallest coin in circulation, and she drops two in the trumpet like receptacle. Jesus tells his disciples she has put in more than all the others. A perplexing comment to an interesting situation.

The widow's gift should encourage us. The widow really had nothing to give. In fact, she gave all she had to live on. In Jesus' time, there were no social programs to help indigent people like her.

There are many who find themselves in similar situations. They may live with spouses who control the purse strings and are bitter toward God. It may be a student who has to fund their education, or an elderly person living on a fixed income. They look at the outgo versus the income, and it does not seem possible or even prudent that they should give to God.

Regardless of our financial situation, God promises that if we give to him he will take care of us. Our financial situation is not an excuse to shortchange God. The widow demonstrates this. God wants us to give freely, sacrificially and joyfully.

The widow's actions rebuke those who have a selfish spirit. So many give out of their surplus, not sacrificially. Jesus said the widow gave all she had. God does not require only large sums from us, but the gift should be in proportion to our income. God will bless us when we choose to make that giving sacrificial.

Reflection: The widow's giving is a challenge to give no matter what our financial circumstances. God has given himself for us through Christ on the cross. We owe him our all. Are you giving cheerfully and sacrificially?

April 13

Living Authentically

I Peter 2:11-12

At 87, Mother Teresa was loved the world over for her charitable work with the poor and destitute in Calcutta, India. Her blue and white sari was familiar to all who saw her. In 1979, she was awarded the Nobel Peace Prize. She walked where others feared to go and believed no one was too wretched to serve. One priest said of her, "She was totally immersed in the experience of seeing Jesus Christ in the poorest of the poor and worshipping God through her love of them." She lived an authentic life.

Webster defines authentic as that "that can be believed or accepted, trustworthy, reliable." Our world needs genuine Christians. How often has our message been tainted because of bad behavior, words or attitudes? Authentic existence is living a clean life. Our lifestyle matters, even to unbelievers. While they do not confess Christ, they have a scenario formed in their mind for those who have. Peter warns Christians to stay away from things that are displeasing to God.

Our challenge is to do this while being tempted by people and situations. We do not live in isolated environments. Jesus calls for us to live in the world but not be of it. Even removing ourselves from other people would not help. Our battle begins in the mind and is exacerbated by our sinful nature.

Authenticity leaves no room for slander. Our standard of living should be above reproach, so much so that no one could find reason to say anything negative about us. Others will talk, but the slander should not be because we have given them occasion to. Plato, famous Greek philosopher, was told of a man who was making slanderous remarks against him. His response was: "I will live in such a way that no one will believe what he says."

We live authentically by doing good deeds among unbelievers. It is easy to serve those who love us, but Jesus said we are to love our enemies and pray for those who persecute us. (Matthew 5:43-48) If not careful, believers can develop tunnel vision-we only see other Christians and their needs. Churches will never be more than they are if they limit their acts of love to the membership only.

Reflection: How about you? Are you living an authentic Christian life that shows others, in word and action, that you love God?

April 14

Overcoming Discouragement
II Timothy 1:5-8

According to a fable, the devil decided to have an auction. He was going out of business, so he would sell his tools. All were laid out on a red plush mat for the throngs of interested observers to peruse. Off to one side was a silver wedge. When people questioned him about it, he said, "That's the wedge of discouragement. I can drive it in and pry open a door, and all the rest of my cohorts can go in. I can break that life down with discouragement."

One of Satan's favorite ploys is discouragement. If he can drive this into believers and churches, he can start us on a downward slide. Discouragement brings a domino effect that destroys our usefulness in God's work, and since Satan cannot steal the salvation God has given us, he will settle for destroying our usefulness. Dismay will take the enthusiasm and excitement God's people should have.

Paul's child in the faith, Timothy, was discouraged for some reason. Paul instructed him to fan the flames of his faith and stir up the gift of God that was in him. The hot coals of his faith were still smoldering, but he needed to blow on them. Churches can become dismayed just like individuals when it appears our efforts are not rewarded-when evil seems to overcome good.

Discouragement can be avoided when we remember the law of the harvest. If we sow, we will reap a return. It is easy to grow weary in our work, but we should never tire of doing good in God's name. God will reward our efforts, here and in eternity. We must adapt our methods to our ever changing culture while keeping the message intact. Spiritual laziness is a danger we must always guard against. God is responsible for the outcome. It is our job to do the input.

We must be careful of the measurement stick we use to gauge success. Success our way is not necessarily success God's way. In most churches, baptisms and new church members are the measurement we use. Location can have a negative or positive effect on this. Spiritual growth is important, and churches can give to those who are working in other areas.

Reflection: In the final evaluation, we must trust God for growth. Trust will also wart off discouragement. While we are his instruments, he brings the harvest.

April 15
God's Program for Greatness
Luke 7:24-28

Billy Graham is an evangelist known the world over. He has advised presidents, met with dignitaries and touched countless numbers of people. Through his preaching, thousands have trusted Christ as their Savior. But unlike many with a famous streak, he has never craved fame or gloated over himself. Graham has simply been steadfast in his ministry.

Jesus said John the Baptist was the greatest man to ever live. We would probably give a different diagnosis. His ministry was not very long, and his appearance certainly was not eye catching. The message he preached was not even popular with the in crowd, so what made him so great?

Do not be overly impressed with who you are. Simply recognize who you are in relation to God. A good vertical assessment will always lead to a spirit of humility. John recognized his job. He was not the Messiah and never claimed to be. He was simply a Jesus pointer whose job was to decrease while Jesus increased.

Jesus moves us from sinners to saints. He accepts us into his family and even makes us his friends. Abundant life is ours for the taking, and heaven awaits us. In spite of all these things we might crow about, humility is the feather we should wear. Never think more of yourself than is reasonable, but never think less of yourself than God thinks of you. Be secure in your position but not infatuated with your power.

Greatness is not shaken by what it sees. John saw a lot. He saw religious leaders who were misleading the people. They burdened them with interpretations of God's laws that even they did not live up to. He saw a brood of snakes who thought they were God accepted because they were Abraham descended. John was anchored in his faith and unshaken by what he saw.

Christians must not be afraid of the evil that seems to swallow up good. Remember God is in control, and he has empowered us to infiltrate the darkness with light. Remain steadfast in what God has given you to do. The mission is not to covet or compare but to allow God to use your unique personality in his kingdom work.

Reflection: Remember that greatness is found only in obedience to God's mission for your life. Faithfully use the talents and gifts you have.

April 16

Missing Lazarus

Luke 16:19-25

How many opportunities have you missed? The Greeks had a statue named "Opportunity." Hair adorned the front of the head, but it was bald on the back. It symbolized that opportunities can be grasped as they come but are often lost when they pass.

The rich man had an opportunity on his doorstep. His name was Lazarus. He lay there longing for the scraps that fell from the rich man's table while the dogs licked his sores. Either the rich man did not see the opportunity or did not care.

Selfishness can lead to overlooking Lazarus. The rich man was certainly this. Life was all about him. Lazarus only wanted scraps. The rich man could have given this and more. Instead, he let the dogs do what he should have done. After all, Lazarus was a diseased beggar. He was unclean.

The rich man's sin was not in being rich or even in how he acquired his wealth. It was that he was selfish and refused to share what God had blessed him with. Wealth does not necessarily equal selfishness. We can be poor and inflicted with the same disease. The question is what we are doing with the opportunities God gives us. A kind word is free.

It is important to see the inner potential of people. The rich man obviously missed this. When he looked at Lazarus, he saw someone who would never be more than he was. He was only worthy of the bread napkin that he discarded after wiping his mouth. But Lazarus might have been something else had the rich man let go of his selfishness and helped him.

How often do we look through the eyes of prejudice? We classify people as lazy, snobbish, from the wrong side of the tracks, or criminals. Stereotyping clouds our vision. We need to see people Jesus died for. We should see a person who can do all things with Christ. When God changes the inside, the outside follows.

Busyness can let opportunities slip by. The rich man lived in luxury every day. He must have been an important person, or so he thought. He had no time for a poor beggar. Interestingly, after he died and wound up in hell, he wanted Lazarus. Nothing is more important than a helping hand in Jesus' name.

Reflection: What is causing you to miss God's opportunities?

April 17

Grace Based Relationships

Luke 2:39-52

Family is on the minds of many today, especially Christians as they see the challenges families face. Churches also find themselves involved in ministries they have never had to worry about before. Stress management, marriage enrichment seminars, and support groups are all examples. Some churches even promote family ministry programs as a drawing tool.

The present scripture gives a rare glimpse into Jesus' family life. As was customary, this family went to the Passover feast in Jerusalem. On the way home, Mary and Joseph notice that Jesus is missing. In our time, such behavior would constitute neglect, but not here. They find Jesus in the Temple debating with the religious leaders. Mary questioned why he was treating her and Joseph like this. He reminded her that he had to be about his Father's business. Then he returned to Nazareth with them.

Love and affirmation are vital to family life. We have every reason to believe that both were present in Jesus' family. Jesus' earthly parents knew God had a plan for their son. As time progressed, Mary must have understood more about his ministry.

Parents should demonstrate both these qualities before and to their children. Psychologists call this modeling. Each child is different.Jesus certainly was. He was the sinless Son of God. He was unlike his brothers and sisters in this way but in other ways also. In return, children should give these qualities to their parents. To honor incorporates both traits.

Relationships need attention. Jesus' parents gave this also. Joseph taught him the carpenter trade. They both looked for him after the feast when they discovered he was missing. Jesus would later return the attention while he hung on the cross by turning the care of his mother over to John.

Parents must nurture their love. Dating is a good method. They must also give needed attention to the children, for neglected children are normally bound for behavioral issues.

Parenting involves modeling responsibility. Jesus was taught a trade, to be obedient, and to obey God's laws. Responsibility is a needed attribute. It forms the basis for healthy families and societies.

Reflection: God, help me to model my parenting on the principles of your Word.

April 18
What Happens When We Mess Up
Luke 15:11-32

The story is familiar to most. A father had two sons. The younger approaches him one day demanding his share of the inheritance. Normally this was done after the father's death. The father concedes, and the son starts off for a far country where he wastes his inheritance on wild living. He started out with pork but soon finds himself feeding porky to keep his head above water. Certainly a reprehensible job for a Jewish man.

Soon the young lad comes to his senses. He remembers that his father's servants have more than he does. Home seems very attractive. While a great distance off, his father sees him, runs to him, and greets him with great emotion. He seemingly does not even hear the son's request to be made a servant but instead restores him to his original position.

The young man's actions teach what God expects when we mess up, and all have. Our greatest transgression against God is our sins. Even after these are forgiven, we still fail God from time to time. What are we to do in such times?

God expects us to take responsibility. This involves repentance-going in a different direction. While we cannot do anything about our sins, we can run to the Father who can. Because of Christ, those sins can be forgiven. Our inability to rectify our sins does not relieve us of responsibility for them. God holds us accountable. After salvation, we are to confess when we sin. It is our acknowledgment to God that we have missed the mark again. The wonderful news, however, is that all our sins are forgiven in Christ. We are no longer under condemnation. The prodigal took responsibility.

We must accept Christ's forgiveness for the mess we have made of our lives. The prodigal's father extended forgiveness, and the son accepted. In fact, the story implies that forgiveness had already taken place before the son asked. In forgiveness, God releases us from the debt we owe because of the sins we have committed against him.

Following this, we must move on. Since God no longer holds our sins against us, we need to release ourselves as well. We should live in the freedom of forgiveness not the slavery of regret.

Reflection: God, thank you for your forgiveness. Help me to live the abundant life you offer.

April 19

Living Victoriously
Ephesians 4:22-24

Imagine you and a friend were at a coffee shop chatting, and she asked, "If you could change anything about yourself, what would it be?" Typical responses might include: hair color, amount of hair, height, weight, body shape, personality characteristics, emotional stability, or spiritual maturity.

Most of the above is society's measure of self esteem. However, most of them have nothing to do with self-esteem in God's eyes. Believers have reason to value themselves because we are the crown of creation. Only humans can testify to the goodness and mercy of God. Healthy self-appreciation is a vital part of our new nature and is tied to living victoriously.

Loving yourself affects abundant living. Jesus taught to love others as we do ourselves. How much we love self determines how much we can love others. Loving oneself is not equivalent to conceit, selfishness, or self absorption. It is recognizing we are worthy of being loved because the God of the universe loves us. The sacrifice of Christ on the cross proved this. Though marred by sin, we are worthy of love because of the image of Christ in us.

God chooses to need us. At some point in eternity's expanse, God chose to create a world and humans to inhabit it. He could have continued to exist without us, but he commissioned us as the agents in his redemptive plan. Angels do not carry the message of salvation. We do.

Since God uses believers in his redemptive plan, we need to find our place in his body, the Church. We are the sweet savor that influences the lives of others. God gifts his people. By belonging to a local church, we are given opportunity to find our niche. This comes from practice and by others in the body recognizing God's gifts in us. Christians should encourage each other to find their place. Just as checks are validated by a signature, so we validate ourselves by recognizing our importance in God's work.

Living victoriously comes when we make realistic demands on ourselves. God does not expect more than he enables you to do. You are not held accountable for opportunities and gifts he has not given. Be only what God wants you to be.

Reflection: Thank God that he enables you to live a victorious life. Find your place in his work, and enjoy the wonders of serving him.

April 20

Missing God's Will

Luke 24:13-32

Have you ever missed out on something important? Maybe you were out sick from school and when you went back the teacher gave a test you did not know about. Or you were off work one day and returned to find that an announcement of a major lay off had been made.Missing out on information leaves a void that can lead to confusion or even anger.

The two disciples on the road to Emmaus missed out on the revolution Jesus had just brought through his crucifixion and resurrection. It would be like living through America's fight for freedom and not knowing about it. We wonder how that could happen.

These followers of Jesus knew about his ministry, death and resurrection, yet they are on their way with sullen faces. Such action appears incongruent. Their shoulders slouched, and their hearts were heavy. Jesus joins the duo, but they did not recognize him. Their hopelessness is found in the words, "We were hoping that it was He who was going to redeem Israel."

God desires that we know his will. Seeking God's will is searching his heart. It is attempting to answer the question, "How does God want to use me?" Jesus had to enlighten these two learners.

God can reveal his will through others. This is why it is so important to associate with a local church. The two disciples had heard the report of the empty tomb. Evidently, they disregarded it. God often enables other believers to see his plan for us. Always consider seriously what a brother or sister in Christ tells you they see God doing in your life.

We know God's will through his Word. It is our lamp, and hiding it in our heart keeps us from sinning against God. It is a two edged sword that pierces to our innermost being. God also speaks to us when we read and study it so we might know his purposes. Jesus used the Old Testament to reveal God's will concerning himself to these sullen converts.

Taking a daily walk with God also reveals his will. Walking with someone requires going in the same direction as Jesus did with these disciples. Doing this requires prayer, time in his Word, and fellowship with other believers.

Reflection: Ask God to reveal his purpose and plan for your life. Then walk with him in obedience.

April 21
God's Commentary on the Cross
Matthew 27:45-46

After the First Continental Congress passed a list of grievances against the British government, Britain decided to force a showdown with their bumptious colonial offspring. Redcoat regiments poured into Boston, but the Patriots were forewarned by Paul Revere. He had made a famous ride crying out to the colonists that the British were coming.

Jesus also made a cry. On the cross, his cry had the potential to affect an entire world; then, now and for as long as time exists. These verses, along with the teaching of Scripture in general, provide God's commentary on what really happened that fateful day.

It had been a grueling experience for Jesus. Scorned, mocked and beaten, he was then nailed to the cross. From noon until three in the afternoon, darkness engulfed the land. It was at the ninth hour that the fateful cry was heard.

Jesus cried out "Eli, Eli" which is "My God, My God." Those standing nearby thought he was crying for the old prophet Elijah. It was an agonizing cry of separation. The division was between Jesus and God the Father. It was necessary because Jesus was taking our sins upon himself, and God cannot look on sin.

Never before in the annals of eternity had such a thing taken place. Neither theologians nor reason can explain the scenario. Since Jesus was

God, how could God turn his back on God? The separation was not in nature, substance or essence, but it happened nevertheless. It was a separation that brought greater pain than the nail, spear or lash marks.

Following the cry, Jesus asks God why he had forsaken him. God is holy. We are sinful by birth and nature. Jesus destroyed the wall of separation and took upon himself our sin. This is why God turned away. Jesus' death was not just some heroic gesture but rather a substitution. He took our place and paid the penalty we owed.

On Calvary the cure was enacted for our sin problem. Though the payment has been made, it is only applied to our account upon request. How great is the God who would deliver us from our own self-inflicted situation.

Reflection: Have you accepted what Jesus has done for you. If not, ask him to forgive you today and accept his gift of salvation.

April 22

Importance of the Resurrection

Matthew 17:22-23

Miss Miller gave her second graders an assignment prior to Easter. It turned out to be one of those life-changing moments. They were to take an empty plastic egg home and bring it back with something in it that represented life. The eggs returned with various items. Jeremy's egg was different. He was a twelve year old terminally student still in the second grade. His egg was empty. Disgusted, Miss Miller scolded him. He replied, "Jesus' tomb was empty too." Three months later, Jeremy's theology was represented at his funeral with nineteen empty eggs placed on his casket.

Herein lies the great hope of Easter: the empty tomb. Various reasons have been proposed to explain the absence of Jesus' body, but Christians reject them all. We believe the tomb was empty because Jesus did what he said-rose again.

Jesus' resurrection assures a new future body. How often we tire of our earthly bodies. This probably started in our preteen years. We began to find all manner of tragic curiosities and wondered why we had to have this body. Things like pimples, wrong hair color, one leg shorter than the other, or uneven ear lobes.

The good news is we do not have to keep this body forever. We are promised a new one in our eternal heavenly home. A body not subject to defects, disease or death. When Jesus appeared in resurrected form, he had a body, and so will we.

The resurrection assures new life. It was God's stamp of approval on what Jesus did on Calvary. It was proof that the Father accepted the Son's payment for our sins. New life comes at salvation when we are granted a new nature that is controlled by holy wants and desires. When we sin, it is temporary insanity. We momentarily do something that does not fit our identity.

Because of the resurrection, we have new opportunities. After his resurrection, Jesus appeared to his disciples and informed them that he was now sending them as he had been sent by the Father. We have the privilege of sharing a living Lord with people, not a dead hero.

Reflection: Thank God for raising Jesus. Had he not, our faith would be in vain.

April 23

Traits of the Crucified Person

Galatians 2:20

In 1998, Milton Garland was honored as America's oldest known worker. At 102, that's not surprising. He has worked for the same Pennsylvania company since 1920. His advice, "Go into something and stay with it until you like it." We might even say he was sold out to his work.

A crucified person is sold out to Christ and works for him with the same enthusiasm as a Milton Garland. The crucifixion of Christ was the end result of a life dedicated to the Father's will. Though he struggled with the thought of it in the Garden of Gethsemane, Jesus was committed to the mission.

Believers have been crucified with Christ. The payment made at Calvary has been applied to our lives. Symbolically, we were hanging there with Jesus. As Christ followers, we must sell out to the mission.

A crucified person faces one direction. Looking at Jesus on the cross demonstrates this very clearly. His face was always set on the Father's will. He moved forward willingly and diligently. Even at twelve years of age, he was found in the temple debating with the religious leaders.

The believer's direction must be forward as well. As recipients of God's grace, we should pursue holiness in actions, attitudes and words. God's will for our life is the compass that guides our plans. Pray daily for God to keep your feet on the paths or righteousness. A one direction lifestyle often includes ridicule and rejection.

We need always remember that tomorrow is in God's hand. Trust in God that he will handle whatever that day brings is the hallmark of our faith.Jesus tells us not to worry about tomorrow but to focus on the day we are currently living. All plans are made with the realization that tomorrow may never come. If it does not, our eternity is secure. In fact, crucified people have no tomorrow, just a few hours.

Being sold out in God's service means putting aside whatever hinders us. The hindrance may not be sinful but merely an obstacle to crucified service. The disciples gave up their livelihood. Jesus rejected some relationships. Whatever slows us down or trips us up must be tossed away.

Reflection: Ask God to give you courage to put away whatever keeps you from living the crucified life.

April 24

Are You Impressed With Jesus?

Mark 1

The process of identification is the manner in which we form and change our attitudes. Our tendency is to identify with people we consider role models. There are things about them that impress us. Identification occurs when we define ourselves in terms of a person or group.

Early role models are usually parents, teachers or famous people. During adolescence it is normally our peers. In college, it might be a professor. On the job, perhaps our boss. For the believer, it should be Jesus.

When impressed with Jesus, obedience follows. While walking by the Sea of Galilee, Jesus called his first disciples-Peter and Andrew. Going a little farther, he called the second set-James and John. They were all fisherman by trade. All four left their trade to follow Jesus.

The Christian life is one of obedience. Jesus says if we love him we will obey his commands. His call is to salvation and service. Once we have obeyed the first, we must conquer the second. Service becomes an honor and joy. Learn to be content with what God is doing in your life. Trust him in the uncertain times. Obey and leave the consequences to him.

Are you amazed with Jesus? While in Capernaum, Jesus goes to the synagogue on the Sabbath Day and begins to teach. There was a man present with an evil spirit. Jesus healed him. Those present were amazed. Here was a man who had authority like they had never witnessed before.

The old hymn says, "I stand amazed in the presence of Jesus the Nazarene." What Jesus did for us on the cross should always amaze us. Realizing our sad state apart from Christ should foster in us an enormous applause of gratitude. We are now saints and no longer sinners. He owed us nothing but gave us everything.

Impression leads to proclamation. As Jesus traveled through Galilee, he happened upon a leper who begged for healing. Jesus granted his request. In return, the healed leper heralded the news.

Jesus has commissioned us to spread the good news about a spiritual healing. What he can do in a person's life is worth sharing with others.

Reflection: Let Jesus be your role model. Be amazed at what he has done in your life, and freely share the good news with others.

April 25

Characteristics of God's Family

I Timothy 3:14-15

Two of my favorite shows growing up were "Little House on the Prairie," and "The Waltons." One was set in the developing Midwest and the other during the Great Depression, but both demonstrated what the perfect family should look like. Family members respected each other and went to church. Children obeyed parents and grandparents. Happiness was not associated with what they had because they owned very little. Spiritual things were important, and they loved their neighbors.

Paul refers to the church as the household of God. As such, it should be a place of caring and sharing. A place where no one bears a burden alone but together. God's church should be the picture perfect family. Billy Sunday, an interesting preacher from the nineteenth century, said, "You can find anything in the average church today from a hummingbird to a turkey buzzard."

Others should know Christ's body for her gladness. In healthy homes, Mom, Dad and the children enjoy spending time with each other. Home is that place we love coming back to even after an enjoyable vacation.

An atmosphere of joy and gladness will attract others to our fellowship. Conflict, strife, bickering and bitterness will drive a wedge between us and those who need our message. Church is the place where we learn to disagree in a spirit of love. The psalmist spoke of how glad he was when he was invited to go to the Lord's house. (Psalm 122:1)

God's family must grow. Church is not about entertainment. Rather it provides an atmosphere in which spiritual growth can and should take place. It provides a location where we can discover, nurture and use our spiritual gifts. Worship is primary as we adore and honor our Creator.

Grace should characterize our churches. Since we have experienced it in Christ, we should dole it out. In a home, position is not earned but birthed. You are a son or daughter. Churches should be known for healing, hope and affirmation. It is where people come to get well not beat up. It is a place where wounds of the world can be healed.

Reflection: What Robert Frost said of home should be true of our churches: "Home is the place where, when you go there, they have to take you in."

April 26

God's Army

Matthew 16:18

One of the most astounding armies ever created in world history was assembled by Adolf Hitler. He built the Nazi party, and in 1933 was appointed chancellor. His name for this new totalitarian Germany was Third Reich. Believing the Germans needed more living space, he set out to conquer other lands. His empire was finally defeated but not before he had killed millions of people, most of them Jews.

The analogy of Christians as soldiers and the church as an army is common in the New Testament. This one verse attests to the offensive nature of the church. Wrongly interpreted, it pictures a church struggling against evil, always on the brink of defeat. Rightly interpreted, it shows the church on the offensive. The forces of evil cannot contain her march.

God's army needs an aggressive mindset. Her mission is not to force her beliefs on others, but we are responsible for making our message known. The church must be alert to the opportunities God places before us and quick to seize the initiative to do this work.

God's church must attack evil on every corner. We cannot be satisfied with our status quo but must advance the kingdom of God at every turn. The church, like believers, is involved in a spiritual warfare against the forces of evil. Our message contains the power to deliver people from the chains of sin.

Abraham Lincoln once remarked to his Secretary of State concerning the sad progression of Union generals, "They al l wait to be attacked. It is not in their nature to attack first."

An effective army will also have a disciplined membership. This is one trait the American military teaches well. The church must too. Jesus gave us a global strategy, but he also said to teach new believers his Word. Not knowing God's Word will create an internal weakness in our ranks.

Successful armies must have adequate resources. The church's strength is not in her numbers or ingeniously designed plans but in the power of the gospel she proclaims.

Reflection: It is an awesome privilege to belong to God's spiritual army. We have the wonderful privilege of sharing the best news people could ever hear.

April 27
The Journey of Humanity
Deuteronomy 6:20-25

John Bunyan's *Pilgrim's Progress* is a classic in Christian fiction. It tells the story of "Christian," a man on an adventurous journey. Christian begins in sin but finds grace. After a tumultuous expedition, he crosses the river to the Celestial City whose builder and maker is God.

Life is a journey, and everyone is on it. The path holds various events for each traveler. There is a final destination, but that too will be different. God's people of the Old Testament also took a journey. The stages they traveled through are some of the same we traverse.

While some of the stages may vary, the first is always identical. Bondage. Israel spent hundreds of years in Egyptian slavery because of disobedience to God. Later they were conquered by the Assyrian and Babylonian Empires for the same reason. The Babylonian captivity finally taught them a lesson about idolatry.

The journey of every person begins in bondage to sin. The Bible says we have all sinned and missed God's goal. (Romans 3:23) The result of our sin is death. (Romans 6:23) The psalmist maintains that he was brought forth in iniquity. (Psalm 51:5) From a young age, children demonstrate this sinful nature. They do not have to be taught to do wrong. It comes naturally. Rather, we have to teach them to do right. This bondage corrupts, enslaves and will doom us for eternity if we are not released. Our deliverance comes through Christ.

Our journey requires instruction. God gave this to Israel in the Ten Commandments and the Law. Over time God's entire Word to humanity was written and collected in our Bible. It is our manual of instruction. If our journey is to be successful, we must follow the handbook. Additionally, God speaks through his Spirit, other believers and circumstances. We need this direction so we can experience the fullness of his will.

Rebellion can also taint the journey. Apart from Christ, everyone is in a state of rebellion, but even Christians can fall into this trap. Israel did on many occasions, and God had to discipline them. Rebellion happens when we go our own way, thinking we know best for our life.

Reflection: God wants us to enjoy the journey of life. This can only happen when we serve him faithfully. Ask him to help you do that daily.

April 28

How's Your Hearing?

Matthew 13:1-9

I remember one Labor Day when our extended family gathered for a meal. Halfway through the meal, Mom asked if anyone needed a refill on their tea. A couple of minutes later, Dad asked the same question. We reminded him that Mom had just asked. He claimed he was out of the room answering the telephone. Not so. Hearing problems. Some choose to address them while others live in denial.

In the parable of the four soils, Jesus tells about hearing problems. In reality, interference was the issue. A farmer went out to sow seed. The seed fell on four types of soil: packed, rocky, thorny and good. Each type represents four states of mind people have where God's Word is concerned.

The unresponsive hearer is the seed that fell on the path between fields. Hard soil kept the seed from penetrating. Birds soon swoop down and devour the exposed seed.

People with hard and unresponsive hearts are like this ground. Spiritual things do not interest them. God's Word is sown by a preacher, teacher, through a television or radio broadcast and they ignore it. Doubt, stubbornness or love of sin afflicts their heart.

Rocky soil reflects a superficial hearer. This soil is not rocky on top but below the surface. As the seed sprouts and develops roots, the rocks prevent the roots from penetrating deeply in the soil. The plant quickly withers and dies. This person seemingly accepts God's Word, but the experience is superficial. When persecution of any sort comes they abandon the faith they never really had. It was only a surface experience.

The thorny soil is the worldly hearer. The thorns or weeds keep the young plant from growing. Weeds envelop the field and no fruit is produced. Such a person really loves the things of the world. This love blinds him to spiritual concerns. The Word bears no fruit.

The receptive hearer is represented by the good soil. This soil has been prepared, receives the seed and fruit results. It is the only soil that reflects a true believer. God's Spirit has convicted them of sin, and repentance has been made.

Reflection: What type of hearer are you? Let God prepare the soil of your heart so your life will bear fruit for him.

April 29

A Living Church
I Corinthians 12:12-27

I once rode with a fellow pastor to see a church he was thinking of starting again. It was a quaint little one room structure with curtain dividers to separate the Sunday school rooms. Out back was the beginning of what was supposed to be a Sunday school complex that was never finished. We visited neighborhood homes to gauge interest in re-opening the church. The answer was always the same: only if Mrs. So and So did not come. A sad commentary.

God's churches should be living breathing organisms. They are not stale organizations that grow cold with time or even close the doors. When believers live in accordance with God's will, our churches will have vibrant existences. Fruit will hang from our branches, and excitement will clothe the fellowship.

A living church realizes it is not a human concoction. It is God breathed. He builds and uses the church no matter who nailed the boards, painted the walls or laid the first brick. Jesus told Peter he would build his (Jesus') church. What God creates will stand against the forces of evil. He calls Spirit guided pastors and leaders to lead the church and members to inhabit it.

Jesus is the head of every living church. It is a sad reality that many churches are controlled by power structures rather than God. It may be a board, committee or prominent family.

A quick study of biology shows the importance of the head. Our skull protects our brain, without which our body would not function. The sensations we receive from stimuli in the environment are transported to the brain. The body is then told how to act or react.

In living churches, all members are important. We are dependent and interdependent on each other. There is nothing quite like a loving church family that cares for the entire fellowship. It makes our burdens lighter and our faces brighter. Though we function in different capacities, each part has its place, just as in the human body. We are important to God, and we should be important to one another.

Reflection: God has given a mission to reach and teach. Ask God to show you where your part is in this great plan.

April 30

Keeping Grass off Your Path

Nehemiah 4:1-6

In one region of Africa, the first converts to Christianity were diligent prayers. Each believer had a special place outside the village for prayer. Paths developed quickly to these prayer closets. If someone became negligent, it became very evident because grass would grow on the path. One of their friends would then say, "Friend, there is grass on your path." A well worn path was a sign of a dedicated follower.

Involvement in God's work wears a path. Inconsistency allows the grass of indifference and unconcern to grow on our paths. God always has work for us to do. He did for Nehemiah. God's people had spent seventy years in Babylonian captivity. The city of Jerusalem was in ruins and so were the walls that protected it. Nehemiah's assignment was rebuilding the walls.

Keeping a clean path involves determination. Against all odds, Nehemiah was determined to rebuild the walls. He was opposed by enemies who wanted to see the work fail. In spite of the intense resistance, Nehemiah and his crew kept up the work. They did not argue or discuss. The result: Success. Be determined and faithful in God's work.

Prayer and preparation keeps grass off our path. One is the logical outgrowth of the other. The opposition against Nehemiah and his workers intensified. Some were killed and attempts were made to do the same to Nehemiah. Rumors flew, and God's people were surrounded by people who hated them. Nehemiah's response was interesting. He prayed and posted a guard.

There is no inconsistency between prayer and preparation. God gives us a mind to use. We pray as if everything depends on God and work as if it all depends on us. Be a good steward of your mind. God created it for you to use. Failing to plan is a plan for failure.

Times of discouragement can dot our path. All the opposition as well as the great task before them caused some of the Jews to grow discouraged. Nehemiah encouraged them by reminding them that God was on their side. We should never grow weary in God's work. It is the most exciting and rewarding work in the world.

Reflection: Whatever God gives you to do; he will equip you to carry it out. Keep the grass off your path.

May

May 1
God's Plan for You
Genesis 15:1-6

Nelaton, great French surgeon, once said that if he had only four minutes to perform an operation on someone who was dying, he would take one of the four to plan the operation. Upon planting, the farmer plans to reap a harvest.

Planning is also carried out by the clockmaker. When he makes all the intricate parts of a grandfather clock, he plans for it to keep time-perfect time. If the clock is not level, it will not run. If the nut on the end of the pendulum is not adjusted correctly, the clock will run fast or slow.

God has a plan for you-general and specific. He did for Abraham also. God told Abraham to leave his homeland for a foreign country he had never seen before. He promised to make him a great nation and give him descendents as numerous as the stars. These descendents would come through a son not yet born.

God's plan is for individuals to be restored to a right relationship with him. Sin has destroyed that union and separated us from God. Restoration comes through faith in Christ. The Bible says, "God is patient with you, not wanting any to perish, but everyone to come to repentance." (2 Peter 3:9) God takes no pleasure when the wicked perish.

There are also specific plans that God has. These entail details of where and how God wants to use you in life. The occupation he has planned for you or the person he wants you to marry. Prayer and time in his Word will reveal these things. Confirmation is found through the still small voice of the Spirit.

We must follow God's plan for success in life's journey. Abraham and Sarai failed initially. God's promised son was not arriving quickly enough, so they took matters into their hands. Sarai gave her servant to Abraham to marry. He could have the son through her. While a custom of the period, it was outside God's plan. Later the child of promise came in God's time.

Following God's plan is important. Following it in God's way and in his timing is equally important. Manipulation is not the answer.

Reflection: God's plan for you will not fail for it is empowered by God. He has your best interests at heart. Search for his plan for you.

May 2

Shape Up!

Matthew 26:36-46

A tour of historical Savannah, Georgia will reveal cobblestone streets. The story behind those stones is interesting. In its early history, goods were brought into this city by ship. To prevent the ship from turning over, rocks were placed in the bottom for balance. Upon arrival in Savannah, the rocks were offloaded with the merchandise. Muddy streets plagued the city. Someone formulated the idea of using the rocks to pave the streets. Bumpy yes, but better than mounds of mud. The rocks shaped up the roads.

Jesus enters the Garden of Gethsemane just prior to his crucifixion. It was a time of intense struggle for him, knowing full well what was just ahead and the agony associated with it. His cry to the Heavenly Father for strength was a plea for God to shape him up for his ultimate mission.

Our shapes often need attention physically but more importantly spiritually. Surveys show a decline in church attendance, giving, faith in God's Word, and time in prayer. God's Kingdom does not advance as it could when we are out of shape.

In-shape believers are holy in lifestyle. God says we must be holy even as He is. Holiness reflects the character and honor of God. Like the adolescent, we can find ourselves in a rebellious mood where this trait is concerned. Our bodies are temples of God's Spirit. He partakes of whatever we put in them. God is never satisfied with a polluted vessel.

Our shape incorporates a concern for the harmony of God's creation. God gave Adam and Eve this responsibility, and it has been passed down to us. Believers should be environmentalists-not radical but sensible. This is God's world, and it should matter how it is treated. What can you do to restore the beauty of God's creation?

Devotion to God is important. The Garden experience shows Jesus' depth of this characteristic. The cup of the crucifixion was agonizing as he thought of it. Yet he was devoted to what the Father sent him to do.

In the Old Testament, this word is used to describe a passion for something or someone. Love and honor God through your actions.

Reflection: God, help me to see my shape through your eyes. Shape me up so I can be effectively used by you. Thank you for the unique personality you have given me.

May 3

How to Have a Beautiful Soul
Romans 5:3-4

Theologians debate whether the human is body, soul and spirit or just body and soul. With our body, we relate to the environment, and with our spirit God. Our soul is who we are. A popular saying is, "Beauty is only skin deep." The soul is at the core of our being.

Beauty of soul should be the Christian's goal. Outward appearance has nothing to do with this and should be secondary to our inner person. Jesus reinforces this by teaching that the inside is important. Soul work is relentless and continuous. Among the first words spoken by Jesus when he began his public ministry was "repent."

Our souls shine when pleasing God above everyone else. Normal behavior pleases the one whose opinion is most important. Since God created us and will give the final opinion on our eternal destiny, it makes sense to please him above all else. Evil within our souls will lead us to substitute gods. It will cause us to lower our sites. Approval of others becomes more important.

Acceptance by others is a basic need. We seek it from parents, teachers, peers, and employers. Make it your goal to please God first and others second.

Responsibility reflects a beautiful soul. We have reared an entire generation who abhors this word. A whole structure has materialized to help people escape it. We are victims of any number of things. Such teaching is contrary to God's Word. While situations may affect our actions, we are still responsible for our sin and the resulting actions. Not accepting it makes us no less responsible for it.

Beautiful souls emerge when we accept ourselves for who God made us. We do not compare or complain. Our standard is God alone. Perceived limitations are only undeveloped strengths. Weaknesses give opportunity for God to be honored.

Confession makes for a beautiful soul. It is the act wherein we recognize our sinfulness and almost daily failure to live up to God's standards. Yet we also recognize the goodness of God to forgive.

Reflection: Thank you God for making me wonderfully complex. A masterpiece in the making.

May 4

Staying Within Reach

I Kings 17:17-24

Summer's bloodsuckers. An apt name for mosquitoes. Actually, it's the female that worries us. Though fertilized by the male, she must have blood to nourish and develop her eggs. Violence becomes a way of life. She inflicts every bite, so she always stays within reach of what she needs to nourish her future young.

Elijah lived in extraordinary times. King Ahab had married the wicked Queen Jezebel. Pagan worship was established on a large scale. God's prophets were persecuted, killed or forced to hide in caves. In spite of the difficult circumstances, Elijah managed to stay within reach of others.

Elijah loved. God sent him to Zarephath where he found a widow gathering sticks. He asked for a piece of bread only to learn that she was about to prepare her last meal for herself and her son. Then they would die. Elijah told her to fix him the bread first. Her flour and oil would not run out until the Lord sent rain on the land. She listened. Later, her son died, and Elijah brought him back to life.

Loving others keep us in reach. We learn to rejoice when they rejoice and cry when they cry. Empathy is learning to feel the pain of others. We must reach people where they are instead of expecting them to measure up to our standards before we help.

Prayer keeps us connected. The widow was naturally grieved when her son died. Elijah takes her son upstairs, lays him on the bed and prays. God answered his prayer, and Elijah returned the young lad to his mother.

Prayer is more than voicing our wants and desires to God. It is intercession for others. We must put feet on the prayers. God gives us opportunities to meet the needs of others we pray for. Prayer pulls us closer to God and our fellow human beings.

Serving keeps us in reach. Elijah served the widow by praying that God would not let her oil and flour run out. He served her again by praying for God to bring her son back to life. Greatness in God's kingdom does not come by how many serve us but by how many we serve. Jesus denied himself, took up his cross and served humanity.

Reflection: Do you see the needs around you each day? How has God equipped you to reach out to the needy around you?

May 5

Requirements of Christian Citizens

I Peter 2:13-17

The Puritans and Separatists were two groups in English history who demonstrated their citizenship in different ways. The Puritans thought the Church of England could be purified and chose to continue association with it. The Separatists thought it beyond repair, and they left it.

Christians have reacted to government in various ways. Some favor separation of church and state while others enjoy a small governmental control. Religious freedom is the shout of others. Some believers are heavily involved in political matters while others take a hands off approach.

Believers are to subject themselves to governing authorities. Believing that God is sovereign, we also believe that officials are under his control. God sanctions government though he certainly does not approve of all leaders. Yet he will use even wicked rulers to accomplish his world plan.

Obedience to the established laws is a part of subjection. The only exception is when authorities ask us to commit actions that are in disobedience to God's laws. Then we must obey the higher law.

Disobedience embarrasses the cause of Christ and is a blot on our record. God uses human rulers to enforce good and punish evil. That is the ultimate function of human government.

Obedience does not mean we cannot react against laws we think are unjust or immoral. But the way we choose to confront those matters must honor God. Murdering abortion doctors because we do not believe in abortion is not an accepted manner.

Christian citizens must do right. Of all people who should be model citizens, believers should rank at the top. Our behavior must be spotless, and we must carry ourselves with the highest degree of integrity. Society needs good examples. Early Christians were falsely accused of cannibalism and immorality, but their excellent behavior nullified the charges.

As servants of God, we live as free people under government institutions. Non Christians often think they are free and believers are chained by the demands of God. In reality, only believers are free. While free to serve Christ, we are not free to disobey the laws of the land.

Reflection: Ask God to help you portray a model citizen. Pray for your leaders. Ask God to grant them wisdom to govern righteously.

May 6

Don't Give Up on Prayer

Luke 18:1-8

A Roman emperor sat snugly in his chariot, part of a parade. On a platform was his family, watching as he passed by in all his pomp. Soldiers were stationed for crowd control. Suddenly a young boy bolted toward the chariot. A soldier stopped him and reminded him that the emperor was off limits. The young boy replied; "He may be your emperor, but he is my father."

Prayer takes us into the place where our heavenly Father dwells. As believers, we have the privilege and authority to enter his Holy of Holies. In spite of this, surveys show Christians spend little time doing it. Even Christian leaders are guilty of neglect.

Jesus teaches the need for persistence in our prayers through the parables of the widow and unjust judge and the friend at midnight. In a certain town there was an uncaring judge. A widow seeking justice from her adversary requests his help. Though he did not care to assist her, her diligence finally wore him down.

Then there was the friend who went to a neighbor at midnight asking for bread. It seems his friend had stopped by, and he had nothing to feed him. Hospitality demanded service. The neighbor told him not to bother him. He and his family were in bed. Determination by the neighbor finally won out.

Both stories teach us to pray and not give up. If the judge finally helped the widow because of her persistence, how much more will our Father who loves us willingly answer our requests? If the friend's pleading led his neighbor to give him bread, how much more will God gladly give us those things that are in his plan for our life? Persistence is necessary because we are not privy to God's timetable. It also demonstrates our faith. God delights in answering the prayers of his children.

Just because God does not always answer immediately does not mean he will not answer. Persistence develops our faith and trust. God sees the entire scope of the matter. Our vision is limited.

Reflection: Make prayer a regular part of your daily routine. No matter what you are facing, prayer will adorn you with a peace that is beyond your understanding.

May 7

Detecting the Truth

I John 4:1-6

How do you detect truth? Better yet, how do you detect error? In order to know error, we must have a standard of truth. Teachers often have a key to grade tests by. The key is the truth that detects error in the student's answers.

Some have trouble with truth. Doubt is prevalent. Things become relative and confusing. The line of demarcation for right and wrong is not clear. Situational ethics enters the picture and blurs the picture even more.

The philosophy of Gnosticism was prevalent in John's time. They proposed to have special knowledge that gained them acceptance with God. The divinity of Jesus was questioned. Some abused their bodies believing that actions of the body had no bearing on one's spiritual state. Religious errors still abound in the twenty first century.

Believers are instructed to test the spirits so we might recognize false teaching. To test the spirits assumes we have something to measure truth by. We do. The Bible. Jesus proclaimed to be truth, so knowing him acquaints us with truth. Elements of truth are found in many places, but ultimate truth is only found in God's Word.

How are we to test these spirits with God's Word? All messages that proclaim Jesus as the Son of God who died for our sins pass the test. Messages that do not fail. The important question to ask is "What do you think of Christ." The answer to that query will separate truth from error. Any message that denies Jesus is from God is antichrist. The spirit of antichrist was present in the first century and is still prevalent.

Our status enables us to detect truth. Those who know Christ as Savior can detect truth. Unbelievers have no means to do this but have been deceived by the evil one. We may divide classes by many measures, but in God's eyes there are only two classes of people: lost and saved. Believers are controlled by God's Spirit, and therefore have the ability to discern truth.

Godly teachers can point us to truth. Teachers are given a great responsibility to disseminate truth. God holds them at a greater accountability. We must attend to those God has gifted to teach his truth.

Reflection: Use God's Word to help you detect truth in a society filled with error.

May 8

Victorious Faith

I John 5:1-5

Henry Ford, the man who made America a generation of car owners, said of success, "It is a matter of adjusting one's efforts to overcome obstacles and one's abilities to give the service needed by others." For many, success is about getting, but in God's eyes success is found in giving-giving away our faith.

Victorious faith comes from God. It enables us to overcome the trials and tribulations of life. Such faith enables us to meet any circumstances with confidence. We can share this faith and thereby make our world a better place. Victory comes by trusting Christ, but other victories result that last over the course of our lifetime. How exciting to be parcel to something alive and growing.

The object of victorious faith is Jesus Christ. This may sound rudimentary to Christian ears, but there are many other things that can be the object of our faith. Creeds, church membership, baptism, or even sacraments can be objects of faith. None will suffice for victory. The message of the New Testament is faith in Christ.

The Pharisees and Sadducees of Jesus' day are prime examples. Their faith was in obedience to God's law. Jesus tried to correct their thinking, but they were securely held by tradition. Nicodemus discovered this when Jesus told him he needed to be born again or from above.

Faith in anything other than Christ is powerless and destined for failure. The early church possessed great power because their faith was not in tradition or religious interpretations but in Christ.

The source of victorious faith is the new birth. This was the proclamation of the early church. When we believe, we are born of God. Imagine that. Birthed by God into his glorious family. Victorious faith is not a worked up attitude. The Bible reminds us that our salvation is a gift, not something we worked for. (Ephesians 2:8-10)

We practice this faith by loving God and obeying his commands. His commands are not burdensome. They are not given to make life miserable but for our protection. The end result of this faith is victory. We are overcomers.

Reflection: Thank God for the victorious faith he gives.

May 9

A History of Love

I John 4:7-21

In Hillary Clinton's book, *It Takes a Village*, she relates an incident from her childhood in Chicago. For a few weeks each autumn, migrant workers would arrive for harvest season. Their children would join her class. After a playground incident that could have led her to dislike them, her mother challenged her to babysit for the migrant mothers while they were in the field. For the first time she saw how they lived. It changed her perspective. Clinton begins one chapter with the following quote from James Kellar: "A candle loses nothing of its light by lighting another candle."

Love finds its perfection expression in God. If we asked for definitions of love, the answers would vary. Looking at actions that are classified as love expressions will readily show that many people have a distorted view of this important character trait.

A look at God's Word and what it reveals about his character gives the only true definition of love. Paul defined it well in his great love chapter. (I Corinthians 13) Love is not sentiment or even how we feel inside. It has nothing to do with sweaty palms, rapid heartbeat or a dry mouth. Love involves action. The motive behind why we express love deeds is important. Love leads us to consider the welfare and happiness of others.

Whenever we see the virtue of love manifested perfectly, it is emanating from God. While unbelievers claim to love, they really know nothing about the trait. They date, marry, have children, do charitable things-all things associated with love, yet they do not nor can they experience the deepest level of love. This only comes from a personal relationship.

John reminds us that love is of God. There is a vast difference between expressions of love and love itself. God gave love in providing his Son as the propitiation for our sins.

Love is formed and transmitted through believers. Edward McDowell said, "In loving one another we bring the invisible God into the realm of human experience." Since God loved us, we must channel the same to others. People only see God through our actions, attitudes and words. We are God's representatives to the world.

Reflection: Have you experienced the love of God? If so, demonstrate that love to others.

May 10
The True Savior
I John 5:6-12

Many people struggle with the same question Pilate asked when interviewing Jesus, "What is truth?" Some say there is no absolute truth. This position leads us down a slippery slope that makes almost anything permissible. Others believe truth is determined by circumstances and situations. This too makes truth relative to individual choice.

A more important question is, "What is the truth about Jesus Christ?" Most religious beliefs are instilled by family and church. We must ask how we can know with certainty that they have taught us the truth.

John refuted the teachings of Cerinthus, a contemporary who denied the deity of Jesus. He proposed that the "Christ" descended on Jesus at his baptism but left him before the cross. Jesus was only a man.

What then is the truth? Jesus was sent from God and came by water and blood. Water refers to Jesus' baptism. If not a sinner, why did Jesus undergo this rite? Our baptism symbolizes death and burial to the old way of life. The rising from the waters projects our walking in new life with Christ. While Jesus had no old life to die to, he underwent the ritual to identify with us. Jesus' death was not to sin but for our sins.

There are three witnesses that confirm the person of Jesus: water, Spirit and blood. The Spirit of God descended on Jesus at his baptism in the form of a dove. It is by this same Spirit that believers are guided and gifted for God's work. His Spirit agreeing with our spirit gives us confidence that our belief is not in vain. The water, as already mentioned, is his baptism. The blood is what he released on the cross for our sins. He was our sinless Substitute.

There is also a three-fold testimony that truth is found in Christ. One is that the gift of God is eternal life. He is the author of qualitative and quantitative life. We do not naturally possess it. Eternal life is found through God's Son. The Bible proclaims only one way to heaven, not many. The final testimony is death or life. Depending on what we do with Christ, we either die or live spiritually.

Reflection: Our belief that Jesus is the way, truth and life is built and based on faith. We cannot prove it with the measurements of science, but it is true nevertheless. Have you accepted truth?

May 11

Sowing and Reaping

Galatians 6:7-10

Charles Stanley, author and pastor of First Baptist Atlanta, says, "We reap what we sow, more than we sow and later than we sow." Farmers make their living by this universal principle. When sowing seed, they plan to reap crops at a later date and sell what they harvest.

The principle of sowing and reaping is akin to the scientific principle of cause and effect. For an experiment to be scientific, the results must always be the same under the same conditions. This principle is one of the great moral absolutes in the world.

Sowing is important. If the farmer sowed no seeds, no crop would result. The spiritual aspect is the same. Whatever we sow spiritually, we will reap. The crop of consequences will be greater than the initial act sowed.

Sowing is not always negative. We can propagate positive things. Believers should disseminate positive qualities in their own lives and in the world. Jesus scattered a crop of goodness throughout his ministry, and many people benefited from it. Some were healed and others came to know him personally. We too should do good to all as God gives us opportunity. When we are allowing God to produce the fruit of his Spirit in our life, good is a natural outflow. We will see others as God does. The Bible says to show ourselves an example of good deeds in all things. (Titus 2:7)

This universal principle teaches that vain pursuits will fail. If we sow to the flesh we will harvest corruption. The "flesh" is the old pattern of acting and thinking that Christians still do battle with. We can either walk by the Spirit or by the flesh. We must allow God's Spirit to subdue evil desires in our life. Anything that degenerates goes from better to worse until it is corrupted. A corrupt harvest will ruin our testimony before others.

Sowing to the Spirit reaps success. The one who scatters in this field will harvest eternal life. The fruits of God's Spirit will hang on our vines for others to admire and partake of. When we give our bodies as holy and living sacrifices to God, we sow to the Spirit.

Reflection: While a great writer, Ernest Hemingway was famous for snubbing his nose at God and morality. His life of debauchery led him to put a gun to his head and pull the trigger. What we sow we reap. What seeds are you planting with your life?

May 12

When a Friend Falls

Galatians 5:26-6:6

Jesus' parable of the Good Samaritan is a beautiful story of friendship. Though from a hated race of people, he stopped to befriend someone who probably would not have returned the favor. His actions demonstrate the characteristics of true friendship. The story also shows the ever present possibility of falling into some misfortune that is not of our own making.

It has been said that believers are the only army that shoots their wounded. The mistake of a fellow Christian becomes an unpardonable sin and we disassociate from them. We may even give them the impression that God can no longer use them. The Bible rebukes our quickness to judge and slowness to forgive.

Sin is a reality in every believer's life. While it will not be a practice, we are not perfect. Additionally, sin is sin. Some sin carries greater consequences, but it is all sin in God's eyes. Rather than shooting our wounded, we should say, "If it were not for the grace of God, there would I be."

We should pick up the fallen believer. This does not involve overlooking, treating lightly or failing to confront the sin they have committed. But we are to restore them in a spirit of gentleness. The goal is moral and spiritual restoration. They have been caught in a trespass because they let their guard down. Letting our guard down always opens the door for the enemy's entrance. Christians are to care for one another.

Believers should hold up the fallen believer. Picking up and holding up are two different things. Picking up without holding up can lead to demise if strength has not been developed. Spiritual muscles can atrophy. Temptations that persist are some of the heaviest burdens we bear. We need other's shoulders to help carry them.

Christians must build each other up. This comes through the sharing process. We share our concern over their sin and teach them how God can help them overcome. All benefit through such a process.

Reflection: Do you know a friend in Christ who has fallen to some sin? Restore them in a spirit of gentleness realizing you could be where they are now.

May 13

Appeals from the Heart

Galatians 4:12-20

Numerous appeals are made on any given day. The pastor pleads with his congregation for greater commitment to God's work. Law enforcement officers appeal to drivers to click it or ticket. Employers demand that employees do more in less time while maintaining quality performance. The lawyer appeals to the jurors to find the suspect guilty or innocent.

Paul makes some appeals to the Galatians, appeals that are pertinent for today. Live as an example before others. This requires living in the spiritual freedom that belongs to believers. The Galatians were tempted to return to the slavery of the law. Paul had to remind them that the sacrifice of Christ had set them free from that bondage. When we exist in this freedom we preach to others that salvation comes through the grace of God only. All the things Paul once depended on for acceptance with God he now counted as loss. They had no value. His Damascus Road experience with the risen Lord had changed his outlook on life.

Our lives are an open book before others. They read us with interest and intensity. We must give them an example of right living and thinking. Our ethical behavior will enable us to be the salt and light Jesus tells us we are.

We need good spiritual models to pattern our lives after. Paul was this. In spite of his bodily illness, he faithfully preached the grace of God to them. He also lived a life of grace before them. Paul had visited this region on his first missionary journey. He suffered from some illness, perhaps malaria.

As Paul was a good spiritual standard, so we need to find good models to pattern our life after. We also need to be proper spiritual models. Look for examples that inspire greater faithfulness to God. Inspire others. Love and service are two character traits found in good models.

Be steadfast in your faith. Though initially overjoyed with the message of grace, many of the Galatians were now returning to legalism. Paul encouraged them to keep the faith. We cannot earn what God must freely give. Avoiding those who would damage us spiritually is a necessity. Use caution when making friends.

Reflection: Do you hear God's appeal? Be a godly model that others can pattern their lives after.

May 14

Security in Salvation
Galatians 3:1-5

Security. It is a basic human need. When children do not grow up in secure environments, emotional problems can result. Our need for security goes beyond childhood. We attempt to find it in possessions, money, investments, stocks, bonds, and life insurance policies. Having our possessions lost, stolen or destroyed seems to affect our identity and sense of happiness.

While a semblance of security can be had in the above, real security that drives away fear, anxiety and worry is found only in our relationship with Christ. The Galatians had accepted this security in Paul's grace message, but some were now dissatisfied and looking for security in legalism-what they could do.

Security is found in our experience with Christ. Paul was shocked that some of the Galatians were attempting to work for their salvation. He wonders who bewitched them. Obviously they were under some spell to make such a foolish mistake. They were trying to add to the work of Christ. William Hendrickson said, "A supplemented Christ is a supplanted Christ."

Our salvation is based solely on Christ's work. We cannot add anything to the cross. Salvation is not grace plus works. Nor is it works plus grace. Christianity is not lived by feelings or emotions but by facts. It is based on truth. No ritual or ceremony can add to Calvary.

Security is based on the work of God's Spirit. Paul asked the Galatians whether they received the Spirit by the law or faith. Salvation is based on faith, and it is through this same act that the Spirit is received. He is our seal that guarantees we belong to Christ. Just as good works do not bring salvation; neither do they result in the coming of the Spirit. The Spirit bears witness that we are children of God.

The Father is also vital in our spiritual security. He gives the Spirit when we trust in the work of his Son. Once again, this wonderful gift is not worked for or up but is simply a present for believing. The power of the Spirit is abundant and generous.

Reflection: What are you basing your security on? Let the reality of God's salvation give you freedom from anxiety, fear and doubt. Rest peacefully in the knowledge that you are his child.

May 15

Is Anything Certain?

I John 5:13-20

Life is filled with uncertainties. Your dependable vehicle may break down tomorrow. Social Security has served Americans well for a number of years, but predictions show it going bankrupt in the future. There are many things in life we take for granted that are really uncertain.

When the famous French philosopher Rene' Descartes finished doubting everything he could, he concluded, "I think therefore I am." He was uncertain of everything except that he was a thinking thing.

Christians proclaim their certainty of many things. Eternal life is one of them. John told his audience he was writing that they might know they had eternal life. Can you know beyond the shadow of a doubt that you will go to heaven when you die? Yes you can. Eternal life is a quality and quantity of life. Eternal life is not measured in time. It is simply unending existence. If you have accepted Christ as your Savior, eternal life is yours. This involves abundant life now with the best yet to come.

We can be certain that prayer is a privilege. Believer's prayers are heard and answered. The answer may not come in the form or time period preferred, but it comes nevertheless. God grants what we ask when it is according to his will. Our feelings do not determine the outcome. God delights in hearing and answering the unselfish prayers of his children.

Holiness is the pattern of the believer's life. Of this we can be certain. The one who has trusted Christ will not continue in a life of sin. Sin from time to time? Yes. But not a pattern. We cannot, for God has forged a new nature in us. Perfect holiness is reserved for heaven, but we have practical holiness now.

We are separated from the world. We live in the world but do not partake of the world's pattern of living. The new birth experience draws a line of demarcation between us and non Christians. This separation will become evident at the final judgment.

Jesus is the true God and our eternal life. His Spirit living in us convinces us that what we believe about him is truth. He is present in our life and gives an understanding of himself.

Reflection: Thank God that you can be certain of whom He is and who you are in Him.

May 16

Building a Good Resume'

Galatians 1:10-24

Resumes are important. Some maintain they are the difference between landing a good job and not. Classes are given and books written on how to prepare a resume'.Good resumes contain personal information, work history, mission statement, references, goals, hobbies and community service. Resumes are built over a lifetime.

Christians also build resumes. And they too require a lifetime to complete. A believer's resume' states they are not a people pleaser. Paul made it clear to the Galatians that his aim was pleasing God not individuals. Before Christ changed his life, he tried to please people. He persecuted Christians to satisfy his fellow countrymen. Not anymore.

It is in our nature to want to gratify others. This comes in part because of our dislike of conflict. We want acceptance not rejection. But if unity or acceptance comes with the price of rejecting Christ, we must welcome conflict or misunderstanding. Jesus himself did not please everyone nor did he compromise God's Word for acceptance.

Our resume' should espouse the goal of speaking God's message. Our message is only as important as the truth it contains. Paul's message was not invented or altered. It came directly from God. Had Paul preached the popular message it would have espoused a work for salvation not a grace based rescue. This message promotes self by way of comparison. If I am better, God will accept me.

A good resume' entails proof of our conversion. Paul's proof did not come from his previous lifestyle of persecuting Christians and working for God's acceptance. His proof was God's grace experienced on the Damascus Road. He was never the same after that. Our actions prove the same. We cannot know Christ and remain the same. We will love, care and serve in greater measure.

Some have trouble trusting Christians. They have known some who let them down ethically or morally. We must be consistent and holy in our behavior and words. The new birth must be proved. Jesus said others would know us by our love for each other.

Reflection: What kind of resume' are you building with your life? Ask God to empower your resume' so it will prove who you are to others.

May 17

How to Win in Life's Game

Hebrews 12:1-3

What will it take for you to win in life? Good job, nice boss, material wealth, good health, secure investments, or owning your own business. People define success with different gauges. God wants believers to achieve success in our work for him.

We must run by faith to win life's game. It is the foundation of the Christian race. Faith not only in a Savior on a cross but also in a Savior risen from the dead. Without it, God will not accept us. As we run this race, a great cloud of witnesses surrounds us. They are the men and women of old who provide encouraging examples for us.

Putting aside things that weigh us down is equally important. No runner can gain as much speed with weights attached or when they are overweight.

Anything that takes your eyes off service to Christ is weight. It is not necessarily a sin, and what constitutes a burden for you might not for me. The effects, however, are the same. Lack of effectiveness.

Some weights are sin, and these need our special attention. Even after salvation, we can nurture pet sins. Though forgiven, they are a part of the old life that we still enjoy. While weights slow us down, sin keeps us from moving at all. God will not use us when we repeatedly indulge in known sin. This is foreign to our nature and forbidden by him.

A part of running is completing the course. All believers will finish, but we want to finish well. It is not competition with fellow believers but a life of obedience to God that results in a good ending. We must run with perseverance and patience. A focused runner keeps his eye on the finish line. How foolish for the stockcar driver to pull off the track in the middle of the race and quit, especially if he was winning.

The endurance to finish begins with training. Lack of training can lead to injuries and failed stamina. Training is required of any serious athlete. You will not make the team without it.

Keep your eyes on the goal. For the believer, it is Jesus, the author and perfecter of our faith. He is our great example of how to finish well.

Reflection: Theodore Roosevelt once said, "No man is worth his salt who is not ready at all times to risk his body, to risk his well-being, to risk his life, in a great cause." Are you running well?

May 18

God-A Mighty Fortress

Psalm 46

Frustration. A part of life. Imagine the high school senior who learns all too late that they did not get accepted at the college of their choice. Or the driver who pulls out in front of you and cruises at 20 mph only to go 50 yards down the road. And the vacation money you have diligently saved only to have it spent it on an unforeseen expense.

What or on whom do you depend when life throws you a curve? Your ingenuity, education, or resources. How do you react? With anger or calm composure. The background of the psalm was probably during King Hezekiah's reign in Judah. The Assyrian army pushed toward Jerusalem and drew up in battle array before its towering ramparts. Hezekiah initially tried appeasing the army but then resisted their demands. His trust in God was rewarded when the angel of God slew the Assyrian army.

The psalmist leaves no doubt as to whom he depends on in times of trouble. God is his refuge and strength. What better person to rely on in times of difficulty. Life's valleys and defeats do not frighten him. He does not abandon us to our frail strength when life knocks us down.

The word for refuge signifies a place to go quietly for protection. The mighty God of creation is this for believers. When disaster is on the way or the frustrations of life get us down, he is our strong tower. Tight spots are of no consequence. God is there too. Our heavenly Father is a permanent refuge. Friends and family may abandon us, but God is the unmoved mover. When others desert us or when we have exhausted our own resources, God is still there.

Though the Assyrians were outside the city, God was inside. Knowing that Assyria would return, Hezekiah took steps to ensure Jerusalem had water. He diverted the spring of Gihon into a conduit that led into a reservoir inside the city. The river made the city of God glad.

As God was in the midst of the city with his people, so he is with us in our time of hardships. His presence makes us glad and gives us assurance and peace even when we do not know what the outcome of our situation will be. He is in your future.

Reflection: God rules and reigns in your life and the world. Have confidence that whatever comes your way, he is in control.

May 19

Who's Your Boss?

Galatians 1:1-5

Bosses are interesting. Some are relaxed while others are quite demanding. They are liked by some and hated by others. Some employees work harder when the boss is nearby and others do not care. While bosses can be difficult or easy to work for, they are the boss. Their word is where the buck stops. Employees can obey or quit.

The characteristics of bosses make them easy to identify. They are the person you report to. If you have a problem, you approach them. More importantly, he is the one who can terminate your position.

Christians have a wonderful boss. God Himself. Paul had religious zealots hounding his footsteps trying to destroy his reputation and message, but he was not worried. He worked for God. We do as well. Even in our churches God is the head, not the pastor, chairman of deacons, prominent family, or organization.

Because of who our boss is, we have authority. Paul claimed authority as an apostle. He was not self appointed as his enemies maintained. God had called him to be one on the Damascus Road. Since that point in his life, Paul had served God diligently and tirelessly.

While we have not witnessed the risen Lord as Paul did, we have a commission from the resurrected Savior. It is the same as Paul's. Take the message to the entire world. He has authorized our work. We can go out with confidence that the message will change lives.

Paul's message, like ours, is not of human origin. It came directly from God. This message provides bad and good news. Bad in that it claims people are sinners. Good in that it shows how to escape that situation. Grace is the source of our salvation while peace is the result. The message of grace puts people in a different situation. It takes them from sinners to saints.

Because of who our boss is, our motive for working is different. Paul's motive was that God receive glory and honor for all he did. That should be our motive. Giving God glory focuses the spotlight of ministry on him. As people see our work, they actually see God in it. No boss favors an employee who is vying for their job. God's work is not about us but him.

Reflection: While God's work is demanding, the work he requires is the most rewarding we can do.

May 20
A Woman of Faith
Ruth 1:1-5

The plight of women and mothers continues. Their contributions are innumerable. The struggles they have faced and overcome are worth noting. Single moms are on the rise. Women still face a glass ceiling though not as fragile as it once was. Moms accept many responsibilities around the home even when Dad is present.

Ruth is a challenging example. She was industrious. A foreigner to God's people, she loved her mother-in-law so deeply she was willing to leave her homeland. Once there, she immediately found a field to glean grain. Being one of two widows in the home, they needed provisions. When the owner of the field questioned his foreman about this woman, he testified to her hard work. She gathered all day and winnowed that evening. Ruth did this until the end of the barley season.

God's Word praises hard work and industriousness. This does not denigrate hobbies, having fun or leisure time. These are equally important as Jesus demonstrated. He took time to escape from the crowds that hounded him. It is through industriousness that we gain those things needed in life. It also fosters an attitude of appreciation not normally acquired when born with a silver spoon. Work diligently at home, church, your job and school.

Ruth was a family person. Word of her commitment to Naomi soon spread to Boaz, the owner of the field and a relative of her deceased husband. Ruth would later marry him. It will take all the resources you can muster to have a healthy family. It is not a natural occurrence. The world is overrun with things that will threaten the structure and fabric of your family. Moms play a vital role in keeping things in order for families.

Women of faith are not afraid to make their futures. Ruth did this. She decided to leave her homeland, stay with her mother-in-law, work heartedly and marry a close relative. With a deceased husband, her future was very uncertain, but she was not afraid to face it. With God as your guide, nothing is impossible.

Ruth had a good reputation. Word of how she related to Naomi was known to others. Reputations take vigilant work, but women with good reputations are needed in society. Young girls need role models.

Reflection: God, help me to be a woman of faith.

May 21
Winning the Fight
I Samuel 17:32-37

"The Man I Should Have Been." A story by Pat Conroy, a draft dodger and anti-war demonstrator, interviewing Al Kroboth, a Vietnam vet and POW. Years later, Conroy now reveres words like democracy, freedom and the right to vote. Concluding the article, Conroy says of his old teammate; "It had never once occurred to me that I would find myself in the position I did on that night in Al Kroboth's house in New Jersey: an American coward spending the night with an American hero."

Memorial Day gives Americans the chance to remember those who have fought well and given the ultimate sacrifice for their country. The story of David and Goliath shows a young lad ready to defend his country and the God they followed.

Sent to check on his brothers who were fighting in the army of Israel, David comes face to face with the giant of Gath and his taunting of the God David served. Israel's army cowered in fear. David was willing to fight for his country, but he was more willing to die for his God. Like David, our ultimate fight is against evil represented in many gigantic forms.

As we fight our foe of many faces, we are assured that God is with us. It was this assurance that gave David the courage to fight the Philistine. He did not need Saul's armor. The small items he selected, along with God, were enough. For David, it was a battle between his God and pagan gods. Our fight is against evil in our own life and world.

Winning the battle means choosing the right weapons. At first glance, it does not seem David has done this. A sling and stones against a spear, javelin and armor. One stone found an unprotected spot. The impact brought the giant to the ground. His head belonged to David.

Our weapons are spiritual in nature. God provides armor that will enable us to fight every temptation Satan sends our way. His fiery darts will bounce off our breastplate of righteousness. Put on the full armor of God.

Victory is assured in our battles. David was convinced it was in his. God has promised that no temptation will be so severe that we cannot wart it off with his help.

Reflection: Thank God for those who have fought for our country's freedom. Then fight the good fight in your spiritual battles.

May 22

Prepared for the King

Matthew 25:1-13

One Andy Griffith episode hosts Buddy Ebson as a vagrant who takes up residence by the railroad track in Mayberry. Andy and Opie meet him while fishing at the pond. Barney arrests him for loitering around the railroad yard. Though Andy tries to give him some work around the house, his true colors come through with his procrastinating nature. His famous saying; "Tomorrow is the most perfect day to start any job."

Some feel that way when thinking of Jesus' second coming, but the parable of the wise and foolish virgins presents a different spin. While Jesus warns that nobody knows the day or time of his return, he at the same time teaches that we should be ready. Otherwise that event will come upon us like a thief in the night.

Jesus emphasizes the necessity of being alert with a wedding parable. Ten virgins with lamps start on their journey to meet the groom. Their job was to escort the groom to the bride's home. One group of five took extra oil for their lamps, the other did not. Evidently the groom was some time in coming because they all fell asleep.

The groom is Christ, the husband of the church. The church is the bride of Christ. Only five of the virgins are true disciples as will be evident in the unfolding of the story.

At midnight, the cry went out that the groom was about to arrive. The virgins awake. The five foolish now discover their mistake. Their lamp oil had run out and they have no extra. Though they plead with the wise to let them borrow some, faith cannot be borrowed. While they were away purchasing oil, the groom came. By the time they returned, it was too late to enter the wedding celebration. Faith must be exercised ahead of Christ's coming. At his arrival, it will be too late.

We cannot buy what is freely given. Faith cannot be purchased. We cannot enter heaven on the coattails of our parents, Sunday School teachers, pastors, or spouses. Nor can we work our way there. The foolish maidens knew the groom was coming. They simply failed to prepare. The Bible proclaims that today is the day of salvation. (II Cor. 6:2)

Reflection: Jesus instructs us to watch because we do not know when he will come. Are you doing this by faith? Be ready to meet Him.

May 23

Spiritual Gifts Part I

I Corinthians 12:1-7

"I ain't nobody's nothing." It was a statement made by a young boy whose dad had been killed in the Royal Air Force in World War II. A British preacher had discovered him the next day after a heavy night of bombing.

The statement is made in different forms in the church. We might recognize such comments as; "I'm just a bench warmer," "I can't pray in public," "I'm not a teacher," or "I don't have any gifts." Maybe you have heard them or even spoken them. Here are some liberating thoughts. God has uniquely created you. None of us are inferior. You are somebody.

Because you are important and useful to God, he has gifted you so you will be equipped for his service. Christians are the only ones who receive spiritual gifts. The Greek word for gifts is *charisma* from which our word charismatic comes. This has nothing to do with our denominational tag or personality. These free gifts are from God to those who are his divine originals. Knowing this should awaken you with vigor each morning as you wonder what God has in store for you today that will further his kingdom work.

Gifts and talents are not identical. A Christian will have gifts and may possess natural talents, but an unbeliever can only be talented. Even the non Christian is a creation of God. Natural talents are used in conjunction with gifts for the believer.

These gifts come from the Holy Spirit, and only believers have the Spirit of God residing in them. God's Spirit is the third person of the Trinity. The Spirit is given the moment we trust Christ as our Savior. He is the ultimate gift. The other gifts ensue after we receive the gift.

Our gifts are diverse. We may have the same gift but use it in different ways because of our unique personalities. God knows us intimately and gifts us according to that knowledge and the opportunities he plans to give us in life.

The purpose of the gifts is not for bragging rights. Nor to earn your name in lights or on a plaque. God's gifts are to be used for his honor and to advance his kingdom work.

Reflection: Just as parents give gifts to their children that fit who they are, so God does with us. Thank him for your gifts.

May 24

Spiritual Gifts Part II

Ephesians 4:4-13

One Andy Griffith episode features Barney as a tenor in the choir. The choir director enlisted him, not knowing Barney's vocal skills were untenable. It only took one practice for him to make the discovery. Then came the problem of getting Barney out of the choir. As usual, Andy fixed the problem and Barney was none the wiser. Singing was not Barney's gift.

Discovering our gifts is important. Trying to use gifts we do not have will only lead to frustration and ineffectiveness. The spiritual gifts are listed in several places. Theologians do not agree on them all and others debate whether all the gifts are even mentioned in the Bible.

We begin with apostle, prophet, evangelist, pastor, and teacher. Apostles and prophets laid the foundation of the church, received and spoke the revelation of God and performed signs and miracles to confirm the message. In the technical sense, these offices have ceased to exist. But in a general sense they have not. We are still commanded to spread the word like the apostles and to speak forth God's message like a prophet.

New Testament evangelists were missionaries and church planters. They announced the good news where it had not been proclaimed before. The central message of the evangelist was forgiveness found in Christ. While this is a specific office that God calls some to, there is a general sense in which all Christians are evangelists. We have good news to share and are commissioned by Christ to do so.

Pastors and teachers are the final offices. Pastor occasionally translates a Hebrew word meaning shepherd. A shepherd tends to his flock, and such is the work of the pastor. He shepherds God's flock, tending to the many needs that are expressed throughout the congregation. Jesus is the chief shepherd, but pastors are undershepherds that are his hands, feet, hands, ears and eyes. Elder and bishop are alternate names used in some denominations. All three words describe characteristics of the office.

Teachers instruct. While this is a part of the pastor's role, God gives many lay people this gift. Leading people to Christ is only part of the Great Commission. They must be taught to obey Jesus' commands.

Reflection: God, help me to faithfully teach others your Word through my actions and words.

May 25

Spiritual Gifts Part III
I Corinthians 12:8-10

Another Andy Griffith episode shows Barney chosen for a lead part in the choir. John Masters, the choir director, discovers quickly he has made a mistake. In the meantime, he discovers Gomer-a county bumpkin with a beautiful voice. Gomer is chosen as the new soloist, but when he discovers he is replacing Barney, he is devastated. In the end, Andy, Barney and Gomer sing the solo. Once again, the cast discovered singing was not Barney's gift.

Sometimes we are guilty of what Barney tried to do: cultivate and use a gift he did not have. Then too, we may get jealous over the one who has a gift we desire. Gomer wanted gifts to be used, but he also wanted unity.

Wisdom is a praised and valued spiritual gift. It can come naturally and through learning. The gift of wisdom comes from God. It is associated with a particular work of God's Spirit. We are able to discover truth in God's Word and apply it to life's situations. Some have the further ability to communicate this to others.

Knowledge is the gift of knowing and then applying God's Word, and in this way is connected to the gift of wisdom. However, one can have knowledge without wisdom. It is the ability to discover the deep truths of God's Word. Knowledge is the foundational gift for those who teach, preach, counsel and serve in leadership roles.

The spiritual gift of faith is not equivalent with saving faith. All believers have that. It is trust in God beyond the norm when going through trying circumstances or requesting something from God. Such faith is often expressed through our prayer life. This person can lay hold of God's promises.

Healing is the first in this list that some theologians consider a temporary gift. It was the ability to heal physical afflictions so as to confirm the message preached. Whether or not the gift is still active does not discount the fact that God still heals.

Performing miracles is a further gift that some theologians consider temporary. Like healing, it confirmed the message they proclaimed. The greatest miracle is salvation, and it still occurs.

Reflection: How has God gifted you? Are you faithfully using your gifts for the glory of God?

May 26

Spiritual Gifts Part IV
I Corinthians 12:10-11; Romans 12:6-8

In yet another Andy Griffith episode, Barney is busy trying out for the Lady's Musicale. The winner will sing before the mayor, the musicale and important guests. Fearing the outcome if Barney wins, Andy encourages Rafe Hollister, a local moonshiner, to enter the competition. He wins, and Barney is devastated. Barney simply did not have the gift of singing.

Discernment is an important spiritual gift. False teaching outside and inside the church has been a problem throughout Christian history. The person who has this gift possesses the ability to discern who false teachers are. Christians have the responsibility to examine what they are taught against the teachings of God's Word. If you think you have this gift, be careful lest you allow it to deteriorate into a critical spirit.

Peter exhibits this gift in the story of Ananias and Sapphira. Many early believers were selling their property and bringing the proceeds to the apostles. This couple did the same. Ananias claimed he was bringing the entire proceeds from the sale when he was actually only bringing a portion. His wife, Sapphira, agreed to the deception. Peter discerned the lie.

The gift of tongues and their interpretation is the most controversial of the spiritual gifts. Charismatic denominations believe the gift is still active, while most Protestant denominations believe it ceased in the first century. Additionally, there is some confusion over the nature of the gift. On the Day of Pentecost, it was languages. On other occasions, it was ecstatic utterances. This much is clear: speaking in tongues should not lead to pride in the believer's life nor should it be done in worship without someone present to interpret.

According to the apostle Paul, it is better to prophesy. When we speak forth the Word of God others can understand. God's Spirit deals with them, and they have the opportunity to accept Christ.

The gift of helping is important. It is the same as the gift of serving. The Greek word gives a beautiful picture which means to take someone else's burden and put it on you. This is probably the most widely distributed gift among Christians.

Reflection: Ask God to help you use your gift to bring unity in his church and to build up his kingdom.

May 27

Spiritual Gifts Part V
I Corinthians 12:10-11; Romans 12:6-8

All spiritual gifts are important. No believer should denigrate another believer for not possessing a particular gift. Nor should we allow pride to enter our heart because of a gift we have. Gifts are given to edify Christ and to build up the church of God. God equips us for his work.

God gives some the gift of leadership. It is a nautical term meaning to steer or pilot a ship. Leaders guide those they lead. They are able to steer a group of people in unity to accomplish a particular goal. Leaders keep God's ship-the church, on course. The early apostles appointed leaders or elders in the churches they founded. Churches do not need dictatorial, egotistical or dogmatic leaders. If leading is your gift, lead with humility, graciousness, kindness and most of all love.

Another gift of vital importance is encouragement. Our world is filled with enough things that discourage people. Depression is widespread. Counselor's offices are filled with people who need skills to cope with life. They have been thrown a curve ball of some sort and cannot adjust. God gives us many opportunities on a daily basis to encourage others. Our life experiences, good and challenging, help us in this endeavor. We can share how God brought us through a situation that may be similar to theirs.

Another spiritual gift is giving. Giving is the responsibility of every Christian. God's Word shows that a tenth of what we make belongs to God. In reality, it all belongs to him, but he asks for this much in return.

Beyond this are the offerings we can give that come through our faith in God to take care of us. Many blessings are missed because we shortchange God. We are to give liberally, cheerfully and in proportion to what we make. People with significant needs fill our world and are often very close to us. Any time God gives you an opportunity to give, do it willingly. Do it with pure motives, and never look back on the act with regret.

Showing kindness relates to ministering to the sick and needy. It often overlaps the gift of serving and can involve the gift of giving. This too is to be done cheerfully and spontaneously. It is not the same as pity for those in dire straits. We are blessed through the act more than the receiver.

Reflection: Ask God for eyes to see the opportunities he gives you to exercise your gifts.

May 28

What It Means to Follow Christ
Luke 14:25-33

Psychologist Konrad Lorenz was a student of animal behavior and a pioneer in this field. He discovered that young geese become attached to their mother in a sudden and virtually permanent process called imprinting. Only a few hours after struggling from their shells, they are ready to follow the first thing that moves.

The same is true upon our decision to follow Christ. We are imprinted after we struggle from the shell of our old nature. The first thing that should grab our attention is the example of Christ. From that moment, our goal should be following him in obedience.

Luke records Jesus' parables of the tower and the king to aid us in discovering what it means to follow Christ. The tower was a protective building that guarded a farm or vineyard. From its peak, one could see enemies who might try to steal from the vineyard. Building a tower was a sizable and costly project.

Then the parable of the king. A wise king who is contemplating battle with an enemy king would first calculate whether he, with his smaller army, could defeat a king with a larger army. If not, the king with the smaller army would send a peace delegation.

We must count the cost of following Christ before making the commitment. A foolish king and tower builder would not. The consequence would be defeat and a half finished tower. Jesus never led people to blindly follow him without directly or indirectly sharing the cost involved. Our cost might be ridicule, a lost job, people who avoid us, family who is ashamed of us, or even our life. But the benefits far outweigh the expenses.

Dedication to Christ must be above family, possessions and even life itself. Our love for him should be so great that it would appear as hated for these other things. We must not let anything or anyone interfere with our service to him.

In our journey with Christ, regular evaluations of our commitment should be made. It is easy to let things or people slip in and interfere with his supreme position.

Reflection: Are you a true disciple of Christ or just an interested observer? Make it your commitment to follow him unhesitatingly.

May 29
Grace and Forgiveness
Matthew 18:21-35

Kevin Tunell mails a dollar to a family he would like to forget. They sued him for $936 to be paid one dollar at a time, every Friday for 18 years. The payment plan was designed to help him never forget that Friday when he was driving drunk and killed their daughter. He is haunted by what happened and tormented by the dollar, but the family will not let him forget.

Unforgiveness is the easy way out when someone hurts us. But the simplicity is very costly. We think we are holding the person who injured us captive when in reality the unforgiveness is enslaving us.

Jesus tells the parable of the unforgiving debtor to emphasize the need of forgiveness. A king decides to bring his accounts up to date. One was brought in who owed him millions. He could not pay and begs for time and mercy. Instead the king forgave the entire debt. This servant immediately leaves and finds someone who owes him far less and demands payment.

The scenario is identical. The debtor begs for time and mercy, but the forgiven servant refused. He has him jailed until the debt could be paid. When the king hears of this, he rebukes the forgiven debtor for his lack of forgiveness.

Unforgiveness is common when someone hurts us. Forgiveness is releasing someone from a debt they owe you because of a wrong they have committed against you. Easier said than done. Instead we devise ways to retaliate or get revenge. Or we resort to silence, nagging and distance.

Like a bad addiction, unforgiveness can ravage our body. We move from anger over the situation to anger at the person. Hate follows closely behind. Both are very destructive forces. Experiencing the grace of God helps us remember that no hurt against us is worth not forgiving when God has forgiven us. Jesus' story is a rebuke to believers who refuse to extend what they have experienced.

The causes of an unforgiving spirit can include abusive parents, a spouse leaving the marriage, a fellow employee taking your job, or bullies at school. No hurt, however deep, can justify in God's eyes an unforgiving attitude.

Reflection: Ask God to help you forgive those who have hurt you so you can experience the abundant life he offers.

May 30
Grace and Getting Along
Romans 14:1; 15:7

An old saying shows the challenge of getting along. "To live above with those we love, oh, how that will be glory. To live below with those we know, now that's another story." Having received the same forgiveness and worshipping the same God should bind Christians together, but often we fight. Churches split over trivial matters. Believers hold grudges. And all the while our testimony before the lost suffers and God's work is hampered.

Grace makes three proclamations: only God can forgive my sins, only God is capable of judging my neighbor, and I must accept all who God accepts (which by the way is everyone). Sadly, we often allow our agendas, personalities and backgrounds to get in the way of unity.

Paul instructs us to accept rather than rock the boat. The church ship is easily tipped by crew members who cannot get along and by a belief that all Christians should hold the same opinions.

On the last night of his life, Jesus prayed for unity among his followers. He prayed that they would be one so the world would believe that the Father had sent him. (John 17:21) He could have prayed for success, happiness or safety, but he prayed for unity. It validates believers.

There is a great need for believers to accept each other. Acceptance does not mean we have to worship in the same fashion or adhere to the same form of church government. We identify with one another because we believe the gospel message and want others to do the same. Unity is important to God. He does not like it when his kids squabble.

Paul Billheimer said, "The continuous and widespread fragmentation of the Church has been the scandal of the ages. It has been Satan's master strategy." Jesus said our love for one another would prove that we are his disciples. (John 13:35)

Unity should be our priority. Love for each other will guide our ship in this direction. Though denominational tags divide us now, there is only one flock and one Shepherd. Believers will not be compartmentalized in heaven. Unity is not about compromising the truth or abandoning our standards. It is about the common bond of Christ.

Reflection: God, help me to remember that I am not perfect. Enable me to get along with other believers so your name can be glorified.

May 31

Implications of God's Grace

Romans 8:31-39

How often we lose our awe of God's grace? Like the child growing up who is no longer overwhelmed by their parent's expressions of love. No hugging or kissing in public. No embarrassing behavior in front of my friends. But the overtures of love must continue, for deep inside a child, no matter what age, still longs for their parent's love. God does the same.

God's grace implies protection. We devise many means to protect ourselves. From carrying a concealed weapon to alarms on our homes, the lists of protective venues we take are numberless. Then Jesus says that we do not have to worry about food, shelter or clothing. If we belong to him, he will take care of that. And after all, our treasures that cannot be stolen or affected by the weather are in heaven, not on earth. Many things can come against us-disease, inflation, natural disasters, exhaustion, fears, but if God is for us none of those things can harm us.

God's grace involves provision. He provided for our forgiveness through his Son's sacrifice on Calvary. This was his foremost act of grace in our behalf because it affected our eternal destiny and our relationship with him. Since God has made the ultimate sacrifice for us, it stands to reason that he will care for our less urgent needs.

Because of God's grace, we can live with an absence of guilt feelings. Before Christ, guilt is the norm. God places this guilt for sin within our being so we will turn to him for help. After forgiveness, we can live without guilt because we are no longer under condemnation for our sin. We will feel guilt when we sin, but we are no longer under a constant canopy of remorse. In Christ, God has declared you "Not Guilty."

God's grace assures abundant life now and unending life in the future. Nothing can separate us from God's love. Jesus said that no one could pluck a believer from the Father's hand. How foolish to think we can lose what we could not work for in the first place. God will not take from his children what it cost him dearly to give. Like the parent's love that continues no matter what the actions of the child may be, so God's love continues to flow to his children.

Reflection: Take time to thank God daily for his provision of salvation and the wonderful promises you have because of this gift.

June

June 1
Lessons from a Religious Man
Acts 10:1-8

Our story begins in Caesarea with a man named Cornelius. A centurion in charge of more than one hundred men, he and his family were devout and God fearing. Prayer and giving to the needy characterized his life. One day, he had a vision in which an angel told him to send men to Joppa to find a man called Peter. Two days later, Peter arrived at Cornelius' house and found a large gathering of people. Peter preached the gospel to them, and many believed.

God's message of salvation is intended for all people. Peter discovered this through a vision from God. A great sheet descended from heaven filled with all types of animals. Peter heard a voice telling him to eat. He protested because many of the animals were forbidden by God's law.

God's vision to Peter was designed to teach him a lesson. It was not about what food he should or should not eat. The lesson was about who God accepted. Cornelius was a Gentile. Peter was a devout Jew, and devout Jews did not associate with unclean Gentiles. But God was about to send Peter to a Gentile's house, and he needed to be prepared. The message of salvation was not for Jews only.

The good news of the gospel is for all people no matter the race, social status, amount of material wealth, political party, or any other factor that divides us. Believers cannot be selective in who we share with. Picking out who would and would not fit in at your church is a direct violation of the Great Commission.

Christian fellowship must transcend racial, social and cultural barriers. Peter limited his circle to Jews. God had to teach him a hard lesson. Our fellowship is based on our love for God. Understanding his love and grace in our personal life aids in destroying barriers that separate us.

Cornelius and his family were devout people, but the story teaches that this is not enough to save anyone. They had to accept the gospel message. Religion does not connect us with God. The bridge is only forded by faith and his grace.

Reflection: Ask God to help you look beyond the barriers that are man-made so you can see people who need his forgiveness. Do not let prejudice hinder your effectiveness for God.

June 2
Christian Liberty
I Corinthians 8:1-13

Over the past generations, Christians have debated such issues as: gambling, smoking, drinking, playing cards, going to the movies, wearing makeup, dancing, listening to certain styles of music, and going to sporting events on Sunday. These and other things are not strictly forbidden in scriptures that begin with "Thou shalt not...." Because of this, Christians have disagreed over whether they are wrong or simply unwise.

Paul faced a similar situation with the Corinthians. Some questioned whether it was permissible for a believer to eat meat sacrificed to an idol. This was a first century ethical matter that cropped up when buying meat at the market or eating at a friend's house who was an unbeliever. While not a present day issue, it leaves behind a principle that deals with Christian liberty.

In addressing liberty, believers tend to follow one of two extremes: license or liberty. Paraphrased this can be translated legalism or grace. For the legalist, everything is black or white. For the one living in liberty, everything is permissible unless strictly forbidden by Scripture. Paul offers another twist: offending the conscience of a fellow Christian. Our liberty can become a stumbling block for one new or either weak in the faith.

God gives knowledge to his people in his Word. These early Christians knew idols were not real. Thus food sacrificed to them was permissible to eat. However, there were some who were young in the faith who believed it was wrong. Our actions must take into consideration those who are babes in Christ lest we offend them by our actions. Our freedom is limited by our love and concern. We can be solid in doctrine but weak in love. Well rounded Christians act conceptually and relationally.

Though Paul knew idols were not real, some of the immature believers still believed in their existence. They simply did not worship them anymore. We must live carefully so as not to lead another believer to sin against their conscience. Our particular action may be permissible and at the same time offend.

Reflection: God gives our conscience as a guide. As we grow in our faith, we understand more of his teachings, but we must never allow our liberty to negatively influence a fellow Christian.

June 3

The Celebration of the Covenant
Matthew 26:20-30

For centuries, Christians have debated the meaning of the Lord's Supper or Communion. Some believe in transubstantiation-that the elements actually become the body and blood of Christ. Martin Luther, proposed the idea of consubstantiation-that the presence of Christ is in the elements but that they do not transform themselves. For many Protestant denominations, the elements merely represent the body and blood of Christ.

Whatever interpretation one takes fades before a more important principle-the celebration reminds us of the great sacrifice of Christ. Preparation should precede participation. Prior to instituting the Lord's Supper, Jesus told his disciples to enter Jerusalem where they would meet a man. Jesus would use his home to observe the meal.

If we are not careful, observing the Lord's Supper can become a habit we partake of without careful thought. Scripture commands us to examine ourselves before indulging. If there are actions or attitudes in our life that displease God, we must confess before observing the feast.

Paul wrote that if we eat the bread or drink from the cup in an unworthy manner that we will have to answer to God. The solution is to examine ourselves first before we partake of the Supper. (I Corinthians 11:27-28) Only then will we observe it in a worthy manner.

The observance reminds us that we are capable of disappointing Christ. As Jesus observed the meal with his disciples, he made the startling announcement that one of them would betray him. While not turning our backs on Jesus as Judas did, we can deny Christ by living in ways that hinder his light from shining through us.

Most importantly, the Supper symbolizes the death of our Lord. Jesus specifically told these early disciples that the elements represented his body and blood that would be given for them. The elements remind us of Jesus' wonderful surrender.

Our behavior after observing the feast proves our love and loyalty to Christ. Like the disciples, we leave to face times of testing that will reveal the depth of our faith.

Reflection: God, help me to remember that the Supper is a stark reminder of what you have done for me.

June 4
Jesus on Judgment
Matthew 7:1-5

How quickly we do this and with a critical spirit. We meet someone who is different, and we critique. Or a person who is challenged, and we pass judgment. It seems our natural tendency is to dig up dirt instead of smooth over faults. Psychologists term what we do projection. We attribute to others bad qualities or issues we have in our own life.

Jesus' intention is not that we fail to evaluate or even critique. We can even pass judgment. It is a particular type of judgment Jesus forbids. Believers are responsible for judging between right and wrong. Failure to do so leads to situational ethics. Had the Protestant Reformers failed to make a judgment, the Reformation would not have taken place. Jesus warns against unjust and hypocritical judgment.

Unjust criticism shows an erroneous view of God. The religious leaders looked through these glasses. They judged with unfairness and hypocrisy. When they brought the woman caught in adultery to Jesus for his judgment, they failed to bring the man. The law commanded both to be stoned. Observing the law was not their concern. Trapping Jesus was.

The religious leaders judged because they thought they were better than the average person. Their judgments were wrong and unrighteous. Outward appearances were important to them. God judges with righteousness and mercy. We should too. He also judges against the standards he has established not tradition. This is also our obligation.

When we judge unfairly, it demonstrates an erroneous view of others. The standard we compare others to is God not us. We are imperfect. Nor are we superior.Judging others by their race, clothes, or social class puts us in the category of unfair judging.

Unfair judgment shows an erroneous view of ourselves. We attempt to remove the speck from another's eye when we have a plank in ours. Jesus said to deal with the plank first. Here the sin of the critic is greater than the sin of the criticized. We must deal with our personal failures before we try to assist others.

Reflection: People need love and concern, not self-righteous judgment. Rather than looking at other's faults, look at who they can be in Christ.

June 5

Called By God

Isaiah 6:1-8

Christ on the cross. It is vivid imagery of what God has done. After accepting this payment for our sin, however, we should become keenly aware of some things related to the call of God. The situation in Israel during Isaiah's time was deplorable. Baal worship was prevalent. Ritual was emphasized over righteousness. In the midst of this, God called and commissioned Isaiah. He still beckons today.

When God calls, we see his holiness. Isaiah saw him on a throne, high and lifted up with the train of his robe filling the Temple. He saw seraphim who cried out "Holy, Holy, Holy."

Christians need a fresh glimpse and realization of God's holiness. He is holy other. He is not the same as us, and we dare not try to bring him down to our level. While merciful, he is also righteous. This trait prevents him from looking on sin. We must fear God. The word carries the idea of reverence, not to be afraid.

Such holiness requires our complete submission. In conjunction with this comes the desire to worship him. Only as his holiness captivates us can we be vessels of use. Billy Graham once said that when true revival comes to Christians they will see a "new sense of the holiness of God."

When God calls, we see our personal sinfulness. Seeing God in all of his righteousness impresses this upon our minds. Isaiah's response was "Woe is me, for I am undone." He felt unworthy to view the scene before him. He found himself in God's presence. One of the seraphim takes a live coal and touches his mouth, and his sins are forgiven.

God's holiness magnifies our sinfulness. We are worthy of nothing but eternal separation from God. But when God touches us, he takes our iniquity away and purifies us as the freshly fallen snow. Recognizing our sinfulness coupled with the holiness of God leads to obedience.

After experiencing God's call to salvation, our eyes are opened to the world around us. Isaiah recognized he lived among wicked people. We too recognize there are many in the same situation that we were in. God can rescue them as he has us.

Reflection: God calls us to go to others with his message of deliverance. Will you say, "Here I am, send me?"

June 6
How to Follow the Example of Christ
I Peter 2:18-25

An old beggar was sitting across from an artist's studio. The artist saw him and quickly began to paint his portrait. When finished, he called the beggar over to look at it. At first, the beggar did not recognize himself. The artist told him it was the man he saw to which the beggar replied, "If that's the man you see, that's the man I'll become." God sees in us what we can become when we follow Christ's example.

Following Christ involves a willingness to suffer. Peter spoke to slaves who suffered a great deal. Unlike now, slavery was an accepted institution. Some estimate the Roman Empire had as many as sixty million in the first century. Slaves had no legal rights and could not marry or vote. The slave was little more than a valued work animal.

In spite of their suffering, Peter instructs them to be obedient to their masters just as a child obeys his parents. Many in turn apply this to the employer employee relationship. We are to live admirable lives even in the midst of suffering. As Jesus suffered, so will we. It is a mark of ownership.

The Greek word translated example appears only here in the New Testament and refers to a writing copy a teacher would give to a beginning student. As the student copies the letters on the paper, so our lives are to copy Christ's. This involves suffering.

Trusting God is a part of following Christ's example. Jesus lived on a divine timetable. His was a life of spotless obedience. He faced the stress of living a godly example in an ungodly world but he did so with patience and courage. He did not return abuse nor threaten those who caused his suffering.

God has a plan for your life. Do you trust him daily to fulfill that plan? The plan will involve suffering and sacrifice, but the rewards are worth it. Peace and assurance will guard you mind.

We must be involved in the healing process. We are healed by the wounds of Christ. By his stripes forgiveness is experienced. He bore our sins in his body on the tree. Having our wounds of sin healed motivates us to heal the wounds of others who are weighed down in sin.

Reflection: Heavenly Father, help me to follow the example of your Son in all areas of my life.

June 7
Reactions to the Savior's Birth
Matthew 2:1-12

Napoleon Bonaparte was born in 1769. By 1796 he was marching across the Alps to crush the Austrians. In 1809, Austria fell. In this same year, a veritable host of statesmen and thinkers were born, but nobody noticed. Names like William Gladstone, Olive Wendell Holmes, Edgar Allen Poe, Charles Darwin and Abraham Lincoln.

Eighteen centuries before Napoleon, the world was watching the splendor of Rome. It was a vast and vicious empire with overwhelming military might. Palestine was under their control. A young couple made an eighty mile trip to Bethlehem where the woman gave birth to a Jewish son. While Rome was busy making history, God arrived on the scene.

The first century reactions to Jesus' birth have been repeated throughout history. Some reacted with hostility. Herod provides this example. He was jealous and suspicious. After the wise men asked him where they could find the baby who was to be the King of the Jews, he issued a fateful order to kill all male children two and under.

This reaction has been duplicated by Communism, which reacts to religion in general with hostility. Voltaire, French philosopher, attempted to destroy it within 50 years. Emperor Julian or Julian the Apostate turned savagely against Christianity and vowed to exterminate believers. Some today have no use for Christ and his teachings thinking they are damaging to the human psyche and society as a whole.

Others react with indifference, as did the religious leaders. When Herod gathered them together to determine where prophecy said this king would be born, they simply named the place with seemingly no excitement. Most of these same people opposed Jesus throughout his earthly ministry. Their reaction to the news is repeated in the minds of many today. They may believe in the historical occurrence but see no historical significance. Just another birth. Just another misguided religious zealot.

The wise men reacted by searching and worshipping. Theirs was the only worthy response. Not only did they worship but they also gave. We cannot stop with believing in the birth of Christ. We must accept him for who he claimed to be.

Reflection: What reaction does the birth of Christ stir in you?

June 8

Responding to God

Matthew 21, 22, 25

Responses to God vary. For some he is a grandfatherly type living in heaven who will eventually welcome all humanity home with him. Others see him as a Santa Claus type. Anything I need he will give if I am good. Some refuse to believe in his existence. God is simply another name for the force of the universe. For Christians, he is our creator, sustainer and Savior.

We can respond to God with a self righteous attitude. Jesus tells a parable about two sons. Their father told them to go work in the vineyard. The first said he would not but later changed his mind. The second said he would but did not. The religious leaders did not see their need for Jesus.

A self righteous attitude prevents us from seeing our need to repent. We may recognize our need for God, but our manner of getting to him is wrong. Good works, good nature, or family heritage may be our path. Our need is Christ's righteousness applied to our life. Faith does this. Our testimony to others includes that we were once where they are. Self righteous attitudes can also blind us to sin. We must let God peel us like an onion so we will be the same through and through. Sin can attach itself in layers.

Others react to God with indifference. A king gave a wedding feast and sent his servants to tell the guests that everything was ready. Some paid no attention to the message. Others seized the servants, mistreated them and even killed some. The king was enraged, burnt down the city of the invited guests and summoned others to the feast.

Many are indifferent to God's call to salvation. Some even react with hostility. God calls his people to go. We are not responsible for the response, just the effort. Even believers can become indifferent to the things of God if we do not constantly monitor our priorities. The world's goods can entice us.

People can respond to God with foolishness. Five of the virgins who waited on the groom took no extra oil for their lamps. They missed the wedding feast because they were in town buying oil. Jesus told often of his coming again and of the need to prepare. Foolishness puts our eyes on other things.

Reflection: Are you responding to God appropriately? Follow him in obedience as you await his coming. Live with eternal not temporal perspective.

June 9
Service of the Believer
I Peter 4 and 5

In severe economic times or in areas where large industries are few in number, the service sector flourishes. Yard care, landscaping, plumbing, heating and air, tree service, and appliance service are a few examples. Service is a vital part of the believer's walk. Christ saves us to serve-him and others.

People have needs that God gives us the ability to meet. We must demonstrate love for one another. According to the great love chapter (I Corinthians 13), love is the greatest gift. Church attendance, tithing, prayer and Bible reading are all important aspects of the Christian life, but we cannot miss love. Love is our essential message, and people will believe it only as they see it expressed in action. Our tendency is to love family, others like us and those with similar interests, but love must extend to all. Ask God to remove prejudices that prevent you from serving.

Peter says we are to use our special gifts to serve others. As we do, we are good stewards of the grace of God. Some think they have no special talents while others believe they can use their gifts as they please. God gifts all his children. Discover your gift and then look for opportunities to employ it in service to others. Serve in love. Believers are the primary delivers of God's love to others.

Like giving, our serving is to be done willingly not grudgingly. When we serve willingly, no one has to pressure us to do so. Like the athlete who loves the sport he plays. No one has to drag him to practice. In fact, he may do more than the coach requires simply because he loves the game. We do not serve for social acceptance or because of peer pressure but because it is what God expects. We should love to serve the one who served us. If the willingness is not there, the effectiveness will diminish.

Serve with humility. Humility is not a trait that normally comes easily, but it is one highly esteemed by God. He will exalt the humble but bring down the proud. Humility is not a trait encouraged by society. This needed characteristic keep our focus on the truth that others are more important than us. Christ thought of others before himself. We should too.

Reflection: Love sent Christ to the cross. It was the ultimate act of service. Serve him and others with a spirit of joy.

June 10

Standing in the Faith

Jude

Some things in life are urgent. A failing heart valve, a gash to the leg, a hand caught in a weaving loom, a child in a car accident are all urgent matters that require immediate attention. But how often the urgent is dismissed for the immediate.

It is urgent that believers contend for the faith. Jude addresses those who are called or sanctified. Christians are set apart for God's work, and only believers can fight for the faith. While wanting to write to these early Christians about their common salvation, he could not. Something was more pressing. People had crept into the fellowship who intended to turn the grace of God into licentiousness. They also denied Jesus. They took the special qualities of God and distorted them. The believers had obviously let their guard down because these people crept in unnoticed.

The enemy creeps in secretly when we let our watch down. Sadly, believers often tire in the fight against evil. Rather than contending for the faith, we let the enemy win. Doctrine is important. We must be serious students of God's Word to familiarize ourselves with doctrine. Then we must earnestly defend our convictions but in a manner that does not disgrace God. There are acceptable and unacceptable ways of doing this.

We contend for the faith by living out our faith in the home. World events are often beyond our control, but what happens in the home is within our power. We can also support political leaders who stand for God's standards.

Stand in the faith by remembering God's judgment. Jude mentions three: the disobedient in the wilderness, fallen angels, and Sodom and Gomorrah. Unbelief, rebellion and immorality brought judgment. False teachers bring lies that will incur God's judgment if believed. God will judge any time we adopt these same actions. It is urgent that believers teach others how to avoid God's judgment and experience his grace.

It is urgent that we build each other up. Our journey is not one of solitude. We need one another. Encouragement is required. Burden bearing is essential.

Reflection: Father, help me to see the urgency of standing strong in my faith, believing you for victory over the enemy.

June 11

The Great Rescue

Exodus 3:1-4, 10

In the movie, *Fireproof*, the main character is a fireman whose marriage is in trouble. His father finally convinces him that his main problem is not knowing Christ as his Savior. Through a dare proposed by his Dad, he and his wife find salvation, and their marriage is healed.

As fireman spend time rescuing people from burning structures and vehicles, so God has entrusted us with the responsibility of rescuing people from their sins. Not that we have the power to do anything about their sin, but we know the One who does.

God had a rescue in mind for Moses. God's children had been suffering in Egyptian slavery. Their cry rose to God, and he now planned to use Moses as their deliverer. He confronted Moses with this mission. Moses was not excited. In fact, he made several excuses as to why he was not the man for the job.

Like Moses, we can make excuses for not doing what God asks. It may be a special assignment or simply using our gifts in a local church. It might be entering full time Christian ministry or just witnessing to someone at work or school.

Moses' excuses were four fold. He was an unknown. Then he asked what would happen if the Israelite leaders did not believe God sent him. He also reminded God that he was not a good speaker. Finally, he pleaded with God to send someone else. What God calls us to do; he equips us to carry out. What excuses are you using to avoid what God wants you to do?

Nor does God ever ask us to go alone. He did not ask Moses to. He promised Moses he would be with him. Additionally, he sent Moses' brother Aaron with him as his spokesman. When Jesus left his followers with the task of spreading his love all over the world, he assured them he would be with them. The promise was fulfilled through the coming of the Holy Spirit.

Obedience to what God asks of us always brings blessings. Moses led the children of Israel out of slavery, through the wilderness and to the Promised Land. We have the blessing of forgiveness, heaven and abundant life now as we use our gifts and talents in God's service.

Reflection: Ask God what mission he wants to send you on. Who does he want you to influence for Him?

June 12

The Growing Church
II Peter 3:18

Who cannot marvel at the growth of our country? The first settlers who crossed the Bering Strait must have gasped at the great expanse of wilderness that met them. Then came the Vikings followed by the Europeans. Columbus made the world aware of a great piece of land between Europe and Asia. In 1607, the first permanent settlement was made in Jamestown, Virginia. In 2009, our population had grown to over 304 million.

Compare that to the church. Jesus chose a small band of twelve men to train. The Holy Spirit came on the Day of Pentecost and empowered believers to take the message worldwide. Estimates now show over a third of the world population claims to be Christian. Technology is taking the message farther and faster than ever before.

A growing church has one driving force. It is found in Jesus' Great Commission. We are to go into all the nations and tell them about Christ. Those who accept are to be baptized in the name of the Father, Son and Spirit. Then we teach them to obey God's commands. Our peace comes in knowing Christ is with us as we go.(Matthew 28:19, 20)

For a small number of believers in the first century, this was a tall order. The command to go worldwide encompassed people they did not particularly care for such as the Samaritans. The commission given by Jesus has been passed to us. When the excitement of this charge consumes us, we will find ourselves perking up and gearing up for the challenge.

Growing churches function through worship, evangelism, discipleship, fellowship and ministry. Worship is encountering God in a meaningful way. It takes place in spirit and in truth. Evangelism is telling the good news of the Great Commission. Discipleship teaches others the commands of God and how to obey them in their lifestyle. Fellowship is needing each other. We care and share our joys and burdens. Ministry involves meeting the needs of those outside the fellowship.

When God's churches grow, there will be numerical growth, spiritual growth, ministries expansion and missions advance. Seeds are designed to grow, and so are churches.

Reflection: God, thank you for allowing me to be part of the greatest organism in the world. Use me to help advance your kingdom work.

June 13

The Way to a Healthier Life

II Corinthians 9:6-15

Sir Winston Churchill said, "We make a living by what we get, but we make a life by what we give." This is similar to Jesus' teaching: "Where your treasure is, there will your heart be also." (Matthew 6:21) American psychiatrist, Dr. Carl Menninger, said, "Money-giving is a good criterion of a person's mental health. Generous people are rarely mentally ill people."

In an effort to form a spiritual bond between Jews and Gentiles, Paul began to take a collection from the churches he had visited on his missionary journeys. Those in Corinth agreed to give but for some reason had backtracked. He encourages them to finish what they started.

Liberal giving leads to healthy living. Paul mentions a law of nature. We reap what we sow. If a kernel of corn is placed in the ground, a stalk of corn results. A bean seed produces a bean plant. Apple trees do not produce oranges nor does a grape vine yield pears.

Our giving is akin to sowing. Giving and the amount of it plants seeds for God in other's lives. Our giving is a true and sound investment. Liberal and generous results come from abundant giving. This manner of giving stores treasures in heaven. The believer should never be able to gauge success by material wealth but rather by their giving. We also lay up a harvest on earth to reap. A giving nature leads to friendships and relationships that often offer opportunity to share the good news of Christ. There is a vital connection between giving and our spiritual welfare.

Liberal givers are strengthened in their spiritual lives. The person we help is assisted with their needs. God is glorified by our giving, and he will in turn give us other opportunities to share.

Give with a smile. Give cheerfully. God is never pleased when he has to pry the bills from our clenched fists. Cheerful giving should be a natural outflow of gratitude to God for our salvation. Children often reluctantly play with a brother or sister or share toys with classmates. God's children should not be childish. Avoid giving for fear of criticism, out of custom or because a reward is expected. Give because God gave.

Reflection: When we give to God's kingdom work with the right motives, God will generously give to us in return. And God is not miserly in his giving.

June 14

What Makes Heaven Rejoice

Luke 15

What makes you rejoice? A new car, a surprise gift, Friday's paycheck, a good test score, a child with a good report card, time with family, or a good cup of coffee. Heaven rejoices over a new child.

Luke records three parables of Jesus in this one chapter. One is very familiar. A shepherd has a flock of one hundred sheep but loses one. Normal behavior was to leave the 99 and search for the one. When found, the shepherd lays it across his shoulders and returns it to the main flock. He calls together his friends and neighbors to celebrate with him.

The parable rebukes those like the religious leaders who were meticulous about keeping the commands but cared little for the lost-sinners as they termed them. Jesus insulted them by associating with such scum as tax collectors. They wanted to kill him because he broke Sabbath laws to heal, physically and spiritually. Misplaced priorities were their bane.

We cannot truly love God's laws without loving people. Neighbors are important. Lost people are more important. When they are found, heaven rejoices. God does not forget the lost. What we do in church is important. What we do outside the four walls can be even more important.

Then there is the woman who loses a coin. Jewish women received ten silver coins as a wedding gift, so losing one could be very distressing. Something of sentimental value was gone. Like losing one's wedding ring. She lights a lamp, sweeps the house and searches diligently for the coin. The coin is discovered, and she calls friends and neighbors to rejoice with her.

Our world is filled with those who fail to recognize their value. We are of great value to God. He has work for us to do and talents for us to use. God looks past our sin to see what we can become. We should see the same in others.

The parable of the prodigal son is all familiar. One son requests his inheritance, travels to a foreign land and blows it on wasteful and sinful living. He finally comes to his senses and returns home to a rejoicing father. We are prone to wander, but God always welcomes us back when we repent and confess our sin to him.

Reflection: God loves sinners. We should too. Ask God to use you in finding others for him.

June 15

When Believing Gets Confusing
John 11:1-44

A struggling family. A mom battling alcohol. A decision to drive while drinking. An accident. A child is killed, and a family ripped apart. In such times, we want to ask God "Why?" Yet out of the ashes emerges a father who recommits his life to God and begins serving him faithfully. There are times when believing gets confusing.

Mary and Martha faced such a situation. They, along with their brother Lazarus, were close friends with Jesus. Lazarus became sick, and his sisters sent word to Jesus. Surely he would come and heal him. But John writes, "Although Jesus loved Mary, Martha and Lazarus, he stayed where he was for the next two days and did not go to them." Lazarus died.

God is always near in our seemingly senseless situations. The Psalmist assures us that God is near to those with broken hearts and those who have contrite spirits. (Psalm 34:18) Jesus was not geographically very far. Then again, he did not actually have to go there to heal. But Jesus was near to the situation. He knew what he was going to do.

Some of life's storms are difficult to understand. Others we cannot. God allows some trials and brings others. We often do not know which is which. But of this we can be certain: he is near and is concerned about every detail in our life. (Psalm 37:23)

God's timing is usually different from ours. His ways are higher and normally beyond our understanding. It must have seemed this way for Mary and Martha as they watched their brother grow weaker by the minute until death overtook him. Where was Jesus? Maybe he was not their friend after all. Jesus did not even show up for the funeral.

When Jesus finally arrived, Martha met him and expressed her belief that even then God would give him whatever he asked. Healing before death would not have the effect it did by raising Lazarus from death. He was a walking testimony of Jesus' power.

We are never in a position to question God no matter how foolish the circumstances appear. Mary and Martha didn't. Jesus' delayed arrival honed their faith.

Reflection: God, help me to trust you even in the times when believing gets confusing and things do not make sense.

June 16
What's So Good About Friday
Matthew 27:32-44

Friday. The day many look forward to. It signifies the end of the work week for a host of people. We look forward to saying goodbye to the boss for two days, resting, doing yard work, or spending time with the family. Who can forget the popular slogan represented by the letters TGIF?

Jesus was crucified on Friday. Christians celebrate it as Good Friday. Studying the crucifixion process makes one wonder why we refer to it as "Good." It was cruel and unusual. It involved public shame. It was slow physical torture. The condemned carried their cross as a public warning to others. Nails affixed the victim to the cross, but since no vital organs were damaged, death came slowly.

Jesus went to such a place. But for what reason? He committed no crime, nor was he placed there for his sins. Jesus carried his cross then was hanged on it because God saw our need. A sacrifice had to be made for sin. Blood had to be shed. This was God's requirement. His love and our need led him to put his Son there in our place. So Friday was "Good."

The concept of sin has been watered down as of late. We have manufactured new terms that are less serious. Mistake, error, slip of the tongue. Making sin seem less severe reduces a person's perceived need of having anything done about it.

God takes a different view of sin. For him it is serious, even life-threatening. Was it not, Good Friday never would have occurred. Sin brings the wrath of God, but it was preceded by an act of love that, if accepted, would curtail the previous. Sin is variously translated as missing the mark, veering from a straight line or moral crookedness. Regardless of our view of sin, God's is important. In fact, it is in our best interest to consider his view since we will one day stand before him to give an account of our lives. Aren't you glad God saw your need?

Even more amazing is that God did something about our need. He placed our sin on his Son. Your sins were nailed to the cross, and the blood of Jesus flowed over them. Two days later, God raised him from the grave to validate his acceptance.

Reflection: We serve an awesome God. Thank him for sacrificing for your sins.

June 17

Characteristics of Good Men
Philippians 2:19-30

Father's Day can bring mixed emotions just as Mother's Day can. Many homes are fatherless or motherless, but the fatherless seem to grab more attention. Studies have shown the damage to a child's emotions that occurs when a father is absent. Single moms struggle when the absentee father does not send support. At the same time, there are many admirable fathers who are stepping up to the plate.

Paul mentions two men-Timothy and Epaphroditus, who were allowing God to work in their life. They were growing in the faith. They were becoming more like Christ. Integrity was their coat of armor. Paul was going to send Timothy to the Philippians because he was genuinely concerned about their welfare.

Integrity brings our faith to life and demonstrates its authenticity to others. It is doing the right thing when people are watching or when no one is looking. Do you obey the speed limit only when you know there is a policeman nearby? Is littering one of those laws you see little need to heed?

Men of integrity can be trusted. They integrate faith into every area of their life. Men such as this are integrated wholes. They are what they appear to be. Faith is the foundation of how they live. Timothy was fully devoted to God and reflected it in his lifestyle.

Good fathers have teachable spirits. We think of fathers teaching their children, but they too must be taught by God and others representing him. Timothy learned everything he could from Paul's example. Following a good example is just another name for discipleship. The disciple is a learner. Men with a teachable spirit will follow Christ's example.

Exemplary fathers are selfless. Life is not about them. Their path follows God first and then takes them to their families, churches, jobs, and social functions. At every point along the journey, they put others first. Selflessness takes extra effort because it goes against our natural bent. Greed is not good. Epaphroditus had a servant's heart. He risked his life in service for God.

Reflection: The acid test of good fathers is endurance. Ask God to help you endure in your walk with him and to let that faith touch all aspects of your life. Live a good example.

June 18
Daring to Dream
Genesis 37:18-20

Dreams are the result of mental activity taking place while asleep. They are often a jumbled mix of things we have thought about or encountered during any given day. That you cannot remember a dream does not mean you have not dreamed. Some dreams are wonderful, but a small percentage are nightmares. Dreams are a form of mental housecleaning.

Then we have those dreams that do not come at night. Maybe at work, driving down the road or while sitting in a boring class. We think about things we want to happen or perhaps places we want to visit before we die. This dreaming is superior because we have control over them.

Joseph was the son of Jacob and Rachel. Known for his dreams, he was also favored by his mother and hated by his brothers. He was a daydreamer. God spoke to him about his future through dreams.

Daring to dream involves envisioning God's future for you. The fact that Joseph dreamed is not what infuriated his brothers. It was the details. Two dreams in particular. They were all binding grain. His sheaf stood up right while theirs bowed down. The second dream was similar. The sun, moon and eleven stars-representing his family, bowed before him.

Both dreams related to Joseph's future. After being sold by his brothers and finding himself in Egypt, the dreams came true. Joseph was elevated to a position of leadership. His brothers bowed before him when they came for grain to keep their family from starving.

What does God have in store for you? God gives special abilities to people and matches them to their personalities. He then provides opportunities. What gifts has God given you? Envision God's future for you in using them.

Pursue God's future in spite of opposition. Joseph was opposed by his brothers. His father rebuked him for the dreams. Affairs in Egypt were not always in his favor. He was in and out of jail before finally being elevated to ruler of Egypt. Let God turn you where he wants you to go even if others do not understand or vocally oppose you. Pursuing God's will is the most important thing in life.

Reflection: Dreams are not impossible when they come from God. Ask God to reveal his future for you.

June 19
A Time for Everything
Ecclesiastes 3:1-7

There is a time for everything, and life validates that. A child is born. Diapers have to be changed. Empty stomachs require food. Financial challenges must be met. Unsatisfactory body shapes mandate attention. And yes, there is a time to die. Death is the great leveler of all humanity. Scientists have not discovered the cure. And they never will. God provides a remedy for eternal death, but physical death will occur as long as time exists.

Since death of family members, loved ones and friends is inevitable, how do those of us left behind cope? We cry. There is a time for this, and it is perfectly acceptable. This was not always the message. It was acceptable for girls to cry, but boys were supposed to be tough. Tears were a sign of weakness. Not so. Society perpetrated an erroneous memorandum.

There is a cathartic effect that materializes when we cry. Crying over disappointment is tolerable. Crying over death should be natural. Grown men included. Repressing grief and sorrow only leads to emotional setbacks. Nor is weeping equivalent to lack of trust in God. Jesus cried when his good friend Lazarus died. He wept over his people's unbelief.

There is a time to remember. When death steals a loved one, memory becomes increasingly imperative. Pictures that have languished in boxes in some closet are exposed to the light of day. Journals are read. Stories are rehashed. Because memories are now all we have. The physical presence has vanished. In that well known shepherd's song, the psalmist remembered all God had done for him. (Psalm 23)

How sad to see diseases rob a person of their memory. This is especially difficult when it involves a family member. Alzheimer's disease is the most popular thief along with senility. Mothers do not know daughters and sons. Dads forget brothers and sisters. In times of loss, remember the memories.

Death provides the time to trust God. While this should be the pattern of our life, death increases the need. An absence occurs that will never be rectified. Our loved one will not return. Pictures, writings, stories and other memories are all we have. No touch. No softly spoken word.

Reflection: Death will come to all who live prior to Jesus' second coming. Are you prepared?

June 20

Ferris Wheel or Safari

Genesis 13:5-9

Ferris wheels go round and round. They never take you very far unless you count the distance upward. Double Ferris wheels take you farther upward but no farther forward. Safaris are different. There is a destination in mind. An African safari for example. You desire to hunt a particular animal, and your guide takes you in the direction where you are most likely to find it.

Christians can find themselves in similar situations. We can go round and round, never making much progress in our spiritual journey, or we can take a safari and make more steps forward than we do backward. Which ride we take is completely up to us. God will not force us on either though he desires the latter. In some ways life is like Forrest Gump's mother termed it: "like a box of chocolates." From a spiritual standpoint, we choose to walk close to God and enjoy his best for us.

Abraham chose the safari. God called him to leave his homeland for a country he had never seen or visited. To his credit, he obeyed. It was a journey of faith that took him in a definite direction, not in circles.

Safaris take eyes of faith not foolishness. Doing what Abraham did apart from direct guidance from God would have been foolish. Doing it at God's directive was wise. God guides our lives. We must simply follow his directions whether others understand or not. Our lives are not lived by chance. We do not gamble on the outcome.

God's guidance is something we must desire and search for. There were many unknowns ahead for Abraham. Technology had not brought the world to his doorsteps. He did not know these people. He was unfamiliar with their land. He did not know the dangerous places to avoid. But he went anyway. We can avoid many wrong turns by letting God direct our steps. The Bible says the Lord directs the steps of the godly.(Psalm 37:23) How foolish to try and run a life you did not create or presently sustain?

Abraham trusted God for direction to the land and protection on the way. He believed God would fulfill his promise to him. We might call it blind trust, but it was faith. God calls each of us to complete confidence in him. He will take care of the details of our life.

Reflection: Take a safari with God and leave the details with him. Trust him in faith.

June 21

Get Into the Deep Waters

Ezekiel 47:1-12

Deep waters have always frightened me. In fact, I am not too excited about shallow water. Baths make me nervous. Not being able to swim does that. Almost drowning when you are young complicates the situation. Then there are the shallow ocean waters and the shark stories. And I think of all the other things meandering around my feet that I cannot see.

Christianity is about the deep waters. Ezekiel discovered that. His guide led him out into the water—water that was flowing from the threshold of the Temple. The farther it flowed the deeper it became. The allegory was plain. When the glory of the Lord returned to the Temple, it would rejuvenate, restore and revitalize the people.

When we wade into the abundant life God offers, the same thing will happen. The power of God will transform us and everything we touch. Others will not fear coming to us with their needs, for they will see our authenticity. Nor will they fear our message because they know our motives.

Unlike shallow waters, deep waters require separation. Since acceptance is one of our core needs, this is a scary thought. Yet the Bible declares that believers are a separated people. We cannot be like the world because we are not like the world. Worldly lifestyles do not fit. Our circles should include unbelievers, but our goal is to influence them to become believers. The utmost caution must be used in these relationships lest we be pulled down. Jesus was successful, and we can observe his example in the gospels. If others do not see a difference, they will not be attracted to Christ.

Deep waters involve dedication. We put energy and time into what interests us. The young girl who loves gymnastics will devote many hours every week to practice. It is necessary to excel in a very demanding sport. God's work requires no less.

Dedication is usually preceded by meditation. Meditating on the things of God and letting God speak to your spirit leads to a more fruitful spiritual walk. It is God confronting us. Prayer allows the power of God to flow through our work for him. When we are in God's deep waters, we will pass on the message.

Reflection: God, help me not to fear the deep waters of total commitment to you.

June 22
Giving God's Way
Luke 21:1-4

The story is told of a son who became seriously ill. His father was forced to sell the family car to pay for treatment. Finally, they had to sell their home. As the sickness progressed, the family exhausted all their funds and went deeply in debt. To add to the misery, the young boy died. As friends came by to console the family, one remarked how disconcerting it must be to have exhausted all your possessions and to know it was for nothing. The father replied; "We made no sacrifice. All we did was love our son."

Nestled in Luke's gospel is the story of a woman who sacrificed. Her example rebukes our often lackadaisical attitude about giving. That is not really important. That other things have a higher priority. That my service at church can take the place of it.

We give because God gave. The story does not explicitly state that, but it is implied. Why else would the widow give? She was poor, a widow, and yet gave all she had to live on. Her intentions were obviously pure. Otherwise she would have received the same rebuke Jesus gave the other givers. Even in poverty, she considered herself blessed by God. God gave in Christ, and he continues to give through supplying our daily needs.

Proper giving includes pain and faith. Giving all you have is painful. It is also a major step of faith. When is the last time you placed an entire paycheck in the offering plate? Faith gives and leaves the consequences to God. Hers was not a cheap offering. She was willing to forfeit her financial security. If our giving costs us nothing, it is worth nothing.

Give sincerely. Imagine the scene as Jesus watched the people toss their money into the treasury. The poor widow must have seemed out of place. Actually, she was the only one in place. Her gift was sacrificial and sincere. She sincerely trusted God to care for her. She would need his help. God looks at the motive in our giving. The amount does not impress him.

The widow gave to God first then trusted him to take care of her needs. Welfare would not. Typical giving of our generation is to pay the bills, budget for our entertainment, then give God a part of what is left. This plan is not biblical. God requires the first portion.

Reflection: Trust God enough to give to him first. He promises that if we do that, he will care for our needs.

June 23
How to Gain Control of Your Life
Romans 6:1-13

When asked what he thought of the Great Emancipator, one Alabama slave said, "I don't know nothing about Abraham Lincoln, 'cep they say he sot us free. And I don't know nothing bout that neither." How tragic to have legal liberty to control your life, not know it, and therefore not exercise the right you have. Many Christians are in the same predicament. Before Christ, we have no control. But after Christ, the situation changes drastically.

Control comes from knowing our position and exercising the rights of it. A dog on a chain makes the same mistake. His whole day is consumed with the length of the chain. Because of this, he often just chooses to lie around. What's the use to get up? One day the owner unleashes him. But he is not aware of his freedom, so he continues to live chained.

When baptized into Christ, we take part in his sacrifice. That sacrifice was for the forgiveness of our sins. Accepting that changes our position from sinners to saints. Once chained. No longer chained. Once knowing nothing about our Great Emancipator, now very familiar with him. We can and should live above the dregs and drags of sin's slavery.

Along with this is considering ourselves dead to sin but alive to Christ. Believers will never achieve sinless perfection. Nowhere does Scripture teach this. But the pattern of our life is not sin. It is righteous living. The Master has set us free. We are not in a helpless situation.

No longer are believers to present their bodies to sin as instruments of unrighteousness but rather to God as instruments of righteousness. We live under the grace of God. We have the power to live a good and upright life that will point others to Christ.

There was a southern lady who married her childhood sweetheart. They had a rewarding life together until a heart attack took him from her. She decided to have him embalmed, placed in a glass case and put just inside the front door of their plantation. Soon she met a man from Europe. After a honeymoon there, they returned home. He was met by her embalmed late husband. After questioning his new wife, he said, "He's dead. He's history." And so are believers to our old way of living.

Reflection: Honor God by living with control over your life. Let him give you power over a sinful lifestyle.

June 24

How to Walk the Ancient Paths

Jeremiah 6:16

The twentieth century witnessed untold changes. The year 1903 saw the Wright brothers fly the first practical airplane. Vladimir Lenin began the Communist Revolution in 1917. In 1953, Watson and Crick mapped the DNA molecule. The year 1969 saw Americans walk on the moon and in 1989, the Berlin Wall fell. A century of change.

The church is also in a state of change. Once the center of communities where most activities were held, it now takes a back seat. Parents once attended and made their children go whether they wanted to or not. Fear of God kept society in check. We can now do almost anything on the first day of the week that we can on the second.

In a generation where many decisions are unwise and ungodly, believers would do well to request the ancient paths. God's Temple in Jerusalem was about to be destroyed and his people taken off for a seventy year captivity. All because of their disobedience. God tells them to ask for the ancient path.

Faith is an old path. In fact, it is the beginning path. It was what led God to reject Cain's offering but accept Abel's. Faith was the reason Noah was delivered from the flood while everyone else perished. Paul followed this path and even wrote that God's grace saves us through faith. All of this is a gift of God. (Ephesians 2:8) In fact, faith has always been the way, as witnessed throughout the pages of Scripture.

On the path, we are greeted by prayer. There was a time when God's people believed in the efficacy of prayer. Wednesday nights at church were established so believers could join together in the middle of the week for prayer. Thus the name-prayer meeting.

Purpose is on the ancient path. It should identify the Christian's life. Jesus exemplifies it. His purpose was to follow the Father's will and to glorify him in the process. Ours should be identical. The Bible says when there is no vision the people will perish. (Proverbs 29:18)

We should walk the path of unity. This is the only way God's church can be successful. Backbiting will destroy our testimony and us.

Reflection: The ancient paths will always lead us to success in God's work.

June 25
How to Survive Life
Matthew 24:13-14

He lived in the 1930's and felt his world was about to disintegrate. He decided to pack his belongings and move to the loneliest place he could find. His journey ended in the South Pacific on a forgotten little island called Guadalcanal. A few years later, he awoke to find World War II in his front yard.

Dr. M. Scott Peck begins his book *The Road Less Traveled* with a simple but profound statement, "Life is difficult." Who ever told us it would not be? If you have lived at all, you have already discovered it. Trials, temptations and turmoil arrive on a regular basis. Even the loneliest island will not help us escape. We live with alcohol related deaths, ill effects of drug use, broken families, unemployment, economic distress and international tension, and we feel helpless to control any of it.

Believers can have victory in spite of life's difficulties. Jesus deals with the end times and events that will transpire. He prepares his followers for things they will face in the first century-struggles that came when the Romans overran Jerusalem in 70 A. D. Ninety seven thousand would be killed and more than a million taken captive.

While life is difficult, victory is assured for God's people. Those who endure to the end will be saved. There will be many battles along the way, but we must carry on. Keep the faith. We can burrow into the cliffs of difficulties and avoid falling. Almighty God is our rock of refuge. Faith is our stronghold.

Accomplishments along the way are also assured. Jesus says the good news of the gospel will be preached all over the world. There was a time when we may have wondered how this would happen. The Internet answered the question. The Jews livelihood would be destroyed, but the gospel would not. Struggles too are our lot in life, but in spite of them, God will use us in his work.

After all these things happen, the end will come. Isn't it assuring to know we worship the One who will end it all? That he will conclude it means he is in control of it. He is the King of Kings and Lord of Lords. It is also calming to know life's difficulties will one day end.

Reflection: Take time daily to thank God for the ability to survive life.
June 26
Responsible Stewardship
Luke 12:47-48

One Andy Griffith episode begins with a farmer on the side of the road, his produce scattered about. It seems someone had run him off the road. Andy and Barney begin the chase and finally catch up to a rich young punk in a convertible who thinks the world revolves around him. His father is well known in the area. Andy takes him to jail, and over the course of the episode teaches him responsibility for his actions.

Jesus tells about two servants. One knew his master's will but did not obey. His punishment will be harsh. The second also was disobedient, but he did not know his master's will. His reprimand will be less severe. Both, however, were responsible. Our rights are matched with responsibility, our obligations with opportunity and our privileges with duties.

We are responsible for the opportunities God gives us. These occasions give us chances to use the knowledge, gifts and talents he has given us. Opportunities only provide two avenues. We can take advantage of the opportunity or let it slip by. We do not all have the same privileges, but we are responsible for those we have.

One said, "Opportunity is a bird that never perches." Lyndon B. Johnson's father used to say to him, "You must seize the moment."

God holds us accountable for our abilities. Like opportunities, these are varied among individuals. Likewise, we are not held accountable for abilities we do not have. We like to say that all people are created equal, but this is not quite true. While created by the same God, we are not all given the same abilities. Wasting them dishonors God. According to Paul "Bear" Bryant, legendary football coach at the University of Alabama, "There are players who have ability and know it."

We are responsible for our resources. These too are diverse. God blesses some with great material wealth while withholding it from others. One day we will give an account to the Father of how we handled them. Giving a tithe is one of the most honorable ways, but our offerings go well beyond that. A consistent program of giving to God and others helps to establish discipline and a right order of priorities.

Reflection: Ask God to help you honor him with your money and resources. Give your offerings first, and trust God to take care of you.

June 27
Starting Over Again
Genesis 13:1-4

How often we start over again. We finish paying for our vehicle, trade it in, and begin with another payment. We sell our house that is paid for and accrue another mortgage payment. Or we change jobs and have to learn new skills. Every four years or, at the most eight, our country starts over with a new president.

Helen Steiner Rice wrote, "It doesn't take a new year to begin our lives anew. God grants us new beginnings each day." And so he does. He is the God of second chances (and third, fourth, fifth, etc.). He was for Abraham. God gave him the chance to leave his pagan homeland and begin anew in the Promised Land.

In the new beginnings, we should love more. "Love makes the world go round." There is never enough of it, and we can always improve on the way we distribute it. After leaving his homeland, Abraham took his nephew Lot with him. In time, their possessions multiplied. Quarreling erupted between Abraham and Lot's herdsmen. The land was promised to Abraham. He could have ousted Lot. But he did not. In love, he gave Lot first choice of all the land. Believers should bestow this trait on each other and unbelievers in great measure.

Give more. Abraham did. He was willing to give Lot whatever part of the land he wanted. It was a great sacrifice and demonstrated total unselfishness. The Bible instructs us not to withhold good from those who deserve it when we have the power to act. (Proverbs 3:27) And that a generous person will prosper because he refreshed others. (Proverbs 11:25) As the church gives, she reaches her potential. And so do individual believers. Our giving demonstrates our genuine love for God and his church.

In those times of new beginning, unity is important. While the herdsmen of Abraham and Lot experienced a lack of accord, Abraham sought harmony through the idea of separation. The bickering was soothed by the salve of unity. Race, class, social status and prejudices all divide us. Believers have the rare opportunity to exhibit unanimity in a divided world. Our relationship with Christ is the driving force of our unison.

Reflection: Thank God for the many opportunities you have to begin again, despite your mistakes and bad decisions.

June 28

The Downfall of a Good Person

II Chronicles 26:16-21

Robert Robinson, author of the hymn "Come, Thou Fount of Every Blessing, lost his happy communion with Christ. In an attempt to relieve his troubled mind, he began to travel. In the course of his journey, he became acquainted with a young woman on spiritual matters. She asked what he thought of a particular song. To his amazement, it was his very song. With a broken voice, he said, "I am the man who wrote that hymn many years ago. I'd give anything to experience again the joy I knew then."

Perhaps you have known a good person who fell into the trap of sin. Maybe it was you. Uzziah, the tenth king of Judah, did. He rose to his position after the murder of his father. The beginning of Uzziah's reign was prosperous. The kingdom of Judah was elevated to a position it had not seen since the time of Solomon. But the seeds of destruction were present.

Pride can bring our downfall. It did for Uzziah. He reigned in Judah for 52 years. Prosperity and peace characterized his long reign. The people of the kingdom loved and respected him, and he brought stability and security to them. He was only 16 when he ascended the throne, but he was obedient to God, and God gave him great success. Then came the tragedy: "But after Uzziah became powerful, his pride led to his downfall."

Pride is the bane of humanity. Why else would God warn against it in so many places in his Word? It is our tendency to think we are better than others, to imagine that we deserve what they have, to connive and cheat to get it. Pride lifts our ego, but God honors humility.

Uzziah's pride led to unfaithfulness. He entered the Temple to burn incense, a job reserved strictly for the priests. Pride led him to think he had rights he did not possess. The priests confronted him about this disrespect and disobedience, but he failed to listen. God requires and expects faithfulness to his commands.

Anger sealed his fate. When questioned about his unfaithfulness, Uzziah became angry. As he raged against the priests, God struck him with leprosy. The priests rushed him from the Temple. He died a leper. Anger over sin is acceptable. Any other form is sin.

Reflection: Pray for God to help you stay on the paths of righteousness.

June 29

The Greatest Giver

John 3:16

She was born in 1910, a woman of Albanian ancestry. In 1928, she traveled to Ireland and joined the Institute of the Blessed Virgin Mary. Six weeks later, she was on her way to India where she moved into the slums of Calcutta-home of the most destitute people in the world. Here Mother Teresa founded the Order of the Missionaries of Charity. In 1979, her work was recognized by awarding her the Nobel Peace Prize.

Though a great giver, Mother Teresa was not the greatest giver. That position is reserved for God. God gave and still gives the greatest love. People seek after love in many places and forms often never realizing it is only a prayer away. God loves with agape' love-love that gives repeatedly and is not determined by a response from the recipient. He does not force his love on others, but it is available to all who ask. As his follower, Christ expects us to demonstrate this same type of love to others.

God gives to the unlovely. He loved the world so much that he sent his Son. The world is not a reference to the physical planet but to the sinful people who lived there. The world encapsulates all races of people. God does indeed love the little children of the world-red, yellow, black and white.

As the greatest giver, God gave the ultimate gift-himself in the person of his Son. The Father, Son and Holy Spirit are all part of the Trinity and thus God. Only a sinless person could die for sinful people. He was the perfect sacrifice that all Old Testament offerings foreshadowed.

A part of God's gift is our ability to believe. So enslaved are we to sin and its dictates that we cannot even believe in God without his help. We must be drawn by the power of God's Spirit. We believe by faith. The gift of salvation is not automatically received just because Jesus died. The Bible nowhere teaches universalism. Faith is part of the process. Out of that belief will flow a mighty steam of good works that testify to our changed lives.

God gives a favorable future to his children. We will not perish but have everlasting life. There is the promise of heaven and of a new earth. Once again earth will be restored to its original intention. Sin will be destroyed and its ravaging effects nullified.

Reflection: Have you received your gift of salvation from the greatest giver? If not, repent of your sins and accept his gift today.

June 30

What is God's Body Supposed to Do?

Colossians 1:18

The little crippled boy sold notions at the train station. It was his only means of making a living. One day a hurried traveler rounded the corner, ran into his stand, and scattered his wares all over the floor. The traveler gave him a dirty stare, as if to say, "Why are you in my way?" Another hurried traveler stopped and helped. Then he gave him ten dollars to cover the cost of the lost and broken wares. As he hurried on the little boy asked, "Hey are you Jesus?" He answered, "No, but I'm one of his followers trying to do what he would do if he were here."

We have certain expectations of our bodies. We assume that all parts are going to work in unison and properly. When they do, we enjoy good health. When they do not, we are usually made aware of it in short order.

The most common analogy of the Church in the New Testament is the Body of Christ. Like us, Christ has certain expectations for his body. The church is not ours to do with as we please. God founded it and Christ died for it. We are Jesus on earth, helping people pick up their scattered lives.

As Christ's body, we should respond to him. What takes place in our heads determines what our bodies do. Messages are sent to all parts of our body. You walk and speak because you have received a command. Christ is the head of the church. What he is thinking, expecting and dreaming for individual churches must be important to us and determined by us. When it is not, we develop mentally challenged bodies. Additionally, fear, doubt, strife, indifference and discord can paralyze our bodies. Failure to respond signals paralysis.

God expects unity in his body. If the human body is not unified, chaos results. One leg moves forward while the other walks backward. One hand reaches for an item while the other tries to put it down. One eye looks left and the other right. God's body has different parts determined by the gifts and talents he has distributed. When we use them in unity, God's church succeeds.

God's body is to serve. Jesus is our great example. His life was consumed with service to the needy. As he served, he witnessed of who he was. We must serve the needy so they can adequately hear our message.

Reflection: "A Christ without hands is no Christ at all."

July

July 1
What's My Purpose in Life?
I Corinthians 10:31

Questions. Socrates, famous Greek philosopher, is famous because he asked all the important ones. Dr. Gregory Stock, in his book, *The Book of Questions*, details over two hundred thought provoking questions. "If you could use a voodoo doll to hurt anyone you could, would you?" "If your house caught on fire and you had the chance to save only one item, what would it be?" Such questions sometime disturb us.

Determining your purpose in life should be the most important question. Why are you here? What did God create you to do? What is the foundational reason you exist? Are you living up to God's expectations for you? The answer is simple but profound. We exist to bring glory to God. Defined, it means to magnify, elevate and shed radiance on him. It is an unnatural experience in our natural state.

We should include God in every segment of life. This does not naturally happen. It must be a conscious decision. It is living daily with the question, "If Jesus was here, would I be doing or saying what I am?" Christianity is not a compartment of our life but a wrap around lifestyle. Habits can be good or destructive. Make a habit of including God in every decision you make.

Refuse any glory that belongs to God. How often we want the praise, pat on the back, plaque or ribbon. Failure to realize that all our accomplishments result from opportunities and gifts God has given steal the glory from him. John the Baptist prepared the way for the Messiah, but when Jesus began his ministry, many of John's disciples followed him. John recognized his position. He had to decrease while Jesus increased. (John 3:30) Commit to God's way rather than going your own.

Fulfilling our purpose involves maintaining a priority relationship with God. Earthly associations are important, but the one we have with God supersedes all others. If not careful, we will find ourselves devoting more attention to earthly relationships. Family, friends, social functions, sporting events, hobbies.

Reflection: God help me not to allow anything to siphon my attention from you. Help my actions, words and attitudes to bring glory to you.

July 2

When Grace Touches Your Heart

II Corinthians 8:1-6

Sam Houston was an important figure in Texas military history and Texas government, but his behavior earned him the nickname, "Big Drunk." He married a devout woman who prayed for his salvation. His decision to trust Christ finally came upon hearing Dr. Rufus Burleson, then president of Baylor University. News of his baptism attracted a crowd. So deeply had grace touched his life, that he was baptized with his wallet. He said, "I'm afraid it needs baptizing too."

Salvation not only affects our eternal destiny but our worldly possessions as well. Houston paid half the pastor's salary and gave financial assistance to ministerial students at Baylor for as long as he lived. The 20/80 principle applies to most churches. Twenty percent of the people give eighty percent of the money and do eighty percent of the work.

Paul refers to the Macedonians. They were experiencing severe economic stress, but in spite of poverty were willing to contribute to an offering Paul was taking for impoverished saints in Jerusalem. Paul was pleasantly surprised by the amount. People give from many motivations: pressure, duty, reward. God wants us to give cheerfully and sacrificially.

Hard times should not keep us from giving. It did not for the Macedonians. Often God gets the leftovers because our creditors have gotten the first portion. Poor financial planning can exacerbate this situation. Our giving will always suffer if we let our economic status determine the amount. We must give believing that God will supply our needs in return.

When grace touches our life, we will not underestimate ourselves. Paul expected a great deal out of himself and others. He continually pressed toward the mark of the high calling of Jesus Christ. But he underestimated the Macedonians. They gave more than he expected. Never underestimate what God can do with what you give. It may seem insignificant to you, but God can take little and multiply it.

Grace also reminds us to give ourselves. Money is not a substitute for personal sacrifice. The Macedonians gave themselves first, then their money.

Reflection: Ralph Waldo Emerson said, "The true gift is the gift of thyself."

July 3

Free At Last

Galatians 5:13-15

The signing of the Declaration of Independence on July 4, 1776 ended a long struggle pitting America against Great Britain. It was the day that America officially became a free nation-free from the injustices of a nation that ruled from far away. One has said, "If a nation values anything more than freedom, it will lose its freedom."

Our country and world have witnessed many freedom movements, but the greatest movement came on Calvary's cross. For here, humanity was delivered from the greatest form of bondage one could ever know. A bondage that delved deeper than society could ever imagine-bondage of the soul.

Living in true freedom means opposing the flesh. The flesh is that residual part of us that remains even after trusting Christ. It is the old patterns of acting and thinking that we have learned along life's way. While no longer chained by the old nature, we are still haunted by the flesh. We must walk by God's Spirit to avoid fulfilling the desires of the flesh. Christ gives us the power to live in this freedom.

In John Bunyan's classic, *Pilgrim's Progress*, Christian is on his way to the City of Zion. He meets Apollyon who accused him of being one of his subjects. Christian replies, "But I have let myself to another, even to the King of princes, and how can I with fairness go back with thee?"

Our freedom involves serving others. Those who fought for our country's freedom were often more concerned for others than for their own personal welfare. Jesus was as the cross proved. We must be too. Serving should be a natural aspect of the believer's life because God has deposited love in our heart. We must leave the high places of intimacy with God and journey to the valley of service.

Freedom is fulfilling God's moral law. Jesus stated that we are to love God with all our heart, soul and being. Then others as ourselves. (Matthew 22:37-39) Salvation frees us to love those we could not or did not want to love before. Our love is then demonstrated through action. When we love others, we will avoid harming them. Their welfare will be our interest. Working together will prevent us from being torn apart by our bickering.

Reflection: Our greatest freedom is found in a relationship with Jesus Christ. Are you following him?

July 4

A Heart for Worship

Matthew 17:1-5

People are different. Not a profound conclusion but nonetheless true. Andy found this out on the high school reunion episode. Barney was moving some of his things when he came across an old year book. They began reminiscing and were soon planning a reunion. Andy was overjoyed when his high school sweetheart, Sharon, came. Marriage was once on their agenda, but it never materialized. Andy liked the small town atmosphere, but she wanted the big city life.

Worship is an area where people have various preferences. Some prefer the traditional services where the old hymns are sung and the preacher preaches. Others want a praise band leading contemporary songs and a preacher who delivers a very practical short sermon. How we worship is not nearly as important as the fact that we do.

We must prepare for worship. And it can happen, and should happen, no matter the style of service we attend. We should come expecting an experience with God. Worship is in spirit and truth. It is not all about our needs. It is more about Him. Anything that hinders that from occurring must be addressed.

Nor is worship limited to certain days. Sundays and Wednesdays are the traditional days that Christians worship, but worship should happen daily. When we spend time in God's Word and prayer, worship should happen. When we are spiritually hungry, we eat spiritual things.

Peter, James and John's worship experience did not take place in the Temple, God's house. It happened on the Mount of Transfiguration where the true person of Jesus was shown to them. The Father spoke and reminded them of who Jesus was and told them to listen to him. Worship is about listening to the Son.

A little boy on a plane was heard to say, "Will they really let me meet the pilot?" The pilot overheard the request, shook the little fella's hand and invited him into the cockpit. With a few exceptions, no other face showed the enthusiasm of the little boys. But he was excited because he had met the pilot

Reflection: Are you excited when you meet the Pilot of your life? Worship him regularly in spirit and truth.

July 5

Choose Honesty

Ephesians 4:25

"Honesty is the best policy." An old but good saying. Some years ago, a bank teller gave me too much money when cashing my check. I did not discover it until after paying my vehicle payment when an extra twenty dollars appeared. Try as I might to justify why I should have it, I could not. I finally returned it to the teller who told me she was twenty dollars short.

When teaching high school, it was not uncommon to have a few students make a habit of cheating on tests. It was not that they were not smart, just too lazy to study. One girl in particular was absent the day of the test. She came in later for a makeup. I was teaching another class, and she did not think I would notice the cheat sheet under her arm. I did. She failed.

How often have you had the opportunity to demonstrate honesty and did not. A cashier charged you the wrong price for an item. You knew it, but hey, they are overcharging you anyway, right? You keep silent. Or you get home, check your receipt and find you were not charged for an item. The store is too far to return to. But the next time you go you fail to mention it.

Paul reminds us that the truth is important. Honesty deals with truth. For many, truth is relevant. It depends on the situation. And after all, what is absolute truth? Does it exist, and if so, where can I find it? Such thinking leads to situational ethics. Which leads to no truth at all. Who then determines truth?

And we are often tempted to classify our lies. White lies are those things we tell because we are afraid of hurting someone's feelings. A friend has a baby and you remark, "That's just the cutest baby I've ever seen" when it is really the ugliest child you have ever witnessed. Then we have the serious lies, such as when a spouse is unfaithful and lies when confronted about it.

Christians of all people should stand for and speak the truth. Honesty should be the hallmark of our life. If we cannot find truth among believers, where else can we look? Just because we cannot see our Judge does not justsify skimping out on truth. We are witnesses, and the world is our jury. As witnesses are called to testify, believers are so called to testify of Christ to the world. Jesus terms us his witnesses.

Reflection: Jesus is our great example of truth. Isaiah wrote of how he had done no wrong. (Isaiah 53:9)

July 6

The Importance of Focus

Ephesians 1:17-18

While in elementary school, I suddenly lost focus. The teacher would write on the board, but I could not see. Just a blur of characters. I sat at the back of the room. My eyes said move forward. My body lingered in the back. So I compromised. I sat in the back, but when the teacher wrote on the board I moved forward until I could write the material down. Then I returned to the back. Soon the teacher began to wonder if I needed glasses and contacted my parents. I have been wearing them ever since.

Focus concerns seeing things clearly. If I cannot see the target clearly, I will miss the center after firing my pistol. If the yellow light is blurry, I may run a red light. Some of your peers in high school were focused. Maybe you were. Maybe not. They knew from an early age what they wanted in life. After high school, they attended college. Following graduation, they got a job doing what they had prepared for. Others just muddle through life.

Focus is no less important for the believer. We need to see clearly God's will for our life. We must see God's will clearly for our churches. Blurred vision leads us in the wrong direction, or we miss things we should have observed. Life is difficult enough without blurred vision making it even more challenging.

Jesus was a man on target, and he accomplished that without any of our modern conveniences. He possessed no GPS system to map his course. MapQuest on a computer did not exist. Paper road maps had not been invented. Yet he managed to consistently do his Father's will. He possessed wisdom, and the eyes of his heart were enlightened. A life void of options or expectations was not what made life easy for him. Expectations were high that he was the political Messiah who would deliver his people from Rome. Some may have wondered why he was not a carpenter like his father.

Jesus lived a life of focus. When he came to the end of his earthly life on the cross, he was able to say that it was finished. (John 19:30) When we come to the end of our earthly time, we should be able to say we have finished what God wanted us to do. We remained on course. We hit the target.

Reflection: Ask God to help you see his plan for you with clear vision.

July 7

Be Happy

Proverbs 17:22

Ben was the opposite of happiness. Of all the characters on the Andy Griffith show, he was foulest. A scowl almost always adorned his face. Smiles came on rare occasions only. From trying to run a door to door salesman out of town to evicting a couple who were experiencing difficult times, his hardened heart showed through. In speaking of him to Barney, Andy said, "You know, when his time comes, he ain't gonna go like everyone else. He's just gonna nasty away."

You have probably known people like that. Their outlook is always pessimistic. Nothing good ever happens to them. They are miserable, and they want you to enjoy their company. When people smile, they want to know why. Complaints roll off their tongues. They are down and want to drag you down with them.

A happy heart is like good medicine. Medicine is always good when it soothes our symptoms. When it relieves the pain. Or cures the disease. Or prolongs our life. Or renews your energy. After all, it takes fewer muscles to smile than it does to frown.

On the other hand, a broken spirit zaps our strength. It dries up our bones. It takes the joy out of living and replaces it with discouragement and depression. Brokenness sends us to counselors, psychologists, or pastors. Since the emotional is tied to the physical, it might send us to the doctor.

The power of choice is one of the most powerful tools God has given us. We can choose to be happy or sad. We can choose to allow circumstances to determine our mood or pray to the God who controls the circumstances and get his perspective. His take will take away our discouragement and replace it with peace. Unexplainable peace.

Jesus tells three parables in Luke 15 that demonstrate happiness. A lost sheep is found, a lost coin discovered, and a lost son returned. All the players are overjoyed when what was lost is found. While happiness should be the normal state for believers, there are special things that should give us more reason to rejoice. People coming to know Christ as their Savior. Backslidden believers returning home. Heaven rejoices. We should too.

Reflection: Let joy be your state of mind as you remember that we worship a God who is in control of all circumstances.

July 8
The Importance of Purity
Matthew 5:8

Greenhouses are a typical part of the nursery business. The temperature is controlled, and flowers are protected from frost and the damaging rays of the sun. Some have them in their yards so they can keep flowers year round. Plants grow faster here and are normally healthier.

But suppose I went out to gather seeds for your greenhouse. I walked along the road and stripped seeds from plants growing there. You might say, "Wait a minute. Those are weed seeds you are gathering." You question

232

my sanity. But I protest, "I do not feel like driving all the way to town to buy flower seeds. These are more convenient." Doesn't make much sense does it?

Nor does it seem right when believers live in impure ways. Jesus says we will be happy (blessed) when we are pure in heart. The heart is the seat of emotions. Our wills. Our character. Our minds. The Bible says the heart is desperately wicked and beyond human help. (Jeremiah 17:9) Only the blood of Christ can cleanse our hearts. When this happens, they are made pure and spotless. The Father sees us through his Son.

Purity is taking the challenge of matching our practice with our position. Living out in action who we are. Jesus tells the parable of the soils, and in it demonstrates that only the properly prepared soil can receive his Word. This equates with the heart that is properly prepared for salvation. The heart has been convicted by the Spirit and is ready for Christ.

Society often makes it challenging for the believer to live in a pure manner. Evil surrounds us. It is our responsibility to salt it and shed light on it. We must manage our minds as the flowers in the greenhouse must have attention. What we allow in will come out. Jesus says what comes out of our mouth is a reflection of what is inside. Garbage in, garbage out. Sow a thought, reap an action. Familiar sayings with enormous truth.

As a bad heart limits us physically, so an impure mind affects us spiritually. God cannot use what is not pure. We purify our minds by filling them with God's Word. When this happens, our resulting actions will also come from pure motives.

Reflection: Submit your thoughts to the authority of Christ. Let him capture those thoughts that would allow impurity into your mind.

July 9

Doing Our Best for Christ
I Peter 1:13-21

Executives at Hitachi often quote the words of the father where preparation is concerned: "Though we cannot live 100 years, we should be concerned with the next 1,000 years."

Jim Davidson, lay preacher and Salvation Army worker, once remarked, "What the future holds for my life is hidden from view, but whatever is ahead, I determine to do God's will."

Second best is never our best. God deserves the best. Peter's readers were in for turbulent times. Severe persecution and even death for some lay ahead. But the best was yet to come. They have a rich inheritance in Christ.

We must strengthen our minds to do our best for Christ. We are to think clearly and exercise self-control. Gird your minds. Roll up your sleeves. In Peter's day, dress was a long robe. Whenever laborious work was done, the robe was pulled up and tucked or tied around the waist area. The person was girded and ready for work.

Improving our mental capacity is important. Research shows it may possibly stave off or at least postpone diseases like Alzheimer's. Spiritually, it helps us prepare to give a defense of what we believe and why. Thinking diligently about our faith will prevent our faith from being shaken when contested. Spiritual maturity should be our goal. Each generation of believers is confronted with different issues-some from within and others from without the church.

When such times arrive, we need self-control. "Don't lose your cool" is a loose translation. Be sensible and calm when the times of testing come. You are prepared because your mind has been strengthened. Our hope is in Christ. He will guide us through the tough times when our faith is challenged.

Our lifestyle is necessary in doing our best for Christ. The term "lifestyle evangelism" was once popular. It describes a living acting faith that points others to Christ. We must leave our thinking about faith and move to action. Freedom in Christ is not unrestricted freedom. It is responsible freedom.

Reflection: In difficult times, remember your Redeemer. He will strengthen your faith and help you remain calm.

July 10
Remember Who You Are
I Peter 4:1-6

In Robert Frost's, *A Cabin in the Clearing*, Mist and Smoke carry on a conversation about the cabin's inhabitants. Smoke finally says, "If the day ever comes when they know who They are, they may know better where they are. But who they are is too much to believe-Either for them or the onlooking world."

It is normal for the adolescent to pass through an identity crisis. They wonder exactly who they are and what their purpose is. It is an ordinary part of moving from childhood to adulthood. Failure to solve this crisis in a healthy manner can lead to an identity crisis.

Peter admonishes his readers to remember who they are. Christians should not have identity crises. We should always be comfortable with who we are-children of the Heavenly Father no longer under condemnation.

As God's children, we are responsible for living according to his will. A part of this is suffering for our faith. Jesus did. He felt the nails and the whip. He endured the crown of thorns and ridicule from the religious authorities. Those who are godly will also experience persecution.

Believers must arm themselves for our times of suffering. The term reminds us of military life where the soldier has to arm himself for battle. The challenge is easier when we are prepared. Our armor is the mind of Christ. A willingness to suffer for our faith is a sign of dedication to the cause. The person who is strong in their faith is better able to resist temptation.

Suffering is a means to an end. Through the process, we are purer and stronger than we were before. A Christian who is willing to suffer is more apt to live according to God's plan. God's will rather than human passion should be the determining force in our life.

We remember who we are by putting our past behind us. Our sins have been cast as far as the east is from the west and thrust into the bottom of the ocean. We have a desire to live according to God's teachings.

Sinful activities such as sensuality, lust, drunkenness, carousing, partying and any form of idolatry should find no place in the believer's life.

Reflection: We will all stand before the judgment seat of Christ to give an account to God. Remembering who you are will aid in living a life pleasing to him.

July 11
Standing for Right
I Peter 3:13-17

Standing for right is always challenging. The 1950's and 60's were tumultuous times in our country. Race relations and women's rights were subjects of fierce battles. Christians had to make a choice-stand for right or go along with the majority. Realize God loves and died for all people or continue to segregate.

The twenty first century still holds challenges requiring a stand-a stand that will often bring suffering and ridicule. Homosexual rights and marriages, abortion, pornography, abuse. Even all Christians do not agree on where we should stand or even if we should stand. The old saying, however, is true: "If we don't stand for something, we'll fall for anything."

We must stand in agreement against those things that God's Word forbids. When we do, suffering will come, but Peter says we will be blessed. Confidence and peace come when we suffer for doing the right thing. Jesus said a similar thing when he proclaimed that those persecuted for righteousness sake would be happy. (Matthew 5:10)

Along with suffering comes opposition. Opposition may not lead to suffering, but it often does. Unbelievers will always oppose believers when we stand against issues they stand for. We will be ridiculed as narrow minded, unforgiving, rigid people. Peter says not to fear this intimidation. Do no fear their fear. Rather, muster courage.

Suffering and opposition give opportunity to give a defense of our faith. Being grounded in our faith and God's Word prepares us to give the apology. This vindication should be given with gentleness and reverence. There is a way to defend our faith that drives others away rather than attract them. An arrogant attitude will deter. We remember that we were once where they are-sinners with no understanding and in need of God's grace. Our testimony is simply that God loves us, sent Christ to die for us, and will forgive our sins if we ask.

Our defense must be supplemented by righteous conduct. This will put to shame those who ridicule and persecute us. It will also prove that our faith is authentic.

Reflection: Remember that persecution and opposition give you opportunity to defend your faith. Stand for the right.

July 12

Teachings from the Example of Christ

I Peter 3:18-22

Consciously or not, we follow examples. We need examples. Parents are often our first standards. They care for us. We might see in them what we hope to become later in life. A favorite teacher might inspire us to follow our dreams. Heroes, good and bad, abound for the young child to emulate.

What better place to find an example than in Christ. He gives us a wonderful model to pattern our life after. He remained on the straight and narrow of following his Father's will and plan.

Christ's example provides a representation of redemptive behavior. Peter reminds us that he died for the just and unjust because each of them was sinners. His purpose was to bring us to God-a bridge that could not be crossed without a sacrificial death. Christ did not die for sins he committed. His death was a propitiation for our sins. He was our Substitute, not just a good example.

Isaiah said Jesus would be pierced for our transgressions and crushed for our iniquities. (Isaiah 53) John concludes that Jesus was the propitiation for our sins and those of the entire world. (I John 2:2) Christ covered our sins through his death in an once and for all event. No further sacrifice was needed.

Christ's death reminds us of the necessity of witnessing about our faith. Verses nineteen and twenty are among the most controversial in the New Testament having at least six different interpretations among Christians. And it is only human to wonder where the Spirit of Christ went between his death and resurrection. Whatever interpretation one might take, the important point is that Christ was concerned for the lost. His ministry demonstrated that. His death was for the sole purpose of bringing the lost to God.

Don Jones was the Youth Minister at Hillary Clinton's church when she was in high school. Under his leadership, they organized babysitting brigades for the children of migrant workers. In speaking of him, Hillary told *Newsweek*, "He just was relentless in telling us that to be a Christian did not just mean you were concerned about your own personal salvation."

Reflection: Commit yourself to following the example of Christ. Love others, and share your faith with them.

July 13
Results of Being a Spiritual Child
Galatians 4:21-5:1

Many blessings are received from our parents. They are responsible for our existence. As we grow, our basic needs are met by them-food, shelter and clothing. Because of their resources, some parents can provide more than others. We inherit traits from our parents. Half of each is in every child. And just perhaps we receive an inheritance when they die.

Being a child of God also has advantages. Significantly more than being a child of an earthly parent. Paul reaches back into the Old Testament and uses the story of Abraham, Sarah and their children as an analogy of the advantages of being a child of Christ.

As God's child, we can expect him to guide us. God did this for Abraham as he led him from his homeland to the Promised Land with the promise of a child from which many descendants would come.

God's plan did not unfold quickly enough for Sarah, so she took matters into her hands and made a mess. Sarah gave Abraham her servant, Hagar, as wife, and a son named Ishmael was born. Later, God fulfilled his original plan and gave Sarah a son whom she named Isaac. Paul uses Hagar and her line as a symbol of those who are lost. Sarah and her line through Isaac symbolize those who are believers.

Abraham was not unique. God's guidance is available for all. In fact, he wants to be involved in every detail of our life. (Psalm 37:23) So often, we, like Sarah, run ahead of God. We manipulate. We take matters into our own hands, thinking we know best. It is always wise to ask God for wisdom.

A rich inheritance awaits God's children. Sarah later instructed Abraham to put Hagar and her son out. He would have no inheritance with her son Isaac. Non Christians have no inheritance with believers. They may persecute believers now, but their eternal destinies will radically differ. All who live outside God's covenant of grace will receive punishment.

God also gives us the power to live for him consistently and faithfully. The new nature that comes with salvation includes the ability to live free from the chains of sin. We can stand firm in our new found freedom. Christ also sets us free from the guilt of past sins and mistakes.

Reflection: Thank God for the blessings that are yours because you are his child.

July 14

Childhood Responsibilities

Galatians 4:1-11

Children reaching a certain age are usually assigned certain responsibilities: taking out the trash, washing and drying the dishes, cutting the grass, folding clothes. Behavior often belies the family atmosphere.

It is the highest privilege to be called a son or daughter of God. John Newton lost his mother when only seven. At eleven, he went to sea as a sailor and became involved in the inhuman African slave trade. He was hardened by his surroundings, and quickly outdid his companions in wicked living. At twenty three, his ship was caught in a severe storm. He cried out to God for mercy and was graciously saved. Never wanting to forget God's mercy, he penned the words to the beloved song, Amazing Grace.

Remembering the source of our sonship is critical. It is none other than the true Son himself, Jesus Christ. In ancient culture, the father established the time when his son would come of age and pass into adulthood. God decided when the fullness of time had arrived. Then he sent his Son to solve our sin problem. Jesus' work and our acceptance of it mean we are now joint heirs with him. Our faith in him leads to adoption.

God, in his wisdom, had engineered the fullness of time. The law was given to God's people to show them their sinfulness. The Babylonian Captivity cured them of idolatry. Alexander the Great had spread the Greek culture and a common language. The Romans built a magnificent system of roads for travel. The time was right for the Son.

We must walk by the Spirit. Upon receiving Christ as our Savior, the Spirit becomes God's gift to us. He is the seal that guarantees our future inheritance in heaven. God gives us a part of himself when he gives the Spirit. Paul writes that we have received a spirit of adoption which allows us to call God our Father. (Romans 8:15) "Abba" is an Aramaic term of endearment used by children that can be translated "daddy" or "papa."

Since we are now joint heirs with Christ, we will inherit the entire heavenly estate of our Father. Everything that belongs to God belongs to us. There are no poor people in God's kingdom.

Reflection: The law proved one could not please God by works. Jesus brought the message of grace. Our obligation is to live as a child of God and thereby demonstrate his grace to others.

July 15

Dependable Salvation

Galatians 5:2-12

Dependability. A good trait but often hard to locate. The young girl is impressed by a date that shows up on time. Employers are overjoyed when employees show up for work and carry out their responsibilities. Every parent enjoys a child who obeys the curfew and them. And a vehicle that cranks on a regular basis is always nice. So is a computer that works.

And so it is with salvation. It is comforting to know that it is certain, that God will not take it away if we sin one time, and that no one can steal it. Living life in a vain pursuit that does not deliver a reward is no fun. If the Bible says Jesus is the only way of salvation, we want to know that is the truth. Wondering if we will make it only leads to discouragement.

Dependable salvation involves some essentials. The basic tenet of Judaism required good works in addition to faith. Paul preached against such heresy. If good works could bring salvation, then Christ died in vain. Nonessentials cannot be confused with essentials. Nor could these first century believers trust in circumcision. True circumcision is allowing God to cut the evil from our hearts.

What brings acceptance from God is our confession of sin and trust in his Son's sacrifice. Nothing can be added to that. That action and belief, and it alone, leads to salvation. Good works are only the proof of the experience. Trusting anything other than the grace of God severs us from Christ. We cannot live by the law and grace. Salvation is either earned or given as a gift. Obedience to outward rules does not bring inner cleansing.

The security of our salvation is not in something we do. We could not do anything to receive it, and we cannot do anything to keep it. God keeps us by his grace. Our security is in him. While twenty first century people do not trust in circumcision, they do in such things as church membership, good works, baptism, and charitable giving.

After salvation, we travel the road to sanctification. Defined, it means set apart. Realistically, it is a life-long process of growing spiritually and becoming more like Christ. It is allowing him to mold us into his image. We must fight against anything that deters us from our spiritual path.

Reflection: Thank God for giving you salvation that is secure. Ask him to help you grow daily in your spiritual walk.

July 16
Faith is the Answer
Galatians 3:6-14

What must you do to be saved? Time has revealed various answers. Some do not bother with the question because they do not think they are lost. Atheists do not concern themselves with the answer because they do not believe in God. Some believe one can work their way to heaven. Others try meditation or some form of Eastern mysticism. The German, Martin Luther, came along and said it was simply by faith.

It was the question asked of Paul and Silas by the Philippian jailer. Arrested for advocating customs not accepted by the Romans, they were beaten and thrown in jail. Around midnight, an earthquake opened the prison doors. Assuming the prisoners had escaped, the jailer was about to kill himself. Paul witnessed his actions, told him all the prisoners were safe, and then had the jailer ask this thoughtful question.

Paul goes to great lengths in this letter to prove that faith is the only way to be saved. It has always been the only way. Abraham provides positive proof of this. Abraham lived before the law was given to Moses on Mt. Sinai. If Paul could prove God accepted him because of faith, then he could dispute the argument of the Judaizers that other things had to be added.

After God gave Abraham the promise of a son and many descendants, the Bible says that Abraham believed God and God counted it as righteousness. (Genesis 15:6) Paul's critics said circumcision then salvation. Paul taught that the reverse was true.

Because we often feel we can pull ourselves up by our own bootstraps, it is easy to believe we can save ourselves. Such is a lie from the Devil. He wants us to think we do not need God. Pride leads us to put faith in ourselves rather than God.

While Abraham provides a positive example from the Old Testament, the Law gives a negative example. Those of Paul's day could no more do what they taught than could Old Testament saints-be saved by obedience to the Law. Our sinful nature pulls us away from God, so it is impossible to perfectly obey him. To have this ability would have eliminated the need for Christ.

Reflection: Faith has always been the way to come to God. Are you taking that road?

July 17
God's Way to Freedom
Galatians 3:23-29

Because many Arab tribes trusted him, the famous British soldier and scholar, Lawrence of Arabia, participated in the Paris peace talks after World War I. Several Arab leaders came to Paris and stayed with him at the hotel. When they went to the bathroom, they were astounded to find an unlimited supply of water by a simple turn of a handle. Upon their departure, they removed the handles and packed them with their luggage.

242

They failed to understand that the handles had to be connected to free the water.

Prisons are establishments where freedoms are severely limited. Prisoners find themselves in the company of rapists, murderers, child molesters, burglars, and homosexuals. When the cell door slams shut, many of the outside world's freedoms are taken away.

The plight of humanity is similar and even more severe. Born with a sinful nature, we are prone to wander away from God instead of in his direction. While it appears we are free to do as we please, we are in fact chained by sin. We may not break the laws of society, but we break the laws of God. Humanity is a prisoner of their own making, being unable to perfectly obey the laws of God. The good news is the grace of God at Calvary.

The Law of God in the Old Testament brought bondage. We might wonder why God gave such commandments. It was a prison but also a guardian. The purpose of the Law was for conviction. When a person disobeyed a law of God, they became aware that they were sinning against their Creator. But it brought bondage. The more they tried to obey, the more they found themselves missing the mark.

God's law made people aware of what his requirements were. Paul said he would not have known it was wrong to covet unless the Law had told him. The Law was also a tutor. As people realized they could not live up to God's standards, it drove them to the grace of God.

Freedom comes in Christ. The Law demonstrated how helpless our cause was. Grace through Christ showed how much God loved us and how far he was willing to go to provide for our salvation. Through God's Spirit, we have an inward guide that moves us toward obedience.

Reflection: All efforts to please God are useless without faith. Trust Christ for freedom.

July 18
Living a God-Approved Life
Galatians 2:1-10

Like acceptance, approval is one of our core needs. We need it from our parents. Failure to feel their approval often leads to self-esteem issues.

Some children go to their grave never believing they had their approval. We like it when our employers approve of our work. We get a paycheck. Pastors enjoy being approved by their congregation.

Approval from God should be our main objective. His approval means more than anyone else's. Our eternity is at stake. His is the approval that counts. Paul sought God's approval rather than his contemporaries. Whether they approved of his ministry was of little consequence.

Paul knew he was approved because God spoke to him. The risen Lord met him on the Damascus Road. For seventeen years, he preached the gospel without human instruction. His message came directly from God. In obedience to God's command, he took the gospel to the Gentiles. Paul listened for God to speak, and then he spoke.

Though direct revelations no longer come from God, he still speaks to his children. God speaks through his Word, prayer, circumstances, and other believers. He speaks by his Spirit. That God speaks to us assures that we belong to him. Our responsibility is akin to Paul's-listen and obey.

Living in liberty assures God's approval. The law of God brought bondage, but the grace of God in Christ brought liberty. Paul's enemies tried to re-entrap the Galatians under the bondage of the law. They wanted to add to what Christ had done. Liberty and legalism are mutually exclusive.

The gospel and legalism cannot coexist. The gospel concerns grace while legalism involves ritual obedience to laws regardless of the inner motive. Jesus said that those who are truly free are the ones that he sets free. (John 8:36)

God's approval gives us confidence in our commission. Paul never doubted what God expected of him. The Light had illuminated his way. Christ's commission to his early followers has been extended to modern day Christians.

Reflection: Thank you Lord for approving of me in Christ. Help me understand that I do not have to work for your approval but that it is freely given by your grace.

July 19
Reaching Your Full Potential
Exodus 3:1-16

Self-actualized. It is the term humanistic psychologist Abraham Maslow used to describe individuals who were healthy and creative. People who were reaching their full potential in life. He chose to study these people in contrast to disturbed individuals as his contemporaries did.

The Army's slogan to "be all you can be" is God's desire for us. It was for Moses. God's people had languished in Egyptian slavery for hundreds of years. While using the Egyptians as a means of punishment for his children's disobedience, he was now ready to deliver them. Moses was the instrument chosen. God spoke through a burning bush and informed Moses of his plan. Moses was not excited. In fact, he offered several excuses as to why he was not the man. God told him he was. Moses would have settled for less than the best. We often do too. Are you reaching your full potential?

We must believe that God can use us. God could carry out his world plan, or he could use the angels. He chooses to use us. Using frail humans magnifies his power and gives glory to him. Moses either did not believe God could use him, or maybe he was just afraid. After all, it was a monumental assignment. From his lack of identity to his plea for God to send someone else, Moses' belief in his inadequacy was evident.

God can and does want to use you. God's plan is as unique as you are. While God rebukes pride, he does not want us to self-abase ourselves. After all, we were created by him, and God does not create just to create. We can feel good about ourselves because of who we are in Christ. We can do all things through Christ who strengthens us. (Philippians 4:13) No matter your background or current situation, believe God can use you.

Reach your full attention by handing God your weaknesses. Moses had to do this before he could approach Pharaoh with God's plan. Every weakness Moses mentioned, God assured him he could take care of. Weaknesses are only strengths we have not developed. God will not call you to a task he will not equip you to handle. Depend on his strength and not your own.

Reflection: Pursue God's plan for your life. Whatever God leads you to do, he will equip you in order that you might reach your full potential in his service.

July 20

Reaching Your Full Potential (Part II)

Exodus 3:1-16

Asthma is a potential stealer. Those who suffer with it find out very quickly there are some activities they cannot endure. Running, walking rapidly, playing sports can all be examples of limitations. Inhalers and medicine are often daily routines. Attacks bring a feeling of being smothered. The desire is there. The ability is not.

Moses had no medical condition that prevented him from obeying God's call. His condition was invented. Concocted because he was afraid and unsure of himself. Eventually, he reached his full potential with God's help.

Filling our mind with God's Word helps in the journey. Every excuse Moses offered was met with a Word from God. God's Word overcame his fear. We have much more of God's Word. The final revelation has come in Christ, and we have the entire New Testament to assure us of God's love and his world plan. What Moses had was only in the making as he lived it out.

It is necessary to make studying God's Word a daily activity. It is one of those habits that have merit. Let it light your path and illuminate your feet as they walk that path. Studies continue to show how many Christians neglect reading the Bible. How sad to disregard what helps us reach our full potential. Establish a daily quiet time for prayer and meditation.

Do not be afraid to pour out your feelings to God. Moses wasn't. He candidly shared with God why he thought he was not the person for the job. We can fault Moses for his excuses, but at least he was willing to express rather than repress. As he poured out his fears, God was able to help him.

God already knows what we are often afraid to articulate. Revealing our feelings is for our benefit, not God's. As we share, we feel his care and concern. Shutting down hinders our spiritual growth.

Reaching your full potential can be painful. It was for Moses. Though he finally obeyed, Pharaoh was not enthused with God's plan. Then there was the forty years of wilderness wandering. Murmuring, backbiting and complaining were on Moses' list of things to hear, probably daily. God's plan for him involved pain. But through the pain, it will amaze us how God uses us in marvelous ways.

Reflection: Are you reaching your full potential as an individual and Christian? If not, let God deal with what holds you back.

July 21

Salvation's Bottom Line
Galatians 2:11-21

Guilt. Throughout time, people have concocted different ways to deal with it. Primitive people tried to alleviate it by sacrificing humans and animals to their many gods. Their gods were angry and had to be appeased.

Modern people try other means such as psychoanalysis, counseling or other forms of therapy. Positive thinking and self-confident living are measures taken. Some use drugs, sex or alcohol to dull their senses and ease their minds. The fact remains: we cannot ignore it. There must be some logical reason for it. Christians accept the fact that God's Spirit brings this feeling or conviction when we transgress God's laws.

These verses give Paul's solution to the guilt we often feel. It comes through salvation in Christ and its ensuing forgiveness. The teaching arises out of Paul's rebuke of another great apostle-Peter. Peter freely associated with Gentiles as long as his Jewish contemporaries were not around. When they appeared, he withdrew, demonstrating a flaw of hypocrisy. Paul rebukes him for this, and in the process teaches how faith can deal with our guilt.

Faith is what justifies us in God's sight. Jesus was born into a time when many had perverted the teachings of the Old Testament. They looked to their own goodness or good works to bring acceptance with God. Their spiritual leaders enhanced the situation. Out of this situation arose the Judaizers who taught the same thing and hounded Paul's steps, trying to compromise the message of grace he taught.

Justification can be defined as "just as if we never sinned." Faith is the only way this can happen. Only forgiveness by God can cover our sins to the extent that we no longer have to feel guilty over failing God. God takes away the guilt, and gives us a new beginning in Christ. All of humanity has a heart problem that only God's grace can mend. Faith is the surgical procedure he uses to cut away the evil.

Hypocrisy will ruin our testimony. It did Peter's. Paul had to remind him of what he already knew. Salvation is not by works or obedience to ceremonial laws. His actions were influencing others thereby leading them into hypocritical actions. We must be consistent in our spiritual behavior.

Reflection: Thank God for justifying you. Remember that your actions always influence others.

July 22
The Eternal Choice
Galatians 6:14-18

Where religion is concerned there are many choices. We can take the Christian religion and choose from many denominations with slightly different ideas about church government and other ideas surrounding the Christian life. Or we can choose from various movements that are normally classified as cults or false religions by Protestant denominations.

While the range of choices may appear wide, there are truly only two choices one has. We can choose a religion that teaches one must work for salvation, or we can accept one that says it is freely given. Only one, Christianity, teaches the latter. According to Bible based Christianity, only faith in what Christ has done on Calvary leads to salvation.

In the final verses of this epistle, Paul tells his readers that he will boast in the cross. For him, it was more than a piece of wood. It was the place where humanity's sins were actually paid for. His Savior died there, and it was there that the unrighteousness of humanity was dealt with. It brought an end to the ceaseless effort of individuals to please God with their good works. Paul would claim that God made his Son who knew no sin to be sin on our behalf. Now we are righteous in him. (II Corinthians 5:21)

The cross possesses power to free us from the world's bondage. On the cross, Paul was crucified to the world and the world to him. When we accept that accomplished work, we are free from evil's rule. People who refuse this offer remain slaves to sin. Though they may be unaware of it, their life is consumed by a desire to gratify selfish and sinful desires. Turning over a new leaf is not the answer. Even better courses of action are haunted by past sin and failures. The Christian is free from the guilt of past, present and future sins. Our slates are clean. Sin is a dead issue.

The cross does for us what the flesh cannot do. Paul's critics were high on circumcision believing it was a necessary part of salvation. It was faith plus this procedure that was now of no value because of Christ. Salvation makes us a new creation. God does not remodel. He creates anew.The Bible says that people who are in Christ are new creations or creatures. (II Corinthians 5:17)

Reflection: The cross brings peace, mercy and salvation. Such is found in no other place.

July 23

The Superiority of God's Promise
Galatians 3:15-22

One Andy Griffith episode shows Barney concerned with the local bank. The guard falls asleep. Cash drawers are left open. It seemed a prime target for robbery. Failing to convince Andy and the bank president to make changes, he concocts a scheme to demonstrate the danger by dressing up as the cleaning woman. The president discovers his plan. "Stop thief" sends Barney into the bank vault with the door closed behind him. Though he beats against the door, he cannot escape.

Laws, and their enforcement, keep order in our society. Those who choose to ignore them or break them purposefully are fined or put in prison. Laws prevent chaos. While jails are a deterrent, only God can place in a person a desire to live morally upright.

Paul has taught that salvation is by faith alone, using Abraham as an example. He further taught that salvation was not through obedience to the law God gave Moses. God's covenant with Abraham was unconditional while the covenant of law made with Moses was conditional. The first was based on God's faithfulness to the people while the second was based on the people's faithfulness to God.

The covenant of promise God made to Abraham was superior because it was confirmed by God. It was irrevocable and unchangeable. God's covenant with Abraham involved a son of promise through whom many descendants would come-physical and spiritual. God accepted Abraham because of his faith. God confirmed the covenant through a ceremony common in the Near East. Though normally all participants passed through the animals, in this case only God passed through.

God's promise was superior because it was Christ centered. Paul states that the seed God speaks of does not refer to many seeds in the plural but to one Seed in the singular-Christ. The covenant made with Abraham was directly related to the New Covenant authored in Jesus Christ. Though the law was given in the intermediate time, it did not nullify the promise given to Abraham. Whether before or after Abraham, salvation has always come through faith.

Reflection: Rather than beating against the wall of your own self effort, trust Christ for what you need in life.

July 24
Walking By the Spirit
Galatians 5:16-25

In spite of the many forms of exercise available, doctors still agree that walking is probably the most effective. It involves low impact but at the same time increases the heart rate. Exercising several times each week leads to better health. We can join exercise facilities, purchase our own exercise equipment or just take a good brisk walk.

Walking by the Spirit is also good exercise. In fact, it is more advantageous than physical exertion. Sanctification is a process that each believer is involved in. We often shy away from the word, but it simply means we are growing more like Christ each day. The course begins at salvation, and is a lifelong journey.

Walking by the Spirit is commanded by God. Many things in life are optional. For the Christian, this is not. Failure to walk by the Spirit results in walking by the flesh. Flesh is our learned ways of acting and thinking left over from our life before Christ. Walking by the Spirit involves relying on God's Spirit as our inward guide.

The book of Galatians is a contrast between living by the law and living by grace. One involves works and ends in futility. The other brings success in the Christian life. God's Spirit enables us to live a holy and acceptable life before God. Many in Galatia were trying to meet God's standards in their own strength.

The word for "walk" refers to continuous and regular action. The pattern of our life is walking by the Spirit. It implies progress. God will not drag us along in this process. He wants the initiative to come from us as we rely on him for the power to do it. When we saturate our thoughts with godly things, the appeal of the flesh will lose power over us.

Walking by the Spirit will bring conflict. Paul was a great man of faith, but even he faced conflict. The conflict was between the flesh and the Spirit. Flesh living leads to many actions we do not intend to do, but we do them anyway because we are being led by the wrong motive. Paul described this battle in Romans when he said he did not do the good he wanted. (7:15) The presence of this conflict is proof of our kingdom citizenship.

Reflection: Many battles are not won in war. In our spiritual war, we are assured of victory. Thank God for victory over fleshly living.

July 25
What Does God Expect of Us?
Luke 16:1-13; 19:11-27

Expectations are a normal part of life. Parents have them for their children. Responsibility, obedience, doing their best in school, and respect are usually on the list. Teachers have them for their students. Timeliness, doing homework, obedience, and staying awake in class normally top the agenda. And employers have some of the same for employees.

God also has expectations. One area is stewardship, and each of these parables of Jesus deal with this area. The first is the story of the rich man who calls in his manager and accuses him of squandering his wealth. Knowing that his dismissal was inevitable, he began making plans for his survival. He assured mercy from the debtors by lowering the amount they owed his master. When his master uncovered his actions, he praised him for his shrewdness.

The second story concerns a man of noble birth traveling to a far country to be appointed king. Before leaving, he entrusted minas to his slaves to do business with. Upon his return, he called the slaves to account. Two had invested well, but the third had hidden his mina in a handkerchief.

Rather than just money and material possessions, all of life is a stewardship from God. Everything that you have belongs to God and has only come to you because of his grace and mercy. He gave you the energy, resources, time and ability to get it, but it belongs to him. God created everything, and all things are under his governing authority. He expects us to realize his ownership so we will use wisely what he has entrusted to us. One day we will give an account of how we have handled what he gave us.

God expects us to be ready to meet him as we use our resources. This happens when we use our assets shrewdly and decisively. Forethought and industriousness with our possessions is expected by God. Make the most of what God has given you.

We must also remember that we cannot serve two masters. While our resources come from God and are to be used in his service, we cannot worship them. We reverence the one who gave them.

Reflection: God will reward us when we use wisely what he gives us. Thank God for your time, talents and resources. Then use them in a way that honors him.

July 26
What is a Secure Investment?
Luke 12:13-21

Experience and history have proven that no investment is secure. Disasters can take them. Robbers can loot them. Even the FDIC places a limit on how much of your investment they will guarantee. Some bonds may be guaranteed by the government, but what if they enact a new policy?

If not careful, we can place too much confidence in things that are not trustworthy. The rich young fool did that. As usual, a crowd surrounded Jesus. One man works his way to the front, hoping Jesus would settle a complaint. His brother would not divide the inheritance with him. After questioning why the man came to him, Jesus tells a story to illustrate the devastating effects of greed.

A farmer's land produced a good crop, so bountiful in fact that he ran out of room to store the yield. He devised a plan. He would tear down his existing barns and build bigger ones. Then he would take life easy. But God appeared and told him he would die that very night. Who would enjoy then what he had accumulated?

Christians must have a different set of priorities. For the rich fool, life was about him. The ground had been good to him. Bigger was better. A life of ease was a worthy goal. While we are required to be good managers of what God gives, serving him must be our supreme priority. We accomplish this by using the resources he gives us.

Our attitude about wealth must be different. Wealth is measured in more than money and possessions. Security is not measured in these things, and greed is the poison of life. Money is not the root of evil, but love of it is. A wrong attitude about wealth motivates a person to use whatever means are necessary to get rich. Jesus said it was easier for a camel to pass through the eye of a needle than for a rich person to enter heaven. (Matthew 19:24)

Security is found in God not our resources. Nor can we serve both at the same time. We will love one and hate the other. Living in an economy that measures wealth by money and resources creates a challenge for the believer. Our security is in our relationship with Christ.

Reflection: Segregation that supposes our religious and business life are separate matters is sinful. Our religious beliefs should mold our attitude about possessions and money.

July 27

What Motivates You?

Galatians 6:11-13

What motivates you to get up and go to work? Money for bills, a desire to get rich, a healthy work ethic, Biblical mandates, you feel better when you exercise. Or coming to church. What motivates you to make that commitment? Entrance into heaven, Mom and Dad make you, business contacts, fellowship, guilt, family tradition.

Paul's arch enemies were giving one message to the Galatians while Paul was giving another. The Galatians had to decide between the two. Did works have something to do with their salvation, or was it all of grace? The motives of the Judaizers were impure and unacceptable while Paul's was honorable.

Humility should motivate our service to God. The Judaizers were no different than the religious leaders Jesus dealt with. They were motivated by selfish pride. A good showing was necessary. Gentiles needed to be circumcised. They depended on their good works, and they wanted others to witness how righteous they were. What others thought mattered immensely to them. Making a good impression was important.

Jesus warned against insincere prayers and actions. His parable of the Pharisee and tax collector was a rich rebuke against those who tried to place God under obligation to save them.

Humility must drive what we do for God. Otherwise he takes no pleasure in it. No church ritual can replace serving God out of a sense of appreciation for our salvation. All that is required for salvation is our faith in God. Nothing more, nothing less.

Bravery should motivate us to serve God. It took this trait for Paul to keep going in spite of severe opposition. Christianity is not for cowards. To be identified as a Christian in the first century destined one for persecution. Nero blamed them for burning Rome and persecuted them mercilessly. Paul refers to his enemies as cowards because they feared persecution.

Serving Christ involves sincerity. This goes hand in hand with humility. Hypocrisy is a constant temptation when doing God's work. We must remember that God sees the inner person.

Reflection: Thank God for the wonderful privilege of serving him. Serve him with humility and sincerity.

July 28

What's So Urgent About Salvation?
Luke 14:15-24; 16:19-31

I once had the unfortunate privilege to witness a terrible accident. One car was traveling down a major highway while another was crossing that same highway from a secondary road. The latter did not see the stop sign. What resulted was a perfectly timed crash that sent a young lady to the hospital with serious injuries. Fortunately, she recovered.

The urgent and the necessary. How easy to get the two confused. Of the first, salvation is the most urgent need of humanity. It was the Sabbath. Jesus was at the home of a prominent religious leader. While there, he told the parable of the Great Banquet. A man hosted a dinner. He sent his servants to tell the invited guests that everything was ready. Excuses were all the servant garnered. Furious, the master instructed the servant to go into the hedges and highways and invite everyone he could find.

The other story is more familiar. It is the parable of the rich man and Lazarus the beggar. The rich man threw crumbs to Lazarus, who was so miserable he could not even fend off the dogs that licked his sores. But both of them succumbed to the inevitable-death. The rich man entered hell while Lazarus was received into Abraham's bosom.

God's invitation to salvation must be accepted. It is not enough to know it is offered. Those who made excuses for not attending the banquet represent those who refuse God's offer of salvation. The rich man assumed his family heritage was enough. Or maybe his wealth would impress God. Christian families are a good heritage, and rearing children in the church is admirable. Neither, however, assures salvation.

Salvation is urgent because the benefits begin on earth. Jesus offers abundant life now. Forgiveness of our sins begins immediately. Salvation is a process that begins with the initial decision to follow Christ, but it continues until we reach eternity. Earth prepares us for heaven.

The urgency is seen in the master sending the servant to tell the guests that the banquet was ready. The time to respond is when God's Spirit convicts of sin. Believers are one of the main instruments God works through. We must carry the message to others.

Reflection: Have you accepted God's invitation to believe? If not, ask him now to forgive your sins.

July 29

The Believer's Position in Christ
Ephesians 1:3-6

Positions in life vary. From the floor sweeper to the CEO who runs the entire factory. From the cafeteria worker preparing the food to the principal who watches over the entire school. Often unsatisfied, we move from position to position searching for identity, security and happiness.

Life should be different for the believer. Chapter one encompasses God's entire plan for humanity, showing the full scope. In the past there was election. In the present, redemption. In the future, inheritance.

We reach our position through election. Election and what it truly means has been hotly debated by Christians. The Bible shows three types of election-national, vocational and salvific. Election to salvation is the controversial of the three. That the Bible teaches election is not the point of debate. How and when that election takes place is the sticking point. Whether it is solely of God or cooperation between him and humans, it is still the process through which we reach our standing of being saved.

One element must be stressed, however. God does not elect because of good he sees in us. That would constitute salvation based on works which the Bible does not teach. Humanity is enslaved by sin. Election then is solely because of his grace and desire to forgive our sin. Though we trust Christ in time, Paul says that our election took place before the foundation of the world. Election is a specific choice of individuals or a plan, not simply foreknowing that someone will believe.

The purpose of our standing is holiness. God had a purpose in choosing. Believers cannot and should not live careless lifestyles. At salvation, we are given a new nature. Our actions from then on should mimic those of Christ.

God's motive in electing us was love. Agape' love. Though we had miserably failed him, he chose to provide a solution for our madness-a perfect sacrifice.

After trusting Christ, he makes us his sons and daughters. We are adopted into the family of God and nothing or no one can ever remove us. From this position, we await the future glory that will be ours in eternity.

Reflection: Thank God that his awesome love motivated him to chose you as his child.

July 30
Walk in Unity
Ephesians 4:1-6

On April 4, 1949, the foreign ministers of the United States, Britain, France and nine other countries signed a compact that created NATO-North Atlantic Treaty Organization. The treaty declared, "The parties agree that an armed attack against one…shall be considered an armed attack against all." It was a treaty that brought together millions of people in a brilliant display of unity.

In many places, God's Word exhorts believers to be unified. It will not automatically happen though it should because of our common denominator. But it can happen with a little work and God's guidance.

We must walk worthy of our calling. The moment we receive Christ as Savior, we become citizens of his Kingdom. Along with that privilege come responsibilities and obligations. Our obligation is to act like the person we now are. This is what it means to walk worthy of our calling.

Paul considered himself a prisoner of the Lord, and we should as well. There were times when he was a literal prisoner, but at all times he was a spiritual convict. Since meeting the risen Lord on the Damascus Road, his entire being was in chains. His life was consumed with obedience to God's call for him to take the message of salvation to the heathens. Our relationship with Christ must be the most important thing in our life. We have been called by the Divine Sovereign of the universe. He deserves no less from us.

Unity will result when we are selfless instead of selfish. A selfless life is a humble life. Bernard of Clairvaux said of this trait that it is the "virtue by which a man becomes conscious of his own unworthiness." It is the most fundamental Christian virtue. Humility puts the rights of others before our own interests.

Gentleness and patience will follow humility closely. We will also bear with one another. If another Christian hurts us, we should endure the wrong and suffer the slight to demonstrate unity to an ungodly world.

Unity must be pursued. With a little effort Christians can demonstrate this instead of division. We worship the same Savior and have the same interests. We are one Body.

Reflection: Make it your priority to live in unity with your fellow brothers and sisters in Christ.

July 31
Handling Tension in the Home
Ephesians 5:22-32

Factors abound that lead to tension in our homes. Dual-income describes most families. A stay-at-home Mom is almost extinct. Latch key kid is a term used to describe thousands of children who come home after school to empty homes. Half of all marriages end in divorce, and of those who remarry, half will experience a second divorce. Abuse of children and spouses is also prevalent in the American home.

Believers have the rare opportunity to demonstrate what a true family looks like. The world should not get their idea of family from television or the theatre. Thomas Jefferson in a letter to Francis Willis in 1790 said, "The happiest moments of my life have been the few which I have passed at home in the bosom of my family."

Tension in the home can be countered with submission from all parties- Mom, Dad and children. Because Christians have been victimized by worldly standards, the mandates of God often seem out of date. Hardly the case. God has assigned the husband headship in the home. Of course, when there is no father in the home, that role obviously passes to the mother.

The wife is to submit to her husband. Not as to a dictator, but lovingly as to one who is to love her as Christ loved the Church-enough to die for it. This type of submission is voluntary and not the same as children give to parents. The wife is his equal, and God has given him the responsibility to care, provide and protect her.

Men and women who enter a marriage submitted to God will have no trouble fulfilling these roles.Mutual submission is as unto the Lord. The husband represents the functional head of the home as Christ is head of the Church. The wife submits to her husband as she does to Christ. Children in turn submit to their parents because of their God given role.

Tension in the home is kept in check when there is mutual love. The husband who loves his wife will never demand anything that would be difficult for her to submit to. Nor will the wife require anything of the husband that would challenge his voluntary submission. Neither will the parents provoke their children to wrath by unrealistic demands.

Reflection: Pray that God would enable your home to be a living testimony of a godly family.

August

August 1
Dispelling the Darkness
Ephesians 5:8-14

Nyctophobia. A fear of darkness. Many have it. Young children normally fear going into dark rooms by themselves. A night light usually provides the solution. Caverns provide examples of pure darkness. At some point in the tour, the guide will turn off the lights. Living in such total darkness for a time would eventually lead to blindness. Genesis says the beginning of time before creation was a time of darkness. (Genesis 1:2)

The most detrimental darkness is spiritual. John wrote that God was light and had no darkness in him. If we claim fellowship with him but walk in the darkness, we lie and do not live by the truth. (I John 1:5-6) How do we dispel this darkness?

We must remember our past condition. Paul reminds his readers that darkness was a former state for them. Things that characterized their previous life were sexual immorality, impurity, greed, filthiness, obscenity, foolish talk and coarse joking.

If we have trusted Christ as our Savior, we can no longer live as those who have not. We dispel the darkness through this act of faith. We continue to dispel it by living in spiritual light. While we can use our past actions in our testimony to show others how God has changed us, we should not dwell on our past condition.

The darkness is dispelled by dwelling on our present condition. In Christ, we are new creations. The old is gone, and the new has arrived. We have died to our old ways of living. Believers are lights in the world that shine forth the grace of God. You are a child of the light. Are you living up to your name?

As children of light, we live with a spirit of thanksgiving. God has blessed us immensely, and we have much to praise him for. Goodness, righteousness and truth will characterize our speech and actions. These traits produce spiritual fruit that cannot be manufactured apart from Christ. We are good in our nature and effectiveness. We do not participate in deeds of darkness but expose them. Let others see the light of Christ in you.

Reflection: Horatius Boner wrote; "I looked to Jesus, and I found/ In Him, my star, my sun;/ And in that light of life I'll walk,/ Till traveling days are done."

August 2

God's Word for the Home

I Peter 3:7

Speaking of Plato, Eugene Debs, the great socialist, said, "Plato was right in his fancy that man and woman are merely halves of humanity, each requiring the qualities of the other in order to attain the highest character. Shakespeare understood it when he made his noblest women strong as men and his best men tender as women."

As Paul does, Peter also reminds women of their responsibility in the home. It is to recognize the headship role God has given the man. Beyond that, they are to lovingly submit to their husbands.

But instruction is also needed for the husband. Sadly, many modern day families experience an absent father. Additionally, child support is often nonexistent making family life even more difficult for those they left behind. Husbands, wives and children all play a part in healthy families.

The marriage union should be viewed and entered into as a permanent situation. While death, unfaithfulness and an unbelieving spouse who leaves breaks the union, God designed marriage to be until death. Two people leave their parents and enter into a permanent relationship with themselves and no other.

Peter's counsel to husbands was very progressive for his day. Women had little if any rights and men were often dictators of the home. The word "likewise" refers to mutual responsibilities in the home. The wife was not to carry all the weight.

Husbands were to keep living with their wives. Here is the idea of permanency. When divorce affects almost half of all marriages, we need to hear this exhortation. Couples should not enter the marriage union with the idea that they can divorce if things get unpleasant. Marriage is to endure through the good and bad times. Nor is living together before marriage an acceptable way to discover compatibility.

Living together in this way requires understanding or consideration. Permanency does not result from romantic feelings or speaking the right words. Clear thinking, good judgment and understanding are necessary. Husbands need to use their minds to discover how best to care for their wives. He must respect and love her.

Reflection: What can you do to make your marriage healthier?

August 3

A Lesson in Humility

I Corinthians 4:6-13

Humility is a difficult virtue to develop. In fact, it is often learned only in the school of hard knocks. It is humanity's tendency to think more highly of themselves than they should. Pride lurks just outside our doors and with it many consequences. It seems to go against our grain to be humble, yet the Bible instructs us in many places that we need this trait.

John the Baptist showed humility. Being the forerunner of Christ, he had a very important responsibility. Yet when Jesus began his ministry and some of John's disciples followed him, he responded with humility. He knew Jesus was to increase while he decreased in importance. (John 3:30)

Peter demonstrated it when Jesus helped him catch a net full of fish when his attempt had previously failed. He told Jesus to leave him because he was a sinful man. (Luke 5:8) The greatest example is Jesus himself. The Bible says that he humbled himself. (Philippians 2:8)

The Corinthians had not learned humility, so Paul rebukes them. Factionalism in their church led to conceit. Some claimed to follow Paul. Others followed Peter and Apollos. They were proud of their leaders and their wisdom. They were arrogant and boastful.

Arrogance and boasting is not for the believer. All we have flows from God, even the breath you are breathing right now. He provides your food, shelter and clothing. All the blessings in your life come from him. Freedom of worship is his gift. Everything we have is on loan from God, interest free.

More importantly, our salvation comes from God. Realizing that God has forgiven the debt we owed him should lead to humility. You could not get to God using your own resources. It took the perfect sacrifice of Christ. You are what you are only because of God's mercy.

The early apostles were good examples of humility. In the world's eyes, they were worthless and peddled worthless ideas. Of all people, they were last in line. They deserved only death for spreading the gospel message. In the eyes of many, they were the scum of the earth. But Paul knew his position in life as one of those apostles.

Reflection: Pride will lead to spiritual defeat, but God exalts those who recognize who they are and remain humble.

August 4

It's Later Than You Think
I Peter 4:7-11

Have you ever been so engrossed in something that you completely lost track of time? Then when you were late for a meeting or dinner and questioned about it, you said, "I lost track of time." The urgent or enjoyable can cause us to lose thought of time.

First century believers seemed to think that Jesus would return in their lifetime. In every generation since then, many Christians have thought the same thing. That Christ has not appeared does not negate the importance of the event nor its certainty. Remember, God operates outside of time, and is not confined by it. With him, one day is as a thousand years.

We live in a state of tension. The already not yet. Christ has already appeared the first time but not the second. His kingdom came in some form with his first appearance, but the fullness of his kingdom is yet to arrive. Something wonderful has already taken place but the best is yet to come.

Realizing the urgency of the time and the certainty of his coming should lead us to a greater level of commitment. Commitment to him personally and to the work he has assigned. Preparation for eternity must be made now. Not knowing the time should not decrease our expediency.

266

In this late hour, we need to pray. Don't neglect your lifeline to God. Through prayer, he makes us aware of opportunities for service. Through prayer, he reveals things in our life that do not fit who we are. We then hurriedly make the necessary changes.

Fervency in love is also important. Serve others in love. Love as Christ did and does. A hurting world needs loving hands to touch it. It will cover a multitude of sins. It is the pulse of our life that will stretch and strain to touch others. They will know us because of our love.

Hospitality should characterize our behavior. Peter is not speaking of social entertainment but ministering to strangers. It also entails taking care of those doing God's work in full time status.

Jesus told many parables that concerned stewardship while we await his return. Peter enforces this message. Use your gifts and talents wisely and faithfully while you wait for Christ.

Reflection: The return of Christ is certain and near. Work diligently in his service as you await his coming.

August 5

Being Christian in a Non Christian World

I Peter 4:12-16

Some things are inevitable. The loss of teeth is one. For a child, it is a certainty. For aging adults, it is a strong possibility. Any parent expects that at a certain age a loose tooth will appear. Weeds in a garden are inevitable. No matter how meticulously the soil has been prepared, weeds and grass will appear. When autumn comes, it is a natural occurrence for leaves to fall.

There are also things that are normal for Christians living in a non Christian world. Testing is one. Peter says we should not be surprised when trials come our way. After all, our world is dominated by evil. Nevertheless, we should still praise, honor and obey God. We find favor with God when we patiently endure. Suffering will actually bring us happiness.

The believers that Peter wrote to were familiar with persecution, and it would soon become more severe. Under Nero's rule, many were burned at the stake. They were blamed for the great fire of Rome. He covered some in pitch, set them on fire, and used them as torches in his garden. Still others were placed in animal skins and attacked by wild animals.

Our suffering identifies us with Christ. Peter's teaching on this subject echoes Jesus' eighth beatitude where he teaches that those persecuted in his name will be happy. They will inherit the kingdom of heaven. (Matthew 5:10)

Rejoicing over persecution seems illogical. Suffering for our faith places us in good company, for Jesus suffered for his. When we suffer for our faith, it enables us to enter more fully into the experience of our Lord. We become partners with him as we go through a small part of what he endured. God assures us that he is present with us as we go through our trials.

The suffering we endure results from our attempt to follow Christ, not for wrongdoing. Wickedness should never be the cause of our suffering. Christians must set a godly example in behavior. In fact, we must avoid all appearances of evil.

Our suffering will glorify God. The spotlight will be focused on him as the reason for our willingness to suffer. This in turn gives us opportunity to witness about our faith.

Reflection: Christ suffered immensely for you. Will you be willing to suffer for him in return?

August 6

Elements of Redemption

Ephesians 1:6-10

I remember when I was young that Greenback stamps were given at the grocery store where my Mom shopped. A certain amount was given based on the amount spent. These in turn could be redeemed to purchase all types of items at the local Greenback Store.

During the New Testament period, the Roman Empire hosted as many as six million slaves. Buying and selling was a major business. Sometime the slave was a friend or loved one. If a person had the means, they could redeem them from slavery.

Redemption is the central theme of Scripture. From a theological standpoint, it speaks of the sinner's vindication, justification and declared righteousness before and by God. It is through this means that God adopts us into his family. It is the process by which we are reconciled to God through Jesus Christ. God redeems us from spiritual slavery. These and many other biblical verses make it clear that Christ is our Redeemer.

In the Old Testament is found the picture of the *goel* or kinsman redeemer. A person fulfilling this role had to meet three requirements. They had to be related to the one needing redemption, be able to pay the price and be willing to pay the price. Boaz did this for Ruth in that beautiful Old Testament story. Jesus fulfilled this role for us.

The redeemed are those who accept the grace of God. We move from being sinners to saints. Since we were dead in our trespasses and sins, we needed deliverance.

Christ's blood on Calvary was the price paid for our redemption. He could pay this price because he was the sinless Son of God. That he fulfilled the entire plan demonstrates his willingness to die for our sins. He was our substitute. All we must do is accept what he has done.

When Christ redeems us, results will emerge. They are forgiveness, wisdom and insight. Forgiveness is immediate upon our asking. Wisdom and insight take longer and depend on our efforts and desire to have them. God will give us the wisdom to live for him and insight into his working in our life. We must simply search for both.

Reflection: A great price has been paid for your redemption. Have you accepted the offer of God?

August 7

Build for Rewards

I Corinthians 3:10-17

Behavioral psychologists believe that rewards and punishment determine our behavior. There is a great deal of truth to this. When people break the laws of society, they are punished through a fine or jail time. The goal is to prevent the repeat of criminal behavior. Child rearing follows the same philosophy.

Before psychology made this seemingly great discovery, God's Word had already taught it. Scripture teaches that God will reward us now and in eternity for doing as he commands. When we willfully disobey him, he disciplines and punishes us. The discipline, however, has a teaching purpose. To show us the benefits of walking the narrow path of obedience.

One of Paul's greatest motivations was his belief that God would reward him for his efforts. He deeply appreciated the fact that God had saved him, and he worked diligently for God. He hoped one day to hear him say, "Well done good and faithful servant."

Believers are master builders. Paul was a contractor and architect. He built the church at Corinth. He organized many churches on his missionary journeys. It was what God had gifted him to do. Foundations are important in building, and Paul was an expert in erecting solid foundations. The churches he began were given sound doctrine. He built where and when God told him to.

Paul began many foundations and others would come and add to his work. We still work that same way. Some sow, others water and still others reap. As we distribute God's Word, we lay a foundation. When we teach and preach the gospel, we build. God's work done in his time and at his initiative will result in rewards. Who gets the credit is not important.

The foundation we build on is Christ and his work at Calvary. Our message is that people are sinful and in need of a Savior. We needed a Substitute. Jesus was that. Following him in faith leads to forgiveness and eternal life. Any other foundation will crumble. We build through faithfulness and obedience and with the right motives.

Reflection: Samuel Johnson once said, "When a man knows he is to be hanged in a fortnight, it concentrates his mind wonderfully." The time is short. Build quickly.

August 8
Characteristics of the New Life
Ephesians 4:25-32

What is it about new clothes that make us feel better about ourselves? I have never understood this mentality, but it must be true. We get a new job and buy new clothes. We get invited to the prom and buy a new dress. We join a social club and buy new clothes. Easter rolls around, and we buy new church clothes. Clothing does make a statement about what we think of ourselves. It describes our inner belief system.

Likewise, when a person trusts Christ as their Savior, they get new clothes. (So buying new clothes for new occasions must be biblical?) God throws away our old nature and gives us a new one. We may look the same on the outside, but we are radically different on the inside. Because of the inner change, there will be some outward alterations. We are new creations.

One outward behavior will be truth. We will speak it and live it. Liars do not inherit the kingdom of God. Believers are not characterized by this trait. Telling a single lie normally leads to telling another to cover that one up. A person can become a habitual liar that no one believes.

Even though lying has detrimental effects, it seems to characterize our society. Unfaithful spouses do it. So do many of our politicians. Occasionally, we hear of church leaders doing it. And what about the test you cheated on or the tax return you falsified. Or the promises we do not fulfill. Lying is incompatible with our new nature. Honesty is still the best policy.

We must clothe ourselves with righteous anger only. It is often taught that all anger is sin. If so, Jesus sinned, but we know that statement is false. Most anger is sin, but anger over sin is not sin. Jesus was the sinless Son of God, yet he got angry when he saw the merchants in the Temple cheating people. Paul says to be angry and sin not. Anger is a natural human emotion like others we have. It is what we do with it and what we are angry over that determines whether or not it is sinful.

Sharing identifies the believer. We work at honest endeavors, and then use our resources to help others who have needs. We should also speak wholesome words. Vulgarity, dirty jokes, cursing, and gossiping should not be a part of our speech.

Reflection: Put on the new clothes God gives in Christ. Be tender hearted and forgiving.

August 9
Discipline in the Church
I Corinthians 5:1-13

Church discipline is a touchy subject. While practiced by the Roman Catholic Church throughout much of Christian history and by emerging Protestant denominations in their infancy, it is rarely exercised by churches today, at least with any consistency. We fear hurt feelings and loss of membership. We worry over diminishing tithes and offerings.

Rules are important in society and families. They are important in churches as well. Without rules and laws, society would melt into chaos. Without rules and discipline families will dissolve into disarray. The same will occur in churches when willful sinful behavior is tolerated.

The church at Corinth was tolerating blatant sexual immorality in their membership but was turning their heads as if it did not exist. A man was living with his stepmother. Paul rebukes them for tolerating such behavior and not reacting.

There is a need for church discipline carried out in love. When believers choose to involve themselves in open and unrepentant sin, the church must confront them. Overlooking it because of who they are or fear of hurt feelings does not justify our lack of interest. Sin in the church is like an infection. It can spread. Just as we should not tolerate sin in our individual lives, neither should we overlook it in our churches.

Alexander Pope wrote; "Vice is a monster of so frightful mien,/ As to be hated needs but to be seen;/ Yet seen too oft, familiar with her face,/ We first endure, then pity, then embrace."

The method of discipline is removal from the church. This is not immediate but the end result when the sinner is unrepentant. Nor is this done to the person who sins occasionally. If so, churches would be empty. It is reserved for the one who continues to sin with no remorse. Jesus gives the pattern. Approach the unrepentant individually. If he does not listen, take several people with you. If still unrepentant, bring the person before the church. If they still do not repent, remove them. (Matthew 18:15-17)

Church discipline must be exercised with love. Our motive is not to destroy but to restore. Knowing that sin is like leaven and can infect the entire church, it is necessary to address it.

Reflection: God help me to be an example in my church.

August 10

Filled With the Spirit

Ephesians 5:18-21

Anyone who has ever witnessed a puppet show understands the concept of filling. A puppet is a lifeless piece of cloth, rubber and hair. Left on its own, it would do nothing but lie in a box. However, when a human hand enters the cloth, it comes to life and can even speak.

Such is the portrait of humanity. Apart from Christ, we are lifeless, good only for lying around and wondering what life is really about. But when the Spirit of God comes, he fills us with vigor and purpose. Paul contrasts being drunk with wine and being filled with the Spirit.

God's Spirit came upon Old Testament figures to empower for a particular job, but at Pentecost the Spirit came in fullness of power to indwell all believers. We receive God's Spirit when trusting Christ as our Savior. But possessing and being filled are two different matters. When we avoid the second, we live as secondary citizens in God's kingdom.

To be filled with the Spirit does not entail a second blessing subsequent to salvation. Nor is it characterized by any particular sign. It has nothing to do with stoically trying to fulfill God's commands. It is not equivalent with baptism of the Spirit for this happens at salvation. Being filled with the Spirit can and should happen continuously in a believer's life. It happens when we repeatedly turn our lives over to him on a daily basis, allowing God to form us into the image of his Son. It is not something we do but what God does in us.

The Greek word for "be filled" carries several connotations. Wind filing a sail, permeation and total control all describe the work of God's Spirit in the believer's life. Failing to let God do this leads to retardation-failure to measure up to all God wants for us. Being filled detaches us from the desires, standards, objectives and fears of the world system. We do not have to pray about being filled because we already know it is God's will.

When filled, we will sing God's praises. Not necessarily in song but by demonstrating his love to others. We will thank God for all he has done and will do for us. Total submission of our life to God's desire will be our goal.

Reflection: Ask God to help you live a Spirit filled life so you can enjoy the abundance of Christianity.

August 11

The Christian and Alcohol

Ephesians 5:18a

Alcohol drives our society in many ways. From alcohol producers paying millions for advertisements to certain sports where drinking it is common. From holiday parties that do not seem complete without it to high society functions that regularly serve it. Drunk drivers kill scores of people each year and often suffer little consequence for their actions.

Alcohol makes a regular appearance in God's Word and is used for good and evil purposes. While we cannot say the Bible teaches total abstinence, it does provide a host of warnings about drunkenness. Drink offerings often accompanied Old Testament sacrifices. Paul told Timothy to use a little wine for his stomach, and the Good Samaritan used wine for the wounds of the beaten man.

People drink for various reasons. Peer pressure. Their lives are filled with problems, and the effects of alcohol help them cope. Some drink to dull a particular pain in their body. For others, it is a part of making social contacts. For the Ephesians and most other pagan cultures, alcohol was associated with idolatrous rites that accompanied their temple worship.

It is important to understand the nature of biblical alcohol. There are several kinds of wine mentioned. One is normally translated strong drink because of the high alcoholic content. The next was new wine. It was sweet and would ferment quickly, so it was often mixed with water. The third type was grape juice boiled until it became heavy syrup. This type was suitable for storage and would not ferment. Even when mixed with water later for drinking, the alcoholic content was very low.

The early church probably used this same procedure of mixing water with wine to dilute its alcoholic content. In fact, the content was probably well below what a drink must contain now to be considered an alcoholic beverage. To get drunk with the type of wine Paul refers to would require consuming a very large amount.

The nature of most biblical wine was very different than modern day alcohol. Even the more civilized pagans of Paul's day would classify the type of drinking that happens today as barbaric and irresponsible.

Reflection: God, help me to remember that my body is a temple of your Holy Spirit. Encourage me to keep it clean.

August 12

The Christian and Alcohol

Ephesians 5:18a

Robert Stein, writing in *Christianity Today*, says that the ancient Greeks, when getting ready to drink unboiled, unmixed and therefore highly alcoholic wine, would dilute it with water as much as twenty to one. While some instances in the Bible demonstrate unbridled use of alcohol, we cannot randomly use its presence in Scripture to justify its use by the believer.

In the first century, drinking wine was almost a necessity. The quality of water was low, making it dangerous and even deadly to consume. Good water either did not exist or was in short supply. Wine was the safest drink, and it was also useful for antiseptic purposes. The wine actually purified the water.

The same is not true today. Our water is good, and there are many other drinks to choose from. We also have good medicine which makes using alcohol for medicinal purposes unnecessary. While believers are not to flaunt our abstinence in a self-righteous manner, we abstain out of respect for our bodies which are temples of God's Spirit.

A question remains. Is there ever a need for alcohol in the Christian's life? In a word, no. Believers differ on this answer. Some have no objections to drinking in moderation and under the right circumstances. Others believe total abstinence is the preferred way. In the Old Testament, the high priests were commanded to refrain from strong drink. The same standard applied to the rulers of Israel. One taking the Nazarite vow obeyed the same guideline.

Christians are a separated people. As such, it seems best for us to avoid all appearances of uncleanness in our practice. Alcohol clouds the mind, and we need clear thinking to do God's business.

There are numerous dangers associated with alcohol. It is habit forming. Social drinking can lead to alcoholism. God is the master of our body. It can destroy mentally, physically and socially. Our drinking can offend other believers. The Bible teaches that we are not to put a stumbling block before another Christian. Finally, it can harm our testimony. When unbelievers see believers drinking, we lose the power of our witness.

Reflection: Through prayer and meditation, ask God to help you avoid the temptation of alcohol.

August 13

A Unified Body

I Corinthians 3:18-23

The created order gives many examples of unity. Day and night come with regularity. Tides rise and fall. Seasons come and go. In spring, trees and flowers begin to bud and the grass grows. In fall, the leaves turn and fall from the trees. Flowers and grass die. Winter brings cold temperatures.

Unity is God ordered in nature. God said to Noah following the flood that as long as the earth endured the seasons would change with regularity. Day and night would never cease. (Genesis 8:22)

Life is simpler when unity exists. When absent, disruption and division occur. A lack of unity in the natural realm would lead to many problems on earth. Even the absence of life. Unity is also important in God's churches. But there are things that must happen for it to occur.

Believers must have a proper view of who they are. Paul says if we think we are wise in this world, we need to become fools so we will then be truly wise. God's wisdom and that of the world are totally different.

The cross is a prime example. Worldly inhabitants would never have imagined it as a solution for man's sinfulness.

Sometimes we are just too impressed with ourselves. Self esteem is not thinking so highly of ourselves that we bump into pride, but it is also thinking as much of ourselves as God does. Unity in the church will never come until we understand that wisdom comes from God and not us. Spiritual wisdom cannot be discerned apart from an encounter with God. This comes primarily from his Word and guidance by his Spirit. Neglecting God's Word opens other avenues for wisdom to come through, which are seldom trustworthy.

We need a proper view of others to have unity. There were factions at Corinth. Some followed Paul, others Peter and still others Apollos. All three were on the same team. The head of the church is Christ. Following anyone else will lead to disruption.

As a church, we have all we need to do God's work. Paul says everything is ours. Christians are joint heirs with Christ. He will give us whatever we need to do his work.

Reflection: Make it your goal to promote unity in your church.

August 14
Comparing the Old and New
Ephesians 4:17-24

One Andy Griffith episode hosts Ernest Tee Bass interrupting a high-class social affair. He was an infamous mountain man who usually only came to town to throw rocks at windows when he was upset over something. On this occasion, he wanted to meet a girl. Andy decides to clean him up and secretly reintroduce him to high society. When Barney arrives to pick up the duo, he initially does not even recognize Ernest Tee. He could not see the old for the new.

A radical transformation takes place when we trust Christ as our Savior. The Bible proclaims that we are buried with him in baptism and raised with him in newness of life. (Romans 6:4) We must walk in this newness of life daily. Our stride is radically changed.

Having been transformed, the believer must not walk as they once did. Martin Lloyd-Jones said, "Our conduct should always be to us something which is inevitable in view of what we believe." Paul instructs us not to walk as we did before Christ. Living for Christ and living for the world are mutually exclusive. They cannot happen at the same time and in the same place. The moment we start living for the world we stop living for Christ.

What are the old ways we are to avoid? Futility of mind. Thinking is important for it is the seedbed of action. Satan's battleground in our life starts here. Ignorance of God's truth. A daily dose of God's Word prevents this. Darkened in our understanding. Our minds have been enlightened through Christ. Spiritual and moral callousness. Following Christ automatically attracts us to good spiritual mores. Depraved in our minds. Our minds have been transformed by Christ. We think on what is good, just, pure, lovely and has virtue in God's eyes. No longer should any of these things characterize your life.

But the old is gone and the new has come. We have a Christ centered attitude. The interests of the world no longer attract us. We possess the ability to know God's truth. We have his Word and his Spirit to guide us into all truth. God has delivered us from the old self. He has made us a new creation. We are a new self created in the image of God's Son. Every day God is working to conform you to his image in your actions, attitudes and words.

Reflection: Live according to the person you are in Christ.

August 15
Defining Salvation
Ephesians 2:1-10

A pastor tells of a young Muslim actor approaching him desiring to accept Christ. He explained the plan of salvation to him, and he prayed to receive Christ. Following his prayer, he said, "Isn't it wonderful. Now I have Jesus and Mohammed" But salvation is not adding Jesus to someone or something we are already trusting in for deliverance.

An actor and an elderly preacher were once asked to recite the twenty third psalm. The actor's recitation was beautiful and received great applause. The preacher's voice was rough and broken, but when he finished, there was not a dry eye in the room. When someone asked the actor why the difference, he said, "I know the psalm, but he knows the Shepherd."

Salvation is from sin. A solid theological concept of sin is necessary to recognize the need of salvation. Sin is missing the mark God has established for humanity. It is moral crookedness and failure to stay on the narrow line God requires. Human nature is not basically good. Nor will humans share and share alike if they are placed in the right environment. We are not just sick but dead in our trespasses and sins. Humanity is out of harmony with their Creator. As the dead person can no longer respond to any stimuli, neither can the person apart from Christ except by faith.

Salvation is by love. Apart from the initiative of God's love, we would remain in our sin. It is through the calling and convicting of his Spirit that we are made aware of our sin and given the ability to come to him. His love is boundless, immeasurable and unlimited. Jesus purported that the greatest love one could have is in laying down his life for his friends. (John 15:13) Our sin has offended God.

Salvation is into life. Through Christ, we are transferred from a spiritually dead state. We are no longer walking corpses. The same power that brought Christ from the grave brings us out of death.

Salvation has a purpose. God desires to restore us to the position we had before sin. The Garden of Eden experience demonstrates the kind of fellowship with God humanity had before sin. Now we can do the good works God designed for us to perform.

Reflection: Thank God for salvation. Live in the power of your new nature.

August 16
God's Prescription for a Happy Home
Ephesians 6:1-4

Norman Wright described four changes that have recently transpired in families. A move toward nuclear families-Mom, Dad and children. This varied from the previous norm of extended families. The second was selection of a marriage partner being left up to the individual. Parents desiring fluid rather than fixed roles. And finally, a change in sexual morality. Specifically, a lack of it.

Family structure, for the most part, has departed from God's intended purpose. The rate of family failure is astounding. Successful families take hard work. Parents cannot do it alone. The old African proverb is true: "It takes a village to raise a child."

God intends for children to submit to their parents. The humanistic philosophy that instructed parents to let their children express their personalities without threat of punishment or discipline did not work. Dr. Spock's method was faulty. While humanistic philosophy liberated children, it freed them from such important things as: traditional morals, values, punishment, patriotism, parental authority and sexual restraint.

God's Word, on the other hand, says parents are to rear their children in the nurture and admonition of the Lord. This includes discipline and even punishment. One has a teaching element, and the other is reserved for willful disobedience.

Children are to honor and obey their parents. After becoming adults, there may be occasions when a child must disobey a parent, but the honor extends for a lifetime. Obedience involves action while honor speaks of an attitude. Learning to honor our parents is the basic foundation of all other relationships. This relationship teaches respect for all authority figures.

However, parents are not to provoke their children to wrath. This involves submission of the parent to the child. Provoking speaks of any ongoing pattern of behavior that builds a deep seated anger in the child that boils over in hostile behavior. Over protection, favoritism, neglect, conditional love and pushing achievement are all ways parents can provoke their children.

Reflection: Thank you Lord for giving me the privilege of being a parent. Help me remember that my child is a loan from you.

August 17
How to Live Triumphantly
I Peter 5:6-14

A marriage on the brink of collapse. Husband and wife were separated, and the local pastor's efforts to help were breaking down. The husband, a salesman, was out of town and contemplating infidelity. Then he attended a revival. A couple of Sundays later, he accepted Christ and his wife rededicated her life. Their marriage was saved. They discovered, although almost too late, what it meant to live triumphantly.

Humility will enable triumphant living. An English poet said of humility that it is the "highest virtue, mother of them all." And the Bible says that the reward for humility and fearing the Lord is riches, honor and life. (Proverbs 22:4) Through instruction and example God reminds us of the importance of this trait. Humility is not low self-esteem but an accurate assessment of ourselves as God sees us. God will exalt when we are humble.

Triumphant living comes when we cast our anxieties on God remembering that he cares for us. In fact, he is concerned about every detail of our life. Cast carries the idea of throwing. The psalmist tells us to cast our burdens on God because he will sustain us. (Psalm 55:22) God's shoulders are broad enough to handle the anxieties of all his children. He will come underneath our burden and help us shoulder the load of life. In place of the anxiety, he will give a peace that surpasses our understanding. Whether trials, temptation or failure to meet unrealistic goals, God is there. Even when the defeat is from our own bad decision, he will still come to our rescue.

We live triumphantly by being vigilant. The reason? Our adversary the devil prowls about like a roaring lion trying to devour our effectiveness for Christ. Our comfort comes in knowing that God will not allow any temptation to become so strong that we cannot endure or escape with his help. Satan will try to trip us up, but God's wisdom will enable us to avoid his traps.

Our lives should be characterized by confidence. The final victory belongs to God and his people. Righteousness will win over evil. Just as

Jesus gained the victory over the forces of evil, so will we.

Reflection: Live each day believing that God has work for you and that you will succeed in your spiritual walk.

August 18

Instructions on Prayer
Ephesians 6:18-24

According to polls, a great number of Americans do it. What the polls often do not show, however, is what god people are praying to, why they are praying, or what theological belief they hold about prayer. A great outcry went up when prayer was removed from public schools. And the subject of prayer often arises when separation of church and state is discussed.

For the devout believer, prayer is our connection to God. We pray and believe he hears and will answer. How he can hear all of his children's prayers at any given time is unexplainable, but we believe nevertheless. Paul never debates the matter of prayer but assumes it should have a place in the Christian's life. Prayer is the spiritual air we breathe. Prayer takes time and sacrifice, but it is an investment with great returns.

Our prayer life needs variety. Requests, petitions and praise should characterize our prayers. So often our prayer life is consumed by requests as if God is a big Santa Claus in heaven. While we are encouraged to bring our requests to him, they should be a small part of our overall prayer life.

Petitions and praise are more valuable. We petition him on behalf of others. Friends, family, work associates, government leaders. Our greatest petition for others is that they come to know Christ as their Savior. Beyond that we intercede for emotional, physical or mental needs they have.

Praise to God for who he is and his blessings should also adorn our prayers. This prepares us for heaven where all the saints of God will praise him for eternity. Additionally, there are many ways and places that we can pray. A good method to put variety in your prayers is the ACTS method: Adoration, Confession, Thanksgiving and Supplication.

Our prayers should be frequent. Paul says to pray at all times and in another place to "pray without ceasing." (I Thessalonians 5:17) Frequent prayer keeps us on the alert for our enemy's snares. While we need to be in an attitude of prayer throughout each day, we do need a specific time and place to pray to our Heavenly Father. A place where we can focus on listening to him. Through regular prayer God will instill wisdom for successful Christian living. Praying at all times means living with a God consciousness.

Reflection: Remember that your prayers have power because of the one they are addressed to. Pray in faith and expect God's answers.

August 19

Living Life to the Fullest

Ephesians 3:14-21

Imagine the person who knows a great deal about cars. They might even be a mechanic. When something malfunctions, they know exactly how to repair it. Such a person could have all this information and skill yet never own a car or even have a driver's license. On the other hand, there are many people who drive every day and know very little about the mechanics of how a car works.

The same can happen in the spiritual realm. It is possible to possess many biblical facts yet not know how to apply them. One can have knowledge but no practical use. When this happens, life cannot be lived to the fullest. God wants us to know the abundant life. He wants us to understand the power we have in Jesus Christ.

We need to pray that God would give us the inner strength of the Spirit. This strength is given when we realize all we are and have in Christ. We are alive in him. We are no longer strangers or aliens but friends. We belong to God's household and are built on the foundation of the apostles and prophets.

Our prayer is for God to help us exercise the power we have. We are more than conquerors in Christ. It is typical to measure our resources by material possessions, but the greatest power we have is in the spiritual realm. Chosen, redeemed, forgiven and eternal life are all terms that describe believers and our inheritance.

Not realizing our resources leads to spiritual poverty and causes those we touch to be poor as well. As we recognize our potential, we begin to touch the lives of those around us. They benefit because we know our identity.

We also need inner strength from Christ. Paul requests that Christ dwell in their hearts through faith. This is not a reference to salvation but sanctification. A sanctified life is a Spirit controlled life.

Recognizing the strength of Christ and his indwelling Spirit brings abundant love, and love leads to a full existence. We experience God's love daily and then share it with others.

Reflection: Remember God can do more through you than you can ever imagine.

August 20

Mandates for God's Leaders

I Peter 5:1-5

Leaders have great responsibilities. They are normally chosen for such positions because they possess "leadership qualities." They are responsible, goal and vision oriented, talented and gifted, and able to motivate others to perform.

Leaders in the spiritual realm are also accountable-to God. God has given leaders gifts for their position, but they must be responsible stewards. Peter speaks to elders and the younger. Elders were older men and leaders in the local church. In the early church, the name was used for an appointed or official leader. It became a term used for pastoral leaders in the church.

Leaders in the church must tend the flock. It is their responsibility to help the church mirror the faith she claims to have. This enhances our testimony before unbelievers. They are responsible to God for their actions and the actions of those God has given them to lead.

Tending the flock is done willingly, not by compulsion. Leaders must have a leader's heart. Leaders are not forced to do what God has gifted them to do. Nor do they do it for pay. While the Bible teaches that those who make their living by the gospel should be paid, pay is not the reason they lead. Tending the flock is not about lording it over those you lead. Being a leader gives no one the power to be a ruthless dictator. People do not normally follow leaders with that characteristic.

In the Greek language, "tend" comes from the same stem that means to shepherd. This is what Jesus told Peter to do with his people. Shepherd them. A shepherd and a dictator are radically different. A good shepherd will lay down his life for the sheep. This analogy is perfect for leaders in churches. They shepherd the flock. It involves work, concern, time and sacrifice.

When leaders fulfill their roles adequately, the Chief Shepherd will reward them. Reward is not the motive behind the leading, but it is the consequence of sacrificial service. All leaders are really undershepherds under the Great Shepherd. The world's crowns will dissolve, but the crown given to faithful leaders will never fade away.

Reflection: Lead with humility. Recognize God has given you the talents and gifts to function in your role.

August 21

Marks of a Spiritual Father
I Corinthians 4:14-21

In Gary Smalley's book, *The Key to Your Child's Heart*, he tells of a professional boxer and his parent's commitment. Without hesitation, he told how his Dad was his best friend and the most encouraging person in his life. When he was nineteen, he went through a real trial, one that some of his family did not understand and one that led others to reject him. "But my dad told me even though he was hurt by what I had done, I was his son. He would always love me and always be there to pick me up."

Paul was a spiritual father to the Corinthians. As a father, he had rebuked them for factions in the church. He was harsh with them, but only because he loved them in the faith. It disturbed him to see ungodliness in their lives, especially when Christ had paid so much to set them free.

A spiritual father will admonish. Love does not negate punishment or discipline. Love does not turn a blind eye to sinful behavior. Love that allows any type of conduct without reprisal only rears a criminal. Discipline is not damaging but encourages one to regain the high ground. Harsh and unfeeling punishment can destroy a child, but discipline teaches.

Spiritual fathers love. The Corinthians were his children in the faith. Love led him to care. He does not reject them, but love leads him to reprove. Love understands, trains, is gentle, worries and is intense.

A spiritual father will beget. We must have children in order to love and admonish them. The church must reproduce. We must have evangelistic zeal. A lack of missionary effort leads to death. The family name must be carried on. Being a spiritual child and a spiritual father are not the same. Paul left spiritual progeny everywhere he went, and our responsibility is the same. Multiply and fill the earth.

We must set a good example. Paul was so bold as to tell them to imitate him. When we live as spiritual children, we can tell others the same and do so in a spirit of humility. Parents should provide good examples.

Spiritual fathers teach. A part of the Great Commission is to teach others to obey God's commands. Telling is not enough. We must teach. As the parent teaches their child, so we must teach our spiritual children.

Reflection: What type of spiritual parent are you? Ask God to help your weaknesses become strengths.

August 22

Our Divine Inheritance

Ephesians 1:11-14

Dennis was a cripple. During high school, he kept to himself, that is, until Stacey came along. He dropped his books one day, and she offered to pick them up. Then she took him skating and swimming. Each time he protested, she said, "I will help you." One day, Stacey was sharing her dreams with him. After she was through, she said, "Dennis, what are your dreams." His only dream was to have a normal body. But Stacey helped him understand that God looks on the inside. He was God's masterpiece and could be used by God. She invited him to church and there he discovered a whole world of people just like Stacey. He wanted what they had and accepted Christ as his Savior. Dennis accepted his divine inheritance.

The ground of our inheritance is Jesus Christ. Our present and future inheritance is based on our relationship with Christ through faith. Our just reward apart from him is condemnation but in him there is freedom. In some sense, each believer has been to the cross with Christ and experienced his death, burial and resurrection.

Our inheritance is not material things but is spiritual in nature. We receive all the blessings that come with being a child of God. The inheritance includes: peace, love, wisdom, eternal life, grace, joy, victory, strength, guidance, power, mercy, forgiveness, and spiritual discernment.

The believer's hope is in Christ and him alone. Hope is not simply wishing something will happen but is a confident assurance that God will give us what he promised. Paul wrote of his confidence that the one who began a good work in him would bring it to completion by the day of Christ Jesus. (Philippians 1:6)

God gives us a guarantee of our inheritance. It is typical of humans to want some type of guarantee if someone promises us something. Ours is the seal of the Holy Spirit. He is God's pledge to us that the eternal life promised will indeed be granted. God's Spirit is given the moment we trust Christ as our Savior. Paul says in another place that the person who does not have the Spirit does not belong to Christ. (Romans 8:9) This seal implies security, ownership, authenticity and authority.

Reflection: The goal of your inheritance is to bring glory to God. At the cross, God rescued what rightfully belonged to him initially. You.

August 23
Servants for Christ
I Corinthians 4:1-5

After the bombing of Pearl Harbor on December 7, 1941, Japanese found themselves being excluded from many aspects of American life. In February of 1942, President Roosevelt established military areas for them on the West Coast. Two months later, another order excluded them from there. Yumi and her family of five shortly found themselves living in a nine by twenty foot horse stall. But a Mrs. Perkins who had known them began to visit. She was appalled. Returning to their previous home, she ripped the linoleum from the floor and brought it to the horse stall to keep them from sleeping on the damp dirt floor. A servant for Christ.

Our identity as God's children is servants. Not a term we are particularly fond of but biblical nevertheless. Jesus taught that a person's measure of greatness was not in how many served him but in how many he served. Quite the opposite of normal world philosophy. We do not usually think of the floor sweeper in a factory as being greater than the president of the company. Then again, Jesus' ways are not the same.

We serve because we have been served by him. Jesus modeled this concept by washing the feet of his disciples. When Peter objected, Jesus told him this was necessary for his followers. A life of service keeps life in perspective. The word Paul used in these verses refers to the lowest galley slave who rowed on the bottom tier of a ship. They were the most menial, despised and unenvied.

Servants are under the authority of another, and for the believer this is Christ. He is our Master, but not a cruel one. In salvation, God makes us joint heirs with Christ which means we own all things. No slave could boast of such a privilege. We serve him out of love, and we serve others because of the love he has deposited in our hearts. A part of our service is dispensing the gospel to others.

As a steward of the grace of God, he expects us to be trustworthy. God has entrusted us with the message of salvation. Further, he has endowed us with spiritual gifts to aid in our service to others. Faithfulness and stewardship go hand in hand.

Reflection: A final evaluation awaits God's servants. Evaluate yourself daily. Is your life exhibiting sacrificial service to others?

August 24

Supporting God's Servants

I Corinthians 9:1-14

On the Happy Days sitcom, Fonzie was the coolest guy in town, at least for Richie and his friends. High school drop-out, motorcycle rider, leather coat. What more could a guy want? And girls came by the handful at the snap of his fingers. Since he was a partially reformed hoodlum, he associated with what some of his former companions would refer to as "nerds." One episode shows Fonzie at the grocery store. Richie questions why he is there. Fonzie assures him that angels did not bring him food.

Paul must have encountered some churches who thought that of their leaders for he gives instructions that they should be paid. Paul himself never demanded it. He was willing to work a secular job so he could preach. His example, however, was not meant to be the norm. Those who make their living by preaching the gospel should be supported by other Christians.

Paul offers the example of a soldier, farmer and shepherd as proof of the need to pay God's servants. The soldier did not fight during the day and work a night job to support himself. Nor did the shepherd. They were paid by those who enlisted their services. Farmers do not plant and cultivate for someone else without remuneration. Those in full time Christian service have the same needs as anyone else and should be compensated.

Support for this reasoning is reinforced by God's law. Oxen were not muzzled while threshing. Eating while working was their pay. The law taught God's concern for animals, but there was a higher principle. He is concerned with those who give their entire lives to doing his work. As employers pay employees, so God's church should recompense his full time servants.

Compensation for service is a universal pattern. Under the Old Testament system, the priests and Levites devoted their time to serving in the tabernacle and later in the Temple. God's law required the people to support them. They received no inheritance in the Promised Land. The people gave them a tithe of their crops, animals and other sacrifices.

The most important reason God's churches are to support full time ministers is because Jesus ordained it. While we have no specific place where Jesus said this, it was revealed to Paul that he had.

Reflection: Be faithful in giving to God's church so God's servants can carry out his work effectively.

August 25
The Believer's Resources
Ephesians 1:15-23

Philip Henry, father of commentator Matthew Henry, had fallen in love with a young lady. She, however, belonged to a higher level of society. While that was not a problem for his love, it was for her parents. "This man, Philip Henry, where has he come from" they asked. She replied, "I do not know where he has come from, but I know where he is going." His resources extended beyond material possessions.

Resources are necessary for life to exist. One cannot live in American society without money. Food and water are essential as are a certain amount of material possessions. But our greatest resources are in Christ. A part of intimately knowing Christ is being aware of what we possess because of the relationship. We know God on a personal level, through our involvement with him and through his grace.

He gives us faith. We exercise levels of faith daily. Faith in the stock market, bonds, our economy, vehicles, locks, and each other. But faith in God takes us to another level. It is through this virtue that we are saved, but the believer lives by faith each day. It is this confident assurance that sustains us through all of life's difficulties. Faith is obedience.

We have love. Our love should extend to all people but especially to all the saints. Our fellowship now prepares us for eternity. We are not free to pick and choose which Christians to love. The Bible declares that we can know we have passed from death to life because we love one another. (I John 3:14) This love is more than a feeling, attraction or emotion. True love acts in behalf of others.

Believers have the ability to know God's plan. Within God's overarching plan is his individual desire for each Christian. We know this plan through his Word, others, circumstances, and the guidance of his Spirit. God will reveal how and where he wants to use you.

We can understand the greatness of God's power and person in us. He indwells us through his Spirit. Physical, psychological and spiritual problems will not appear so large when we have an accurate view of how great our God is.

Reflection: God has given you all the resources you need to be the person he created you to be.

August 26
The Bible Speaks on Celibacy
I Corinthians 7:1-7

There was a time in our country when marriage by a certain age for a woman was expected. Girls married in their teenage years and before. Waiting until they were in their twenties would have them classified as old maids. People would wonder what was wrong with them. In like manner, a man who did not marry by a certain age was looked on with odd stares. In spite of changing trends, it is still a fairly normal expectation that men and women will marry and have families.

While the Bible has more to say about marriage, it does contain some teachings about those who do not. Much of what Paul says here is taught against a very immoral and pagan background which the Corinthian believers lived in.

Scripture teaches that celibacy is good. Society should not discriminate against one who makes such a decision. However, the person who chooses to remain single should also choose to remain celibate. Sexual relationships outside of the marriage union are wrong in God's sight. Nor does remaining single place one on a higher spiritual plain, but it does give a person more time to serve God since they do not have family responsibilities.

The Genesis account of the first marriage records God saying it is not good for man to be alone. Marriage, then, is the most fulfilling type of companionship. This does not mean, however, that God does not allow for singleness.

A word of warning. The single and celibate life is tempting. It is a natural part of our makeup to be attracted to the opposite sex. Homosexuality is not only a violation of God's law but it is also not normal. Because of the natural tendency of the sexual relationship, the celibate person has to deal with this temptation.

Celibacy is also wrong for the married person. Sexual relations are normal and expected by God in a marriage. He designed them for our pleasure and for procreation. For marriage partners to withhold this from the other, except for a short period for the purpose of prayer, is wrong and places one partner at a higher risk for temptation.

Reflection: If you have chosen to remain single, use your time to effectively serve Christ.

August 27

The Christian Example

I Corinthians 6:1-11

Corruption abounds in our society. Politics is the normal place we complain about. Many times political leaders do not have the best interests of their constituents at heart. Greed is rampant, and many of the bad actions we see result from this trait. Waste is found in businesses and schools.

Corruption should not be found in God's churches or among his people. Cyprian was an early church leader who lived in a corrupt world. In spite of his surroundings, he wrote of Christians, "But I have discovered in the midst of it a quiet and holy people who have learned a great secret. They have found a joy which is a thousand times better than any of the pleasures of our sinful life."

These early believers that Paul addressed were ruining their reputation by taking one another to court. They were accustomed to the arguing and bickering because it was part of their former life. But now in Christ, it was not the avenue they should have taken to settle their disputes.

Believers must remember their rank. Sinner is no longer a classification that fits. We are termed saints for we no longer stand under God's condemnation. Knowing this, in most cases, we should not take our disagreements among ourselves or in our churches before unbelievers for settlement. It was not that Paul was worried that the believers would not get a fair ruling. It simply ruined their testimony before the unbelieving world. How could pagans settle Christian disputes?

Taking other believers to court demonstrates that revenge and our rights are more important than unity in the body of Christ. God has given us gifts and resources, and as much as possible, we should settle our disputes using them. We should not air our dirty laundry before the world. Because of our judicial system, there are occasions when Christians must come before unbelieving judges, but even in these instances our actions should not demonstrate selfish greed.

So important is our testimony that we should allow ourselves to be wronged before we go to court and subject ourselves to an unbelieving legal system. Forgiveness helps us along this road.

Reflection: We can identify an animal with certainty that has fur, four feet, and barks. It is a dog. Can others identify you as a Christian?

August 28

The Christian's Benefits

I Corinthians 1:1-9

Benefits are important and enticing. When considering a job opportunity, the benefit package is usually a calling card. Health insurance, retirement programs, and life and dental insurance are welcome additions to any job offer. Most jobs that are void of benefits also do not pay enough for the employee to purchase their own insurance.

Christians have a wonderful benefits package. It has nothing to do with our job title or how much our salary is. It has to do with whom we belong to. No matter how often we change jobs on earth, the benefits remain intact.

The greatest benefit we have is grace-God's unmerited favor. A sound theological concept of sin will lead to a deep appreciation of this trait we have received from God. Observing what the Bible says about how sin has infected the human race helps us love God more. There was nothing good in you or me that led him to the cross solution. He simply loved us with his grace. God's grace is free and unearned.

Grace cannot coexist with guilt, merit or obligation. Guilt over sin disappears at salvation. No longer should the believer fret over past, present or future sins for the righteousness of Christ has been given to him. This is not to say we should adopt a relaxed attitude about sin. We simply do not live with guilt which leads to fear. Meditation on what God has forgiven hinders God from using us in the present and future.

Nor is grace related to merit. We did not nor do we deserve what God has done for us. We cannot earn what must be freely given. God will not threaten to take away what he has given when we fall into occasional sinful acts. Neither can we place God under any obligation to rectify humanity's self inflicted mess. We are responsible for our rebellion.

Grace has a purpose. God wants us to do good works. It is by these that his Kingdom is advanced and his name honored. He desires for us to touch the world with his goodness. God enables this to happen by giving gifts to his children. There is nothing the believer lacks to live for and serve God. We are complete in Christ.

Reflection: Thank God for his wonderful grace and that you do not have to live with guilt but can live in true freedom.

August 29

The Dangers of Sexual Sin
I Corinthians 6:12-20

Breaking down the barriers that bind them. Throughout history, people have done this in one way or another. The sexual revolution of the 1960's and 70's was an example in American history. We are now reaping the results. Sexually transmitted diseases are rampant. AIDS is a result of unrestrained sexual forays. Teens are having sex at younger ages, and teenage pregnancies are at an all time high.

Like ours, the Corinthian society was notoriously immoral. Temple prostitutes abounded. Sexual promiscuity had been the believer's former way of life, and no doubt they were still tempted by it.

Sexual sin harms. It breaks down the moral fabric of society by destroying families. A lackadaisical attitude about sex before marriage destroys the foundation of society by diminishing the importance of family. God designed marriage and sex within that union. When the attitude of society does not enforce the importance of that concept, we cannot expect our youth to naturally generate in that direction. The church must play the major role in emphasizing this truth.

Relaxed attitudes about sex confuse the love message. Sex and love are not the same thing though one does flow from the other, but the first does not mean the second is in place. While sex is designed for the pleasure of the married couple, it is also for procreation. God designed this method to populate the earth.

Unfaithfulness within marriage through immoral sexual relationships often destroys the union. Few marriages survive this act of treachery. A deep trust factor is broken that will take hard work and time to heal. It is often more convenient to just walk away, and many do. Sexual sin never delivers what it promises.

Sexual sin also controls. People can become addicts to this behavior just as they can to illegal substances. Perverted behavior is often repeated by sexual offenders. Child molesters do not usually stop with one act. Sexual sin will destroy all it touches. Thousands of children are affected yearly by the sinful sexual acts of parents.

Reflection: Sexual sin perverts God's intentions for our bodies. Remember that your body is a temple of God's Spirit.

August 30

The Divided Church

I Corinthians 3:1-9

One explains his new found faith this way; "It is rather like a cyclist, who, when he is climbing a long hill, thinks he will be able to freewheel down the other side. It is not until he reaches the top that he sees that his task has only just started and that the road winds on with steeper hills that the one he had just climbed."

Indeed, the believer's life is divided. Trusting Christ as our Savior places us in a battle zone we did not face before. Prior to Christ, we were enslaved to sin. After salvation, we are driven by a new nature but still haunted by temptation to return to our old ways. Like the salmon, we find that gravity and the current are often against us.

The division that assaults the Christian will sometimes meander into the church. Bickering and splits result. Some just walk away from the church altogether. Others choose to remain and target the one who offended them with gossip and neglect.

Divisions arise because of the flesh. Flesh is not skin but rather our old patterns of acting and thinking that we have learned before trusting Christ. While Christ gives a new nature that pummels us in new directions, the fleshly side still disturbs us. It is this part of our makeup that Satan works through with his temptations.

While the flesh cannot totally dominate the believer, it can exercise a great deal of pressure. Sin will not be the pattern of our life, but a fleshly controlled life will lead to more and more sinful acts. If we walk by the Spirit, we will not fulfill the desires of the flesh. (Galatians 5:16) Spirit filled living means leaving the elementary truths of the faith, reaching farther into the deeper truths of God's Word, and starving the flesh. As memory is enhanced by rehearsal, so is life in the Spirit as we study God's Word daily.

The symptoms of division are jealousy and strife. Immaturity in the faith can lead believers into such behavior. So can living in the flesh. This in turn infects the church. Immaturity is a choice. All believers are given the resources to develop and grow in their faith.

Reflection: The cure for church division is remembering that our work is to give attention to God and not ourselves. Glorify God in all you do in your church.

August 31
The Gifts of Christ
Ephesians 4:7-11

Gifts are often associated with special occasions: graduation, birthday, Christmas, birth of a baby, or wedding. Perhaps Christmas is the time when the most giving takes place. In fact, some incur a huge amount of debt during the Christmas season. Giving with pure motives is a wonderful exercise that helps us better appreciate what God has given us.

The greatest failure in church history has been referred to as the "clerical domination of the laity." It was a period when the functions of the two were separated. The clergy was supposed to lead while the laity followed like docile animals. But such is not the picture of the church presented in the New Testament. Only as all believers use their resources can the church make a worldwide impact.

Christ has the right to give gifts to his children. His work on the cross and the coming of the Spirit at Pentecost brought spiritual gifts to believers. The resurrection validated this authority. Jesus maintained that those who believe in him will do the works he did and even greater works because he was going to the Father. (John 14:12)

God gives special gifts to some for leadership. While all believers have gifts, these gifts are given to the leaders. Paul mentions apostles, prophets, evangelists, and pastor-teachers.

In its strictest sense, an apostle had to witness the risen Christ. There are some instances where the word was used in a more general sense. Prophets foretold and forth told the message of God. Many theologians believe these two offices have ceased to exist and are now replaced by evangelists and pastor-teachers. The evangelist spreads the gospel while the pastor-teacher leads the local church.

Gifts are also given to individual believers. In fact, all believers have at least one spiritual gift and many have more. They also come from the Spirit of God that indwells us. Christ knows our personality and the opportunities we will have and gifts us accordingly. Additionally, the same gift can be and is used in different ways according to each believer's unique set of circumstances. We are to use these gifts in unison in God's work.

Reflection: Discover the gifts God has given you, and use them in conjunction with your brothers and sisters in Christ.

September

September 1
The Key to Good Relationships
Ephesians 6:5-9

For the first 246 years on this continent, African Americans were treated as possessions. While the Declaration of Independence said that all men were created equal, a man was defined literally. Women, slaves, and landless people were not equal. In fact, the Constitution would define a slave as three fifths of a man. Slaves could not vote or own property. They could not marry the person of their choosing. The slave market separated families.

Slavery was a popular institution in Paul's day. Estimates show the Roman Empire having around sixty million slaves, but if we are looking for Paul to condone it we will be sadly disappointed. The Bible's teaching that all men are made in the image of God would suck the very lifeblood from the institution and eventually dismantle it.

Since slavery is no longer an issue in America, most scholars now take these verses and apply them to the employer employee relationship. Employers want more productivity, profits and control of practices and policies while employees want higher pay, better working conditions and more benefits.

While there are many differences in that relationship and slavery, there are some important principles that we can glean. The common denominator between then and now is still greed. Masters wanted more from the slaves so they could have more for themselves. Employers fall into the same trap. Socialists, Communists, Fascists and other philosophical advocates have sought solutions to no avail. The solution begins in a relationship with Jesus Christ.

Just as husbands, wives and children all have a special place and responsibility in the family, so employees and employers do as well in their capacities. Employees must submit. Viewing what we do as unto the Lord will help us submit to those we work for. They are not our true boss. Do your work as if you were working for God. You are.

Employers should submit as well. They must recognize that their position has been granted by God and the people who work for them are

301

made in his image.

Reflection: Whatever work God has given you to do, do it honestly and joyfully, remembering that you are working for God not men.

September 2

The Mystery Revealed

Ephesians 3:1-13

On one Andy Griffith episode, Andy meets Karen, a cousin of Thelma Lou's. Andy invites her for supper, and she notices that Andy is reading a mystery. He asks if she likes mysteries too. Her reply, "Yes, and the scarier the better." Many people love a good mystery.

In the middle of his prayer, Paul gets sidetracked and feels the need to explain a mystery. The mystery had to do with Jews and Gentiles. In the Old Testament, God chose the Jewish people. He gave his laws to them, gave them the Promised Land, and promised to bless them and make them populous. However, they came to believe that they were special just because of this covenant relationship with God. The great mystery was that Jews and Gentiles were one. They were both created in God's image.

We are prisoners of the mystery. That is, we are prisoners of Jesus Christ. Paul believed this. While he was once a prisoner of Judaism, he was now a prisoner of Christ. God gave him this ministry on the Damascus Road. God delivered him from persecuting Christians and led him to become one of their greatest proponents. He was sold out to service for his Lord.

The salvation of a believer is just as monumental as Paul's Damascus Road experience. While not blinded by a light as he was, God still speaks to our heart in a life changing way. From then on, our goal in life should be to sell ourselves out for him. We are bound to do his will using the special gifts and talents he gives. We must minister within and without the family of God. Peter says we are to employ our special gifts by serving one another. This makes us good stewards of the grace of God and magnifies his name. (I Peter 4:10)

The plan of the Jews and Gentiles being one in Christ was not known in Old Testament times. Before the church age, not even the great prophets knew of this mystery. God had told Abraham that all the nations of the earth would be blessed through him, but it was left to Paul to interpret the meaning of that promise. Faith was always the way that one was justified in God's sight. Nationality had nothing to do with it. It still doesn't.

Reflection: The wonderful mystery of God is that all people are loved by him. We have all been created in his image. Share his love without discrimination.

September 3
The Prepared Christian
Ephesians 6:10-20

John Nyland was a former lineman for the Dallas Cowboys and later the Philadelphia Eagles. He believed there were only two kinds of sports: easy and contact. The easy anyone could and did play. The contact was only for men over two hundred pounds.

The Christian experience is a contact sport. A war and battle on a grand scale. It is only for the strong and durable, and only those who are prepared can hope to endure to the end. Those who are not equipped will be blown about by every wind of doctrine. (Ephesians 4:14) All believers have two common enemies: Satan and themselves. Satan will tempt, but he will work through those spiritual areas in our life that are most susceptible to his plan to kill, steal and destroy.

Fortunately, Christ gives us armor to fight our battle. To wear it is to be prepared for the conflict. To toss it aside will lead to certain defeat. God gives us the girdle of truth. Robes were common attire in the Middle East. But when doing work or having to hurry, they could be cumbersome. To solve the problem, the robe was lifted and tucked in the girdle around the waist. It was referred to as "girding the loins."

We fight our spiritual battles with truth. Jesus did this when tempted by Satan in the wilderness. For every temptation, he responded with God's Word. Truth is not relevant to the situation or circumstance. Believing that it is places us on a slippery slope that leads to destruction and no firm belief in anything. It also makes truth relative to individual preferences.

Believers also have the breastplate of righteousness. Every Roman soldier had one to cover the torso thereby protecting his vital organs. Our righteousness is not self attained but given to us when we trust Christ as our Savior. On the cross, God took the righteousness of Christ and gave it to humanity. We must live out in practice who we truly are.

Our feet are shod with the gospel message. Shoes were important for the soldier. They protected his feet as he walked over hot roads, jagged cliffs, and through rocky streambeds. Christians take the gospel of peace to the world. It is a peace that results from knowing Christ as Savior.

Reflection: It is a wonderful privilege to join the army of the faithful. Make sure you are prepared to do battle.

September 4

The Prepared Christian

Ephesians 6:10-20

Following the death of his father, Alexander the Great extended his empire from Greece to India. As he marched toward the Danube, he had to cross the main Balkan range. Here lay the Thracians who decided to hold the pass against him. It was a clever move because there was no alternate route. One of the things that made Alexander such a great warrior was his ability to calculate the moves of his enemy. By preparing his army, he was able to deliver them from certain destruction.

We too must anticipate the moves of our enemy, and God gives armor to prepare us for battle. He offers the shield of faith. Soldiers used a shield in hand to hand combat. Faith joins us to Christ and carries us through our spiritual journey. It is by faith that we trust God for daily provision and strength in times of trouble and temptation. Our shield of faith helps us ward off immorality, greed, hate, envy, anger, covetousness, pride, fear and doubt.

Our minds are protected by the helmet of salvation. Helmets were important for the Roman soldier. They were often made of leather and covered with metal plates. Cheek pieces were also typical on the soldier's helmet.

A part of our salvation involves our mind. The mind is the battleground of our enemy. All temptation begins here, for Satan knows that what we think about long enough we will act on. Thoughts lead to emotional feelings which in turn lead to actions. We are to think on those things that are true, noble, just, pure, lovely, and that have virtue and are praiseworthy. (Philippians 4:8) When thoughts come that are not from God, we are to take them captive under the authority of Christ.

The sword of the Spirit is vital in preparing for spiritual battle. This is God's Word, and no battle can be won without it. It pierces to our innermost being and shows us the thoughts and intents of our heart that we might judge them in light of God's teachings. We must hide God's Word in our heart so that in times of temptation his truth will rise up to meet the enemy. Truth will always expose error.

Reflection: As you pray each day, ask God to adorn you with his full armor.

September 5
The Sharing of God's Mind
I Corinthians 2:6-16

Extrasensory perception was a common phenomenon of years ago. Defined, it is an awareness some people claim to possess that goes beyond the usual means we gain information. One form of ESP was telepathy or mind reading. While some desire to read other's minds, we might imagine what kind of society we would build if we all had the ability to discern what each other was thinking. Fights and arguments would surely multiply as would crimes. Most of the population would probably be mad at one another.

God, of course, knows the human mind because he created it. More importantly, he gives us the opportunity to know his mind. While we cannot know his mind fully-this would make us as advanced as he is, we can know enough of his mind to discern his plan for us. In order to have interaction with our Creator, we must know something of him and his expectations. This understanding does not come from our sensory perceptions.

We can know the mind of God through revelation. Revelation means to reveal, and God has revealed information about himself to us. This revelation comes through the agent of his Spirit. He takes up residence in our life at salvation and is the one who inspired the authors of God's Word. We can trust him for guidance and help in understanding biblical teaching.

The Spirit knows the mind of Christ. As we have the ability to know what we are thinking at any given moment, so the Spirit knows what God is thinking and can reveal that to us.

The mind of God is revealed through inspiration. Theologians differ in how they define inspiration. The ideas range from writers taking dictation from God to theories that relegate the authors to no more than modern day authors. A weak view of inspiration leads to a weak view of the Bible. Inspiration is the process by which God reveals his Word to humanity. His Spirit acted upon the writers giving them the words God wanted recorded. That being said, Scripture is reliable, trustworthy and without error. Though God did not remove them from their time period or negate their personalities, he did move upon them with his Spirit in a manner that has not happened since.

Reflection: Take a moment to thank God for giving you his reliable Word and for giving you the ability to understand it.

September 6
The Wisdom of God
I Corinthians 1:18-2:5

The ancient Greeks had a love for wisdom. Their culture was built around philosophy. They asked questions about questions. But the wisdom they sought was human and not godly. Their society hosted as many as fifty philosophical parties, each with different ideas about humanity's origin, significance, destiny and relationship to the gods and society.

While human wisdom is good in some respects, godly wisdom is better. We seek some of the same answers the early Greeks did, and like them, many look in the wrong places for answers. We can depend on wisdom from doctors, scientists, politicians and lawyers without consulting the One where true wisdom is found. Doing this will lead to disappointment. It is characteristic of humanity to think their wisdom is superior to God's. But when we compare ours with God's, we will discover that we have only discovered foolishness.

God's wisdom is far superior to man's. The cross is a prime example. Man would never have dreamed up such a plan to save himself. He would have appealed to a works driven salvation, which is evident by all who try to approach God in ways other than the prescribed manner. A god who takes on human flesh and pays for something he did not do makes no sense to the darkened mind.

Man would devise a gospel that is much more difficult than the simple message presented in Scripture. Paul had encountered such people in Athens. The Bible says when they heard about the resurrection of the dead that they sneered. (Acts 17:32)

The wisdom of God is permanent. Philosophies come and go. The wisdom of humanity-which is really foolishness, will one day be destroyed. God will reign supremely as King of kings and Lord of lords. We are prone to solve problems our way without consulting God for wisdom. We depend on transitory wisdom. Our efforts have failed in large part for we still encounter many of the same things that have plagued humanity throughout its existence. Human wisdom only sees the problems while God's wisdom helps us view the root causes.

Reflection: The power of God's wisdom is seen in the change that takes place at salvation. Those who trust his wisdom find true freedom.

September 7
The Wisdom of God
I Corinthians 1:26-2:5

Human wisdom does not always get us what we want. One Andy Griffith episode introduces a spoiled brat named Arnold. He gets an enormous allowance and has a dad who gives him almost anything he wants. If he does not, Arnold pitches a fit, pouts or holds his breath. Opie decided he would try those measures to get an increase in his allowance. Trouble is, it did not work with Andy.

Some of the first century Christians may have lost some prestige, influence and income when they trusted Christ, but Paul reminds the Corinthians that very few of them were in that category. Neither did Jesus choose followers characterized by such traits. His disciples were just run of the mill men and women.

The paradox of God's wisdom is that he usually does not choose those who are wise in the world's eyes to be his followers or do his work. Choosing people who have many resources often leads to them getting the rewards, praise and accolades. It is not normally the Phi Beta Kappa's, millionaires, famous athletes, entertainers, or noted statesmen that are making strides for God. But when God takes the poor, untalented, and unrecognized people and uses them, then he gets all the glory.

The nature of philosophy is to doubt and try to explain. But there are many things in the spiritual realm that must be taken by simple faith. Pride and dependence on accomplishments keep many from the kingdom of God. The simple person who has nothing to brag about in life is far wiser than the philosopher who doubts the gospel message. God takes the world's nobodies and makes them somebodies who will impact a lost world.

God's main purpose for his wisdom is to bring salvation. This then leads to a higher purpose of bringing glory to himself through that process. Our life becomes a living testimony to the unsaved that God can take the sinful, weak and unwise and make them righteous, strong and wise. .

As we understand and accept God's wisdom, we come to see that we must offer it to others. Paul did not go to Corinth as a philosopher but as a messenger of God's grace. We must testify of what we have experienced.

Reflection: Thank God that he takes the unknowns of the world and uses them for his glory and in his work.

September 8
Unity in Christ
I Corinthians 1:10-17

For those who remember the cold war years between America and the former Soviet Union, June of 1995 was an important month. On the twenty ninth of that month, six Americans and four Russians entered the Mir space station. They exchanged grins, handshakes and hugs after the docking of the Atlantis space shuttle. It was a major step toward building an international space station, which later was completed.

The Corinthians were doing what many people still do-quarrel. Sadly, the bickering often enters Christian relationships and churches.

Remembering our unity in Christ helps stem the flow of such divisive mentalities. Quarrels come because of our selfish egotistical nature as we let our interests outweigh that of others.

Humanity's sinful nature is the root cause of divisions. Even though Christ heals this at salvation, our learned fleshly patterns from that time in our life can cause us difficulties if we do not learn to live a Spirit filled life.

Paul makes a plea for the Corinthian Christians to agree. Our unity enhances our testimony for him, while factions and bickering tear down our witness. The name of Christ is damaged when his children do not learn how to play together. While we may disagree on some particulars of the faith, these disagreements should not escalate to the point that we break fellowship.

Our divisions can place a barrier between unbelievers and the gospel message. Christians can have different interpretations and their own opinions on matters the Bible is not explicitly clear on, but unity must be maintained on the core doctrinal beliefs. This leads to effective, healthy and harmonious fellowship. Our temperaments and personalities may differ, but we serve the same Lord. The psalmist wrote of how good and pleasant it was for believers to dwell together in unity. (Psalm 133:1)

The unity of believers is based on the oneness of Christ. Christ is not divided, and his people should not be either. No human leader should gain the trust and loyalty that only Christ deserves. Paul wanted no part of a faction named for him. A divided church is a contradiction.

Reflection: Paul said that all believers are one body in Christ. (Romans 12:5)

September 9
Walk in Love
Ephesians 5:1-7

Only July 14,1861, Major Ballou of the Union Army, penned the following words to his wife, Sarah. It was one week before the Battle of Bull Run. "If I do not (return), my dear Sarah, never forget how much I love you, and when my last breath escapes me on the battle-field, it will whisper your name." Love. Young hearts blossom with it. In spring, it seems to float in the air. It is a wonderful emotion but often misunderstood.

God desires that his children walk in love. Love for him and love for each other. Love should characterize our daily lives, and it also fulfills God's law. Paul wrote in another epistle that the commandments not to steal, not to murder, not to commit adultery, not to covet and any other commandment was summed up in the one rule to love our neighbors as ourselves. (Romans 13:9)

Walking in love requires tapping into the source of true love-God. Only as we understand the love God has for us can we adequately love others. His love demonstrates itself in tenderness, kindness and forgiveness. All that God does for us, in us and through us is because of his love. God's love moved him to create. More importantly, it prompted him to intervene in our self-inflicted sin problem. It was the love of God that raised Jesus from the dead, thereby validating the work on the cross.

God wants us to mimic him, and we are able to do this as we allow him to conform us to his Son's likeness. It is important to know the teachings of Scripture, for it is here that we see the picture of God.Recognizing our sad state before Christ helps us identify with those who are still in that position themselves.

We walk in love by following the pattern of Christ. Jesus once ate at the home of Simon, a Pharisee. While there, a prostitute entered and anointed Jesus' feet with tears and perfume. Simon questioned why he would let a woman like this touch him. She was unclean. Jesus told Simon a story about a moneylender who forgave two people the debt they owed. Love is always willing to forgive. Love loves the unlovely. Love is more than a feeling or emotion. It is giving portions of us to others. And it is unconditional.

Reflection: Remember God's love for you. Love him in return, and love others in his name.

September 10
Walk in Wisdom
Ephesians 5:15-17

The opposite of a wise person is a fool. Webster defines a fool as "a person with little or no judgment, common sense, wisdom, etc." The Bible says that fools believe in their hearts that there is no God. (Psalm 14: 1) Fools are corrupt and do abominable deeds. They cannot understand the things of God.

Foolish people act foolishly. They commit crimes, are unfaithful in their marriages, and argue and bicker over insignificant things. But the greatest act of foolishness is the person who will not acknowledge Christ as their Savior. They deny God with their words and through their actions. Since the foolish person denies God, they must invent something or someone to fill the void. They become their own god and authority.

Wisdom is the opposite of foolishness, and it begins with fear of the Lord. (Psalm 111:10) Acknowledging God and his ways makes us wise. The ancient Greeks looked to sophistry and philosophy for their wisdom, but Paul looked to God. So should we.

Wisdom involves monitoring our lifestyle. We are children of light and must pay close attention to our words, actions, and attitudes. The wisdom to walk like this comes when we trust Christ as our Savior. Jesus forgave the woman caught in adultery but then told her not to sin anymore. Forgiveness implies a different lifestyle.

God continues to increase our wisdom as we grow spiritually. The Bible instructs us to grow in the grace and knowledge of our Lord and Savior Jesus Christ. (II Peter 3:18) James reminds us that if we ask, God will give more wisdom in a generous manner. (James 1:5) We must live circumspectly, always on guard against people or things that would cause us to stumble and sin against God.

With the wisdom of salvation has come the privilege of making the most of our time. All people have boundaries. The believer's boundary is limited time on earth. What we do for God, we must do quickly. We only have so many opportunities for service.

Reflection: Napoleon said, "There is in the midst of every great battle a ten to fifteen minute period that is the crucial point." Make the most of the time God has given you to do his work.

September 11

Defining the Child of God

Ephesians 2:11-22

Barriers are the bane of human history. They divide and can even shut out completely. Throughout much of history, they divided slaves and free persons. Barriers have led people to look down on women and those of other races or cultures as inferior. The ancient Greeks viewed their language as that of the gods. Sir Philip Gibbs, in his book, *The Cross of Peace*, said, "The problem of fences has grown to be one of the most acute that the world must face."

Barriers are a source of heartache for God, for all of humanity has been created by him. He desires for all people to live at peace as far as is possible, and he certainly expects his children to be unified. Realizing who we are in Christ helps us along this path.

Believers were once alienated from Christ. Karl Marx, founder of Communism, used the word alienation to describe what happens between workers and owners. When the worker produced, a part of what they produced was in the product, which was sold. This would alienate the worker from himself.

In the early Church age, the alienation was between Jew and Gentile. While God chose to work through the Jews until the Church age, it was never his intention that only they could know him in a personal relationship. Instead of being a light to the nations, they developed an attitude of superiority. Jonah typifies this attitude when he got angry when God did not destroy the Ninevites.

Our alienation from God meant we were without hope. Our sins weighed us down and made us odious in God's sight. The Bible classifies our position as dead in trespasses and sins. The Christian's eyes need to see all people apart from Christ as in this condition. Race, ethnic group or social status has no bearing on this condition. Seeing all people in these dire straits will make it easier for us to minister to them physically and spiritually.

While alienated apart from Christ, we are all unified in him. In Christ, any existing barriers are manmade. The blood of Christ brings all people near to each other. Paul said that believers are all one in Christ. (Galatians 3:28)

Reflection: Ask God to help you see that he loves all people.

September 12

Guidelines for Marriage

I Corinthians 7:8-16

Marital failure is almost epidemic. Half of all first marriages end in divorce and a large part of second marriages do as well. Many suggestions are given for this. Some say a lack of proper counseling before marriage. Others marry for the wrong reason. Easy divorce leads many to just walk away when problems arise. Lax moral standards in society as a whole lead people not to fear being ostracized by society for their behavior.

God's Word gives guidelines for all groups of people where marriage or singleness is concerned. Paul says it would be better for the single person and widows to remain as they are: single or single again. This group could also include those who had divorced before their salvation experience.

Society and family members often rush people into marriage. They want to play the matchmaker. Paul reminds us that it is acceptable to remain single. One does not have to feel guilty about being single. In fact, it gives a person more time to serve the Lord. Nor do widows who have lost a spouse need to rush into another marriage. The church was responsible for ministering to their financial needs.

Marriage is not superior to singleness, but if a person cannot control their sexual desires, they need to marry. Sexual expressions outside the marriage covenant are forbidden by God. The person who does not have the gift of celibacy will become frustrated trying to live the single life. But neither should one in this situation marry simply for sexual expression. Marriages based on this alone are destined for failure.

In a Christian marriage, the union should be considered permanent. Jesus had taught the same when he said that what God had joined together man should not separate. (Matthew 19:6) Certainly, God is not part of many marriages, either in the beginning or later. The foundation is cracked.

If one spouse leaves, Paul says they should remain unmarried or reconcile. Neither should one spouse send the other away. Jesus added to this teaching by giving adultery as grounds for divorce. The implication is that the offended party can remarry. Another instance we might consider is when severe physical or emotional abuse is present.

Reflection: Recognize that the marriage bond is serious in God's sight and should not be entered into lightly.

September 13

Guidelines for Marriage

I Corinthians 7:8-16

How tragic that many no longer enjoy lifelong marriages. Not because death takes one partner, but because it simply did not turn out as they imagined it would. Or one partner was unfaithful and chose not to repent and mend the marriage. Or because they just tired of their partner and wanted someone new. What does God's Word have to say?

If a Christian is married to an unbeliever, and the unbelieving partner wants to remain in the marriage, then the Christian should honor that request. Perhaps both were unbelievers when they married, but one chose to trust Christ and the other did not. Or one may have been a believer when they married but did not understand the biblical teaching not to be unequally yoked.

The Christian in the marriage puts a holy influence in the home. This not only influences their marriage partner but also the children who otherwise would not receive godly teaching. Hopefully, the believing spouse will lead their partner and children to a relationship with Christ.

A marriage between an unbeliever and a Christian should be avoided at the outset. Christian parents should teach their children to only date other believers. Much heartache can be prevented when mixed marriages are avoided. More often than not, it is the believer who suffers in these relationships. They have a partner who will likely not support them or join them in their faith experience. Prevention is the best medicine. Yet one Christian in a home can greatly sanctify that home for Christ.

Unequally yoked marriage partners can also face another scenario. The unbelieving partner may want to leave. If this is the case, the believer is not under obligation and must let them go. Paul now adds another justification for divorce in addition to Jesus' reason of unfaithfulness. The believing partner really has no recourse, for one cannot force a partner to remain in a marriage. The believer can encourage their partner to stay and even agree to counseling, but in the end the other partner makes the final decision. Again, the intimation is that the abandoned partner can remarry.

Reflection: While God's ultimate desire is for marriage to remain intact until death, the Bible does give three exceptions for termination: death, unfaithfulness and when an unbelieving partner wants to leave.

September 14

Mary's Lessons on Faith
Luke 1:26-45

Shortly after Dallas Theological Seminary was founded in 1924, it almost folded because of financial needs. On the day the creditors were ready to foreclose on the school, the founders met to pray for funds. At the same moment, a tall Texan strolled into the office, told the secretary he had just sold some cattle, and that God told him to bring the money to the school. She quietly entered the prayer room and handed them the envelope. As the president looked at the check, he found it to be the exact sum needed to satisfy the debt. Coincidence? The founders had faith it was God.

There are many events surrounding the Christmas story that require faith. Angels announcing a birth. A virgin giving birth to a sinless baby. Wise men who saw a different type of star. Angels appearing to shepherds in the field. Mary had faith.

Faith believes that something is true. An angel-Gabriel, was sent to the village of Nazareth where Mary lived. He announced to her that she had found favor with God and had been chosen to birth God's Son, the Messiah. Even though Mary questioned how this would happen since she was a virgin and not married, she believed when the angel told her it would be by God's power.

Faith is more than an academic nod. There is a great deal of theological data in God's Word to go along with the stories. We must take this material by faith. Faith believes what we cannot see or prove with scientific methods. Faith makes a difference in our life. It is the confident assurance that what we hope for will happen. (Hebrews 11:1)

Faith is yielding our life to what we believe. Mary went a step beyond listening to what the angel told her. She accepted her position as the Lord's servant and told the angel she would do whatever God wanted. Faith has two sides. We believe then act on the belief. We must allow God's truths to have an effect on the way we live.

Faith looks for the fulfillment of the promises. Mary anticipated the birth of her Son. God's Word is filled with promises to believers. We must trust him to fulfill each one. God is faithful to his word.

Reflection: Are you living by faith each day? Trust God with every detail of your life.

September 15
Mary's Lessons on Fear
Luke 1:26-45

I once watched a television show about teens and their fears. The results were interesting: losing a parent, loneliness, academic failure, AIDS, and school violence. But fear does not stop with childhood or adolescence. Fears follow us into adulthood.

Fear leads to holding on thinking we are in control instead of allowing God to accomplish his perfect will in our life. We fear what he might ask. What he wants might radically change our plans. As a result, we often give God only portions of our life. Mary had to overcome her fears so God could accomplish his plan in her life. She was a young woman. Some scholars think maybe only fourteen years of age.

Mary could have feared the supernatural. After all, the events taking place were of that nature. We often dismiss or explain away the supernatural simply because we cannot understand it. Since the angel told Mary not to be frightened, it stands to reason that she was. Put yourself in her position. Her willingness to accept God's plan shows she overcame her fear.

We must overcome this fear. His sovereignty, omniscience, and omnipotence all witness that he is supernatural. The entire salvation process that we base our faith on is supernatural. Only by supernatural power could the righteousness of Christ be applied to sinners. Rather than fear, we should stand in awe of the mighty God we serve.

Inadequacy can also make us afraid. Mary was a young poor female. In her society, any of these were reason for fear. Then for the angel to announce God's plan only added more occasion for fear. She would be pregnant and not married. In our own strength, we are inadequate, but in Christ we can do all things he asks of us. His Spirit in us gives all the strength we need to carry out the work he assigns. We are complete in Christ.

Fear can accompany change. Mary's life was about to undergo change in a radical way. We are creatures of habit. Change interferes with our routines. But change is always involved in God's work. God is constantly working to alter attitudes and actions that should not be in our life.

Reflection: Thank God that he is able to help you overcome all fears. He has not given us a spirit of fear but of power and of love and of a sound mind. (II Timothy 1:7)

September 16
What's So Great About Salvation?
John 6:35-51

One of the great disasters of the twentieth century was the sinking of the *Titanic*. It was one of the worse maritime disasters where over 1500 of the 2000 persons on board died. The most recent movie features a wealthy girl and poor boy falling in love. Jack and Rose are together to the very end. In spite of Rose's efforts to hold onto Jack, he eventually slips below the water's surface and perishes. The movie depicts the utter depletion of hope for many, and such is the same sad state for humanity apart from Christ.

Jesus, however, proclaims himself as the bread of life. Bread nourishes and is a cheap fix for filling if money is short and nothing else is available.

317

Sit down hungry at a table with yeast rolls, eat a few of them and see what happens to your appetite. Bread can save from starvation, and Jesus can save from hell.

Salvation reminds us who we are. It is not a pretty picture, and some even deny the Bible's portrait of humanity. But the picture cannot be modified. We are enslaved by sin. It is our master, and we will perform his dictates no matter how diligent our efforts to the contrary. The consequences of our actions will lead to death-physical and spiritual. We are not able to pull ourselves up by our bootstraps as Enlightenment thought taught. Rather, it is our boots caked with the crud of sin that bogs us down. A daily perusal of news events demonstrates the truth of what Scripture teaches: we are all sinners.

But salvation reminds us of who we can be. If we eat of the Bread of Life we will never hunger or thirst again. The hunger and thirst are spiritual in nature. Intellectual knowledge does not discount the need to visit the grocery store. Jesus told the Samaritan woman that he could give her water that would forever quench her thirst. (John 4)

Jesus is a perpetual spring welling up in us. He is the only thing that will continually satisfy all the needs we have. In him, we can be all God created us to be. Life in its fullest is only experienced in a relationship with him. You are important to God. Jesus even calls you his friend.

Reflection: Salvation reminds us that we are totally dependent on God. Self-confidence is permissible but only when based on the belief that all one's power comes from God. Thank God for his wonderful salvation.

September 17
What's So Important About Priorities?
John 6:1-15

One Andy Griffith episode shows the Town Council deciding to sell the old canon. It was an eyesore and cracked to boot. Andy and Barney were assigned the task of finding a buyer. They carted it all over town. No luck. Finally they happen upon an antique dealer passing through town. After an embellished story of the canon's history, Andy persuades him to buy the relic. What is important to some is not to others.

Priorities. They can be misplaced or absent altogether. They can be rearranged or never considered. Priorities are those things of vital significance, and Jesus had his in place. Only one miracle made it into all four gospels-the feeding of the five thousand. Jesus' popularity was at its height. Throngs of people hounded his steps. He wanted time alone. But no secluded time was to be found.

The crowd is enormous; the day is almost spent, so the issue of food arises. One suggests sending them away so they can get food in town. Jesus takes over and has the crowd sit in groups. Then he takes five loaves of bread and two fish and feeds them all. Seeing the miracle, the crowd wants to crown him king, but Jesus retreats into the hills. What was important to some was not to him.

Priorities are imperative, but having the right priorities is even more important. Imagine a life where cutting the grass is just as essential as spending time with your spouse or children. Or when cooking supper is more critical that visiting a sick friend. Or when feeding the dog is as crucial as feeding your family. All things are not equally important.

Jesus had priorities. The crowd was important, but he knew many in the crowd were there for the wrong reasons. Time alone with the Father was more important. Ministering to those who truly believed in him was vital. God, family, church, and others is a worthy list to consider.

It is entirely possible that others will not always understand our priorities. They probably did not with Jesus. If you had thousands following you, would you retreat to the hills? Our priorities should be God-given. What is important to God should be central to us. Then when others do not understand, it gives opportunity to explain our convictions.

Reflection: Examine God's Word for biblical priorities.

September 18

Life's Final Appointment

Hebrews 9:27-28

There is a legend of a rich merchant in Baghdad who sent his servant to the market. While there, the servant was jostled by Death. He hurried back to his master and requested a horse that he might flee to Samaria.

Later, the merchant went to the market, found Death, and inquired as to why he was bothering his servant. He replied; "I was startled to see him in Baghdad because I have an appointment with him tonight in Samaria."

Appointments are part of life. Doctor, dentist, job interview, meetings, church, dinner. Most of life's appointments can be canceled, postponed or even rescheduled. But not death. It is life's final appointment.

Death is not an appointment most care to keep. Even believers are not usually eager to hasten their entrance into eternity. There is a great deal of unknown that surrounds the issue. We have not talked to anyone who has been to heaven and returned.

Death brings a change in environment. Global warming, pollution, overcrowding, greed, selfishness, crime are all negative aspects of our environment. Heaven will be different. Sin will be absent, and righteousness will prevail. In describing this place, John wrote that the home of God would now be among his people. He would live with them forever. God himself would be there, and he will remove all our sorrows, crying and pain. The old world and all its evils will be gone forever. (Revelation 21:4) How wonderful to know that this world is not all we have to hope for.

Heaven will usher in a change of nature. We are all born with a sinful nature. At salvation, God gives a new nature and makes us a new creation. The sinful nature is gone, but the fleshly temptations are still there. In heaven, the spiritual battle will end. Satan will be cast into hell forever and sin will be destroyed. Our natures will be perfect, and God will restore us to what he originally intended us to be.

A great family reunion will take place in heaven, unlike any earthly family reunion we have ever attended. All of our loved ones who believed will be there. We will interact will all the great saints.

Reflection: The greatest part of the final appointment is that it will usher us into the very presence of Jesus. We will see the one who gave his life for our salvation. Are you ready to meet him?

September 19
Doing the Impossible
I Samuel 17:41-50

Intelstat was a 4.5 ton telecommunications satellite that was useless. It was out of orbit 230 miles above the earth. It was up to Endeavor astronauts to do the seemingly impossible. Swaddled in 255 pound rubber suits, and suspended in midair with no net, they wrestled the satellite into the shuttle's cargo bay, attached a booster and sent it into its proper orbit.

Some things in life appear impossible. Saving enough for our children to attend a reputable college. Making ends meet each month. Taking on a new responsibility at work. Going back to school as an adult. Teaching a Sunday School class. Leading the church choir.

What God calls us to do can also seem impossible. It must have for young David. As he takes food to his brothers in Saul's army, he hears the taunts of the Philistine giant, Goliath. The Israelite army cowered in fear, and he wondered why they were not standing up for their God. David did what seemed impossible. Donning only the garb of a shepherd, he marched up to the giant and imbedded a stone in his forehead.

Doing the impossible requires acting responsibly. David was a conscientious shepherd. He cared for his flock protecting them from wild animals that would kill them. He showed responsibility by obeying what his father asked him to do, getting up early in the morning to take food to his brothers. The walk was a long one.

Acting irresponsibly leads to defeat. We must prepare to meet what appear to be hopeless situations in life. God will never desert us, but he does expect responsible behavior on our part.

The impossible involves courage. David certainly needed this to face the giant. Giants come in all shapes and sizes in our life. One of the Marine's famous sayings is, "If it's hard we will do it today. If it's impossible, it may take a little longer." Believe that God will give you the courage to do whatever he asks.

Faith is most assuredly involved in doing the impossible. David believed the same God who delivered him from the bear and lion would help him defeat Goliath. The Christian life is lived by faith.

Reflection: With God all things are impossible. Like David, he will enable you to serve him in all the capacities he requests.

September 20

Components of Biblical Self-Esteem

John 14:1; 16:33

In April of 1996, the world mourned the death of Commerce Secretary Ron Brown and 34 others who were killed in a tragic plane crash in Croatia. They had gone there to help rebuild Bosnia. As their bodies arrived at Dover Air Force Base, President Clinton was there to console the families. In part, he said of those killed, "They went to help people build their own homes and roads, to turn on the lights in cities darkened by war...They were all patriots." They could feel good about what they were doing.

Yet research continues to discover a host of people who do not feel good about themselves. People whose self-esteem has hit rock bottom. They visit counselors, pastors and psychologists. They take medicine to help them cope. Still many cannot escape the dark cloud that hangs over them.

Religion has not always helped this situation. Messages have often seethed with negativity. Apart from Christ, our plight is indeed hopeless. But in Christ the situation is entirely reversed. We can feel good about ourselves because of Christ in us. Christ overcame the trials and tribulations of this world, and we will too. He will return for us.

Humanity has inherent worth. While not negating the sinful nature that we are born with, we can still learn to see the good in people as we look at what they can become in Christ. After creating humanity, the Bible reminds us that God created humans in his own image as male and female. (Genesis 1:27)

What gives us inherent worth is the image of God in us and that God cared enough to create. Being made in God's image can mean several things but the most important is that we have something the animal kingdom does not. We can think, reason, feel and perform at a higher level.

Still more important is our ability to relate to a higher Being-God. We are created to care for his creation, to control his creation, and to relate to him as we do. Our worth is not based on our performance or other's opinions but on who we are in Christ. Learn to accept yourself because of what Christ has done in you. Then look at others in the same light instead of with disdain, prejudice or a judgmental spirit.

Reflection: Thank God for making you so special. Remember he cared enough to create you and to give you forgiveness.

September 21

Components of Biblical Self-Esteem

John 14:1; 16:33

On April 6,1996, in Oklahoma City, President Clinton, along with others, remembered the 168 people who had been killed one year earlier in a terrible bombing incident. Speaking to their survivors, he said, "What you have done has demonstrated to a watching and often weary and cynical world that good can overcome evil, that love can outlast hate." It is acceptable to have a healthy dose of self-esteem.

God gives a sense of security. This is a necessary component of feeling good about ourselves. After telling his followers that their work was to extend to the end of the earth, Jesus promised them he would always be with them. He is always with us every day of our life. We are never alone. Additionally, God promises to supply every need we have.

God wants us to have a strong self concept. He told Jeremiah that he knew him before he was formed in the womb. He had also consecrated him. (Jeremiah 1:5) God has a purpose and plan for your life. You are not a mistake. Parents may tell children that, but our heavenly Father never looks on a child in that manner.

We can have a sense of purpose. God does not save us just so we can bask in the joy of our salvation. He has work for us to do. There is a world who needs to hear of his saving grace. Technology gives us opportunities unheard of before. Use your gifts and talents to carry out God's work in your part of his creation. Trust God for the strength to do what he calls you to do. And never stop serving God no matter what age you are. Believers should never enter into spiritual retirement.

Believers should have a sense of belonging. We belong to the Creator, God Almighty. When we accept Christ as our Savior, he accepts us into the best family possible. All believers become our brothers and sisters in Christ. We share a common bond and will share the same eternal destiny. We have the awesome opportunity to impact people's lives for eternity.

Christians are also empowered. We can do all things through Christ. We can feel competent in the work we do for God. He has authorized us and given us his Spirit for strength and guidance.

Reflection: Thank you Lord for making me your child. Help me to understand that I am complete and whole in Christ.

September 22

God's Way for Church Growth

Matthew 16:13-20

It happens in churches all across our land every Sunday and Wednesday night. The faithful gather for worship and prayer. The trouble is, only a small portion of them show up. A perusal of church life will show that Sunday morning is the largest attended service. Church records in a majority of churches will reveal few if any baptisms. The large majority of Protestant churches are either plateaued or declining in attendance.

On the other hand, God intends for his church to grow, individually and universally. Jesus said the gates of hell would not prevail against it. God's church will grow but we must work diligently to see that the growth is significant and qualitative.

Persistent prayer is a key ingredient. Our prayers do not change God's mind about whether or not he wants a particular church to grow. Prayer clues us in on what God wants us to do. Our opportunities are different. Our communities vary. And so do our resources. Not all churches can do the same thing in the same way and expect the same results. There is no program that is a one size fits all.

Prayer prepares us for the work God has in store. No effort should be undertaken without bathing it in prayer. We often move forward and then ask God to bless our efforts. We need guidance before taking the first step. Just as prayer is foundation for our individual spiritual growth, so it is with church growth.

Churches need positive leadership. Smaller churches understand this even more, for most of their leaders are volunteers. Nehemiah is a positive example. He motivated the people to rebuild the walls of Jerusalem. God's leaders should have a spirit of love, joy, fellowship and excitement. Programs are not as important as the leaders who inspire them.

Proper perspective is important in church growth. A congregation with the right perspective can experience growth. Growing churches have a can do attitude that sees them through any potential pitfalls and problems. They believe in a God who has no boundaries. The church is filled with expectancy. They make adjustments and move toward positive solutions.

Reflection: Growing churches are passionate about reaching others with the love of Christ. Help your church realize its full potential.

September 23

Church: The Reason Why
Acts 2:41-47

A synonym for objective might be purpose. One thing a teacher does in teaching a particular course is set forth a list of objectives. Some will be general while others are very specific. Some will pertain to the course itself while others will speak to the student. At the end of the year, she can look back and evaluate whether the objectives were met.

Similarly, churches should have goals and objectives. The two basic goals any church must have are to reach and teach. Leaders in that church are responsible for evaluating the activities of the church to see if the church is adequately fulfilling those God-given objectives. In the Great Commission, Jesus gave his followers the responsibility to tell others of his love and then teach them his commands.

Worship is a main function of any church. The early believers devoted themselves to the apostles' teachings. They had intense and full hearted devotion to worship. They broke bread together. Fellowship meals are not a modern invention. As they worshiped together, there was an awesome awareness of the presence of God. Are you excited to have the opportunity to praise God? Worship must be in spirit and truth, and when it is it ushers us into the very presence of God.

We live in a time when churches have to sponsor many programs and activities to attract congregants. There is nothing inherently wrong with this, but churches must always guard against the entertainment factor. If we have to entertain people to get them there, we will have to entertain to keep them. Church is not about entertainment but worship of Almighty God.

It is a church's responsibility to instruct in biblical doctrine. We must teach others the deep truths of Scripture. As babies grow, so must believers. Spiritual immaturity is not acceptable and is avoided when God's people not only learn the Word but use their gifts. Doctrine is vital. Worship is not just about good fuzzy feelings. There must be sound instruction.

Fellowship is important. The Bible instructs us not to neglect the gathering of ourselves together. We must then express our faith to others. This part of our Christianity is done throughout the week.

Reflection: God allowed Jesus to give his life for the church. Will you work to see it be successful?

September 24
A Contagious Church
I Thessalonians 2:1-13

When something is contagious, it has one of two effects. It either draws or repels. When someone has a contagious disease, it repels. Anytime fall arrives and a new strain of flu erupts, it is common to see people wear masks when in crowds or at medical facilities. On the other hand, when something is contagious and exciting, people are attracted to it. They put things aside to join. They rearrange schedules and juggle priorities.

The church has both affects on people. The excitement in some churches leads the worshippers to advertise their church. The excitement catches on and before long a crowd grows. But in other churches, people stay away. It may be that they have interacted with some of the worshippers during the week and observed them living in unChristlike ways. Or the church has gained the reputation of being a troubled church.

A contagious church will love God's Word. We have been entrusted with the greatest message of hope. It is a trustworthy guide that will never fail and will never lead us astray. God's Word tells the way to salvation. Then it gives instruction on how to successfully live the spiritual life. The Word is actually a person: Christ. And the church exists to proclaim him to others.

There are several word pictures that apply to God's Word. It is like a rail that keeps a car from running off the road and plummeting down the mountainside. It is similar to a sand trap that stops us when life seems to careen out of control. It can be compared to a lamp that shines the love of Jesus into a world darkened by sin.

Contagious churches are authentic. There is no hidden standard. They truly want to touch others with the love of Christ because they have experienced it themselves. They want to teach others how to live by God's principles. God's church has no room for hypocrites, except those who need to know Christ.

A contagious church will have a gracious attitude. Their existence is based on God's grace, and they understand how to share that with others. A church is a family, not a corporation.

Reflection: Contagious churches recognize the need to be relevant. They determine the needs in their area then meet them with godly principles. Help your church be contagious.

September 25
Giving That Pleases God
Romans 14:10

C. S. Lewis in his book, *The Joyful Christian*, said, "I do not believe one can settle how much we ought to give. I am afraid the only safe rule is to give more than we can spare." This one verse reminds us that one day all people will stand before Almighty God to give an account of our lives. One area that believers will be examined in is stewardship. Daniel Webster once said, "The most serious thought of my life is that I, as an individual, am accountable to God."

Godly giving is possible when we remember that everything we have belongs to God. He is the author of your financial and material resources.

But he is also the originator of your time, talents and opportunities. Your life has been designed by him, and he has selected you to have those things needed for your particular opportunities. He has given you the ability to gain what you have, but this does not negate the fact that he is the author of it all.

Our giving will please God when we learn to budget ourselves. Budgets are guidelines built with flexibility. They normally relate to our finances and show us what goes where, when and how much. Our time in God's work must be budgeted. We can wear too many hats. We can also neglect other important things for church. We must have balance.

Balance comes when we examine the gifts and talents God has given us. Then we look for areas to work in that allow us to use those gifts. This can be in and outside the church. Just as much, if not more, of God's work takes place outside the walls of the church. On the other hand, we can give so much of ourselves to outside activities that we have no time for God's work.

Proper giving always involves motives. Jesus said the giving of the widow was more than what all the others had put in the Temple treasury. The amount is not as important as the motive behind it. Many small gifts are large in God's sight. Motives also determine whether or not we will be rewarded for the giving. Why do you give? To earn God's approval or the praise of others? Is it out of habit or because you feel guilty?

Give liberally. We cannot out give God. Faith will enable us to give in this manner and with the right motive. God does not need our money, but he does use it to advance his Kingdom.

Reflection: Commit to giving of your whole person to God.

September 26

Building Families of Faith

Genesis 18:1-5; 9-14

Mothers and fathers have a great impact in the family. The type of character behavior often witnessed in children who come from broken homes enforces that conclusion. Chuck Swindoll said of the family, "Whatever else may be said about the home, it is the bottom line of life."

While Abraham is considered the father of the faithful, he had some family problems. His promised son was not arriving quickly enough, so he and his wife took matters into their own hands, making a mess in the process. But then as Forrest Gump once said, "God showed up."

Families of faith know God will provide. As faithful as Abraham was, he seemed to forget this one golden nugget. When the promised heir did not arrive as quickly as Sarah wanted, she gave her servant to Abraham as his wife. It was an acceptable custom but not part of God's plan. Abraham went along with the bad plan.

Later when it came time for the promised son, Isaac, to marry, Abraham sent his servant to his homeland to find Isaac a wife. He did not want him to marry from the pagans that he lived among. And God provided a wife for Isaac in Rebekah. She too was initially barren. But perhaps she and Isaac learned a lesson from his parents. Isaac prayed to God about the situation, and God provided her with a child.

God will provide for your family. The God who knows when one sparrow falls to the ground knows about the needs in your family. Finances, loss of a job, a child rebelling, or frightening news from the doctor. God knows and cares. Trust him.

Families of faith believe in God's protection. Moses is an example of this. He was born when the ruler of Egypt had declared that all Hebrew boys were to be killed. His mother hid him in a basket and placed him in the Nile River. Pharaoh's daughter found him and rescued him. He was raised in the finest splendor of Egypt.

There is certainly nothing wrong with taking measures to protect our family. But God is our ultimate shield. From the first day they go to school to the wedding day, we have to trust God to protect our children.

Reflection: Your family is under the providential care of God. Trust him for wisdom to guide your family along spiritual paths.

September 27
Dealing With Discouragement
Nehemiah 4:6-14

Life is filled with discouragements and discouraging news. AIDS runs rampant and takes the lives of many innocent children in the process. Seniors suffer with Alzheimer's taking away their ability to function on their own and even recognize their own family. We get discouraged at school when our grades are not what we desire. And at work when the boss seems unreasonable and the hours required are long.

Like the man standing on the bridge preparing to jump. A passerby happens upon him and questions why the discouragement. He told him there was just too many things wrong in the world to keep living. After ten minutes of listening to his discouraging report, they both jumped.

Discouragement is a deadly and pervasive disease. It is universal, affecting all classes and cultures of people. It is reoccurring. Getting over it one time does not mean it will not appear again. It will. It is also very contagious. But it is one trait we do not want to catch.

God's people had just returned from seventy years in Babylonian captivity. The walls of Jerusalem lay in ruins. Nehemiah returns to help rebuild the walls. It was not long before the builders encountered opposition. Any time we are doing God's work, the Enemy will strike.

Fatigue can lead to discouragement. Because of their enemies' opposition, the workers had to guard the city day and night. They were tired. Lack of rest altered their perception of the situation, as it will ours. God's work is important, but so is rest so we can adequately complete it.

God designed our bodies to rest. Eight hours of sleep is recommended. This may mean rearranging some priorities. In fact, when the body has received enough sleep, it will wake on its own. Some would say, "Sure, my kids would never make it to school on time," or "I would lose my job after two days." But research proves the point. There was a time before alarm clocks, and people worked and had families.

Frustration can lead to discouragement. The work of rebuilding the wall was proceeding well but not quickly enough for the builders. Deal with the things in life that frustrate you.

Reflection: Look to God in times of discouragement so you can have proper perspective on life's circumstances.

September 28

Dealing With Discouragement
Nehemiah 4:6-14

A magazine editor told of a miserable Easter. Her daughter's husband of only one year had left. She was almost immobilized by shock and sorrow. Her job required minute focus. As Paula stopped to buy souvenirs for her grandchildren, the store clerk remarked about God's beautiful world. Paula shared her daughter's troubles, but the clerk reassured her, "Oh, but God is good. He will work on your daughter's behalf." An encouraging word for discouraging times. How often we need that.

Fear can lead to discouragement. The builders in Nehemiah's day feared their enemies. They feared they could not muster the strength to move the rubble and complete the walls. They even feared death.

Fear can immobilize us. We find ourselves running from what God wants us to accomplish. We simply do not perceive that we have the abilities needed, so we make excuses or just ignore him. At church, we turn down opportunities. At work, we do not put in for promotions. At school, we avoid the challenging classes. Fear can lead us to give up. To jump off life's bridge.

Discouragement can be dealt with by reorganizing. To complete the work in the midst of threats, this was necessary. Nehemiah stationed guards while the workers built. This gave them a sense of relief.

Lack of time can lead to discouragement. Rearranging priorities is always in our power. While there are some things we have to do, we tend to accumulate unnecessary or less important things along the way. Sometimes we need a yard sale, but not from junk in the closet. Allow God to help you establish priorities that honor him.

Nehemiah instructed the builders to remember the Lord they served. What they were doing was at his behest, and he would protect them as they completed the task. Their God was great and glorious. Yours is too. In fact, he's the same One. God's Spirit constantly abides with us enabling us to do what God requires without getting discouraged.

Resisting is a cure for discouragement. The builders had to resist their enemies. We too must resist the Devil so he will flee from us. He is the author of discouragement. He tempts us to give up, to walk away.

Reflection: Whatever life throws your way, depend on God to help you face it without discouragement overtaking you.

September 29

Doing Missions Jesus' Way

Acts 1:4-8

Stunted growth. Maybe we have known a child who had a physical defect that prevented them from developing normally. Some have bodies that grow while their minds lag behind. Others have sharp minds but deformed bodies. Whatever the case, it saddens us when we see children that do not develop properly.

One fear believers have is living their entire life and missing God's purpose for them. A fulfilled life is two-fold. It begins by accepting Christ as your Savior but it continues by doing missions or ministry. It is equally important to do our ministry God's way. Jesus is our prime example.

Jesus did missions where others refused to go. In John chapter four, we read of Jesus leaving the region of Judea for Galilee. On the way, he had to go through the area of Samaria. The "had to" was not a geographical "have to." Like other devout Jews, he could have crossed the Jordan River, bypassed the region of Samaria then reentered Galilee. The Samaritans were a mixed race and hated by most Jews.

Jesus went through Samaria to meet a woman at a well who needed to hear of and accept him. Following Jesus' example will take us to mission fields that other Christians may avoid. We shun these fields for various reasons: race, culture, or social status. If we are not careful, we can become exclusive in our reach. Or we can do like a group from Burlington Street Ministries in Vermont who decided to do ministry on a nude beach.

We need to talk to people that others will not talk to. Jesus did that with the Samaritan woman at the well. Being a rabbi, it was not proper for him to do so and definitely not in public. The woman's reaction when Jesus spoke to her illustrates he was doing something out of the ordinary. When the disciples returned from town, they too were disturbed over

Jesus' actions. A perusal of the Gospels will show Jesus made it a habit to shock others by things he did and said. Who do you need to talk to?

Jesus also helped those others would not assist. Lepers are a good example. They were outcasts, but Jesus healed them. Whose life do you need to touch?

Reflection: Only when we do missions Jesus' way will our lives be fulfilled and complete.

September 30

Hey God! We Have Some Questions

Genesis 1:1; Psalm 53:1

Does the topic make you a little uneasy? Probably so if you, like many, were taught that you should not question God. But questioning acts of God and asking questions of God are two different matters.

The Bible is filled with believers who asked questions of God. Some nonbelievers simply question God. After all, we do not know anyone who has actually seen or talked to him. We pray and feel God listens and speaks back, but we never hear an audible voice. Barna Research Group once performed a study that showed thousands who attend church consider themselves atheists or at least agnostics.

History demonstrates that people have different ideas about God. Some believe everyone is God. Others believe he exists and will accept us based on good works. For some, God is simply a higher state of consciousness. And then there are those who believe in many gods. A humanistic psychologist might believe God is a crutch we invent.

Then come the age old questions. Why do bad things happen to good people? If God exists, how can he allow sin? Is heaven real? Was Jesus really divine and human? Why does God allow natural disasters to take the lives of many innocent people? How would God answer our questions?

God would remind us that he does exist. There is no scientific proof, but there is also no proof that he does not. Faith takes us out of the realm of science. This does not mean that faith is unreasonable, but it operates on another level. We cannot know God by sense perceptions. Just because we have not seen God does not means he does not exist.

Most of us have never seen one million dollars either. But it exists. God does not prove his existence to us through a personal appearance but in nature and through salvation.

God would also tell us he is sovereign. He controls the world and all things that happen in it. This should give us the utmost confidence that things are not spinning out of control.

The most inspiring thing God would tell us is that he is knowable. For him to exist and humans be accountable to him but for him not to be knowable would be a terrible experience. We can know him through Christ.

Reflection: God loves you beyond your ability to comprehend. But you can know him by faith in his Son. Trust him. Believe he is in control.

October

October 1
How to Handle Life's Pressures
Mark 6:14-29

Can you relate? A mom who feels she cannot satisfy the demands of her son. A son who is pressured to take over the family business but wants to move in a different direction. The young woman at college who is pressured to live with her boyfriend. The husband complaining that his wife never satisfies him. The secretary who is completely tired of the phone. The wife married to a man who thinks her faith is silly.

Herod caved in to pressure. He was involved in an illegal marriage to his brother's wife. John the Baptist seemed to constantly remind him of his sin. Herod's wife did not appreciate these reminders and looked for an occasion to get rid of him. She found it at Herod's birthday party which was attended by some important people. Herodias sent her daughter in to dance for Herod. She pleased him so much that he asked her to request anything she wanted. At the prompting of her mother, she asked for John the Baptist's head on a platter. Not wanting to embarrass himself in front of his guests, Herod granted the appeal.

What we do when life's pressures mount? Don't give in. Herod did because he feared embarrassment. Herod faced the pressure of maintaining his popularity with the Jews and the Romans. Popularity is one of the main peer pressures for adolescents. And politicians. Everyone wants to be liked. At work, pressure comes in wanting the boss to like us. But Herod was willing to murder an innocent man to save face.

Herod faced the pressure to conform. John wanted him to conform by fixing his illegal marriage. His wife wanted him to conform to her plans to get rid of John. The guests expected him to conform to the promise he made. Then there was the pressure to accept John's religion. Do not give in to the pressures of popularity, conformity or acceptance of false religions. God gives us the power to stand firm against ungodly pressures.

Life's pressures keep coming. God also grants the ability not to give up as we continually face them. Many of our pressures can be relabeled temptations, and God has promised that he will not allow these to be greater than we can deal with. He will also make the way of escape.

Reflection: Thank God that no matter what the pressure, he is there to guide and strengthen you.

October 2

How to Know You're Alive

I John 5:11-13

There are ways to know you are alive. Medical professionals refer to them as vital signs. Blood pressure, pulse and responsiveness. Suppose a terrible crash occurs on the interstate. As the ambulance and police arrive, they notice two cars with people inside, but no one is moving. As they approach the vehicles, they observe the victims have been thrown around and there is blood on the seats. The first thing they will probably do is check for vital signs. If there is no blood pressure or pulse, the person is not alive.

Similarly, there are ways to know a person is spiritually alive, and it has nothing to do with the signs we check for physical life. Blood pressure and pulse can be healthy and strong and the person be spiritually dead. Spiritual life is not as easily discernible. Some do not know whether they are spiritually alive. Others are not sure, and still others think it is impossible to know. But we can know beyond the shadow of a doubt.

We know by checking the manual: God's Word. John says God has testified that eternal life is found in his Son. Where does God testify of this? In his Word. Just as the medical student learns how to know if a person is alive physically, so God tells us how to know if we are spiritually alive.

The main sign of spiritual life is what a person has done with God's Son. Accepting him and what he did on Calvary moves us into spiritual life. People make this decision when God visits them by the convicting power of his Spirit. Christ was qualified to make this sacrifice because he was the sinless Son of God. He was our substitute who took our sins and gave us his righteousness.

A further sign of spiritual life is the presence of God's Spirit. This person of the Trinity is sent into our lives when we trust Christ as our

Savior. The person who does not possess the Spirit does not enjoy spiritual life. When God's Spirit lives in us, our lives will show love, joy, peace, patience, kindness, goodness, gentleness, faithfulness and self-control.

Though the Manual tells us what it takes to have spiritual life, we have to check our pulse to know if we do. It is each person's individual responsibility to make sure they are rightly related to God.

Reflection: Have you checked your spiritual pulse lately? Have you accepted Christ? Is your life producing spiritual fruit?

October 3

Stewardship Questions We Must Answer

II Corinthians 9:6-10

On one Andy Griffith episode, Andy is elected chairman of the needy children's charity drive. Donations were received among the townsfolk and at the local schools. But to Andy's surprise, his son Opie had only donated three cents. He was devastated and reminded Opie how bad that made him look as the sheriff. Little did he know that Opie was saving his money to buy a needy girl in his class a winter coat.

One said, "Money isn't everything, but its way ahead of whatever is in second place." Then there is the business person who said, "We operate our business by the golden rule. Whoever has the gold makes the rules."

The religious leaders of Jesus' day were noted for their strict adherence to God's laws, some of which required tithing of their money and goods. Yet Jesus would rebuke them for being good at this but neglecting mercy, justice and faith. This reminds us that stewardship is more than just money. It includes time and the use of our gifts. God's work requires money and workers. Jesus did not throw money at the cross but gave himself.

An important question is, "Why should I give?" We give because we have been given to. God is the author of all you have. You may have exerted time and energy, but he gave you life and skills to use. Since God gave, God owns. From your lawnmower to the curling iron, it all belongs to him.

Because God is the owner, we should give to him first. Tithes and offerings do not come out of the check after all other bills and entertainment costs are subtracted. This type of giving leaves none or, at the least very little, for God. We give to him first then trust him to care for our needs. We are then accountable to God for how we handle what is left. Giving is also done because God commands it.

The need of humanity is a further reason to give. Jesus reminds us that the poor will always be with us. God blesses us with resources, and he expects us to use them to help others. Additionally, there are still many who need to hear the gospel message, and it takes money to fund such outreach ministries.

Reflection: When we give and do so from the right motives, God promises to open the windows of heaven and pour out a blessing on us so great we will not be able to contain it. (Malachi 3:10)

October 4
Where Do We Find True Meaning?
John 17:1-5

A thought provoking question to say the least. And many vain pursuits have been made trying to do just that. A special spouse or child. Large homes. Land. Material wealth. The right job. A good church home. Social contacts. Addictive habits. Many have tried all or some of these. How sad to live out our years on earth and miss the meaning of life.

Shakespeare has Macbeth say of life, "It is a tale Told by an idiot. Full of sound and fury Signifying nothing." Mark Twain said shortly before his death, "They (men) vanish from a world where they were of no consequence....a world which will lament them a day and forget them forever."

In this prayer, Jesus prays for his current disciples as well as those who would be his followers through the ages to come. His desire was that his Father would keep them safe from Satan's power and would set them apart as pure and holy. But also in the prayer, he tells where the true meaning of life is found. The answer is found by telling what the true meaning is not.

The meaning of life is not found in general knowledge. Our world places a great deal of emphasis on knowledge. We feel it is important for our children to have this and to have it in the correct areas.

Knowledge in general will never lead one to Christ. We can study the humanities in depth and still miss the meaning of life. Science and math can be deeply ingrained in our minds, but the subjects will not guarantee salvation. John faced the Gnostics in his time. They believed special knowledge guaranteed them interaction with God. They were wrong.

Nor is the meaning of life found in the pursuits of this world. In fact, the Bible tells us not to love the world or the things of it. (I John 2:15) The world entices our lust for physical pleasures, material pleasures and pride in those things. The Book of Ecclesiastes shows how Solomon tried all of these things and found they were vanity. Like chasing the wind.

The true meaning of life is only found in a relationship with Jesus Christ. Eternal life is knowing God and His Son whom he sent to die for our sins.

Reflection: Trust Christ as your Savior today. If you have, ask him to help you live the abundant Spirit filled life he offers.

October 5

A Pattern for Prayer

Matthew 6:9-15

Charles Spurgeon, famous English Baptist pastor, said, "A prayerless church member is a hindrance, he is in the body like a rotting bone, or a decayed tooth." James Leo Garrett, Jr., noted Baptist theologian, concurs, "Prayerlessness is the taproot of the Christian's sins and failures."

There is much about prayer we do not and cannot understand. If God is sovereign and controls all things, how can our prayers change his mind? Does prayer really alter anything? Do diligent prayers by God's people modify a course of events? Or maybe the only thing prayer changes is me.

While we may never understand all the dynamics of prayer, it is a certainty that the Bible encourages us to pray and do so diligently. While this prayer is usually referred to as the Lord's Prayer, it is actually the believer's prayer. The Lord's Prayer was made in the Garden of Gethsemane prior to Jesus' arrest and crucifixion. Here he requested the cup of suffering be taken away if possible. It was where he submitted to the will of the Father. Nor would Jesus ask for his sins to be forgiven since he was the sinless Son of God.

Jesus spent an enormous amount of time in prayer, and we should as well. It is the spiritual air we breathe. A regular dose keeps us in tune with God's plan for our everyday life. Regular prayer time also gives a place where God's Spirit can speak clearly to us. In this prayer, Jesus does not teach that we have to repeat these exact words every time we pray. Rather, it is a model which we add to.

Our prayers should recognize the Fatherhood of God. The prayer is not a recognition of this concept in that all people naturally belong to him. It is not a prayer that validates universalism. It simply recognizes that he is the Creator. In this sense, he is the Father of all. But this is a believer's prayer, and from this standpoint, God is only Father to his children. Like a respectable father, God does for us what all good fathers do for their children. As our father, he takes away our fears, uncertainties, loneliness and selfishness and replaces them with resources that enable us to obey him. He will care for us now, guide us through life and provide for us in eternity.

Reflection: How wonderful is the privilege of prayer. Commit to spending time daily with your Heavenly Father.

October 6
A Pattern for Prayer Part II
Matthew 6:9-15

An old saint said of prayer; "True prayer brings the mind to the immediate contemplation of God's character and holds it there until the believer's soul is properly impressed."

Prayer recognizes that God's name is hallowed. Though Jesus says believers are his friends, this is not an authorization to treat God's name lightly. He is not our good buddy. He is our Creator and the Sovereign of life. True prayer does not bring God's desires in line with yours but just the opposite. It also leads us to reverence him and stand in awe of who he is. Hallowing God's name begins in the heart and then transfers to our actions. We will desire a set apart life as well as one that draws him into every area.

Our prayers clue us in to God's program as we pray for his Kingdom to come. God's kingdom is referred to in the past, present and future tense in different scripture passages. All three aspects apply. God's kingdom is his rule. He has always ruled over his creation, he still does, and he will one day rule supremely as King of kings and Lord of lords.

Prayer recognizes God's plan. That his will be done on earth as it is in heaven. In some respects, this is happening. There are certain unalterable aspects of God's plan that humanity cannot change by their actions. Such as the Second Coming. On the other hand, there are actions we can take that interfere with God's plan for our individual lives. Like acts of disobedience. God's ultimate will is that people come to know his Son and use their gifts in serving him. Answers to our prayers are not nearly as important as a deepening dependency on God. Prayer brings that.

After recognizing the position and plan of God, we ask him to supply our daily needs. God's Word promises that he will for his children, but the request acknowledges our dependency on him. Many people have never experienced a time when they actually did not know where the next day's food would come from. But at the same time, there are thousands over the world who do not know. As God has taken care of his children in the past, so he will in the present and future.

Reflection: As you pray, thank God that he is in control. Involve yourself in his world-wide plan of redemption, knowing with assurance that he will supply all your needs.

October 7

A Pattern for Prayer Part III
Matthew 6:9-15

Sin. No matter how diligently we may try to avoid it, there will still come occasions when we will commit acts of sin. It is not necessarily our intention to fail God, but Satan moves into the weak areas of our life, and we cave in.

A vital part of prayer life is confessing sin to God. We ask for forgiveness even as we forgive others. As God forgives us, he expects the same from us. The parable of the unforgiving debtor, as told by Jesus, illustrates this. The master forgave a servant who owed him a large sum of money. The servant demonstrated his misunderstanding of forgiveness by finding a fellow servant who owed him far less and demanding payment from him. Though the servant begged for time and mercy, he showed none.

God forgives when we acknowledge our sinfulness and ask forgiveness. There are no conditions other than believing in his Son's work on the cross. Once forgiven, we must forgive. Jesus reminded Peter of this when he told him that his forgiveness must be unlimited. (Matthew 18:22)

Forgiveness is releasing someone from a debt they owe you for a wrong they have committed against you. Unlike trust, forgiveness should be instantaneous. When we have been deeply wounded by someone, we may have to forgive them more than once. Only God can enable us to release those who have hurt us. But remembering how great our sin was against God and how he freely forgave will help us forgive others. No offense against you will ever compare to your offense against God.

Forgiveness demonstrates our relationship with God. Failing to forgive will take away happiness and peace. One Puritan writer said, "There is none so tender to others as they which have received mercy themselves."

Prayer also requests God's protection. The greatest danger we face is not from nature or others but from Satan. We need God's strength so we will not yield to his temptations. God promises a way of escape. He also promises that he will not allow temptation to be so great that we cannot help but give in. Avoid those situations and places that will make it easier for Satan to tempt you.

Reflection: Pray without ceasing. We do not always have to close our eyes. Be in an attitude of prayer throughout your day.

October 8

A Wise Warning

Matthew 7:15-20

Life is filled with warnings. Cigarette packs show various warnings about potential health problems. They also warn pregnant women against smoking. Advertisements warn against drinking and driving. Stock portfolios warn that past gains do not ensure future profits. Certain medicines carry warning labels for those who have other medical issues.

Jesus cautions against those who would deceive us. False prophets were not new to the Jewish people. Moses had forewarned the people against them in the early pages of the Old Testament. Jesus told of how many would come claiming to be the Christ. (Luke 21:8) John reminds us to test the spirits to make sure they come from God. (I John 4:1) Paul refers to them as savage wolves that will devour believers if they are not alert. (Acts 20:29)

People are always looking for something or someone to believe in. How else do we explain the millions that followed Hitler even in the midst of the atrocities he committed? He proposed an idea to elevate the German people after their humiliating defeat in World War I. They believed him.

False teachers are dangerous when they claim to be sent from God. They can be found in God's churches and will wreak havoc if not exposed and removed. The religious leaders of Jesus' day were prime examples of how Satan can use religious people. They were wolves disguised in sheep's clothing. A firm foundation in God's Word will help us easily recognize those who espouse false information. David Koresh and Jim Jones are examples of false prophets who were successful in leading many astray and even to their deaths.

Our own identity is revealed by examining ourselves. Just as a tree is known by its leaves or fruit, so the believer is known by the fruits of the Spirit that grow on their branches. These are produced because of our relationship with the Vine. Grapes are not gathered from thorn bushes or figs from thistles. Your motives, standards, attitudes and fruits will show where your loyalty lies. That great reformer, John Calvin, said, "Nothing is more difficult to counterfeit than virtue."

Reflection: Jesus issues a warning to those who are deceivers. They will be judged by God. Let others know who you are by your spiritual appearance.

October 9
Abstaining for God
Matthew 6:16-18

Fasting. Or even cutting back. Popular and unpopular subjects. That is, we talk about it and even make many resolutions to do better but often break them before the ink is dry on the paper. Most Americans eat too much and too much of the wrong things and as a result develop health issues that could be avoided. But enough of that depressing subject.

Mahatma Ghandi was famous for his fasts. He did it so Indian textile workers could get a raise. He did it for Indian independence from Britain. It is amazing how one man's fasts unto death could bring owners and governments to their knees as they feared he would actually starve himself to death.

Fasting is spoken of in the Old and New Testament but is a practice that probably very few believers undertake. Jesus even fasted. We can fast from many things, but the idea here is from food. The intended result is some element of spiritual growth. The religious leaders of Jesus' day were good at fasting. The trouble was that they did it for show. This is the reason for Jesus' rebuke and his instruction not to let our fasting be obvious.

Fasting was a practice observed by many Old Testament saints. It was voluntary except on the Day of Atonement. All Israel was to abstain on that day. People fasted during times of repentance, when mourning over sin, or when national disasters occurred.

By the time of Jesus, fasting had been perverted. It was a ritual to gain approval from others. Some practiced it in an attempt to win God's favor. People would put on old clothes, mess up their hair, put on makeup and cover themselves with dirt and ashes.

Early Christians fasted not over sin but to gain God's direction for their life. Cornelius sent for Peter to bring the gospel to the Gentiles, but the instructions came to him while he was fasting.

While fasting is not commanded of Christians, neither is it forbidden. It can be very appropriate if God is leading you to this practice for a specific purpose. It must be linked to prayer and a sincere heart. And there are things that we can fast from other than food.

Reflection: Remember that fasting must result from our desire to see God and his will for our life more clearly.

October 10
Good as Your Word
Matthew 5:33-37

Many can remember the time when a person's word was all that was needed to seal a contract. At the most, the deal might be finalized with a handshake. But no more. No longer can a car or home be purchased with a promised word but no signed contract. Mounds of paperwork now greet us.

Paul Harvey once told of four high school boys coming in late for school. When the teacher questioned them, she was told they had a flat tire. To test their truthfulness, she sat each one in a different corner, gave them a piece of paper and pencil, and asked, "Which tire was flat?" English poet, Chaucer, said, "Truth is the highest thing that man may keep."

In the Old Testament, God provided for oaths to be made using his name. When sending his servant to find a wife for his son, Abraham made him swear by God's name that he would not find a wife among the pagans. When promising to bless Abraham and multiply his descendants, God swore by his own name.

Since God knew humans were prone to lying and deceit, he allowed the using of his name in making oaths. An oath would increase the motivation to tell the truth. But oaths are only as reliable as the people who make them. Peter, under oath, denied that he had been with Jesus. The oath did not make his statement true.

Like many of God's laws, this one was also perverted. Any vow was permitted as long as it was fulfilled thus making vow making meaningless. Oaths became so commonplace that no one took them seriously. As in saying, "I'm sorry" but continuing in the same behavior. Then came a further perversion. Honesty behind a vow was only necessary when it concerned a matter pertaining to God.

Jesus says we do not need to make any vows. When you are as good as your word, there is no reason for an oath. Just mean what you say, and say what you mean. There are times when we have to take oaths, such as in court, but Jesus was addressing the flippant and hypocritical attitude that had developed. Our thoughts, words, and actions always need to be clothed in truthfulness.

Reflection: Make it your commitment to always tell the truth. Be as good as your word.

October 11

Responding to Enemy Behavior
Matthew 5:43-48

Suppose you were a lifeguard at an ocean resort. As you looked across the ocean waves, you saw a person in trouble. It was a good friend of yours. Or it was your son. You would quickly exit your post and make every attempt to rescue the drowning person. But what if the person was someone you did not care for. They had wronged you. Better yet, you knew they had just been released from prison for child molestation. Would it make any difference in your effort? Would you even leave your post?

According to Jesus it should not matter. God loved us while we were still sinners. He even sent his Son to die for us. (Romans 5:8) The people had been taught to love their neighbors and hate their enemies. But Jesus reminds them that was not what the Old Testament taught. They were supposed to love their neighbors as they did themselves. For those of Jesus' time, anyone who was not an Israelite was an enemy.

We are to love our enemies. As hard as that is, Jesus commands this of believers. It is the heart of the New Testament. Jesus does not ask something of us that he is not willing to do himself. His ministry demonstrated this willingness, and the cross was the ultimate picture. Love always involves action, so to love our enemies means to act in their behalf. Our love must overlap the barriers of race, nationality, culture, sex or political party. Enemies will hate us and act accordingly, but our desire must be to love away that hate.

We can pray for our enemies. Jesus did that for those who were crucifying him. There will be forms of persecution that we will have to undergo for our faith. It may be physical but more likely will be things like being made fun of, people avoiding us, or being overlooked for a promotion. In spite of opposition, we must pray that they would come to know the forgiveness of Christ as we do. We must desire that God's love be deposited in their hearts.

Our enemies need to see our relationship with Christ. They need to observe the Golden Rule exemplified in our lives. Most do not love and pray for their enemies. When we do this, we stand out in the crowd.

Reflection: When people oppose you because of your stand for Christ, return that anger with love and prayer for them.

October 12
How to Be an Effective Influence
Matthew 5:13-16

The famous saying by John Donne reminds us that "No man is an island." Elihu Burrit wrote, "No human being can come into this world without increasing or diminishing the sum total of human happiness."

Influence is one of those things we do intentionally or unintentionally. But regardless of which way we do it, we still have one on others. It can be positive or negative, encouraging or discouraging. It can be consistent or inconsistent. This is one of those life matters in which we do not have a choice. You cannot choose not to have an influence on others.

Believers have an awesome responsibility to have a good influence on others. Our actions and response to them may very well determine their response to the gospel. Our challenge is to influence rather than reflect their lifestyles. We are not to love the world but rather persuade those who are controlled by the world's philosophy.

That we need to be salt and light to the world presupposes there is something wrong with the world. It needs some flavor. There is a pervading darkness. What is wrong is sin. Sin has corrupted this world, and it is the Christian's responsibility to influence our society for Christ.

While humanity has advanced in many ways, the sinful nature is still there. We will not "evolve" to a point where we lose this as some evolutionists say we have other body parts. As long as time exists, man will be born sinful and in need of salvation. Our increase in technology has only created more ways to sin. David recognized he was sinful from birth, even from the time his mother conceived him. (Psalm 51:5)

As disciples of Christ, we are to dominate our world for him by being salt and light. This is not a suggestion but a command from God. So the question is how effective are we being as salt and light. Salt can kill, enhance and preserve. Our influence should preserve and enhance. We are the only hope the world has. Rather than letting others influence you, be the influencer. God does not ask us to do this alone but together in force. We are not individual grains of salt or rays of light. It was said of Helen Ewing that "she left the fragrance of Christ wherever she went."

Reflection: Ask God to help you remember to shine your light and sprinkle your salt every day. Be a positive influence for Christ on others.

October 13

How to Handle Anger
Matthew 5:21-26

"He makes me so angry." Have you ever made such a statement? A cruel remark by a friend or work associate. Gossip behind your back. Your peer at school. And anger begins to boil within you, and before long you have said or thought something you should not have.

In reality, no one can make you mad. Just as forgiveness is a choice, so is anger. Others may create situations that enhance the possibility of anger, but we still choose to exhibit that emotion. It is one of those emotions that then leads to the flight or fight syndrome. We retaliate or walk away.

Nor is anger a sin but can quickly lead to sin. (Ephesians 4:26) Anger is an emotion that God created in our human makeup. Jesus himself became angry over the merchants cheating people in the Temple, but his anger did not lead to sin. (John 2) Nor does ours have to. When we become angry, we are to process it quickly and in a godly manner.

Anger is a dangerous emotion. It can destroy our relationship with others and God. It can even destroy us physically. Anger can lead us to have a judgmental spirit. It can lead to rifts between people. It most certainly hinders our ability to worship God. While Jesus is concerned with the inward state of our heart, he is also concerned with our outward actions.

The first responsibility we have when angry is to admit it. This seems like a simple solution, but is often very difficult. Admitting our anger also involves confessing that we were wrong about something that led to the anger. We may have thought or acted in an inappropriate manner. If we hold our anger inside, it will eventually erupt in unhealthy ways. Anger repressed or expressed wrongly can damage relationships, harm us physically and disrupt our walk with Christ. Anger not admitted and dealt with grieves the Spirit of God and places us outside the realm in which he can use us.

If possible, we are to correct the situation that led to the anger. We cannot adequately worship God when we are angry. Religious acts cannot compensate for reconciliation. Reconciliation is not always possible, but we must make the attempt.

Reflection: Remember that anger is a choice. When situation arise that can easily lead you to become angry, ask God to help you respond in love.

October 14
How to Inherit God's Kingdom
Matthew 5:1-3

Happiness is the mad pursuit of many. From money to notoriety to relationships, we search for that one thing or person who will help us feel fulfilled. But happiness is not found in people or things. It is discovered in a relationship. Asking Christ to forgive our sins and be our Lord leads to a fulfilled life. Living our faith in practical ways leads to joy.

Jesus gives a conditional set of sayings referred to as the Beatitudes. This refers to a state of happiness or bliss. God's desire is for us to know happiness. Sadness is not a sign of godliness. Happiness is not conditioned by outward circumstances. It is an inward state of contentment that remains constant no matter the outward situations.

God's kingdom is not something we inherit ourselves. We must be poor in spirit to have it. This poverty is not financial. Additionally, rich is static in its definition. Those considered poor in America would be rich in developing countries. While wealth often gets in the way of following Christ, selling all we have is not a mandate to be his disciple.

The poverty Jesus speaks of is in spirit. It can be translated as "Blessed are those who realize their need for him." Poor should bring to mind a beggar who does not know where his next meal or night's sleep will come from. It describes one who has nothing at all. Nor is Jesus saying we should be poor-spirited in that we lack enthusiasm and drive.

Spiritual poverty is what Jesus has in mind. Only those who have such an attitude will come to Christ for help. It involves an attitude of humbleness where we let go of pride and allow God to fill us with godly humility. We must realize that we are bankrupt when it comes to entering God's Kingdom. It is only through the grace of God that we have any hope at all. God's standards are impossible for us to live up to without a new nature.

Inheriting God's kingdom means emptying ourselves. Self effort must be abandoned. When we become spiritually poor, God will bless us with unexplainable happiness. Emptiness comes before the filling as does repentance before forgiveness.

Reflection: Poverty of spirit will only come when you confront a Holy God and realize who you are as opposed to who He is. Thank Him that heaven is yours because of his forgiveness.

October 15

How to Know Who You Are

Matthew 7:21-29

Dietrich Bonhoeffer was a German theologian who was keenly aware of the deception and delusion of the Lutheran church of his day. He described their teachings as "cheap grace." While a profession of faith was carried out and good works were taught, many of the people were simply not born again.

Many today live self-deluded lives where Christianity is concerned. Some think living in a Christian nation is enough. Others believe their good works will compensate. Or that the coattails of others will usher them into the kingdom of God. I will never forget the testimony I once heard from an older gentleman who told of how at a certain age he had walked the aisle and joined the church. Church membership will not suffice.

Spiritual self deception can result from several things. A false doctrine of assurance believes acceptance with God is based on walking an aisle, taking the hand of a preacher, joining a church, saying a prayer or being baptized. Others have failed to examine themselves. The Bible commands us to do this to see whether or not we are of the faith. (II Corinthians 13:5) And then some concentrate on religious activities. They attend church, give, pray, read God's Word and do other religious things. There is also the idea of fair exchange where good outweighs bad.

We must look beyond a verbal profession. Jesus says that not everyone who says to him "Lord, Lord" will enter the kingdom of heaven. As these individuals stand before his throne, they will claim to have done many good things in his name, but he will declare that he never knew them. They thought they knew who they were, but they were mistaken.

Verbal professions do not necessarily equal faith. Such professions can be coerced or entered into because others were doing it. Pressure from peers or emotional highs can lead to unauthentic statements. Obedience to God's commands is the proof. Those who obey are like the wise man who built his home on a solid foundation. Faith is the only secure foundation. Intellectual knowledge without faith represents the man who built on the sand. His home was less secure than he imagined.

Reflection: Examine yourself. Are you in the faith? When obedience and good works follow your faith, then you can know who you are.

October 16

How to Receive God's Comfort
Matthew 5:4

Comfort is a commodity we all need at some point in life. The loss of a spouse, child or job. Unacceptable test scores. Rejection from our college of choice. Children in rebellion. A good friend moves away. Those times in life when we need a shoulder to cry on come more than we would like.

The psalmist expresses how we often feel. If he had wings like a dove he would fly away and be at rest. Or he would wander off and remain in the wilderness. He wanted to run away from the storm and tempest.

(Psalm 55) We have all been introduced to times of disappointment and have been tempted to walk away or just give up.

According to Jesus, mourning is the key to receiving God's comfort and the key to happiness. Sadness and happiness are opposites. But once again, a spiritual concept is in view. Improper mourning is feeling sad when the evil plans of wicked people go astray. Times of loss can lead to improper mourning. It is natural to grieve, but mourning that never ends, or grief that keeps a person from being able to function is improper.

The believer's mourning should be for others. While we should grieve for and with those who are traveling through life's difficulties, our greatest grief should arise for those who do not know Christ as their Savior. It is only natural for us to want others to experience what we have. The wickedness in the world should disturb us, but we should love those who are committing it. Our eyes should see what they can become in Christ.

Our walk with our Savior should produce a sound social conscience. Often, secondary needs must be met before the primary need will be realized. Believers should never criticize those movements that honestly endeavor to meet human need.

The primary meaning of Jesus' teaching is for us to mourn over sin. While Christians have had their sins forgiven, we still commit acts of sin. Sin should always disturb us as we recognize it is a failure to live up to God's standards. It leads us to miss his blessings. We should endeavor to always see sin through God's eyes, lest we lose sight of its seriousness.

Reflection: Comfort comes in knowing that our sins are forgiven, that the unrepentant will be punished, and that wrong will one day be forever rectified.

October 17
Investing in God's Program
Matthew 6:1-4

One of the most significant events of the late nineteenth century was urban and city growth. Immigrants and those from rural areas began to pour into the cities. Better education was available, and they could enjoy culture-theaters, museums and art galleries.

It was an exciting time, but with the influx came many problems. Transportation was inadequate, and health problems arose. Slums developed, and crime was on the rampage. To their credit, churches responded with a giving spirit. The social gospel gained momentum, and people were concerned with the poor.

Jesus speaks of the giving spirit his people should have. Some say a giving spirit comes naturally because of innate goodness, but a sharing spirit comes because of our relationship with Christ. People are naturally stingy. Any small child playing with toys will illustrate this truth.

Our giving spirit should emanate from a surrendered life. Giving can be hypocritical. We can give expecting a reward, recognition, out of a guilty conscience or because we want to impress someone. We can even give to decrease the amount of taxes we owe. Cain is an early example of giving with the wrong motive. When God confronted him about it, he got angry and killed his brother.

When we share to show off, it magnifies us and not God. Our giving is to honor and glorify him. Hypocritical giving brings us only one reward-other's recognition. God is not impressed. Our offerings are an investment and should be sacrificial.

We should look for spiritual rewards when giving rather than material. Whatever we sow we will reap. And the attitude in the sowing affects the harvest. The task of responding to the burdens around us can become wearisome, but we cannot grow weary in doing good for others. Remembering our ultimate goal will furnish us strength.

Proper and adequate giving always requires sacrifice. Good intentions and warm feelings are not enough. We must look for practical ways to meet other's needs.

Reflection: God delights in your acts of mercy. Give in a spirit of love as Christ has given to you.

October 18
Jesus Speaks on Adultery
Matthew 5:27-30

Nathaniel Hawthorne's *Scarlett Letter* comes to mind. Hester Prynne was sent to America ahead of her husband who was to follow later. After two years, her husband had still not arrived. Hester is found pregnant in a time when this was highly unacceptable. Evidence seemed to support the preacher as the father. Hester was found guilty of adultery. Rather than death, she was sentenced to wear a scarlet "A" over her breast for the rest of her life.

While attitudes about sex before marriage and unfaithfulness within marriage have changed greatly, God's ideal has not. Adultery is sexual relationships between two married people but with someone other than their spouse. Fornication is sex outside the marriage bond. Both are wrong.

Once again Jesus goes to the inward motives that precede the outward actions. On occasion, the outward act never occurs, but because of the inward thought the person is just as guilty as if they had acted. Lusting after a woman falls into such a category.

There is more involved in obedience to God's commands than the just the letter of the law. Jesus is not referring to men or women who glance at members of the opposite sex because they think they are attractive. Lust is dwelling, making plans or imagining.

Nor does Jesus espouse a return to Victorian attitudes about sexual relationships. Sex was created by God as a part of the marital union and for procreation. As a part of God's creation, it too was pronounced good. Society, on the other hand, uses it to sell products and push materialism. Believers must provide the proper teaching and examples. We cannot leave it to our schools, government, health centers or society to teach the proper role of sex.

The cure for lust is dealing with the desire. Committing the physical act of sex will not cure the disease. It will only return. The lustful look does not lead to sin. Rather the sin leads to the lustful look. We must ask God for the strength to deal with the desire. If married, our eyes should be for our spouses only. If single, we should avoid those situations that lead to lustful thoughts.

Reflection: Remember that sin begins on the inside in our minds. Be careful where and how you look.

October 19
Jesus Speaks on Rights
Matthew 5:38-42

On May 10, 1775, the Second Continental Congress met in Philadelphia. They appointed a committee to justify independence from Britain, and appointed Thomas Jefferson to prepare the draft. His statement has inspired the oppressed for years: "We hold these truths to be self-evident, that all men are created equal, that they are endowed by their Creator with certain unalienable Rights, that among these are Life, Liberty, and the pursuit of Happiness."

Since this time, people have used this statement to expand their rights. Our society seems consumed with rights, often at the expense of consideration for others. Anything that gets in the way of my rights is viewed as disposable. While used to support many movements, these verses show rights we must give up in serving Christ.

The "eye for eye and tooth for tooth" comes from the Old Testament and is known as the law of *lex talionis*. It stated that the punishment should fit the crime. It would be easy for vengeance and personal retaliation to take place, especially when a crime was committed against a friend or loved one.

Jesus says to turn the other cheek if someone slaps us on one cheek. In other words, don't do what comes naturally. He is not speaking of letting evil run rampant without a response but is speaking of personal retaliation. We must remember that vengeance belongs to God. His standard is that we are to love and care for our enemies. (Proverbs 25:21-22)

While we must resist evil in our personal lives and in the world, vengeful retaliation must be left with God. Christians must overcome evil with good. We do have a right to be treated with dignity, consideration and respect, but the emphasis is on how we react when we are not.

We must be willing to give up our right for security. If our shirt is taken, we should give our coat too. We must go beyond the fair legal agreement to show how sorry we are over the disagreement. Additionally, we must give up our right to time and money. Be willing to sacrifice your time for others. Remember that everything you have belongs to God, so share with those who have genuine needs.

Reflection: God, help me to be more concerned with other's rights than my own.

October 20

Keys to a Satisfied Life

Matthew 5:6

Hunger is a chronic problem that affects people and countries at various times and in different locations. In 436 B. C., famine came to Rome and caused many people to throw themselves into the Tiber River. There have been several occasions when all of Europe has suffered from famine. Even with the technological advances of recent years, hunger still stalks.

While physical hunger is dangerous and very real, there is a greater hunger with more far reaching consequences. It is spiritual hunger. In his usual twist of words, Jesus tells us this kind of hunger leads to a satisfied life. This hunger comes when we put aside our selfish pursuits, sins and eagerness for power. Putting these pursuits out of our life opens the door for us to bring in attitudes and practices that bring contentment.

Jesus speaks here of intense hunger and thirst, the type few of us have ever experienced. Unless we have lived through a famine, we will not fully understand his meaning. Our hunger and thirst to be more like Christ must be as intense as the hunger of a famine stricken individual. As they continually long for their stomachs to be filled, so we must for God's Word.

Unfortunately, studies generally show that Christians have a very weak desire for spiritual things. Bible reading is sporadic and so is prayer. Church attendance lacks consistency. Our lifestyles are not much different than the nonChristian. We need a strong passion to live as Christ expects. Like an addict, we need addiction to spiritual things. Believers must never reach a state of satisfaction. Do you have a passion to grow closer to God?

Seeing the need of this spiritual hunger is very important. Spiritual hunger is all around us. Sadly, people usually turn to other things to satisfy it: drugs, alcohol, immorality, destructive relationships. All of this and more is an attempt to satisfy a void that can only be filled by God.

As a child of God, we are admonished not to love the world or the things of it. Such should be foreign to us. All that belongs to the world system is passing away. A spiritual hunger proves our profession. Spiritual hunger leads to salvation and then to sanctification. A steady progress of becoming more like Christ.

Reflection: Remember that true satisfaction in life comes from pursuing the things of God not this world.

October 21

Life's Most Important Choice

Matthew 7:13-14

Decisions. Life is full of them. Choices come each day. British poet John Oxenham, in his poem "The Ways", wrote, "To every man there openeth/ A Way, and Ways, and a Way,/ And the High Soul climbs the High Way,/ And the Low Soul gropes the Low,/ And in between, on the misty flats,/ The rest drift to and fro./ But to every man there openeth/ A High Way and a Low/ And every man decideth/The Way his soul shall go."

Of all the choices that life holds, the choice to follow Christ is the most important. It has eternal consequences. While in the wilderness, God spoke to his children through Moses and told them he had set before them life and death. (Deuteronomy 30: 19) After entering the Promised Land, Joshua confronted the Israelites with a choice. They had to choose who they were going to serve. (Joshua 24: 15)

Jesus says we must choose between his ways and other ways. Between his standards and standards established by society. He appeals to a wide and narrow gate. The gates are not for us to stop, ponder and adore. Neither is entering an option. In life, we will go through one or the other.

Entering through the narrow gate results in eternal life while the wide gate leads to death. The narrow gate is hinged by a narrow gospel message. It is a message that states Jesus is the only way to salvation. There is eternal life found in no other. Nor is he one of many ways but the only way. The wide gate is represented by all other means people use to get to God other than through Christ.

There are several requirements to enter the narrow gate and walk the narrow path. We must enter alone. We cannot slip in on the profession of anyone else. It is also entered by repentance of sin. We must recognize we have offended God and choose to go in a different direction. We also enter devoid of self effort. It is only by God's grace that we can be saved. We must deny ourselves, take up our cross and follow him.

Charles Spurgeon said, "You and your sins must separate, or you and your God will never come together." The narrow way requires self denial and diligent work. It is a life of sacrifice. The broad way is easier and more attractive. But there is no security in numbers.

Reflection: Enter the narrow gate by Christ and find life.

October 22

Living the Merciful Life

Matthew 5:7

Mercy is a wonderful thing to receive in time of need. In December of 1620, the Pilgrims landed on a bleak shore in Massachusetts. It was a winter of hunger in which half of them died. As fortune would have it, there was an Indian in the area named Squanto. He served as an interpreter and showed them how to plant, cultivate and fish. The Pilgrims worked hard, got their crop in the ground and enjoyed a bountiful harvest the following November to which they invited their Indian neighbors.

Happiness is found in showing consideration to others even as Christ has shown us at the cross. When we realize our spiritual poverty apart from Christ, it will be much easier to demonstrate this mercy. Nor is thoughtfulness an option but something Christ expects his followers to give.

Mercy carries the idea of being charitable or beneficial. We are to show compassion. We are to help those who are afflicted with the pains and problems of this world. Jesus gives us a wonderful example of such compassion in the cross but also in the mercy he shows daily to his children.

The benevolence we show must evolve from proper motives. A guilty conscience or a desire to impress will not impress God. We love others because God has deposited his love in our hearts. And this mercy must be extended even to those who do not deserve it or who show no appreciation for it. Whether mercy comes from others is immaterial. We will always receive mercy from God when we show it to others. His spiritual blessings are abundant.

Doing good deeds for others always brings a sense of happiness. Often we train our focus solely on how difficult life is for us. Using our resources to help others helps relieve our burden. Life is not about looking out for number one.

We can show compassion in several ways. Kindness can be shown through physical acts. Feeding the hungry. Providing clothes to the needy. Visiting the sick and those in prison. We show mercy by letting go of resentment and grudges. Most importantly, we show mercy by loving the unsaved. Pray for them, and look for opportunities to share your faith.

Reflection: Thank God for his mercy, and look for ways you can show love to others.

October 23

Perspectives on Possessions

Matthew 6:19-24

The Kung San were a foraging people of the Kalahari Desert. They hunted and gathered and used their leisure time to cultivate fulfilling relationships. But then consumer items from the West began to pour in. They began to farm, herd and put up fences. Neighbors and family members grew farther apart. The South African army recruited them for soldiers, and they used their pay to buy more material things. Drunkenness and violence became a way of life. Whereas they were once very peaceful, they were now violent. They had a wrong perspective on possessions.

It is quite natural for us to be thing oriented. Our society promotes such an attitude. Most of what we go after in life are not needs but simply wants. These things place us on a different rung of the social ladder or make us feel better about ourselves. Some even believe that wealth, health and prestige are signs of God's approval, but this is not necessarily so. Jesus reminds us that our treasures should not be stored on earth but in heaven.

This teaching of Jesus reminds us that earthly possessions are transitory. Our treasures should not be garnered on earth. To lay up means to hoard or stockpile. It is a picture of excess wealth. We have it to show off or to create an environment of laziness.

On the other hand, the Bible does not teach that believers should be poor. Jesus did not specifically require his followers to give up all they had. And God does want us to enjoy what he gives. Scripture teaches us to work hard and to follow good business principles. It is nothing wrong with saving for our children or retirement. And it is certainly nothing sinful about having more than we need so we can use the excess to help others in need.

Still we must understand the temporary nature of what we own. They are subject to destruction by moth and rust. Thieves can break in our homes and steal our belongings. Leave something made of metal out in the weather long enough and observe the result. The Bible reminds us to cast but a glance at riches because they will sprout wings like an eagle and fly away. (Proverbs 23: 5) The Old Testament character of Job is a perfect example. All he had was taken in a moment.

Reflection: Ask God to help you remember that what you have is momentary. Our true wealth is found in our relationship with him.

October 24

Perspectives on Possessions
Matthew 6:19-24

The stock market crash of 1929 and the ensuing Great Depression was a stark reminder that neither possessions nor money is permanent. It was a time of great economic failure where one in four Americans was unemployed. People lost homes, farms and money. Businesses failed. Banks closed. And some took their lives because they could not cope.

Out attitude about wealth shows the state of our heart. Jesus says to store our treasures in heaven. They are safe there. But how do we put our stuff there? He also reminds us that we cannot serve two masters. We will either hate one or love only one. We cannot serve God and money. In time the word "mammon" came to mean that in which a man trusts.

When our attention is always on getting more, it demonstrates that our heart is not right. Giving our allegiance or attention to anyone or anything else other than Christ shows misguided perspectives. These two masters call us to do different things. One says walk by faith while the other says trust in what you have. One says to be humble while the other spews pride. One says to look below while the other tells us to keep our eyes on the sky. And one says to love light while the other says to pursue darkness.

Our attitude about possessions also reflects our spiritual vision. Our eyes are the lamps of our bodies. Clear eyes mean bodies full of light. Bad eyes mean bodies full of darkness. The eye illustrates the heart, which is not a reference to the organ in our body but to who we are. Our character. Our personality. Our intentions. When our eyes are clear, we possess single minded devotion to God. If our eyes are blurry, it means our life is crowded with a wrong perspective on material things and our spiritual life is suffering. Our attitude about possessions reflects our spirituality.

A proper perspective on possessions will lead to a generous spirit. Believers should understand that all we have belongs to God and comes from God. We need healthy eyes so our bodies will be full of light. Words closely related to the word used for healthy carry the idea of liberality. Since the eye represents the heart, Jesus is teaching that we should have generous hearts. Generosity should always characterize the Christian.

Reflection: God, help me remember that all I have comes from you. Give me opportunity to use your possessions to help others.

October 25
The Christian Marriage
Matthew 5:27-32

In Nathaniel Hawthorne's *Scarlett Letter*, Hester Prynne is forced to wear an "A" on her breast because she was an adulteress. In Christian circles, we often want to put a "D" on those whose marriages have failed. Half of all first marriages fail. Many of these believers are then relegated to second class citizenship in churches. Those in Christian circles have not always been friendly to those who have experienced marital failure.

Certainly divorce was not in God's plan. Marriage is designed for a lifetime, but sin mars the perfect picture. The sin of divorce is no greater than any other sin and is certainly not unpardonable. Believers should be sensitive to the effects divorced persons have to endure. Depression, radical change in financial states, and behavioral issues with children.

Believers hold different views about divorce. From thinking it is never permissible to believing it is for any reason, the opinions run the gamut. Then whether the divorced person should remarry and under what conditions also enters the picture.

Marriage is a divine institution. We can never understand divorce without first understanding God's view of marriage. God instituted the first marriage between Adam and Eve in the Garden of Eden. When united in marriage, the man and woman become one in the eyes of God. They do not lose their own identities or personalities, but they become one.

Marriage is the norm in any society. While some have the gift of celibacy, most people fall in love, get married and have children. God designed sexual relationships to take place within this covenant for the purpose of pleasure and procreation. Sexual relationships that do not fit this agenda are forbidden and sinful. Marriages where God is the head and the participants fulfill their God given roles are bound for success.

Marriage is holy and sacred and is a union of body, soul and spirit. A deep love must pervade the relationship. This love must go deeper than sexual attraction. Marriages based on this alone are bound to malfunction.

The union is intellectual and spiritual. More importantly, a Christian marriage is a picture of Christ and the church.

Reflection: Make every effort to keep Christ first in your marriage. Only He can help your marriage know success.

October 26

The Importance of Peacemakers
Matthew 5:9

Though America is a peace loving country, our nation and world has known little peace. The terrorist attacks of 2001 show how quickly peace can escape. Since 1945, there have been more than seventy wars and some two hundred outbreaks of violence. In our country alone, we have fought a Civil War, two World Wars, a Korean and Vietnam War, a Persian Gulf War as well as a war in Iraq and Afghanistan.

And then there is the search for peace in our individual lives and that of our families. This too often escapes us. Witness the many marital failures, suicides, and the number of people who visit counselors and psychologists.

Yet Jesus says we are to be peacemakers. As far as is possible, we are to live at peace with others. (Hebrews 12:14) It is the key to finding happiness. A true picture of peace is found in the early chapters of Genesis as Adam and Eve lived in the Garden. They walked and talked with God.Sin stole the peace. However, in Revelation we again read of the harmony that will be enacted at the end of time. (Revelation 22)

Peace is not found by escaping the world through confinement to monasteries and convents. Those peaceful surroundings do not change the outside society. Peace comes when we are willing to confront difficult situations and bring the peace of Jesus as a solution. As we try to bring outward tranquility we demonstrate the inner peace we have with Christ.

Those in Jewish culture greet each other with the word "shalom." It carries the idea that individuals have all the peace and goodness God can give them. Jesus is teaching that we are to establish love and harmony between individuals. Believers must be involved in resolving wrong attitudes and actions. Holiness will aid us in this pursuit. Lives void of this trait will stir up strife and react with vengeance and retaliation.

Striving for peace is not equivalent to peace at any price. We cannot overlook or approve evil so peace will result. The end does not always justify the means. We attempt and offer peace on God's terms. Since sin always robs us of peace, we must point others to a relationship with Christ.

Reflection: Ask God to enable you to be a peacemaker where you work and at home.

October 27

Knowing the Peacemaker

Matthew 5:9

A Chinese proverb captures the essence of this Beatitude. "If there is righteousness in the heart, there will be beauty in the character. If there is beauty in the character, there will be harmony in the home. If there is harmony in the home, there will be order in the nation. When there is order in the nation, there will be peace in the world."

To be a peacemaker, we must know the peacemaker. Jesus demonstrates this in his encounter with the Samaritan woman at the well. (John 4) There was no peace between Jews and Samaritans. Samaritans were half breeds and hated by Jews. But Jesus offered her a peace that reached beyond the boundaries of nationality. He offered her peace found in a relationship with Him.

To have harmony, we must know the peacemaker. This is why the efforts of so many are futile. They are searching for peace in the wrong place. Lack of serenity in our world results from lack of God in people's lives. Christ reconciles us to God. Then we can be reconciled to others. Christ can lead you to peaceful relations with people you thought you could never get along with or forgive. The shape of the cross itself shows peace with God and others. A vertical relationship is vital for horizontal relationships to flourish. On the cross, the righteousness of Christ overcame the problem of sin. The Father is the source of peace. Jesus manifested peace, and the Spirit brings peace in our life so we can channel it to others.

Christians have a unique peace. We often define peace as an absence of turmoil. But the peace Christ gives is stillness that transcends circumstances. We know God is in control no matter what happens. His peace is beyond our comprehension.

We are responsible for carrying this peace to others. Rather than looking down on others for various reasons, we see the peace they can know in Christ. Except for God's grace, we might be in their position. They can then carry that peace to others, and the process continues. Even when others reject our offer of peace in Christ, we can still find points of agreement. We must live with those who chose to reject him without being contentious.

Reflection: How much more enjoyable is the life lived at peace with others. When we do, God will call us his children.

October 28

The Importance of a Gentle Spirit
Matthew 5:5

Aristotle was a noted Greek thinker and philosopher.For him, the virtues of life were defined as the mean between an excess of the virtue and complete lack of it. Courage was the mean between cowardliness and foolish actions. Generosity was the mean between stinginess and waste. And gentleness or meekness was the mean between excessive anger and the inability to show any anger at all.

Gentleness is not high on most people's list of sought after virtues, and it was not in Jesus' day either. Rather, we are taught to look out for our interests. If people treat us unfairly, we should retaliate. The Jews of Jesus' day had similar attitudes. The Romans ruled over them, and they despised the oppression. They looked for a Messiah who would conquer these foreigners and right their wrongs. This attitude is in part why they misunderstood Jesus. He did not fit their preconceived notions.

Jesus had a meek spirit, and he instructs us to as well. Meekness comes from a supernatural work of God's Spirit.It is not a normal or natural human trait. It means to be mild or soft and is pictured by a soothing medicine or a gentle blowing breeze. When applied to individuals, it means to be tenderhearted, submissive or quiet in spirit.

Meekness does not mean to be cowardly, weak, indolent or spiritless. A meek person actually has courage and great strength. Jesus displayed the trait perfectly. He was tenderhearted and compassionate as he ministered to people's needs, but he also demonstrated courage as he confronted the hypocrisy of the religious leaders and more so as he endured the agony of the cross.

Having a gentle spirit will lead us to be polite, balanced and well mannered. We will behave like the animal who listens to the commands of his owner. It will also guide us to a spiritually subservient and trusting attitude. Meekness is power under control. We have rights, but we learn to defer them in the best interests of others. Not only is the power under control, but it is submitted to God. Meekness is necessary for salvation, witnessing and for honoring God with our lives.

Reflection: Only as we have a meek spirit can we truly inherit all God has in store for us.

October 29

The Lasting Word

Matthew 5:17-19

The Bible has been the most revered and most hated book of all time. Voltaire said in his day; "In one hundred years, the Bible will be an outmoded forgotten book, to be found only in museums." Yet it lives and is now in the language of more people groups than ever before. There is no divine power within the book itself, but it lives because of the One who authored it and has preserved it.

God's Word will last because it is preeminent. Jesus reminds us that he did not come to destroy the law and prophets but to fulfill them. This does not mean that the ceremonial aspects of the Law of Moses are still binding on Christians. The sacrificial system pointed to the one final sacrifice made in Christ. The feasts were to remind the people of Israel of what God had done in their history. But the moral law of the Old Testament is still in force.

Societies must have rules to function and to stem the tide of anarchy and chaos. These rules must be based on truth, and this truth must be absolute. Having no absolutes or letting truth be determined by the individual is not truth at all. Removing God from the equation destroys all hope of having or knowing truth.

God's Word is preeminent because it is authored by God. Jesus did not come to destroy the Ten Commandments or the Law and Prophets. God acted upon the men who wrote the Old Testament (and New) by the power of his Spirit. He inspired them to write what he wanted written. Paul reminds us of this when writing to Timothy that all scripture is inspired by God. As such, it teaches us doctrine and at the same time reproves, corrects and instructs. (II Timothy 3:16)

The prophets of old affirmed God's Word. They reiterated and reinforced what God had spoken. They used it to remind the people of their sins. They expanded the law for the people. Warnings of judgment were given for failure to repent. Then Jesus came and fulfilled the law. By teaching, clarification and by keeping it himself, he fulfilled the law of God.

As Sir Walter Scott, a Scottish writer, lay dying, he told his servant to bring him the book. The servant asked what book he was referring to. He said, "My friend, there is only one Book-the Bible."

Reflection: What difference does God's Word make in your life?

October 30

The Lasting Word

Matthew 5:17-19

Discoveries of the twentieth century have served to solidify Christian's confidence in God's Word. As older manuscripts have been found, believers have seen that God's Word has been accurately preserved over thousands of years. This should not surprise us because we know the One who has preserved it. Translators have continued the effort to put God's Word in the everyday language of the people.

God's Word is permanent. Jesus reminds us that not one jot or tittle will pass from it as long as heaven and earth exist. God's Word will outlive time because the eternal Word will always exist to complete it. The jot was the smallest letter of the Greek and Hebrew alphabet and is about the size of our apostrophe. Tittles are small marks used to distinguish one Hebrew letter from the other.

Jesus' use of the jot and tittle remind us that all parts of God's Word are significant. We cannot pick and choose what to believe. It is all profitable for our spiritual journey. God's commands are just as binding on modern day believers as they were on the Old Testament saints.

The Bible leads us to new life in Christ and gives us food for our spiritual sustenance. Since we know God inspired the writers, we can trust what they wrote. Christians should obey, honor, defend and proclaim the Word. Charles Spurgeon said, "The everlasting gospel is worth preaching even if one stood on a burning fagot and addressed the crowds from a pulpit of flames."

God's Word is pertinent. Those who break his commandments and teach others to will be least in the kingdom. But obedience leads to greatness in God's kingdom. While some desire no rules or accountability, rules are necessary in life. The character of God's Word makes it pertinent. It is God's word to us. The prophets magnified it, and Jesus accomplished it.

The Bible is pertinent because it carries consequences. Our obedience or disobedience determines the outcome. We must teach others to obey God's commands. This is a part of Jesus' Great Commission. If we live carelessly and lead others to, we will be held accountable by God.

Reflection: Study God's Word and let its teachings permeate your life.
October 31
The Secret of Effective Prayer
Matthew 6:5-8

Prayer is more than a form of meditation to cleanse our body, spirit and mind. It is communication with God. Communication is a two way street. Talking to oneself is not really communication. Someone else must talk too. And it is the same with prayer. Not only do we speak to God but we also listen for him to speak by his Spirit. Sadly, we can miss out on many opportunities because we fail to hear what God is saying.

There can be much confusion that surrounds prayer. We can overemphasize the sovereignty of God and thus see no need for prayer. Or we can have a weak view of his reign and believe everything depends on our prayers. In reality, we must align ourselves with what God has determined to do. Prayer changes us not God. But God does respond to our prayers. Jesus tells us to keep asking, seeking and knocking. (Matthew

7:7) How this command and the teaching of God's sovereignty interact is a mystery.

One elementary truth about prayer is that it is directed to God. To say this almost seems unnecessary until we read Jesus' story about the Pharisee and the publican. Jesus' take on the story was that the Pharisee stood and prayed to himself. (Luke 18) And of course there are other false gods that one can pray to. We can even pray to a piece of wood which is what many have done as they worshipped their idols.

Some have even construed these verses to mean we should not pray in public, with others or even have prayer meetings. While Jesus' teaching certainly does not forbid this, it does remind us that we need quiet time alone for prayer with God. Our prayers bring us into the presence of a merciful God who stands ready to answer and give us guidance. Prayers are not about our wish list but rather looking for spiritual guidance for daily living. There is a place, however, in prayer for making requests of God.

We gain access to God in our prayers through Jesus. We come to the Father in the Son's name. We are able to do this because of his work on the cross and our faith in that. The atoning death of Christ makes prayer to the Father possible. On this basis, we understand that prayer is only for believers, except for the sinner's prayer for forgiveness.

Reflection: Pray with confidence. As God's child, he hears and will answer your prayers.

November

November 1
Aspects of Kingdom Faithfulness
Matthew 5:10-12

Savonarola was an Italian preacher and great reformer in church history. He condemned personal sin and ecclesiastical corruption in his day and paved the way for the Protestant Reformation. In the end, he was convicted of heresy, hanged and his body burned.

Persecution is one aspect of the Christian life we would rather not discuss. No doubt we have read or heard of the many that have and still suffer for their faith. Even in modern times, some still give their lives. Yet, we often think of this persecution as far away and something that only happens to full time missionaries. But suffering is part and parcel for the believer who walks in faith. Our leader suffered, and we must have that willingness as well.

Living a godly life entails confronting evil head on. This always causes friction, for darkness hates light. Abel discovered this in the beginning of time. He lived righteously, and his brother killed him. While the forms and times of persecution will differ, the suffering will come nonetheless. Being overlooked for a promotion or even turned down for a job. Peers at school making fun of you. Bullies beating you up. People not wanting to be friends with you because of your convictions. Whatever form it takes, persecution is evidence of your salvation. People can get confused or even angry when we refuse to listen to off color jokes or reject sexual advances.

Expecting persecution does not mean we adopt a martyr complex or even become obnoxious about our faith. We can act in such a way that we turn people away from Christ. Jesus was a friend of sinners, but he never indulged in their sins. Don't conceal your beliefs. But do not be surprised when persecution comes for them. It may be physical or verbal. People may make false accusations against you. Stand firm in your faith. And remember that the persecution is not really against you but the one you serve.

Our reward for persecution is happiness and inheritance in the kingdom of heaven. Christians receive a double blessing. God will comfort you in such times and give you the strength to endure. We can rejoice and be overjoyed when we are called upon to suffer for our Savior. Our suffering will never compare to what he has done for us.

Reflection: Stand firm in your faith even when you know it will bring ridicule and persecution from others.

November 2

Results of God's Love

Matthew 7:7-12

Prayer and a Christmas list are not the same. To hear some prayers, we might think they are. While God invites us to bring our needs before him, his will is to form us into the image of Christ. Any request that does not fit that schemata or that is selfish in nature will not be granted. Thus the teachings of these verses must be taken in context with other verses that teach how we must pray according to his will.

Because of God's love, we can have success in life. Jesus says to ask, seek and knock. He is not giving a blank check, but it does relate to persistence in prayer. It also shows God's willingness to give what he sees as in our best interest. It is a great and comprehensive promise. And our Father has blessed us in many ways. Foremost was his willingness to let his Son pay for our sins. Beyond that are the daily blessings.

Wisdom and closer fellowship with Christ are two things that we should ask, seek and knock for. When Solomon assumed the throne after his father David, God told him to ask for anything he wanted. He chose wisdom, and God commended him. We need wisdom to live the Christian life. God also wants to draw us into closer fellowship with him. This closeness tunes us in to his will. His Spirit encourages and strengthens us for service.

Jesus' instruction for us to ask, seek and knock is a command made to believers. The unsaved are given no assurance that God will answer any of their prayers except the one of repentance. But there are conditions even for believers. We must live in obedience, ask with the right motives and be submissive to his will for God to answer. God often gives us the ability to help affect what we request. If we are asking him for a job, we should be looking.

Doing what Jesus instructs will lead to liberality in our giving. When we ask for the right things with the right motives, it will lead us to be channels of the same to others. God gives us good things. A father will not give his child a stone when he asked for bread. Nor a snake if he requested fish. Ask for the right things and God will use you to bless others. There are no limits to God's treasure house. Learn to treat others as God does you.

Reflection: Learn to pray in God's will. Your prayers will be answered. Then ask God to give to you in such a way that you can share with others.

November 3

Worry in the Christian's Life

Matthew 6:25-34

We all do it even though we know we shouldn't. But one widow had learned the key. She had raised six children and adopted six more. Quite an unusual woman. A reporter visited her to find out the key to her success. Partnership was the answer. She said to him, "Partnership. One day a long time ago I said to the Lord, 'Lord, I'll do the work if you do the worrying.'"

Worry has been called one of the most debilitating ailments of our time. All of us face situations that can easily lead to worry or anxiety. How we look at and respond to these circumstances determines whether or not we will step on this explosive trait. While it is natural for us to be concerned about things on earth (after all, that is where we live), we should not worry.

Worry demonstrates unfaithfulness. It shows disobedience because God commands us not to do it. It also testifies to a lack of faith in God's provision. Since God is our master, anxiety is foolish. The command to stop worrying carries the idea that we are to stop what we are already doing.

Jesus instructs us not to worry about life. Life entails the physical, emotional, spiritual and mental aspects. Our whole person. No matter what our circumstances, it does not justify worrying. Yet it is probably the sin believers commit most often. Worry comes from a German word meaning to choke or strangle, and the definition is a perfect description of what worry does. It can choke mentally and physically.

Contentment is the better choice. Several things help us reach this state. Remember that God owns all things. He will not take from us what belongs to him. He is in control of all matters. Why worry about what God is taking care of? Remember Daniel in the lion's den. It was not Daniel but the king who lost sleep that night. God is also the provider. He has promised to give us all we need in life-food, shelter, and clothing.

Worry is unnecessary. Jesus uses several illustrations to drive home this point. Birds cannot sow or reap, yet God provides for them. We are more important than animals. The days of our lives are in God's hands. While we should maintain healthy habits, God knows the length of our days on earth. God will also clothe us as he does the lilies of the field.

Reflection: Remember that worry is inconsistent with your faith in God. Trust God for every need you have and every situation you face.

November 4
Casting the Net
Matthew 13:47-49

Tommy walked into his Theology of Faith class. He had long hair and was an atheist. He wondered if God would find him. He graduated but then contracted cancer. Tommy later came to his professor's office with a body badly wasted. He told his professor how God had indeed found him. He wanted Tommy to share his story with his Theology class but he never made it. The cancer took his life but not his message.

Christianity is about casting the net. It is about finding those God is dealing with who need him. This parable of Jesus is about judgment but also about spreading God's love. It tells of what will happen to believers and unbelievers at the end of time. Several of Jesus' disciples were fishermen and many in that area were as well, so a parable about fishing fit perfectly.

God casts a net for humanity. From the very moment man sinned against him in the Garden of Eden, God has pursued him. Since Christ is referred to as the Lamb slain before the foundation of the world, God knew ahead of time that we would rebel. The net is a dragnet for the area that needs fishing is enormous.

Currently, God is allowing unbelievers and believers to exist side by side. The net will only be cast for a time. At some point, the net will be drawn in and the separation made. God receives no joy when the wicked perish. (Ezekiel 18:23) They are his creations. At the same time, he cannot allow them to enter heaven in an unrepentant state. Peter reminds us that God is currently giving time because he is patient with the wicked. (II Peter 3:9)

Those you meet each day are in God's net. Believers are there too. The unsaved swim around in the net as if they are free. At times they bump against the net. It may be a tragedy in their life, and they begin to consider their immortality. Then the circumstance passes, and they ignore the net again. God often gives people many opportunities to bump into the net. The drawing of the net is equivalent to the end time judgment or the end of life judgment, whichever comes first. John describes a Great White Throne judgment where all unbelievers will appear before God to receive their final destiny.

Reflection: Cast your net as God does by spreading his love over those in your reach.

November 5

When the Net is Drawn

Matthew 13:50-52

Imagine a man in a boat casting a net for shrimp. He throws it in a circular motion, allows it to float on the surface then sink. After a few moments, he pulls it in. Hopefully, it will be full or at least partially full. At that moment, the life of the shrimp ends. The catch is sold, cooked at some restaurant and eaten by seafood lovers.

God through us is casting a net over humanity. For some, it is still floating. For others, it is sinking. And then there are those for whom God is about to draw the net in. Once the net is drawn, all hope is lost. This reminds us of the urgency of our message. We must invite others to Christ before the net is drawn.

Peril awaits unbelievers when the net is drawn. Jesus says they will be thrown into the fire where there will be weeping and gnashing of teeth. It is a picture of hell. Not a popular subject and one we hear little of in sermons, but one that Jesus speaks of often.

Opinions of hell vary. Annihilation is one. Death is it. There is nothing after our heart stops beating. Some believe earth is hell. Hell is spoken of as a place of fire and brimstone. Christians differ in how they understand this. Some take the literal interpretation while others refer to the darkness there and say fire and darkness cannot coexist.

Whatever else hell may be, it is the absence of God. It will not be a place where the wicked can continue to commit dastardly deeds with pleasure without threat of punishment. The desires will remain, but they will not be able to act. Contrary to what some think, hell will not be fun.

Hell is a real place where body and soul will experience torment and agony. Fire will burn but not burn up. The degree of punishment will vary. For the one who had many chances to trust Christ but blatantly refused, the horror will be greater. Punishment of a lesser degree will be reserved for those who had less light. Nevertheless, the torment will be everlasting.

Understanding what the Bible teaches about the destiny of those apart from Christ should encourage us to cast the net repeatedly and consistently. The gospel is an offer of heaven and a warning against hell.

Reflection: Do you know Christ as your Savior? If so, warn others of the danger of refusing him.

November 6

End Time Instruction

Matthew 13:24-29

The little boy proudly showed his mom his new beagle puppy. Looking at his sad face, the mom remarked; "He has such a sad face." Looking at the wagging tail, the little boy retorted, "But he has a happy ending."

Believers look forward to the same. Our world is often filled with misery. While we can live in a state of happiness as Christians, we must still exist in a society that is unfriendly and hurtful in many ways. As we face hardship and turmoil, we too look forward to a happy ending. James instructs us to be patient while we wait for the Lord's coming. (James 5:7)

Jesus tells the story of a man who sowed seed in his field. While he slept, his enemy went to the field and sowed weeds. When the wheat sprouted, so did the weeds. His servants were disturbed and wanted to pull up the weeds, but the master told them to allow both to grow together until the harvest. Pulling them up now would also uproot the wheat.

The story reminds us that good and evil are growing at the same time in our world. Jesus has sown good seed through placing believers in the world. But Satan has sown wicked people, and he uses his evil servants to influence them. At present, God is allowing both to exist.

Why God allows evil is an age old question, and the Bible does not answer the irony of it. We must believe that in some way it is serving God's sovereign purpose in the world. Evil does magnify good. And God promises to bring good out of evil. While Satan is the ruler of all that is evil in our world, God is still in control. In the end, he will redeem this world and all sin will be banished forever.

You and I are here for a purpose. We are to sow light in our actions and words. Jesus reminds us that we are the light and salt of the world. (Matthew 5:13-14) Ours is a divine assignment in which we are to be permeating influences. As we grow and mature in our spiritual walk, we are to reflect God's standards and will to others. We need enthusiasm in the work God has given us.

Reflection: As Jesus began the sowing process through the birth of the church, so we must continue his work. Sow each day as if it was your last opportunity.

November 7

When the End Comes

Matthew 13:30

Believers have looked for the end of time since Christianity began. And with good reason. Wickedness makes it very difficult to live in our world. We read of heaven's description, and we long to go to a place where sin will be absent and where the hurts of this world will be eradicated.

When the end comes, there will be a separation. The wicked will be divided from the righteous. In the parable, the master allowed the wheat and tares to grow together until harvest. At harvest time, the weeds were gathered, bundled and burned. Then the wheat was gathered into the barn.

Jesus interprets the story for us. The wheat is believers while the tares are the wicked. When he comes again, those who have refused him will be gathered and assigned to their eternal destiny in hell. But God's children will be gathered into heaven.

The type of weed Jesus refers to in the parable was difficult to distinguish from wheat. At least, initially. But as the two grew, the difference became evident. The wheat produced grain while the weed produced nothing.

Ours is the day of evangelism. It is not up to believers to carry out the judgment reserved for God. Rather than spending our time trying to judge who is and is not a Christian, we should be sowing the seed. We cannot force our beliefs on others, but we must present them with the opportunity to believe.

History warns us of the danger of trying to force others to become Christians. In the fourth century, the Roman emperor, Constantine, forced all kingdom inhabitants to profess Christ. Those who refused were killed. Then came the Crusades of the Middle Ages where unbelievers were murdered, especially Muslims and Jews. Later the Inquisition would come as a reaction against the Protestant Reformation.

We must speak words of grace and forgiveness to the lost and leave the judgment to God. We are not avengers but agents of truth. When we are faithful to the work God has given us, he will reward us. Our greatest reward will be eternity with him.

Reflection: The end may be nearer than any of us think. Be diligent in telling others about God's grace and mercy.

November 8
Equality in God's Kingdom
Matthew 20:1-16

I once spent a few months at a local plant working as a temp. The circumstances seemed unfair. I did the same work as the other employees but did not receive the same benefits. The company did not pay my insurance, allow me to invest in a 401k plan, give me any vacation or sick time or pay me when the plant shut down for holidays. Some of the other temps and I often discussed the unfairness of our plight.

Then it dawned on me. This company did not owe me a job. They were allowing me to work there and paying me when they did not have to. While my services helped them produce their product, they could have found somebody else to fill my shoes if the unfairness was more than I could bear.

The employer Jesus speaks of seems unfair. He hires workers at different times of the day, but at the end of the day pays them all the same wages. Quite naturally, those who had worked all day were not happy. But the owner reminds them that he paid what they agreed to work for.

Unfairness is part of our society. For hundreds of years, different minority groups have experienced discrimination. Since our Constitution stated that "all men are created equal," it was not until 1920 that women gained the right to express their voices through voting. Even after African Americans received the right to vote, they faced many hate groups that kept them from the polls. Many other examples could be given of unfairness.

Understanding the elements of the parable is important. The vineyard is the kingdom of God. The landowner is God. Jesus is the foreman, believers are the laborers and the pay is salvation.

In the parable, Jesus teaches that God initiates and accomplishes salvation. It is not cleverly devised methods and presentations that result in people trusting Christ as Savior. It is God's Spirit convicting and convincing a person of their sinfulness that leads to a decision. God does work through our methods, but our plans do not confine him. The landowner went out looking for workers, not the other way around. Jesus reminds us that people cannot come to him unless they are drawn by the Father. (John 6:44)

Reflection: As you share your faith, remember that it is God that will bring that person to belief in Him. Thank God he allows you to be his instrument.

November 9

Equality in God's Kingdom

Matthew 20:1-16

In *Raisin in the Sun*, an African American family inherits $10,000 from their father's insurance policy. The mother, daughter and older son all have ideas about how they want to use the money. Against her better judgment, the mother gives the money to the older son to invest in his own business. Before long, his so called friends had taken the money and skipped town. The desolate son returns home only to be scolded by his sister for his foolishness. But listen to the response of the mother; "There's always something left to love. And if you ain't learned that, you ain't learned nothing." How wonderful that God sees us as worthy of his love.

Salvation's terms are established by God. We often want to come to God on our own terms. We think our good works should impress him or our winning personality. Since we sinned and rebelled against God it makes sense that God makes the conditions on which he will accept us. The only way is through Christ, and this is what we must share with others.

In the parable, the pay was salvation, and it was the same for all. No matter how bad or good a person is before they come to Christ, he gives grace to all who ask. Salvation is complete for all people. Sometimes we want to cry unfair like the laborers, especially if it is a notably wicked person. But God saves the murderer who asks just as he does the person who is morally good but not a believer. God's grace is extended equally and freely to all.

The story also teaches that God continually calls people into his Kingdom. He will do this until the end of time just as the landowner did by revisiting the market throughout the day. There should never be a time when Christians cease to invite others to trust Christ. There have been times in Christian history when evangelism has not been emphasized. On occasion, it was because of a misrepresentation of God's sovereignty. When this happened, churches died. God continues to call because of his patience.

Day laborers were completely dependent on someone to hire them. We are too when it comes to salvation. Since we cannot deliver ourselves, we must depend on the One who has the power to forgive sins. As the landowner hired all who desired to work, so God will save all who ask.

Reflection: The landowner expected all he hired to work. Be diligent in your work for God.

November 10
God's Great Reunion
Luke 14:15-24

Family reunions are fun and challenging. Sadly, many families, including mine, have discontinued their yearly reunions for lack of interest. Reunions may be the only time during the year that we see some of our relatives. But the reunion organizer has a great responsibility in contacting all the participants and encouraging them to attend.

Jesus finds himself at the home of a Pharisee for a meal. He probably thought of those who had not been invited. Only the elite would have been invited to this home. As Jesus looks over those who were there, he tells his host he should have invited the poor, crippled, lame and blind. In response, one of the guests says, "Blessed is the person who will eat at the feast in the kingdom of God." And Jesus tells about a great banquet.

God's kingdom is like a banquet or party. It is the reign of God in human history to redeem humanity through Christ. God is king, and is actively working in the world to bring it to his intended goal. While God's kingdom has always existed, it took on a new phase with the work of Christ. It will come fully when time has ended and a new heaven and earth is created. We enter the kingdom by faith.

Belonging to God's kingdom is festive and delightful. It provides a wonderful time for fellowship. The Christian life should be fun, not boring.

We do not have to frown to belong to the family of God. Believers do not have to be ascetics. God has provided good things for our bodies to enjoy. Our joy in all circumstances will make others notice a difference. God has created a beautiful earth. We should enjoy nature. It points to a magnificent God.

The life of Jesus demonstrates that he enjoyed life. We often find him at parties and fellowships. He enjoyed being around people. How else could he distribute his message? He was a friend of children, tax collectors and sinners of all types. We can have a good time in life without being involved in sinful behavior. Jesus desires that we enjoy abundant life. We can be happy because of forgiveness, the indwelling presence of God, his comfort, the fellowship of other believers, and the peace of God that passes all understanding.

Reflection: Make plans now to attend God's reunion. In the meantime, enjoy each day of life God gives you.

November 11

Why We Miss God's Reunion

Luke 14:15-24

One wrote; "The clock of life is wound but once, /And no man has the power/To tell just when the hands will stop,/At late or early hour./ To lose one's wealth is sad indeed/To lose one's health is more./To lose one's soul is such a loss/That no man can restore."

While at the banquet, Jesus takes the opportunity to tell a story of another banquet. When the meal was ready, the host sent his servant to tell those previously invited that it was time to come. The servant was greeted with excuses. One had purchased a field and wanted to see it. Another had bought some oxen and wanted to try them out. A third had married.

The jest of these excuses is some of the same reasons people still offer for not trusting Christ. The excuse of the field and oxen translates into earthly possessions. While not a sin to have possessions, if we are not careful, this pursuit can take our eyes off more important things-spiritual matters. Rather than finding security in material things, we should ask God for opportunities to use our money and possessions to help those with needs. Jesus tells us to lay up our treasures in heaven where they are safe. (Matthew 6: 19-20) Enjoy what God gives you, but do not let it interfere with your service to him.

Family was another excuse for not attending the banquet. One man had just been married, but surely the host would have invited the wife. The Old Testament did excuse a newly married man from military duty. Family is the fabric of society, but it is not more important than God.

Jesus taught that if anyone came to him and did not hate his father, mother, wife, children, brothers, sisters, and even his own life that he could not be his disciple. He certainly was not advocating hate of family. But our love for him in comparison to our family should seem as hate. In your priority list, make sure God is above family matters.

When those previously invited refused to come, the host sent the servant into the streets, alleys, roads and country lanes. This reminds us that God's invitation to trust Christ goes to all people. It is our responsibility to make that message known.

Reflection: God, help me not to let anything or anyone precedemy devotion to you.

November 12
God's Invitation
Matthew 22:1-14

Invitations. Some we like. Others we could care less about. For instance, an invitation to a golf tournament would mean nothing to me. Why? I have no interest in golf. On the other hand, an invitation to the mountains would be accepted immediately. Or an invitation to meet the president. After all, he holds the highest office in the land.

But of all the invitations we might receive, the one to trust Christ is the most important. Jesus' parable illustrates this invitation but also issues a warning against rejecting it. This is one of his most powerful parables. It issues a strict warning to unbelieving Israelites and the religious leaders about rejecting the message of Jesus.

Many stood in awe of the miracles Jesus performed. He could heal people who had been born blind or who had gone blind after birth. He could cause the lame to walk. Demons were no match for his power. He could even forgive sins. But many followed him for superficial reasons. They liked to see the miracles. Or to watch him embarrass the religious leaders. While Jesus gave of his complete self to others, only a small number actually accepted him. He did not fit their preconceived notions of who the Messiah was.

Here a king gives a wedding feast for his son and sends his servant to tell those who had been invited that it was time to come. They refused. The king must have been a patient man for he tells the servant to go again with the invitation. But again the invitation was ignored. So the king sends the servant into the street corners to invite anyone and everyone.

The feast God has prepared for those who follow him is great indeed. It includes forgiveness of sins, peace of conscience, favor with God, exceedingly great promises, access to the throne of grace, the comfort of the Spirit as well as the promise of eternal life.

The king in the story represents God. In the strictest sense, the invitation was given to the nation of Israel in the Old Testament, although foreigners could come too. But with the coming of Christ, the invitation now extends to all people.

Reflection: Take a moment to thank God for his wonderful invitation. As a believer, he invited you to his grand feast. No longer are you a pauper in this world.

November 13
God's Invitation
Matthew 22:1-14

Susan was a 51 year old pharmaceutical consultant planning a high school reunion. She especially wanted to see Bennett Scott who suffered from kidney disease. He was on dialysis and awaiting a transplant. In school, they had sung in the school chorus, worked on the school newspaper and practiced under the same piano teacher. Now Susan finds herself offering him a kidney. At first he refused, but as his condition deteriorated, he finally accepted. Bennett said, "How do you thank someone for giving you back your life?" God does that when we accept his invitation of salvation.

But in Jesus' parable, many refused the invitation to the wedding. They represent people who are preoccupied with selfish interests and daily living. Those who have no time for God. They are secularly minded and want to do their own thing in life.

Like the king's servant, believers are servants of God given the responsibility of inviting others to God's feast. The command is expressed in the Great Commission which instructs us to invite the entire world. No one is beyond the reach of God's grace. We do not have the authority to categorize people as worthy or not worthy of our attention.

The servants who carried the message were treated shamefully and some were even killed. This made the king furious, and he mustered his army to destroy the murderers and burn their city. God invites because of his grace. However, when we choose to ignore the invitation, punishment will result. We can choose to receive God's grace or his wrath. The ultimate expression of his wrath is hell. Not because he wants people there but because sin must be paid for. If we choose to reject his solution in Christ, we must settle for the other.

As the king looked over those his servant had finally garnered for the banquet, he noticed one not wearing proper clothes for a wedding. Instructions were given for him to be bound and cast into outer darkness. Jesus knows those who are his true followers. Hypocrites will be exposed at the final judgment. Not all who call him Lord are his followers. The only proper garment is righteousness, and this is given by Christ.

Reflection: Have your accepted God's invitation for salvation? If not, ask Christ to forgive your sins and give you his righteousness.

November 14
Happiness from Holiness
Matthew 5:8

John Wesley was a great evangelist. While at Oxford University, he joined a group of men who led lives of strict spiritual discipline. The methodical manner of their spiritual exercises, charitable giving and devotional practices earned them the name "Methodists." But Wesley had no joy in his life. In fact, he even doubted that he was a Christian. One day he was listening to a reading from Martin Luther's "Preface to the Book of Romans." He came to realize that holiness was birthed in the heart first and then was shown through actions. When he finally understood that the blood of Christ made him holy, he said, "I felt my heart strangely warmed."

What Wesley discovered is the teaching of Scripture. It is Christ that makes us holy. We are not saved by our good works but rather by grace. It is from that relationship that charitable deeds flow in the right direction. And it is from that relationship that true happiness is discovered.

Jesus introduces no new concept when he speaks of holiness. It is the scarlet thread that runs through the Bible, and is God's goal for all people. The political and economic problems the Jews were currently facing did not compare to a greater problem-weakness in spiritual matters.

Jewish history was filled with stories of vacillation between obedience and disobedience. The people wanted to obey and please God, but God's teachings had been so distorted and misinterpreted that it seemed an impossible task. Their understanding of how to be holy was distorted even as Wesley's was. Their religion needed an overhaul. This probably explains why a lawyer once asked Jesus what the greatest command was. (Matthew 22:36)

Our efforts will not lead to holiness. We do not have the means within ourselves to reach up to such a high calling. Placing our faith in Christ allows his holiness to be applied to our life. This is a holiness God recognizes. Jesus says we need to be pure in heart. Heart in this sense is our inner feelings. It is the seat of our attitudes and motives. It is the center of our personality. Thus our feelings, motives and attitudes need to be pure.

To be pure is to be single minded. Our devotion to God must be undivided. The believer must strive for spiritual integrity.

Reflection: As a believer, you have been made pure in Christ. Ask God to help your motives be pure in all your acts of service.

November 15
Holiness in Life
Matthew 5:8

Imagine being able to look at your heart. The literal organ. It may appear normal with the right color and seem as if it is beating properly. You might conclude, "I have a healthy heart." But a trained cardiologist might see a totally different picture. He might notice a skip in your heart that could lead to future cardiac issues. He may see valves that are not opening and closing properly and therefore restricting blood flow.

While others only see our outward actions, Jesus looks on the heart. He can see when the motives and intentions behind our actions are impure. He often did this with the Pharisees of his day. Like white washed tombs, they looked good on the outside, but the inside was full of dead rotting bones.

There are six types of holiness mentioned in God's Word. Primal purity is possessed by God alone. Created purity was the state enjoyed before man fell into sin. Positional holiness is give to us when we trust Christ. Actual purity comes from the new nature given at salvation. Practical purity is our daily effort to live out who we are in position, and ultimate holiness will be known in heaven. Practical purity should be your goal.

People have tried different avenues to attain such holiness. Some have tried literal separation from the world. But separating ourselves from others does not separate us from ourselves, and therein lies the problem. While we are influenced by our environment, these elements only intensify what already resides inside. (James 4:1)

We must constantly feed on God's Word for strength to live pure lives. Prayer is also necessary as is reliance on God's Spirit indwelling us and living through us. Not only does God's Spirit enable but he also convicts when we go astray of our goal to be pure in practice. Victory is possible.

There have been several periods of monasticism in history. During the sixth, tenth, eleventh, thirteenth and sixteenth centuries, individuals separated themselves from the world in convents and monasteries. The world was renounced and personal solitude sought in an attempt to attain holiness. It did not work. The problem is not the lack of holiness on the outside, but the manner of impurity on the inside.

Reflection: Rely on God's power to live in practice who you are in position. This is possible by daily relying on the Spirit's power.

November 16

How Important is Your Influence?

Matthew 13:31-35

One Andy Griffith episode has a hobo coming to Mayberry. His character is immediately revealed when he steals their lunch from the patrol car while they are fishing. Barney later arrests him for loitering and vagrancy. To keep Barney from repeatedly arresting him, Andy offers him a job doing yard work around his house. Before long, Opie is picking up on his bad habits. He teaches him to steel, procrastinate, and cut school. Andy finally determines that he must remove the bad influence. While the hobo thought the solution was to let Opie choose the best way, Andy knew better.

Influence is not an option. We do it whether we intend to or not. What kind of influence are you leaving with those you interact with? Are others convicted of wrong when around you? Do they behave more appropriately? Are you trying to bless others by serving their needs? Do you ever feel as if your influence is insignificant?

Take for example Jesus' disciples. Just a hand full of men against the entire nation of Israel and the pagan Roman Empire. We can imagine how they must have felt when Jesus issued the Great Commission. But what appears to be a small influence can really have amazing effects. Our alphabet only has twenty six letters, but every poem, great work of literature, history book, letter and essay has been composed using only these letters. Your world of influence may seem small, but determine to make a large impact on that small world. As all believers do this, we touch the world.

God is demonstrating his influence through the church. While many individual churches may be in trouble because of changing communities or unchallenged members, the universal church is marching forward triumphantly. In the first century, a handful of inept and weak believers turned their world upside down for Christ. God's kingdom will grow despite Satan's opposition. In fact, God's kingdom will ultimately permeate the world.

Jesus used leaven (yeast) and the mustard seed to demonstrate this. A small amount of yeast can permeate an entire loaf of bread, and a tiny mustard seed can grow into a large plant. God's kingdom may appear small, but we have the God given ability to take our influence to the world.

Reflection: How are you impacting your world for Christ?

November 17

Little is Much With God

Matthew 13:31-35

My paternal grandfather was a humble but godly man. He was well known in his area because he had been a milk and later ice cream man for over forty years with the same company. He was a quiet man but one of great influence. I recall him telling the story of visiting a local diner for coffee. The waitress had a joke she wanted to tell another patron but would not until my grandfather left. Influence. What difference is yours making?

The mustard seed was the smallest used in Palestinian gardens, yet it would yield a bush of from twelve to fifteen feet. Jesus also mentions leaven or yeast. His listeners were familiar with this too for bread was a major food source in his time. Women would save a small piece of leavened dough from the current loaf for the next batch of bread. That small piece of leavened dough would permeate the entire loaf.

Both illustrations show how wide our influence can be. Since God's kingdom appears small, our influence is important. Evil seems to outpace good. God's people have always been in the minority, but our impact can be monumental. Appearances can be deceiving. In Revelation, John tells of how the entire world will become the kingdom of our Lord and Christ. He will reign forever and ever. (11:15) The mustard seed and yeast represent God's kingdom.

The work we do for God will cause his kingdom to grow until it permeates the world. Not everyone will be saved, but our work will go forth with power that the forces of hell cannot stop. Hundreds of new churches are started each week. Most of the world's people groups have the Scriptures in their own language. Millions are being reached with the gospel through television, radio, literature and now the Internet.

Influence can be positive or negative. The Church's must be positive as that of the yeast and mustard seed. Our influence is positive when we live in obedience to God. We can lead the way in political, economic, legal and cultural areas. We can look for ways to let our standards influence education, the justice system and the halls of Congress. Society always benefits when Christian standards are adopted.

Reflection: Your influence is important because it comes from within. Look for ways you can impact your circle of influence.

November 18

In Debt-What Now?

Luke 7:41-43

Debt. Most Americans are in it. We have more charged on credit cards than we would like to discuss. And then there is the car payment. We do not want something that gets good gas mileage. We would rather have room and convenience, so we go big and fancy. The mortgage or rent also takes a hunk of our monthly income. So we live in debt and are enslaved.

Then there are those ways we try to eliminate our debt. Thousands of Americans get in over their head and feel bankruptcy is the only option. Others borrow from their retirement. Or we transfer debt from one credit card to another that offers a lower interest rate.

The American society encourages debt. Credit cards send offers to college students who have no income. We do not encourage people to save, so the saving rate of the average American is very low if they save any at all. Most Americans have to incur some debt for large ticket items such as a house, car or furniture. Advertisers appeal to our greedy spirit. We are encouraged to spend money we do not have to help an economy in recession.

Debt can lead to depression and short tempers. Financial struggles are one of the main reasons for marital discord and even break up. One's credit rating can be ruined if payments are not made or made on time, and jail time can even result in extreme cases.

Simon, a Pharisee, invited Jesus to his house for a meal. As he is reclining at the table, a sinful woman comes in. Perhaps she followed Jesus in off the streets. She has an expensive bottle of perfume that she washes Jesus' feet with. Her tears provide the water. Then she dries them with her hair. Allowing her to do this proves to Simon that Jesus was surely not a great prophet, for he would not have allowed a woman like this to touch him.

So Jesus tells a story. A man loaned money to two people. To one he loaned 500 pieces of silver and to the other only 50. Neither could pay, so he forgave them both. Then came the convicting question. Who would love him more for cancelling the debt? Simon said the one who owed the most. Then Jesus rebuked Simon and forgave the woman.

Reflection: Of all the debt you could incur, the greatest is what you owe God for your sins. Thank him for forgiving that debt and setting you free. Are you showing your love to him in appreciation for what he has done?

November 19
In Debt-What Now?
Luke 7:41-43

Simon belonged to the sect of the Pharisees. Like most, he probably thought too much of himself. Though he did not wash the dust from Jesus' feet when he entered his house, he scoffed at the sinful woman who did. In her actions, Jesus recognized her perceived need for forgiveness. The story of the two debtors served as a rebuke to Simon's pharisaical attitude.

The story serves to remind us that we are all in debt to God. Unlike financial debt, it cannot be paid off. The Bible terms this debt sin, and it places us in far greater restraints than a debtor's prison. We are in stocks and chains. In the story, God is the man who loaned the money, and we are the debtors who cannot pay. Sin is in our nature and has been since the rebellion of Adam and Eve. Simon the Pharisee had not recognized this yet, but the immoral woman had. Sin is like a bad habit we just cannot rid ourselves of.

Paul reminds us that we have all sinned and fallen short of God's glory. (Romans 3:23). And again that the penalty for this sin is death. (Romans 6:23) While we have different financial debts in life, the sin debt runs equal among individuals. Simon thought the woman owed God more. She was a sinner. From Jesus' perspective, the debt was the same.

Thankfully, God offers a means out of our debt. Nothing we can pay but something he paid for us by sending his Son to the cross. A perfect person paying a debt he did not owe. Though this is the only way the debt can be paid, history provides examples of how people have tried other avenues. Doing good deeds is the major way. God does not operate that way, and the debt cannot be paid by actions but only by faith.

All that God requires for the debt to be erased is what the immoral woman did. She demonstrated her grief over sin. She brought something expensive and washed Jesus' feet with it, then dried them with her hair. It is a wonderful picture of sorrow for sin. She did not have to say anything. Jesus knew her heart, and forgave her sins. He will do the same for us when we repent and ask his forgiveness. He takes all our sins-past, present and future, and casts them into the bottom of the ocean.

Reflection: Have you realized your debt to God? If not, ask him to forgive your sins right now. If he has already done that, serve him with appreciation.Use your gifts and talents to influence others.

November 20
God-Our Debt Releaser
Luke 7:41-43

On one Andy Griffith episode, Andy saves Gomer's life. Andy had visited the service station to deliver a letter from Barney. Gomer's boss had thrown a cigar butt in a can of oily rags. Smoke was boiling out when Andy entered. He quickly extinguished the smoldering rags. For Gomer, Andy had just saved his life, and he had to repay him. He tried to do this through good deeds on Andy's behalf. Andy finally had to concoct a way to supposedly save Gomer's life to get rid of him.

When God forgives our sins, we can show our appreciation. The contrast between Simon the Pharisee and the immoral woman is very distinct. Simon was a religious leader. He was looked up to by the average person and had to be very careful to obey God's written law. The woman, on the other hand, was immoral and classified a sinner by Simon.

There was also a stark contrast in the actions of these two players. Simon invited Jesus to his home but did not perform the customary service of washing the dust from his feet. But the woman's every gesture demonstrated her humility and unworthiness. The woman did not perform her acts of service to get forgiveness but in recognition of who Jesus was. She had a greater love than Simon. She was the one who owed more.

The immoral woman provides a wonderful example. If our sins have been forgiven, we need to show our appreciation to God. How can we do this? By spiritual acts of discipline like reading his Word, praying, witnessing, serving and fellowshipping with other believers. In all of these ways, we show God our appreciation. The immoral woman desired to spend time with Jesus, even as Mary did while her sister was busy preparing. (Luke 10: 39) Are you spending time at Jesus' feet?

The story reminds us that we need to include others in God's love. The Pharisees were exclusive and majored on those things that excluded others. Jesus included those they considered the scum of the earth. Remember that God's love extends to all. Who is it that you are excluding from your Sunday parties? And why?

Reflection: We can never repay God for forgiveness, but we can show our appreciation by serving him faithfully and including others in his love.

November 21
Jesus on Prayer
Luke 11:5-8; 18:1-8

A beautiful song entitled, *A Child of the King*, says, "I once was an outcast stranger on earth, A sinner by choice, and an alien by birth, But I've been adopted, My name's written down, An heir to a mansion, a robe, and a crown. I'm a child of the King, A child of the King: With Jesus my Savior, I'm a child of the King."

As a child of the King, we can approach him with pride and confidence. Prayer is our lifeline to God and the way we discover his will. It is our source of comfort and strength for our spiritual journey. It moves us through the trials and tribulations of life. Without a vibrant prayer life, you will never attain all God wants for you in life.

Through the story of the friend at midnight and the persistent widow, Jesus shows how important it is that we pray and not give up. The friend at midnight continued to knock until the man got up, risked disturbing his family, and got him food for his midnight visitor. The widow pestered the judge for justice until he finally gave in. He did not care about her situation. He just wanted to get rid of her.

God loves to answer our prayers. Isn't it wonderful that we do not have to beg God to listen or answer us? One of the prime means of discovering God's best is through prayer. God is not like the inhabitant of the house or the unjust judge, both of whom did not want to be bothered. God loves to listen to your prayers. We have the wonderful opportunity to come before a rich throne of grace that is adorned with mercy. He delights in our praises and requests. Having an adequate understanding of God's character changes our perspective on prayer.

While God may not answer immediately, the answer will come. The widow and friend were both persistent until they got what they wanted. God may tell us to wait, or the answer may not be what we desired, but his answer is always best, so we must accept the answer as it comes.

God will reward us when we pray with persistence. Jesus reminds us to keep asking, seeking and knocking. As we pray with persistence, we must be careful to pray according to God's will. This assures an answer.

Reflection: Take advantage of the privilege of prayer. Talk to your Heavenly Father on a regular basis.

November 22
Jesus' Picture of God
Matthew 21:33-46

Most of us have heard the old saying that a picture is worth a thousand words. Some people are very diligent in picture taking. They want an abundance of them, so they fill up albums, phones, and computers. But then there are pictures in the form of paintings and portraits. Some portraits bear a striking resemblance. Paintings do the same, but others are abstract.

People paint different pictures of God as well. Some of our founding fathers were Deists. They saw God as the master clock winder who started all things, then stepped back. The world is now winding down without his intervention. Their views represent one of two opposite extremes- that God is involved in the world or he is not. Animists see God in everything-trees, flowers, rocks, etc. Atheists totally dismiss God. Even Christians have different views of God's working. Some see all matters predestined by God while others believe God changes his plans according to human actions.

Through this story, Jesus tells us what God has done, is doing and will do. He relates some of God's characteristics and warns us at the same time. This is necessary because some of the portraits we draw of God are not biblically accurate.

Jesus tells of a landowner who plants a vineyard and then builds a wall around it. He constructs a pit for pressing out the grapes and also a lookout tower. Then he leases the farm and moves to another country. When harvest time arrives, he sent servants to collect his share of the profit. They were treated in various ways. His own son was killed. The owner would punish them for such behavior and then lease the vineyard to someone else.

The picture painted by the parable reminds us that God makes provision for his people. How wonderful to worship a God who promises to supply our every need. While unbelievers may wonder how they will get by in life, the Christian is sure that God will take care of them. The greatest provision came in Christ, for all our physical needs pale in comparison to our spiritual need. He enables us to do his work. And beyond this and the promise to meet our physical needs are many more blessings.

Reflection: Thank God that he has made provision for you. For your salvation and for your every need. No matter what life throws your way, remember that he will care for you.

November 23
Jesus' Picture of God
Matthew 21:33-46

Opie once brought home a run away boy. Unknowingly, Andy had promised not to call his parents. In the meantime, the report was out to be on the lookout for him. Barney had composed a picture based on the description. As Andy, Opie and the boy sat on the front porch, Barney came over and presented his portrait. He said, "I could pick him out anywhere." Andy replied, "Could you pick him out on a front porch?"

If our picture of God is correct, we should be able to pick out his work as we see it around us. The key to success in the Christian life is seeing where God is at work so we can join him in the effort. Not only does God provide for his people, but he is also patient.

When harvest time arrived, the landowner sent servants to collect his profit. Those who had leased the vineyard beat some, killed one and stoned another. Finally, he sent his son thinking they would respect him, but they killed him. That the owner continued to send servants shows God's patience. The son represents Jesus, and reflects God's ultimate sacrifice.

The rejection of the servants and the killing of the son remind us that our message will not always be accepted. In fact, we may even suffer harm in telling our story. But as God exercises patience we must too. It brings him no joy when sinners refuse to repent and seal their destiny.

Parents are well aware of this trait. It takes great patience to rear a child. We must teach them to listen. We must teach them the difference between right and wrong and how to make good decisions and at the same time model all of the above in their presence. Even when they rebel against everything we have taught them, we must continue to be patient.

God is also a God of judgment. We do not like this part of the picture, but we cannot leave out this stroke. While love motivated him to send his Son, those who refuse to believe must face his wrath. We can have the blood of Christ cover our sins or we can chose to pay for our sins. The owner of the vineyard would punish those who rejected his servants and killed his son. While believers are no longer under condemnation, we too can receive discipline when we fail to be faithful to the work God gives us to do.

Reflection: How wonderful to experience God's patience. He loves us even when we fail him.

November 24

Jesus on Money Management
Luke 16:1-9

I recall a sitcom about two sisters, one a good steward of her money but the other loved to spend. The one who lacked good financial sense opened a checking account. During the month, she just kept writing checks. When she got her statement, she could not understand how she could be overdrawn when she still had checks. Sometimes we do not do a good job of managing our money.

This story is very perplexing. It is about a wealthy man who commends his steward for dishonesty. This manager had control of the rich man's estate. But he was dishonest, and word of this had reached his employer. He knew he would lose his job, so he begins to make arrangements for his well being. He began to falsify the amounts of the rich man's debtors. That way, he would find favor with people who would in turn care for him. When the rich man discovers what he had done, he commends him.

All of us wish for better practice in financial management. It is not that we usually make bad decisions out of ignorance. We know better but act anyway. We may have a perfectly good automobile but just decide we want a new one, so we saddle ourselves in debt. Or we tire of one home and buy another. And then there are all those technological gadgets that keep appearing to tempt us. Especially a new cell phone or IPod.

So we spend money we do not have to get what we want instead of being satisfied with what we have. It is the American way. But it is not God's way. We can all look back on decisions we have made that we wish we hadn't. Often these unwise decisions are made in youth. With age comes wisdom.

The religious leaders were once again in the background of this parable, for they were lovers of money. If we are not careful, money can take up the wrong seat in our life. While having money is certainly not sinful, the love of money is the root of all evil. All the players in the story were dishonest, so what could Jesus possibly teach or value in this story? It is a story about prudence and managing our money well. It is about faithful devotion to our duties.

Reflection: Our money is given to us by God. Ask God for opportunities to use your finances to help others in need. Also ask him to help you manage well what he has entrusted to you.

November 25
Financial Management
Luke 16:1-9

While in high school, my daughter took an elective in Financial Management. She was planning to major in Accounting in college, so the course fit well. One part of the course taught them to balance a check book. The teacher had them all draw slips of paper that would show their weekly income. Hers was $160. She remarked that she was already in trouble for she had spent money and incurred debts that exceeded her income. Many of us can identify. The income does not go far enough. The wise saying is true: "If your outgo is greater than your income, your upkeep will be your downfall."

Though all the characters in this story were dishonest, there are some positive lessons we can learn from their sinful actions. The owner was wrong for commending dishonesty. The manager was wrong for being dishonest, and the creditors were wrong for agreeing to a dishonest plan.

In managing our money, we must be prudent or cautious. We need sound judgment in practical matters. Especially in a society that is based on the dollar but also greed. Even though he was dishonest, the manager was prudent in looking out for himself. He needed people to care for him.

It is unfortunate but often true that non Christians exercise more energy and foresight where earthly things are concerned than do Christians where heavenly things are in view. Jesus even says that the citizens of this world are shrewder than the godly. In essence, believers should do more for the God we serve than the world does for the gods they serve. We should show prudence in heavenly things because we know they are lasting. When we dedicate ourselves faithfully to God's work, we store our treasures in heaven. Do you give more attention to your job and its requirements than to God's work? Do your selfish endeavors take precedence over prayer and the study of God's Word?

We must also be prudent with God's resources. God enables the church and believers to do his work by providing us resources. We must be wise managers of what he gives, for he holds us accountable. The resources are material and spiritual, but we must give careful thought to both as we carry out his plans.

Reflection: Realize that all you have comes from God. Ask him to help you be cautious and prudent in your use of his resources.

November 26

A Thankful Spirit
Psalm 100:4

Thanksgiving Day is a legal holiday observed in the United States on the fourth Thursday of November. It was first celebrated by Pilgrims and Native Americans in New England in the early seventeenth century. They had endured a tough winter in a strange land, but their crops had produced and they were thankful for the bounty. In 1621, William Bradford, Governor of New England, proclaimed a day of "thanksgiving" and prayer to celebrate the Pilgrim's first harvest in America.

But a spirit of thankfulness extends farther back than the seventeenth century. It is evident in the Bible from the very beginning and should be an attitude that characterizes all believers. After God finished creation, he proclaimed it good. Then he created humans to care for it, and we should be thankful for that responsibility.

We can thank God for our families. Family was created by God. God saw man and said it was not good for him to be alone, so he created a woman. God performed the first marriage ceremony. In spite of the challenges our families face, family is a wonderful thing. Thank God for your family. Ask him for wisdom to lead your family to be a spiritual example to others. Let love and appreciation flow freely.

Thank God for salvation. When Adam and Eve rebelled against God, he could have left them to die in their sins, but he provided a sacrifice. He then spoke the Protoevangelium which told of the future Sacrifice of his Son. How wonderful that we have a God who loves us in spite of our sin and made a way that we could be reconciled to him. Thank him for taking the righteousness of his Son and giving it to you.

Freedom is another thing we can thank God for. Freedom in our country is an awesome privilege. We do not have to fear persecution when we worship our God. We can witness to others. In spite of the challenges that separation of church and state can sometimes bring, we have freedoms that others countries can only imagine. Freedom in Christ is an even greater honor. All our sins are forgiven, and we have abundant life.

Reflection: Choose to live with an attitude of thankfulness. Even when things seem to go wrong, we have the assurance that God will work good even out of tribulation.

November 27
Managing Our Money
Luke 16:1-9

"I bet he has the first dime he ever made." Have you ever heard that said of someone? The statement can mean the person is frugal or cheap. Or perhaps they are worried about their future financial state so they save everything they can. They want to be able to enjoy their retirement years, or they fear Social Security will go bankrupt.

We should manage our money well. In the parable, the rich man commended his manger not for his dishonesty but because he handled his accounts well. It was not actual money that was owed him but rather goods. But the principle is the same.

While money is not evil, it can lead us into evil practices if we are not careful. Greed can sneak into our life. Material possessions can become too important. We can hoard instead of share. We can live for money. Jesus warns of this when he says it is easier for a camel to go through the eye of a needle than for a wealthy man to enter heaven. (Matthew 19:24) Money often diverts our attention from more important things.

There are several principles that will enable us to handle our money well. Remember that it is temporary. We cannot take it with us when we leave earth at death. It will be left for others to fight over. This is not to say we avoid saving. Undue concern with the temporary often leads to misuse.

Our wealth belongs to God. By giving you talents, time and opportunities, he enabled you to accumulate what you possess. We are only managers like the man in the parable. God has loaned us our money, and he expects us to use it wisely. Jesus says we should use our worldly resources to make friends and benefit others. We are channels. He is not teaching us to use it dishonestly as the manager did. Use your money to bless others. Think of ways you can give that will advance God's Kingdom.

In our position as stewards of God's monetary blessings, we need faithfulness. A good manager is loyal and faithful with what is entrusted to his care. Jesus ends the parable by reminding us that we cannot serve two masters. We can serve God or material things but not both. However, we can use our material wealth in God's service.

Reflection: Ask God to show you ways to use your resources in his work. Be faithful with what God has given you.

November 28

Lessons on Forgiveness

Matthew 18:21-35

For three days a fierce winter storm traveled across the North Pacific from Alaska. The snow was piling up in the Sierra Nevadas. Father O'Malley sat in his bedroom writing Sunday's sermon. Suddenly the phone rang. It was the local hospital. They had a patient wanting his last rites. After the prayer of last rites, the bitter patient told O'Malley of an incident that happened thirty two years ago. He was a switchman on a railroad. It was a stormy night, and all of the crew was drunk. As he pushed the switch for the northbound train, he did so in the wrong direction. The oncoming train slammed into a car killing a family. To O'Malley's surprise, the incident he confessed had happened to his own family. But he forgave the dying man.

Forgiveness is releasing others from debts they owe us. But how often do we have to do this? According to Jesus, there is no limit. Peter offered seven times, thinking that was a gracious number. But Jesus says seventy times seven. Not a literal number but one that signifies no limit on our forgiveness. After all, that is how God responds to us. No matter how often we fail him, his forgiveness continues to flow. His forgiveness is complete in that he erases all our sins-past, present and future.

The parable is almost inconceivable but all too true in life. A man begins to settle accounts with those who owe him money. One is brought in who owed a great sum but cannot pay. He begs for mercy and time. The master instead forgives the debt. The forgiven servant finds a fellow servant who owes him a far lesser amount. The scene repeats itself but with different results. Instead of forgiving as he has been forgiven, he has the servant cast into prison until all could be paid. But the scene did not escape the attention of others, for they reported these actions to the master, and he delivered the unforgiving servant to the tormentors until he could pay the debt.

The nature of our debt to God is unpayable. The amount the first servant owed the master is not a literal amount. It represents an amount that could not possibly be paid. Such is our debt to God. Our debt is represented by sin, and we cannot erase that debt. Thankfully, God chose to pay it for us through his Son. We deserve hell but God offers forgiveness and heaven.

Reflection: Who do you need to forgive? Ask God to help you forgive that person even as he has forgiven you.

November 29
God's Forgiveness
Matthew 18:21-35

One has said, "Forgiveness is like the violet sending forth its pure fragrance on the heel of the boot of the one who crushed it." Jesus instructed Peter that forgiveness should be limitless. Commenting on the scarcity of such behavior, John Wesley said, "If this be Christianity, where do Christians live?"

God's forgiveness is merciful and just. Such was the king in the parable. He had life and death authority over those who owed him money. The first owed him a sum that could be calculated in today's terms as millions of dollars. He could not pay. Initially, the king ordered that he, his family and all he had be sold to pay the debt. But in response to the servant's plea for time, the king decided to simply forgive the debt.

While this is a picture of what God does for us in salvation, the parable is meant to teach about forgiveness among believers. Having Christ's nature, we have the capability to be merciful, just and forgiving. Our forgiving nature reflects the character of Christ. It is the key to unity in God's churches. Forgiveness tears down barriers that sin erects.

The most striking example of forgiveness is Jesus on the cross asking God to forgive those who were crucifying him. (Luke 23:34) The early apostle Stephen also shows this trait. As he was being stoned for his faith, he prayed almost an identical prayer. (Acts 7:60) Joseph in the Old Testament also demonstrates this quality. After being sold into slavery by his brothers, he is later promoted to ruler in Egypt. When famine strikes the land, his brothers appear before him for food. He could have had them killed, but he forgave them.

Sadly, it is our tendency not to forgive. Even after receiving our new nature, it is still difficult to forgive those who hurt us, especially those who do so deeply. This is shown by the forgiven servant who was unwilling to forgive a fellow servant. It serves to remind us that the power of the flesh can control us if we are not prepared. We must walk by the Spirit so we do not fulfill the desires of the flesh. One of which is unforgiveness.

Reflection: Unforgiveness will place you in an emotional prison that will damage your relationship with God. Choose to always forgive no matter how intense the pain of the offense.

November 30

Lessons on Religion

Luke 18:9-14

Have you ever met someone who was not what you initially thought? I once had what I thought was a good friend. One day I opened the local newspaper to find he had been arrested for exposing himself to two young girls selling doughnuts. Then I discovered that it was not the first time. He had previously served jail time for a similar offense.

Things and people are not always what they appear to be. The world looks flat from our perspective, but Columbus found out differently. We can draw lines where one appears longer but really is not. The magician can seemingly cut someone in half. And yes it is possible to pretend to be a Christian when you are not. It is also possible for churches to be dead when they appear alive.

The story Jesus tells is about pretense and misinformation. A Pharisee and tax collector both show up at the temple to pray. The Pharisee moves down front and begins to tell God how good he is and all he has done for him. He thinks he deserves acceptance because of his good works. The tax collector's prayer was quite different. He knew his position. He was a sinner in need of God's saving grace. Jesus says he went home justified. The Pharisee just went home.

Jesus speaks of certain ones who trusted in themselves and despised others. While this line certainly characterized the religious leaders, it is possible that it did some of his followers as well. It is possible for a person to associate religious activity with salvation. While one flows from the other, the first does not result in the second. We can be misled by our own lack of understanding or the teachings of others. While a believer should not doubt their salvation, we do need to examine ourselves to make sure we are of the faith. (II Corinthians 13:5)

In speaking to the early church at Sardis, Jesus told them he was aware of all they did. They had a name for being alive but they were really dead.

(Revelation 3:1) There is a stark contrast between religion of the heart and that of mere form. True religion makes a difference in our lifestyle.

Reflection: Examine your life to see if there has been that time when you have asked for God's forgiveness. Make sure you are not depending on religious activity to save you.

December

December 1
Religion or Christianity
Luke 18:9-14

The study of world religions is very interesting. As you study the records of ancient people, we find one thing in common. Almost all of them worshipped something. It may have been figures that represented gods, or they may have worshipped the sun, moon, or stars. Sometimes it was a combination of the two. Judaism and later Christianity are unique in their worship of only one God and in the belief that their God is still alive.

What is it that makes individuals recognize that there is something beyond us? Christians believe it is because of a spiritual void created in us that can only be filled by worshipping God. But because people have not heard of him or have rejected him, they choose other things.

In our story, the Pharisee trusted in his religious deeds and position. He belonged to an elite sect and was a separatist. They were the heroes and backbone of Jewish identity. His list of good deeds was extremely long. This probably explains why he went down front to pray. But the tax collector left the temple justified. The Pharisee just prayed with himself.

The publican realized that religion cannot save. We must too. If it could most of the world's population would be secure, for most all people are religious to a degree whether they have trusted Christ as Savior or not. It is possible to be alive religiously and dead spiritually. We cannot equate good works with salvation, though one will proceed from the other.

According to Jesus, some who think heaven is a sure thing will be disappointed. He said that not everyone who called him Lord would enter the kingdom of heaven. Only those who did his Father's will would have that privilege. (Matthew 7:21) True religion is faith in what Christ has done on Calvary. We must depend on God's grace, for nothing else will do. Jesus reminded Nicodemus that we must be born again. (John 3)

True religion involves repentance and faith. The Pharisee thought so much of himself that he saw no need of repenting. Only sinners needed to do this, and he did not belong to that class of people. The publican did. He knew who he was and what he needed to do. He cried out to God for mercy.

Reflection: Are you religious but lost? Is your religious experience based on repentance of your sins and faith in Christ? If not, make that decision to follow him now.

December 2

The Impeccable Word

II Timothy 3:16

There are many great works of literature. We are introduced to some of the classics early in our educational journey. If our journey takes us to college, we will read more and most likely the entire story. We will learn of the different interpretations and the historical background. Sadly, the greatest work to ever be written is normally omitted-the Bible.

A study of God's Word and how it came to be in the form it currently enjoys is remarkable indeed. From the original manuscripts-all of which have been lost, to the copies made by the scribes to our modern bound Bibles in many translations, the Bible has remained the most beloved book of all times. Christians depend on it to guide their lives, though we may differ in some of our interpretations. And even though some believers see errors in God's Word, they all believe it points the way to God.

The Bible claims it was inspired by God though written by men. To be inspired means that God acted on those people who wrote the Bible by his Spirit. He gave them the words to say. Christians differ in how inspiration took place. The most extreme position is that God actually dictated the words. The opposite extreme is that inspiration was no more than a modern day writer being moved to write some work of literature. In between the two extremes are more moderate theories. One is that the words written are the words God wanted penned but that he did not take the writer out of their environment or change their personality. Another proposes that he even let the writers choose their own words.

One's view of inspiration is important because it determines how much faith is placed in God's Word. A low view of inspiration leads to a liberal view of Scripture. If God's Word is subject to any error, then how can we believe anything it says? How can we know that the way it proclaims for salvation is truly the right way? How can we make sure it is not filled with myths and legends?

A productive Christian life can only be lived when we have a strong faith in God's Word. It is true, dependable, trustworthy and without error. Living by its principles will lead to salvation and abundant life.

Reflection: How important is God's Word to you? Make a commitment to believe all of it by faith.

December 3

Perils of a Fruitless Life
Luke 13:6-9

Disappointments and unmet expectations are a regular part of life. Imagine the woman who cannot get pregnant but greatly desires a child. A great deal of money is often spent in any adventure that might result in pregnancy. Or the child who is extremely intelligent but whose parents have no money for college. Or the person who is diligently trying to establish seniority at his job but repeatedly gets laid off.

In this story a man who owned a fig tree was disappointed. For three years he had been looking for fruit but found none. His solution was to cut it down. But the caretaker of the vineyard suggested some fertilization and one more year. If it did not bear fruit after that, he would cut it down.

Jesus taught that others would know us by the fruit we produce. That fruit should be love, joy, peace, patience, kindness, goodness, faithfulness and self-control. (Galatians 5:22-23) Such fruit can only be born when connected to the vine, which is Jesus. (John 15:5) So why do believers often not produce fruit or the amount of fruit we could?

Failing to realize our true identity hinders the fruit from growing properly on our branches. The tree in the story represents believers. The resulting fruit comes from godly living. God planted the tree, and cutting the tree down represents discipline resulting from a fruitless life. The extended time frame for fruit symbolizes God's patience with the human race.

What is the believer's identity? We are God's children, accepted into his family. It is the largest and most exciting family in existence. Jesus even goes so far as to call us his friends. It is not a friendship in which he loses his authority over us or where we come to look on him as our "buddy," but it is a friendship nevertheless. While once called sinners, we are now classified as saints. We were once unrighteous, but now the righteousness of Christ has been applied to our life. Our life may have been a miserable existence before, but we can now have abundant life in Christ as we allow him to live through us. Most of all, we look forward to eternal life in heaven. God will create a new heaven and earth for all of his people to enjoy. No longer do we grovel in the dust before God.

Reflection: Realize who you are in Christ so God can use you fully in his marvelous work.

December 4

Fruit Bearing Christians

Luke 13:6-9

Identity is one crisis we must solve for a fulfilled life. This crisis is typical for the adolescent. The "Who am I" question must be answered. Are they are a carbon copy of their parent, or can they make their own way in life? Some never solve the equation and carry the uncertainty into adulthood where it leads to further problems. Depression, low self-esteem, low energy and reduced enthusiasm can all result from not knowing who you are.

Knowing our identity as a Christian is directly related to productivity for God. The opposite is also true. If we do not know who we are and are not aware of the ammunition God has given us, our fruit will be almost nonexistent as it was on the fig tree.

Not producing fruit in our spiritual life is a serious thing as shown by what the landowner suggested doing to the tree. As God's children, we are no longer under condemnation. However, God does use discipline when our lives are not producing fruit. His discipline can come in many forms but always arises out of his love and desire that we enjoy all he has to offer. The discipline carries a teaching element designed to move us in a different direction.

The Church's example of fruit producing is not much different than Israel in the Old Testament. Their pattern was disobedience, discipline, a return to God, then disobedience again. Ours is often the same. God has to send his discipline on a regular basis to encourage us to bear fruit. How much better to bear the fruit and enjoy God's best for you.

Fruit results when God's Spirit resides in a person. This takes place when we trust Christ as our Savior. He is not received at a subsequent time. We get all of God all at the same time. This does not mean we always live a Spirit filled life, but we do possess him. This being said, we realize that it is not us that bears the fruit but rather God who bears the fruit through us. We do not have to strive to bear fruit, we just allow God to let happen what should naturally result because of our connection with him. As his life flows through us, it becomes evident to others who we are.

Reflection: Coals that are separated go out. The closeness keeps the fire going. Involve yourself in those spiritual disciplines that will keep you connected to God so fruit will hang from your branches.

December 5
The Almighty God
Genesis 1:1

The beginning. When was it? How was it? Until Charles Darwin, many assumed the beginning happened just as the Genesis account proposed. With his findings, opinions changed. Long held beliefs were seriously challenged. No longer was the world thousands of years old. Now it was billions. No longer was man created complete and intelligent. He had to evolve into that position over millions of years.

But the Bible says God was in the beginning. Not chance. There are not many gods. Nor is our God bereft of intelligence. People could not always enter a personal relationship with a pagan god. They were distant deities not very concerned with the humans they had made.

The God of the Bible is intelligent. In fact, this is one of the most convincing proofs of creation. Looking at nature and how it interacts to ensure continued existence should be evidence enough to prove God. Our God is wise. All his decisions that relate to his world and us are made in advance. He is proactive not reactive. His will is not determined by our actions. He does not rearrange his plans based on our decisions.

Not only did he create but he also preserves his creation. More importantly, he is a personal God that we can have a relationship with.

Our God is characterized by the following words: omnipresent, omniscient, and omnipotent. God is everywhere at the same time. He operates outside of time but also in it. In fact, he created time and will one day bring time to an end as it is absorbed into eternity. He is in your future as well as in your past and present. Nothing you do surprises him because he already knows. You cannot disappoint God. There is nothing God is unaware of. His knowledge is complete. He is also all powerful. There is nothing God cannot do except those things that would violate his nature. He is more powerful than all those things we fear.

God represents himself in three persons but at the same time is one. God the Father rules over his creation. God the Son has made the redemption of humanity possible, and God the Spirit resides in our life enabling us to live as Christ desires.

Reflection: God is God, and there is no other. Worship him with all you are.

December 6
Preparing for Christ's Return
Matthew 25:1-13

Aunt Bee is called away to care for a sick relative on one Andy Griffith episode. Andy and Opie are left as bachelors for several days. While they started out good, cleaning deteriorated as the days progressed. They planned to pick up just before Aunt Bee arrived but were surprised when she called to say she would be home in a few hours.

Believers are often tempted to the same actions. Time continues and still Christ has not come.So we get careless in our lifestyle. Others even dismiss the Second Coming entirely. Careless lifestyles and last minute clean up is not what Jesus has in mind for his followers.

Jesus illustrates the need of preparing for his Second Coming through the parable of the bridesmaids. Five decided that the oil in their lamps would be enough while the other five took extra oil. When the oil in their lamps was used up, the five foolish had to go into town to get more While they were gone the groom came, and the five wise were ushered into the marriage feast. When the foolish bridesmaids retuned, they found themselves shut out of the ceremony.

While we are warned about trying to know the exact time of Jesus' return, the warning does not include a lackadaisical attitude about the return itself. After all, the when is not nearly as important as being prepared. The groom is a picture of Christ who is the husband of the church, and the bridesmaids are believers.

Part of preparation is acknowledging the imminence of his coming. The five foolish bridesmaids thought they had plenty of time. When their oil ran out, they went to town to buy more. Since Jesus has been a long time in coming, we have no reason not to prepare. His coming will be sudden.

Repentance and faith are the initial and elementary acts of preparation, but they must be followed by a life of obedience. And the preparation must be individual. Preparing for Christ's return must be done now. There is no Purgatory wherein we might be cleansed and made ready for heaven.

Reflection: One has said, "Tomorrow is the most perfect day to start any job." But it is not the most perfect day to prepare for Jesus' coming. Today is the day of salvation.

December 7

Man-God's Creation
Genesis 1:27

According to most Science textbooks, man is the result of years of evolution. At some point, he became human instead of primate. From there he developed into the modern form he now is. Thanks to Charles Darwin and his discoveries, this theory is widely held among scientists. Thanks to God-who was there when it happened, we can consider another view.

While some theologians hold to Theistic Evolution or at least Progressive Creation theories, many believers still take the Genesis account at face value. According to God's Word, man is a unique creation made from the dust of the ground, not a product of evolution. Nor did he have animal-like characteristics that had to be shaken off over thousands of years.

The Bible says that we are created in the image of God. This in itself makes us very different from the animal kingdom. While the animal kingdom does have senses and can even reason to a degree, man is different. Being made in the image of God entails having some of God's characteristics in us that animals do not have. The most important is our ability to relate to God. We also have a soul and/or spirit that will live on after death. When animals die, their existence is over, but not for humans.

Man is the crown of God's creation. As is evidenced by the story of Adam and Eve, man was created with the freedom of choice-at least initially. Eve and Adam chose to disobey God's command. At this point, sin entered their life and resulted in death. Though they did not die physically at that moment, they did spiritually. They were separated from God.

Because of our first parent's sin, all are now born with a sinful nature. The Bible reminds us that sin entered the world through one man but did not stop there. It spread to all people thereby bringing death to all people. (Romans 5:12) How that sin nature passes to each individual is a matter of debate among theologians, but it is there nevertheless. God does not hold us accountable for the sins of our first parents, but we do reap the harvest of their sin. We are held accountable for our sins which began to manifest themselves at a very early age.

Reflection: God's grace is the solution to humanity's sin problem. Thank God that he loved us enough to send his Son to pay for our sins so we would not have to.

December 8
Responsibility-What God Expects
Luke 19:11-27

Responsible money management. Not a subject we normally like to discuss. Why? We probably do a better job talking about it than actually doing it. There was once a show named "Millionaire." Each week a millionaire would look for someone to give a million dollars to. He discovered that some people were very frugal with it while others were foolish and wasteful.

So how is it with you? Are you responsible with what God has given you? Do you pay your debts on time? Do your credit cards go into shock every month because of the load they carry? And what about those checks that we don't have funds in the bank to cover? Or all those things we buy that we do not need?

God has expectations of us where our resources are concerned. The parable teaches that. But we are also accountable for the gifts, talents and abilities we have. And with our spiritual disciplines, such as Bible reading, prayer, serving and faithfulness to gathering with fellow believers. If your example was all that others saw, how would it influence their spiritual journey?

Those in the parable faced the same question. A master went on a long journey to be crowned king. Before leaving, he entrusted his servants with money. They were to invest while he was gone. Some did a good job while others did not.

God expects us to be responsible with what he gives us. While we may have the same gifts, we use those gifts in different ways because we have different opportunities and unique personalities. We are not responsible for opportunities we do not have. The same is true with our talents and resources. We are not cisterns to hold but channels to flow through.

After returning, the king called in his servants for an accounting. The first reported a one thousand percent profit. The next five hundred. The third brought back the original amount. He did not even put it in the bank where it could have drawn interest. The rebuke from the king enforces the conclusion that God expects us to use what he gives.

Reflection: What gifts and talents has God given you? Discover them, and then use them for his honor and glory.

December 9

Responsible Stewardship

Luke 19:11-27

Regis Philbin once hosted a show entitled "Who Wants to be a Millionaire." Contestants were asked questions with each correct answer bringing them closer to the million dollar question. Some chose to quit while they were ahead rather than risk losing what they had already accumulated. But others risked the question in hopes of winning the grand prize. One wonders how the winning contestants chose to use the money.

The nobleman called to a distant country to be crowned king expected his servants to use their money wisely. When he returned, he discovered that some had but others had not. His rebuke of the one who did nothing reminds us that God expects us to be responsible stewards. After the coming of the Spirit at Pentecost, gifts were given to believers. These gifts are still doled out according to God's plan for us.

Think of how much God must trust us or the high hopes he has. He has entrusted his entire work to frail human beings. But the picture is not actually that bleak, for his Spirit empowers us. As we let God's Spirit work through us, we are instrumental in advancing the kingdom of God. It is not news catching accomplishments that we must make but small ordinary things we do each day that proves our faithfulness. Our small deeds of mercy increase the investment that has been left with us. This does not mean that God is not still in control. His overarching plan will come about. He simply uses us as the instruments to make it happen.

The responsibility God expects of us requires courage and it means taking risks. Joshua was chosen as Moses' successor to lead his people into the Promised Land. God instructed him to be courageous. It would take that to conquer the land and all the pagan inhabitants. God's work is not for the faint of heart. It takes a strong will to live for God consistently. It is often easier to give in to the temptations which in turn lead to acceptance and approval by others. We risk rejection and persecution as we tell of his love. We may even lose friends and family.

At the end of our lives, we will give an account of our stewardship. Our goal should be to hear Jesus say "Well done, good and faithful servant."

Reflection: What gifts do you have that could be used more effectively in God's work? Ask God to show you where he wants to use you.

December 10
God's Salvation
Ephesians 2:8-10

My daughter's cross country coach once endured the greatest heartache a parent can have. He lost his daughter. They lived in a safe subdivision, but one day she was riding her bike when a resident accidently ran a stop sign and hit her. Her life ended, and a part of his did too. There was absolutely nothing he or anyone else could do to save her. She got what she did not deserve.

In the process of salvation, God gives us what we do not deserve. We do not warrant it because we have sinned against him. When Adam and Eve rebelled in the Garden, God could have ended the human race. During Noah's time, when the inclination of people's hearts was always on evil, God could have let the flood destroy all life. But he chose to save.

When Nicodemus came to Jesus at night for a conversation, Jesus immediately went to the heart of the matter by telling him he must be born again. Salvation is the basic need of every person. Trying to live right, doing charitable deeds, nurturing the environment, and giving to charitable causes are all good. But none of those things can touch our deepest need.

When God saves us, he redeems our whole person. We are saved spiritually, physically, mentally and emotionally. The offer is free but it cost God dearly. He was willing to give up his only begotten Son for your sins. Jesus was willing to leave the glories of heaven to come to a sin cursed world and be nailed to a cross. But God's love for us is so immense that he willing to make such a sacrifice. All who receive it will be saved. This carries the idea of being rescued from imminent peril. True gifts are always free.

Jesus was the propitiation for our sins. There are different theories surrounding the atonement. Some would say his death was just a good example. But Jesus' sacrifice was a substitution. Him for us. Either he died for our sins, or we had to. He actually took your place and by doing so satisfied God's wrath. While God is a God of love, he cannot overlook sin. It must be punished, but in his love he allowed his Son to take that punishment. Through the atonement, we are made at one with God. The relationship that sin destroyed is restored.

Reflection: Thank God daily for his wonderful plan of salvation that allows you to go free and enjoy God's love.

December 11

What Salvation Accomplishes

Ephesians 2:8-10

The call comes into the local fire station. A house fire. The firemen quickly suit up and man the trucks. In a moment's time, they arrive to find a mother and father standing outside, yelling for them to rescue their child who is trapped inside. One brave fireman enters through the front door, crouches low to the floor, searching through the flames for the child. Finally, he sees her lying on the floor overcome by smoke. He quickly snatches her up, brings her out and gives her oxygen. She recovers.

The above is similar to what God does in salvation. He sees us overcome by sin and knows the damage it can inflict. He sends his Son in to rescue us and administers his blood to cover our life threatening wound.

While salvation is a process, it is also a one-time event. Salvation involves that one moment when we ask Christ for forgiveness and share with him our desire to serve him obediently. But at the same time it involves more than that.

The process of salvation involved regeneration, justification, sanctification and glorification. All of this is accomplished through faith in Christ. He is the only way of salvation. Regeneration is the process we normally refer to as the new birth. Repentance and faith are involved in this process, though the act itself is the result of God's conviction in our life. God is also the one that gives the new nature. We are not saved by good works. We cannot labor for what is free, nor can we work to keep what was freely given. Repentance is sorrow for sin and involves going in a different direction and having a change of heart. Instead of loving sin, we hate it. Instead of having to sin, we now have the choice to be obedient to God.

Justification is also what God does. It can be defined as "just as if I never sinned." Once forgiven, God looks on us through Christ. His righteousness has been applied to us. Our position is holy. We are now his children. Sanctification is a life-long process. It involves becoming more like Christ each day. It is not a second work of grace but a daily dying to self and living for God. We grow in grace and are set apart for God's principles.

Reflection: The end of salvation is glorification. It is the great hope we look forward to. An eternity in heaven with our Lord. Take a moment to thank God for saving you.

December 12

Take the Adventure

Matthew 25:14-30

Some people love taking adventures. Every spring a large number of people gather in Georgia to begin a thru hike of the Appalachian Trail. It is a six month or longer journey of living in and traveling through rugged mountains. Carrying all your belongings on your back, sleeping in mice infested shelters, sore feet, blisters, and a host of other challenges explain why only a few of the many ever make it to Maine.

Then there are the adventures that come with cheap thrills. Binge drinking. Using drugs or misusing legal drugs. Committing illegal activities and then trying to escape the authorities. Immoral activities like prostitution or pornography. Gambling and cheating. A life of crime.

But none of the above is the greatest adventure in life. The greatest exploit begins with a decision to follow Jesus Christ. Names for this adventure include salvation, regeneration or the new birth. Many toy with this adventure, but things crop up that make them change their mind. Others begin but fall by the wayside. True believers follow to the end.

Jesus speaks of a man who takes a long journey. Before leaving, he gives money to his servants to use while he is away. One is given five talents, another two and a third one. When he returns, he discovers that the servants given the five and two talents had doubled theirs, but the man with the one had hid his in the ground. He hid the talent because he feared his master.

It is a privilege but also a responsibility to use what God entrusts us with. The man on the journey is Christ and the servants represent believers.

425

Jesus said that after he ascended back to the Father that his people would do greater works than he did while on earth. Not greater in measure, but we would go into regions he never reached. His ministry was confined to a small area. And indeed we have. We have taken the gospel almost to the ends of the earth as instructed in the Great Commission. Technology and the Internet have in large part made this possible. Faithful giving to mission work by God's people over the years has made a great impact. And God gives us the privilege of impacting our little worlds by using the talents, gifts, and resources he provides.

Reflection: Are you on the greatest adventure in life? If not, decide to follow Christ today. Use your resources to touch others.

December 13
On Adventure With God
Matthew 25:14-30

Imagine cancer ravaging the body of a young child. No cure is currently available, but there is a doctor who is working diligently on a possible solution. Finally, he seems to have found it. But he is a selfish man. Though he has taken the Hippocratic Oath, he does not really care for people or about helping them. So he decides to keep the news of the cure to himself. An unimaginable scenario. Are you keeping a cure to yourself?

We are responsible for sharing God's love in practical ways. He entrusts us with capabilities to do that. It takes no effort to do as the third servant did-hide your talent in the ground. Any time you turn down an opportunity to work at church, you have hidden your talent. When you do not go on the mission trip you feel God prodding you to sign up for. When you fail to give to the mission offering, knowing you have the resources to really make a difference. In all these ways and others, we can hide our talent.

It takes courage to go on adventure with God. The Good Samaritan did. While the priest and Levite would not help the hurting man, the hated Samaritan did. The Bible reminds us that the person who knows right but fails to do it commits sin. (James 4: 17) Are you sharing the cure for the greatest disease in life? Christians can be bandits. We plunder and loot by not using what God has given us. We can embezzle by living for self and not God.

Sometimes we know what our gifts and talents are but we cannot see they are needed. Every local church gives opportunities to use them. In any given church twenty percent of the members do eighty percent of the work. There are always hats to share. The man with the one talent obviously had no confidence in himself, so he did nothing. In your power, you cannot do what God requires, but in his power you can do all things he wants.

When we fail to use what God has given us, we can lose it. Such is what happened with the one talent man. His talent was taken away and given to the one with five. All God asks from us is faithfulness. God knows we are powerless in and of ourselves. But he grants us strength for the adventure. All you need he will supply.

Reflection: Believe that you are worthy of being used in God's kingdom work. Ask him for strength to do what he is leading you to do.

December 14

The Purpose of God's Grace

Ephesians 1:4-6

Something that serves no purpose is useless. It normally finds itself in the trash can or in a yard sale. Unless there is some sentimental value, it will be discarded. But things of use are different. They have purpose, and we keep them around for that very reason. A hammer is a useful tool around the house and in the yard. Even if the handle breaks, another one can be secured.

God's grace is made known through election, and it has purpose. Election has been a hotly debated and misunderstood subject for many years. Early church reformers had different understandings as do theologians and Christians today. It is an important subject, and the Bible speaks of it in many places. It must be distinguished from the election of Israel as God's people in the Old Testament. That was national election, but there is an election unto salvation and it is individual.

The early battle was between Augustine and Pelagius and resurfaced hundreds of years later between John Calvin and Jacobus Arminius. The question was what part man had in salvation. Was he predestined to salvation whether he wanted to be or not, or did he have free will? And then there were some moderate or middle ground positions. While Christ was the elect of God, and it was God's plan that people come to know him, this still did not explain individual election. And then too there was the debate over whether election was based on foreknowledge. Or was it based on some good in the person.

A God who predestined some to heaven and others to hell, then created them to live out that destiny seemed harsh and foreboding. On the other hand, a God who allowed anyone to enter heaven regardless of their wickedness did not fit the biblical picture. A harsh definition of predestination often led to lack of missionary zeal in some denominations. The opposite extreme of universalism led in the same direction.

This much is conclusive. If you are a child of God, you are because God's electing grace worked in your life. Were it not for God's Spirit drawing you, you would never have approached Christ. God could have let you wander in your sins until you paid the final consequence, but he didn't.

Reflection: Thank you Lord for loving me. Help me to live for you so that others can see your love in me. Amen.

December 15

God's Wonderful Grace

Ephesians 1:4-6

Grace is God's unmerited favor. It is a word used over and over in the Bible. And there are many stories that demonstrate God's grace. Imagine a young man caught stealing. He is brought before the judge. The evidence is overwhelming. The judge pronounces sentence but then steps from behind the bench and tells the young criminal he will accept his sentence. He did not deserve those actions, and neither do we merit salvation.

That God's grace comes to individuals is uncontested. How it comes has been hotly debated. It is by election that God regenerates, justifies, sanctifies and glorifies. Whether or not this is consistent with free agency is the contested element. Strict Calvinism states that true freedom was lost after Adam and Eve fell into sin. After that, all of humanity has been enslaved by sin and will perform its dictates. That God elects any at all does not make him unfair but rather quite gracious. After all, he is under no obligation to save any. Staunch Calvinism sees God predestinating people even before he creates. This view appears quite contrary to the Bible. But neither is universalism the answer. Nowhere in Scripture does it teach all will be saved. A modified position seems to fit better.

Take for example a woman who goes to an orphanage to adopt a child. She looks over all the children and chooses the one she wants. The paperwork is completed, and she takes the child home. Is she being unfair because she did not take them all home?

By electing us, God shows his goodness and sovereignty. Election may never be understood fully, but we can see the result of it in our life. Our wants and desires change. No longer do we want to live for self. We have a purpose, and it is to live for our Savior. God's electing grace also forms humility in us as we come to realize that salvation is all of God. Even though you believed in faith, he enabled you to do that.

We are secure in God's grace. When God draws us into his family, he keeps us there. We will not want to leave, and he will not let Satan snatch us out of his Father's hands. Your eternal destiny is secure. To prove this, he seals you with his Holy Spirit.

Reflection: Bask in the goodness of God's grace. Worship and serve him faithfully in appreciation for his goodness.

December 16

Who's Your Authority?

Matthew 21:23-32

I recall one episode with my daughter where I had restricted her Internet use to between the hours of eight and ten at night. One morning I saw her on the computer and questioned her about it. She said, "Oh, I'm just checking my email." I reminded her of the rule, but she kept checking. I said, "So I as a parent make the rules, but you decide whether or not you want to obey them? I guess she thought about it because she did not check her email.

We all have authority figures in life. Even if you are your own boss, there are still people you have to answer to, like the government. Some people go into business for themselves because they do not like to answer to anyone else, but they quickly discover that there is always someone or some organization telling them what to do.

God should be your ultimate authority figure. He is the one to whom we ultimately have to answer, but not everyone views life this way. We are raising a generation of young people who have different views about God. As they become adults, this will affect how the adult population views God. In a poll taken by George Barna ten years ago, more than half of teenagers agreed with the statement; "All religious faiths teach equally valid truths."

In part because of the Internet, our youth are being exposed to pluralism as no generation before. But God is not just whatever works. And it is not up to us to define religion just any way we desire.

Authority is a strong word that denotes power and privilege. People in authority have the duty of exercising control over the lives and welfare of other people. This is why no society can be a pure democracy. We have too many different opinions. An absence of authority leads to anarchy and chaos.

As Jesus returns to the temple to teach, the religious leaders question by whose authority he had recently drove the merchants from the temple. Instead of a direct answer, Jesus asks them where John the Baptist's baptism came from. To answer heaven was to condemn themselves for not believing him. To answer earth would start a riot because the people believed he was a prophet.

Reflection: Realize that God is the ultimate authority in life and eternity. It will not do to believe in any god or a number of gods. God is God, and there is no other. Submit your life to him.

December 17

To Obey or Not to Obey

Matthew 21:23-32

Authority figures fill our lives. Unless we are reared in an orphanage or foster care facility, our parents are our first authority figures. Then we start school and are introduced to teachers. After graduation, or even before, we encounter another authority figure-the boss. When we move out on our own, we quickly discover that there are even more authority figures.

After embarrassing the religious leaders with his question about John's baptism, Jesus tells a story about a father and his two sons. He went to the first and told him to go work in the vineyard. He initially told his father no but later changed his mind and went. The second son told his father he would go but did not. Obviously they both had trouble with authority, and the only obedient one was the son who actually went.

It is vital that we recognize authority. In fact, we cannot live in society with recognizing its organizational structure. If we ignore it, thinking we can do as we please, we will probably end up in jail. Kids who have trouble with authority figures in school usually drop out or fail classes. There are many bodies of authority that exercise some control over our lives. God designed it that way. His Word teaches that we are to honor and obey those who have authority over us as long as it does not require disobeying him. We can chafe under that power because we may not like a certain person who is in office, but it does not change the command. The better way to deal with such a situation is to pray and seek change in an honorable way.

Our greatest authority figure is Christ. Jesus was not just a man. He was God incarnate. He is the ultimate authority whether we recognize him or not. All people will one day answer to him whether they accept him or not. We need to respond to him in a positive way. Many of the common people accepted Jesus and became his followers. Even some of the religious leaders did. But many rejected him. When we fail to actively respond to him, we rebuff him. Allowing him to have full control of your life is the only adequate response. Jesus reminds us that we cannot serve two masters. (Matthew 6: 24) Our natural tendency is to disobey because of sin's consequences in our life. We must choose to obey.

Reflection: Give God complete authority in your life. Recognize him for who he is, and serve him with all your heart.

December 18
God's Church
Matthew 16:18

It is the tendency of people to want to belong to organizations. Barney Fife was once excited because he and Andy had been invited to the capital with the possibility of joining an elite social club. Barney tried so hard to make a good impression that he made a fool of himself and was turned down for membership. He was devastated.

While God's church is not an organization, it is the most exciting thing that we can belong to. The church is an organism. It lives, breathes and changes in degree to meet ever developing and changing beliefs and standards in society. While the message it proclaims never changes, its methods must or she will lose her effectiveness.

Jesus died for the church. The church was established on Peter's profession that Jesus was indeed the Messiah and not just some miracle working prophet. As such, the gates of hell will not prevail against it. The picture is not the church on the defensive but rather on the offensive. As we push forward with the message of God's love, all the wickedness of hell will not be able to stop us. The church will be successful?

God's church is universal but only in the sense that it is composed of individual bodies of believers. There is no overarching authority that governs the church other than Christ himself. Not all denominations adhere to this principle, but it is biblical. Churches are not ruled by priests, bishops or popes. Christ is the head.

The requirement for belonging to God's church is faith in what his Son has done. Accepting Christ as Savior should be followed by baptism, for Jesus commands us to baptize those who express faith in him. The method of baptism and when it should take place has been disputed throughout church history. Methods include dipping, pouring, sprinkling and immersion and are practiced by various denominations. When baptism should occur seems conclusive by the example of New Testament believers observing the rite after they believed in Christ. Baptism before that time carries no meaning since the rite itself demonstrates that we have died to our old way of life and are now living in a new manner.

Reflection: Have you joined God's church? If so, look for ways to use your gifts so you can be instrumental in helping his kingdom advance.

December 19

Why God Searches for Us

Luke 15:1-10

Hide and seek is an old game that has been passed through the generations. The seeker counts while the hider hides. Then the hunt is on. The reward: the person found has to seek. And then there is the deer hunt. Hunters are lined along a highway or field while dogs are released at another point. Hopefully, the dogs will run a deer and a kill will be made.

The greatest search is the one God makes for us. God performed this search in the very beginning when Adam and Eve chose to rebel. Though they tried to hide from God, he came in the cool of the evening and asked that monumental question, "Where are you?" It was not a geographical question but one with spiritual aspects. God's desire was to restore them.

There are some profound statements where God's love is concerned. God loves you where you are, but he loves you so much he will not leave you where you are. Nothing you can do, whether good or evil, will make God love you more or less than he already does. His love is a constant. You are a unique creation of God, and his love for you is beyond your comprehension.

These stories are not as familiar as the one that follows about the prodigal son. But they all teach the same truth. God is searching. The man who has one hundred sheep is not satisfied if he loses one. He will search until he finds him and then will call his neighbors to rejoice with him. Nor will the woman with ten pieces of silver be satisfied until she finds the one piece she lost.

These two stories have been called the gospel within the gospel because they tell us so much about the nature of God. They remind us that it is impossible for us to come to God unless he first comes to us. He does this by searching our hearts and convicting us. This is done by his Spirit.

Jesus often searched for lost people, and he spent time with them. This caused much ire from the religious leaders, especially since he claimed to be a great teacher and prophet. Many of the people Jesus hung around with were considered the scum of the earth. But this is where he needed to be. We might say Jesus jeopardized his reputation among the church crowd because of who he hung around with.

Reflection: Take a moment to thank God that he searched for you. Because he did, you are the recipient of eternal life.

December 20

God's Search

Luke 15:1-10

One has said, "A man is known by the company he keeps." I suppose this is why many of the religious leaders mistrusted Jesus. He associated with them on occasion, but often fellowshipped with people they did not care for. Sinners. Prostitutes and adulteresses. Even tax collectors. The religious leaders were so concerned with the trivial aspects of the Law that they had no time to actually do what the Law required. They had no time for such people.

God searches because something is lost. It was for the sheep owner and the woman with the silver. They searched because what they lost was important to them. God searches because what is lost is important to him. We are what is lost. The prophet reminds us that we have all gone astray just like sheep often do. (Isaiah 53:6) Paul reinforces this when he writes that there is not even one righteous person. (Romans 3:10)

Every person born is under the condemnation of sin. We are lost and without hope apart from God. All humanity was represented in Adam, and when he and Eve sinned, they inherited that sinful nature. All we have to do is observe human actions, and we will conclude that this is true. Repentance is our only hope. When we recognize our sinfulness and confess our sins to Christ, we receive his wonderful forgiveness. Christ becomes the Savior of those who confess but is the judge of those who refuse.

God searches because of his love and because he knows we need deliverance. We have no hope apart from his convicting power. If he did not come to us first, we would never approach him. You might say, "Well, I came to him." But the Bible reminds us that he came to us first. Jesus said no one could come to him unless he was first drawn by the Father. (John 6:44) Both the sheep owner and the woman made an anxious search for what they had lost. One has even termed God the "hound of heaven."

The search God makes is by his Spirit. It is his voice of conviction that we feel and hear when we have sinned against God. As believers, we are the instruments God's Spirit uses. Through us, God speaks to people who need him as Savior.

Reflection: There is rejoicing in heaven when people come to know Christ. Thank God that he uses you in the searching process. Who do you know who needs Christ?

December 21

Baptism and the Lord's Supper
Matthew 26:20-30; 28:19

All religions have ceremonies they observe in conjunction with their religious practice. The ceremony may result from tradition, or they may view it as having some salvific significance. Baptism and the Lord's Supper are two sacraments related to Christianity. The Roman Catholic Church added more sacraments as well as viewed God's grace coming through the sacraments. This led to individuals needing the church to enter heaven.

Mainline Protestant churches do not see God's grace emerging through these two ordinances but do believe they are important. They possess no saving grace but are commanded by our Lord. The Great Commission reminds us that we are not only to tell the good news but also baptize those who accept it. And Jesus tells us to observe the Supper until he comes again.

That baptism has no saving power is portrayed beautifully by the thief on the cross with Jesus. He accepted Jesus, and Jesus told him he would be with him that day in paradise. (Luke 23:43) Baptism is symbolic of what has happened in our life when we trusted Christ. This eliminates the need for infant baptism. Though some Protestant denominations practice this rite, there is neither scriptural justification nor command to do so. The New Testament clearly shows people being baptized after trusting Christ not before.

Baptism symbolizes the magnificent change in our life after Christ. The practice of baptism by immersion beautifully displays this change. We are plunged beneath the water symbolizing death to our old way of life. Rising out of the water portrays our desire to walk in newness of life. While other forms of baptism are used, immersion seems to be the proper form. Using other methods, however, should not lead one to question their salvation. Baptism does not save us. This is done by God's grace.

The Lord's Supper reminds us of Christ's work on the cross. The bread represents his broken body while the juice reminds us of his shed blood. Partaking of the supper helps us remember the great sacrifice he made on our behalf.

Reflection: Pause to remember the great importance of these two rites.

December 22
Stinky Days
Romans 8:28

My morning walk once took me down a road that meandered through pastures and over hills. This particular morning was extremely foggy. All of a sudden, a skunk appeared. I crossed to the other side of the road and continued walking. I had not gone far when another skunk appeared. And then another. I concluded: "Some days just stink."

Have you ever had stinky days? From the moment your feet hit the floor things begin to go wrong. The pipes froze overnight because you forgot to listen to the forecast and leave your water dripping. Junior informs you he forgot to do his homework that you asked him about three times. You forgot to wash your work uniform. And then there are the cookies you forgot to bake for Susie's class at school.

Problems. They are a part of life. We tend to think that sin only affected Adam and Eve and their descendants. That is, it only touches an individual life. But creation itself was affected by sin. This is the reason we have natural disasters and why rust corrupts. Paul speaks of the entire creation groaning as it awaits future deliverance. As Christians, we do too. (Romans 8:21-22) We look forward to that day when we will receive bodies that do not ache or break down and die.

When trials and tribulations come your way and the day really stinks, remember that God is sovereign. Nothing takes place that is not under his control. Now you may ask, "Well does God bring these bad things into my life?" And the answer is no. He is not the author of temptation nor of anything that violates his character. Satan is the instigator of all things evil, but God is still in control. He allows Satan to do his dastardly work. Remember the example of Job. If things were occurring outside the control of God, we would be in terrible trouble. So even our stinky days are allowed by God, but for a purpose, not just to aggravate you.

Remember that God promises to bring good out of everything bad in life. He can take the evil devices and plans of Satan and turn them for your good. Through the dark periods in life, God can grow us spiritually if we will respond correctly.

Reflection: Thank you God that you can take my stinky days and make them smell like a rose.

December 23

The Lord's Day

Acts 20:7

Over my years in the ministry, I have heard many excuses from people about why they do not attend church. The most popular is that the church is full of hypocrites. This usually stems from their encounter with someone from the church who they have witnessed doing something they should not have. It is also a very weak excuse to just not attend church. Of course, the main reason people do not attend church (whether they will admit it or not) is because their relationship with Christ is not in order.

The Jewish people worshipped on Saturday during the Old Testament period. God commanded them to keep the Sabbath day holy. (Exodus 20:8) Early Christians changed that practice to commemorate Christ's resurrection from the dead which occurred on the first day of the week-Sunday. Though many refer to Sunday as the Sabbath day, this is an incorrect reference. Sunday is the first day of the week, not the seventh.

The writer of Hebrews reminds us not to neglect the assembling of ourselves together. (Hebrews 10:25) I have also had people tell me they do not have to go to church to be a Christian. Technically this is true. But so is the opposite. If you are a Christian, you will have that heartfelt desire to worship with God's people. When we gather together, we do so to collectively worship our God. This is our main purpose in going to church. God desires that we worship him in spirit and in truth. We have oneness of spirit, and we feel his Spirit in our presence. Our worship is based on the truth of God's Word and is not just a feel good experience.

Believers also gain another advantage from joint worship. We can encourage one another and share each other's burdens. In the New Testament, Barnabas was an encourager. We all need encouraging on a regular basis. As we face trials and tribulations in life, they are made easier when we have others to share words of comfort and offer help. Christians should share burdens. We are on the same spiritual journey, and a burden shared is always lighter.

Reflection: Some habits are good, and attending church is one of them. While church membership has nothing to do with attaining salvation, it is a sign of your commitment to God. True friends are made at church, and it provides a place where children can be nourished in the things of God.

December 24
God's Special Gift
Luke 2:1-16

That special gift. All of us have received it at some point. It may have come from a parent, sibling, spouse, child or friend. It was that something we had wanted for a long time. We did not think anyone knew what it was. As we opened the present, we had no idea our prized possession was at our fingertips. When it made its appearance, we were overcome. Our mouths dropped open. We were speechless.

God gave us a very special gift in the Christ child. We might wonder why God proposed such a plan to save mankind. There were other ways that seemed more logical. After all, why does a person have to die for other people for them to be saved? But this was God's way. The Bible

438

reminds us that without the shedding of blood there is no remission of sin. (Hebrews 9:22) The sacrifice also had to be perfect. No human qualified. So God decided it must be his Son, but how would he get him to earth? The same way anyone gets here. Through the procreation process, only in this birth a man would not be needed. He would accomplish the conception by his Spirit.

Most scholars think Mary was a young girl when she was approached by the angel announcing to her that she had been chosen to birth God's Son. We can only imagine the thoughts that ran through her mind. She was not married. To walk around pregnant in her society would surely subject her to ridicule and whispers of contempt. How would she explain her pregnancy to her parents? And what about her finance' Joseph? He would assume she had been unfaithful to him. An angel took care of explaining that for her. To his credit, Joseph accepted the situation and did not put her away.

As the duo arrived in Bethlehem, they faced a crowd of people who were there for the same reason they were. There was no room for them in the inn. God's Son had to settle for a cattle stall. It was a fitting place to illustrate how far he was willing to go. He left the portals of heaven for a sin cursed earth. He knew humble beginnings.

His arrival was heralded by angels who appeared to shepherds living in the field. The shepherd quickly left their flocks to find the babe wrapped in swaddling clothes lying in a manger. God's special gift.

Reflection: As we approach the Christmas season, thank God for his special gift. By accepting his gift we are given eternal life.

December 25
Small Beginnings
Luke 2:1-20

If he were alive today, he would be the product of a broken home. An illegitimate child who never saw his mother, his father later married a sixteen year old girl. He was first reared by his grandmother and later two aunts. Later he went to live with his father and step mother. His early life was very unsettled, but the young lad had an active curiosity and soon began to roam the countryside. He later became an authority on scientific and artistic subjects. We know him best as Leonardo de Vinci, the renowned painter of the well known and intriguing, "Mona Lisa."

Our Savior also had small beginnings. Not only was he born in a stable, but he later lived in the little respected town of Nazareth. Jesus' birth gives a lesson in humility. Caesar Augustus issued a decree for a census to be taken. Everyone had to return to his own town to register. Since Joseph was of the lineage of David, he and Mary returned to Bethlehem. While there, the time came for her to deliver the Christ child. Since there was no room for them in the inn, she gave birth in a stable.

Jesus was not afraid to be humble. Humility does not mean we are weak or that we never stand up for our rights. It does mean we remember who we are in relationship to God. He is God and we are not. He is our Creator, Sustainer and the one who grants each breath we take. When the vertical view is correct, the horizontal relationships will be characterized by humility. When we humble ourselves before God, he will lift us up. (James 4: 10) Humility leads to a successful life.

The birth of Jesus also familiarizes us with holiness. He was born of a virgin and therefore did not inherit the sinful nature all others receive. He was the sinless Son of God. Christ was conceived by the power of God's Spirit. He was Immanuel, God with us. His name means "Yahweh is Salvation." It was a fitting description for salvation of humanity was the reason for his coming. Because he was sinless, this qualified him to die for our sins.

Reflection: The birth of Jesus teaches us about miracles. Never has a child been born without a man's contribution. That is, until Jesus. He was a miracle from God. Thank God for the greatest Christmas present that anyone could ever give.

December 26
Experiencing God's Grace
Ephesians 2:8-10

Grace. God's unmerited favor for humanity. It is a scarlet thread that runs throughout the Bible, but one that has been clearly misunderstood and misinterpreted as a glance at church history will make evident.

440

The theme of God's grace begins in Genesis with the creation of humanity. God had existed from eternity and had angels for fellowship. In fact, since he is a triune God, he needed no one to complete him. For whatever reason, he chose to create with humans being the crown of that creation. Not under mandate to create but choosing to nevertheless is a picture of his grace.

Through deception and willful disobedience, Adam and Eve chose to go their own way. They immediately recognized their mistake, but the damage had been done. As God covered them with animal skins, he demonstrated that a sacrifice had to be made for sin. This is later reiterated by the writer of Hebrews who tells that forgiveness of sin is not possible without the shedding of blood. According to the law, almost all things had to be cleansed with blood. (Hebrews 9:22)

God's grace was also shown shortly thereafter by the pronouncement known as the Protoevangelium. God said to the serpent that he would put enmity between him and the woman. This enmity would also be exist between him and the woman's offspring. Her offspring would eventually deal a death blow to man's enemy. (Genesis 3:15) It was a prophecy of what would happen to Satan, that old snake. His blow to Christ was not lethal. Though death took him on the cross, he rose again three days later to demonstrate his victory over death and also to show that God had accepted his payment for sin. This is known as propitiation-that satisfaction of God's wrath against humanity.

God's grace continues to run throughout the Old Testament and finds its fulfillment in Christ. God gave the Law of the Old Covenant in part to show people that they could not live up to his standards and commandments.

Reflection: The sin nature that infiltrated Adam and Eve's life because of the choice they made to rebel would now be passed to all of humanity. But thank God for the cross.

December 27
God's Unmerited Favor
Ephesians 2:8-10

Our sin nature, coupled with the temptations of the enemy, would show man how hopeless his situation was. Many prophecies in the Old Testament foretell how the coming of the future Messiah would rectify our sin problem.

In the fullness of time, God sent his Son as the ultimate expression of his grace. This was his intent all along. He did not change his plans when he observed that the Law was not working. Christ was the lamb slain from the foundation of the world. (Revelation 13:8)

On the cross, humanity witnessed the grace of God and the great lengths he would go to demonstrate his grace to us. Allowing his Son to undergo such shame and persecution was God's loud shout to humanity that they are loved by him.

Sadly, this grace that is so aptly demonstrated in God's Word became distorted and misinterpreted. Much of history and even Christian history demonstrates this truth. Through the growth of the Western Roman Empire, the Holy Roman Empire and the control of Roman Catholicism, the message of God's grace was mired in tradition, legalism, and church control. When the Holy Roman Empire finally ended, it fulfilled what Voltaire had earlier said of it. It was "neither Holy, nor Roman, nor an Empire."

During the years that the Roman Catholic Church was dominant, grace was distributed through the church represented by the pope and priests. If one did not belong to the church, they had no hope for

salvation, for this came through the sacraments that could only be administered by the church. An individual's eternal existence, then, was not an individual choice unless they chose to obey the mandates of the established church.

It took the Protestant Reformation in the sixteenth century to question the teachings of Roman Catholicism. Martin Luther and other reformers believed that salvation was solely by the grace of God and did not depend on sacraments delivered by a priest.

Reflection: How wonderful to know that we do not have to depend on a human to intercede for us with God. The grace of God allows us to go boldly before God's throne with our needs.

December 28

Lessons from Job

Job 1 and 2

Who would you rather learn lessons from? The person whose life always went smoothly and had everything fall into his lap. They never had to work for anything. Or the person who traveled through monumental storms and came out stronger rather than defeated? The latter is the better choice.

When life goes sour, advice is prevalent. There are always those who think they know why we are going through this trial. Or they have been through something similar and have an answer to help us cope. Job had so called friends who gave him abundant advice-not all bad, just not the correct advice for his particular situation. When storms come, go to God in prayer. It is nothing wrong with sharing with a few godly friends, but limit how much and who you share with. Seek advice in God's Word and through prayer. He knows the source, intensity and purpose of the storm.

Storms can discourage us. Job would not have been human if his storms had not caused some of this, but he did not allow discouragement to paralyze him. He trusted that God would deliver him. Discouragement can be debilitating and can even lead to depression. If we are not careful, storms can take our focus off what God wants to teach us through the trial. It has some purpose. Rather than asking God why ask him what.

When storms come, it is always appropriate to remember how God has delivered you in the past. History is important. Reliving how he has done this will give us strength for the present challenge. As David faced Goliath and was ridiculed by his brothers and King Saul, he recounted how God had delivered him from the bear and lion that attempted to kill his sheep. Past deliverance gave him hope for his present situation.

Storms always have the possibility to increase our dependence on God, and this is one of God's desired outcomes. Whether he brought the trial or allowed it is not the issue. Do not spend a great deal of time investigating the source. Let the storm drive you to him. Anything that draws us closer to God is worth going through. Let the storm enhance your prayer life and cause you to seeker deeper truths from his Word.

Reflection: When the storm is over, victory always comes if we respond to God in the right manner. Weather the storm with faith so God can become more real in your life.

December 29

The Dangers of Compromise
Matthew 27:1-26

Compromise is all around us. It is the idea that doing or saying something just one time will not hurt me. A single drink has led some to a life of alcoholism. One act of unfaithfulness can destroy a marriage. One sexual encounter can lead to an unwanted pregnancy.

Pilate, the Roman governor, compromised when it came to delivering Jesus up for crucifixion. The chief priests and elders delivered Jesus to him, but he was smart enough to know that this was a religious matter. Jesus was stealing their followers. It was the custom to free a prisoner during the Jewish feast of Passover. He knew Jesus was innocent but because he feared the Jews he delivered an innocent man to death.

King David compromised with Bathsheba. She was the wife of one of his soldiers. Instead of joining his army in battle, David stayed behind. While walking on his roof, he saw Bathsheba bathing, sent for her and committed adultery with her. This sin led a domino effect of consequences in his life. He found himself lying. He even murdered her husband.

Compromise weakens our Christian testimony. Even unbelievers, while not concerned about their actions, have certain expectations of Christians. They know enough to realize whether or not we are living as God expects. When we do not, it reinforces their doubts about Christians.

Compromise is a selfish pursuit. It reveals our desire to go our own way instead of God's. We choose to deny his principles to gratify selfish desires. And often we think that God will somehow overlook this.

Acceptance and a sense of belonging are strong needs that God has created in us. When children are not finding that at home, it makes it easy for them to give in to peer pressure. This can even follow us into adulthood.

One act of compromise often sets off a chain reaction. Not only is our character weakened, but because we have deliberately disobeyed God and not repented, his truth becomes hard for us to digest. We do not like to be reminded of our sins, so we neglect his Word and even fellowship with other believers.

Reflection: God is a God of forgiveness. If you have compromised in some area, confess that to God and ask him to restore you to that right relationship with him.

December 30

Our Priceless Inheritance

I Peter 1:4-6

A family inheritance. The effects can be good or bad. Many families have been destroyed when the patriarch or matriarch dies. Siblings are divided and may even stop speaking to each other. One thinks the other received more. An inheritance can change one's life. Inheriting a large sum of money or land can alter perspective and financial situations.

God has reserved a priceless inheritance for his children. It is not one that we will squabble over. Our inheritance may vary where rewards are concerned, but the ultimate inheritance will be the same-heaven. So much of our attention is given to earthly pursuits that we occasionally forget that life is a journey of preparation for heaven. Seeing Jesus, living with him for all eternity and serving him faithfully is at the end of our life's journey. Life is not about prestige, power or the accumulation of material possessions.

Our inheritance is pure and undefiled. Neither will it change or decay. Worldly things are not pure. And they will decay. Paint or some type of finish may delay the process, but decay will take place. This is why Jesus tells us to store our treasures in heaven.

God's people under the Old Covenant looked forward to their inheritance in the Promised Land. But that land was not pure and undefiled. In fact, it was inhabited by pagans. God's people were often guilty of compromising by mixing their religion with theirs. The result was catastrophe. The inheritance that Christians look forward to will not be defiled in any way. Sin will not be present, and sin is the corrupting force in our current world.

God promises to protect us until we receive our inheritance. Our spiritual journey is splattered by trials and temptations. Even persecutions. God's mighty power will keep us safe until we reach the end of our journey. Ours is a journey of trust. The trust begins when we accept Christ as our Savior, but it continues each day as we depend on him for guidance by his Spirit. Learn to listen to God each day. Learn to hear his voice even in the midst of life's clutter.

Reflection: The joy we will experience in heaven is unlike anything we have ever known on earth. Thank God for the priceless inheritance that awaits you.

December 31
The Final Journey
II Timothy 4:6-8

In May of 2009, my father made his final journey. Following an earlier heart valve replacement that did not work well, he was referred to Emory University in Atlanta, Georgia. While the second operation went well, infection soon set in. It was an aggressive type that ravaged his body. Our family had to make a decision. In reality, Dad had already made the choice. We had to decide to honor his wishes. He was ready for the "final move."

My father had been a pastor almost all my life-for over forty years. It was his desire to preach until his life ended, and he did. Though he had been retired for several years, he continued to fill pulpits in the area. Just before he discovered he would have to have a second surgery, he had agreed to pastor a small church in the area. God allowed him to share the gospel until he died.

As our family viewed how the infection was progressing, we decided to let him go home. It was his wish. He had fought the good fight and finished the race. There was a crown of righteousness reserved in heaven for him. He would hear Christ say, "Well done good and faithful servant."

The time of death is near for us all. Each day brings us closer. We never know whether it will come in our younger years, senior years or somewhere in between. It may come peacefully or through pain and tragedy. The question is whether we are ready. Salvation is the only way to prepare. As a young lad of nine, my father took me into his study one day and explained to me the message of salvation. I realized my need for Christ.

Believers must fight a good fight. This is done by living faithfully for Christ each day. Satan tries to distract us, get us off course and ruin our testimony, but God's Spirit will move us around those traps if we rely on him. Our fight will include trials, tribulations, temptations and even persecution, but God gives us a suit of armor to combat whatever the enemy sends.

At the end of the race, we want to be found faithful. Christians never go into spiritual retirement. There is always work for God's people to do, no matter our age.

Reflection: Have you prepared for the final journey? If so, there is a crown of righteousness awaiting you along with the words, "Well done, good and faithful servant." See you later Dad!